Social History of Africa

LITIGANTS AND HOUSEHOLDS

Recent Titles in
Social History of Africa Series
Allen Isaacman and Jean Allman, Series Editors

LITIGANTS AND HOUSEHOLDS

AFRICAN DISPUTES AND COLONIAL COURTS IN THE FRENCH SOUDAN, 1895–1912

Richard Roberts

Social History of Africa
Allen Isaacman and Jean Allman, Series Editors

HEINEMANN
Portsmouth, NH

Heinemann
A division of Reed Elsevier Inc.
361 Hanover Street
Portsmouth, NH 03801-3912
www.heinemann.com

Offices and agents throughout the world

ISBN: 0–325–00259–2 (cloth)
ISBN: 0–325–00258–4 (paper)
ISSN: 1099–8098

Library of Congress Cataloging-in-Publication Data

Roberts, Richard L., 1949–
    Litigants and households : African disputes and colonial courts in the French Soudan,
1895–1912 / Richard Roberts.
        p. cm.—(Social history of Africa, ISSN 1099–8098)
    Includes bibliographical references and index.
        ISBN 0–325–00259–2 (alk. paper)—ISBN 0–325–00258–4 (pbk : alk. paper) 1.
Domestic relations—Mali—History. 2. Customary law—Mali—History. 3. Colonies—
Law and legislation—France. I. Title. II. Series.
    KST54.R63 2005
    346.662301'5'09041—dc22   2004028022

British Library Cataloguing in Publication Data is available.

Printed in the United States of America on acid-free paper.

07   06   05   04   03 SB   1   2   3   4   5   6   7   8   9

Copyright Acknowledgments

The author and the publisher gratefully acknowledge permission for use of the following
material:

Sections from *The End of Slavery in the French Soudan, 1905–1914,* ed. Suzanne Miers and
Richard Roberts (Madison: University of Wisconsin Press, 1989). © 1989. Reprinted by per-
mission of The University of Wisconsin Press. Sections of "Disputes over Property in the
French Soudan at the Beginning of the Twentieth Century," *African Economic History,* 1996.
Reprinted by permission of University of Wisconsin-Madison. Thanks also to Cambridge
University Press for permission to reprint sections of "Women's Wealth and Women's Prop-
erty: Maraka Household Textile Industry in the Nineteenth Century," *Comparative Studies in
Society and History* 26 (2) (1984), and "The Banamba Slave Exodus of 1905 and the End of
Slavery in the Western Sudan," *Journal of African History* 21 (3) (1981).

CONTENTS

ILLUSTRATIONS

FIGURES

TABLES

MAPS

PREFACE

This book has its origins in conversations between social historians, anthropologists, and legal scholars about what we can learn from the study of court records. This conversation has a long and venerable tradition in the humanities and social sciences, but my entry into it was occasioned in 1988, when Kristin Mann and I organized a conference on Law and Colonialism in Africa at Stanford University's Humanities Center. While most of the participants at that conference used court records in some way, few had made systematic use of them. One of the challenges we raised for ourselves—and the field of African social history more generally—was how should we extract social history from African disputes recorded in colonial courts. This book is my response to this challenge.

For any project that extends over nearly 16 years, we accumulate many debts. And these debts come in a great variety of forms. As in all intellectual endeavors, this book is really a collaborative project. Whether they intended it or not, my colleagues and students have become deeply implicated in the shape and substance of this book. I have benefited from sustained conversations with Kristin Mann, Martin Klein, Allen Isaacman, David Cohen, Bill Worger, David Abernethy, Zephyr Frank, Tim Broderick, Jonathan Greenberg, Erik Jensen, Thom McClendon, Lynn Schler, Emily Osborn, Benjamin Lawrance, Rachel Jean-Baptiste, Emily Burrill, and Rachel Petrocelli, some of whom have been forced to endure a reluctant apprenticeship with court records. My colleagues, Lou Roberts, Philippe Buc, and Joel Beinin, have guided me into some of the debates in French, medieval, and Islamic history regarding the law and legal studies.

The Malian court records I use in this project have been painstakingly copied by Timothée Saye, whose labor on behalf of this project I greatly appreciated. Timothée has been assisting scholars at the Archives Nationales, République du Mali, for many years. Ali Ongoiba, the director of the Archives Nationales, Mali, graciously gave me permission to use these court records and to have them copied. These records form a precious body of data and I am currently working with Ali Ongoiba on the next stage in making these documents available to a wider body of researchers. I am especially appreciative of the efforts by Dr. Saliou Mbaye, the director of the Archives Nationales, République du Sénégal, to promote the study of colonial court records. In December 2003, I assisted Saliou and an international team of scholars and archivists in a major conference in Dakar that was designed to stimulate research in judicial archives.

Access to court records and coding them constitute the twin foundations of the work of this project. Besides Ali Ongoiba and Timothée Saye of the Malian archives, I want to thank Karen Fung, curator extraordinaire of the Africana collections at Stanford, for her support of this project. Stanford University Libraries and the Dean's Office of Humanities and Sciences helped me acquire the copies of the court records and together with grants from the office of the Vice Provost for Undergraduate Education contributed to the labor of coding the court cases. All the court records used in this project have been coded into a FileMaker Pro database and to date, we have coded over 4,000 cases. I have used only half of these for this project; we continue to code the entire run of all the civil disputes heard at the provincial tribunals throughout the French Soudan. Once completed, this database consisting of some 8,000 cases will constitute a remarkable collection of the entire run of all the available entry-level civil disputes for all the districts of the colony. I want to thank Lynn Schler, Rachel Jean-Baptiste, Emily Burrill, Fayelle Ouane, Marie-Jo Sofianna Mont-Reynaud, Mari Webel, and Sophie Roberts for their help in coding these cases. The broader project on using court cases to stimulate research has found a welcoming home at the Stanford Humanities Lab, where the next stages of this project are being developed.

As academics know all too well, access to the raw material of historical sources is only part of the task of the historian. We need to struggle with the data and with our interpretations and test out our ideas on a regular basis. I have benefited from feedback from colleagues at Stanford, at the African Studies Association, from the participants at the Stanford-Berkeley Symposia on Law and Colonialism in Africa over the past dozen years, and from my students in my course on Law and Colonialism in Africa. I have come to appreciate just how much my students actually teach me in the process of my teaching them.

Being ready to write does not translate into being able to write. Research support for scholars is crucial in providing a sustained opportunity to deliver on the promises we regularly make about what we plan to do. I received generous grants from The National Endowment for the Humanities and Stanford's Institute for International Studies, where I spent the 2002–2003 academic year affiliated with the Center for Democracy, Development, and the Rule of Law. Stanford's Hewlett Fund had supported a research trip to Mali in 1996, when I first immersed myself in this project.

Some of the court records I used in this project dealt with household tensions stemming from husbands taking new wives. It may have felt a little like that in my household as I sought to establish another "household" that grew out of my research on court records. Amy, who shared with me my very first fieldwork in Mali in 1976–1977, continues to share our lives as our household goes through its own development cycle. As our son prepared for his own wedding, I gained new insights into the nature of marriage and bridewealth that I was investigating in the court records. Our daughter helped with the coding and designed the Web site for the Stanford Humanities Laboratory court project. She may not have liked the coding, but she has been bitten by the muse of social history.

I want to extend a very special statement of gratitude to Allen Isaacman, Jean Allman, Luise White, Jean Hay, and Jim Lance for making the Social History of Africa Series into the major vehicle for the development of African social history. Their tireless efforts have helped a generation of young scholars weather the challenges of academic publishing in a period of major retrenchment throughout the world of academic publishing. We thank them indeed.

A NOTE ON COURT RECORDS AND PRIVACY

I wish to express my thanks to Ali Ongoiba, the director of the National Archives of Mali for granting me permission to use colonial court records. In this book, I adhere to the 2002 regulations issued by the Republic of Mali governing the use of records held by the National Archives. These regulations restrict the use of any records that may "implicate the private lives of citizens." To that end, I have used surname pseudonyms whenever I cite actual court cases. In Figure 1.3, which is an image of actual court records, I have followed the practice of the United States Freedom of Information Act (title 5 of the United States Code, section 552) in providing information but blocking out the surnames of the litigants in order to protect their privacy. I also adhered to the stipulation in Article 22 that records of judgments that name litigants are restricted for "60 years or more following the case." The records I have used in this book are 92–100 years old.

Current practice in French West Africa and internationally regarding public access to court records is changing dramatically as a result of scholarly interest in court records and innovations in digital technologies involving storage and dissemination. Dr. Saliou Mbaye, the director of the National Archives of Senegal, has encouraged scholars to study judicial archives and made them available according to the standard 30-year rule of access. A consortium of British universities and research institutes are in the process of providing access to the entire run of court records from Old Bailey, mostly criminal cases, which will be a searchable database consisting of "the largest body of texts detailing the lives of nonelite people ever published, containing accounts of over 100,000 criminal trials held at London's central criminal court" (www.oldbaileyonline.org). The United States Federal Judiciary has recently introduced electronic access that allows users to obtain case and docket information from civil, bankruptcy, and criminal case files with "appropriate privacy safeguards." Several judicial decisions have reasserted the principle that court proceedings are presumed open, unless specifically closed by law or a party proves that "an overriding interest in justice requires closure." Such overriding interest involves situations where a defendant's constitutional rights to a fair trial may be threatened.[1] Judgments and court transcripts are of course open. This is exactly what the Maryland Judiciary reasserted in Rule 16-1002 (a): "Court records maintained by a court or by another judicial agency are presumed to be open to the public for inspection."[2]

For information other than court records, The Freedom of Information under the Privacy Act (title 5 of the United States Code, section 552a) provides the government with some exemptions to the disclosure of personal information regarding individuals. Exemptions 6 and 7 (C) prohibit a federal agency from releasing information that would be "a clearly unwarranted invasion of personal privacy" such as medical and financial information. Information in personnel files might fall all under these exemptions as well. Other information regarding individuals, however, is not restricted.

The intention of the architects of the colonial native courts in French West Africa was that these courts were to be open and justice transparent. Court records were to be maintained to ensure accountability of the judges and court officials and these innovations were to mark colonial justice as different from precolonial practices. Litigants came to the courts fully aware that these were public occasions and that the power of the colonial state stood behind the judgments rendered. In the civil cases examined in this book, litigants had to state their names and their residences, and, in the course of their testimonies, they revealed the most intimate aspects of their lives in order to convince the court of the validity of their claims. Any reasonable interpretation of the present day practice of protecting human subjects would realize that these litigants were willing and ready to reveal their identities and thus waive their rights to anonymity. This was part of the transaction costs of going to the colonial courts.

For the student of social history, court cases are a potentially vast and exquisitely rich body of evidence about historical actors with real disputes. While I have respected the regulations governing access to the court records held by the National Archives of the Republic of Mali in protecting the privacy of individual litigants at the beginning of the twentieth century, I would have preferred to let the litigants speak for themselves in so far as the records allow.

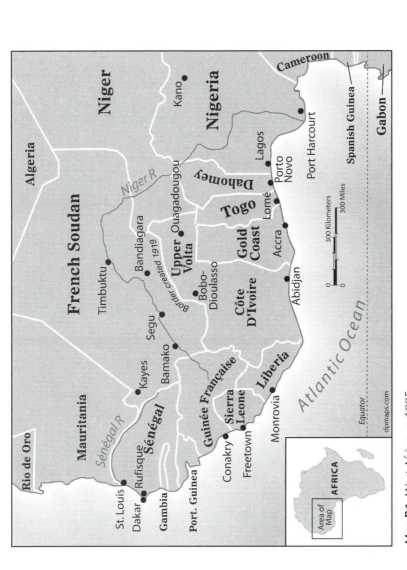

Map P.1 West Africa, c. 1905

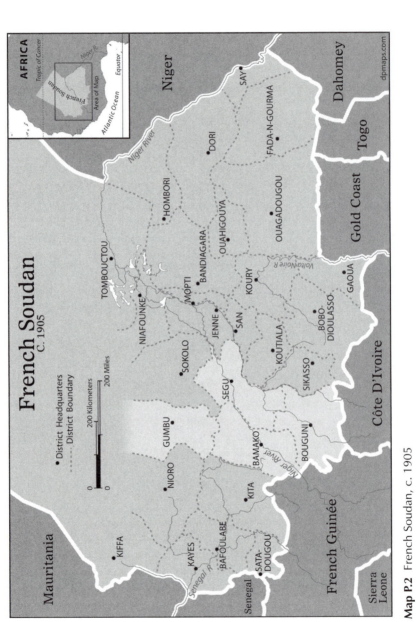

Map P.2 French Soudan, c. 1905

1

INTRODUCTION: "DISPUTES WITHOUT SIGNIFICANCE"—AFRICAN SOCIAL HISTORY AND COLONIAL COURTS AT A TIME OF SOCIAL TRANSFORMATION

France's leading scholar of the principles and legislation of colonization reminded his readers that imperial nations must "respect the double organization of the family and property to which the natives are accustomed and attached. Europeans have absolutely no interest in needlessly disturbing the natives' practices." Arthur Girault argued that doing so might well contravene both moral obligations as well as written treaties that required the French to respect the indigenous inhabitants' practices.[1] One year after Girault published the original version of his *Principes de colonization de et legislation coloniale* in 1895, Lieutenant-governor Trentinian of the French Soudan warned his administrators not to get involved in adjudicating disputes among natives. "The natives have become accustomed to bring even their smallest dispute before the jurisdiction of the commandant, who is reduced to the role of a simple justice of the peace. . . . Do not get mixed up in the many disputes without significance, which demand understanding of the morals and traditions of the population." Trentinian urged his administrators instead to pass these disputes on to our "native leaders, who are our indispensable intermediaries."[2] Despite these admonitions of "must" respect and "do not" get involved, colonial administrators throughout the French Soudan found themselves increasingly involved in resolving the most ordinary disputes over family and property relationships among Africans. They did so because Africans brought their disputes to French administrators and after 1905 to the newly created native courts.

This book examines the evidence of Africans using colonial courts to resolve their most intimate domestic disputes and uses this evidence to examine tensions within African households during a moment of rapid social change. The establishment of the native courts in 1905 coincided with the beginning of the exodus of slaves throughout the French Soudan. Court cases from this period provide a lens into the social and economic changes set in motion or accelerated by the departure of many thousands of slaves in a relatively short period of time.[3] These court cases not only provide a lens, but they provide precious data about actual social relationships within households as women and men struggled over the nature of their relationships and access to economic resources.

Court data, as I will argue, are not transparently easy to use, and this book establishes a methodology for using colonial court records as sources for African social history. The methodology I apply moves back and forth between aggregate trends in African civil disputes brought before the native courts and individual cases that compose these trends. Aggregate data derived from over two thousand civil cases and individual cases reflect very different registers of social meaning and African agency. Both are central to this study. To interpret the trends derived from aggregate data and individual cases I apply the concept of "trouble spots," developed originally by Lloyd Fallers for his study of disputing among the Basoga. As I will elaborate more fully in later sections of this introduction, Fallers's innovation in legal anthropology was to shift the emphasis from the individual case to a body of disputes that clustered around specific fault lines of social and economic change in an African society during the colonial period. To identify the clustering of disputes provided significant sociological insights, but it left unstated how and why Africans acted upon their grievances.

To complement the analytical insights I derive from using the concept of "trouble spots," I apply the idea of a "landscape of power" to interpret how and why women in particular took their disputes before the newly created native courts when they could have brought their disputes before a host of other fora designed to reconcile their grievances. I elaborate my thinking on both of these concepts later in this introduction, but first a word on the structure of this book.

This book is primarily a study of the two thousand civil cases that compose the entire run of cases brought before the provincial level native court (*tribunaux de province*) of the French West Africa Federation (AOF) in four districts in the French Soudan. Court data for 1906 are missing from all the district files. As I will argue in Chapter 3, as part of the debates surrounding the establishment of the new native courts, the attorney-general (*procureur-général*) was given authority to oversee the operation of the courts. I have found traces of the 1906 court registers in the Senegalese National Archives, which suggest that all the 1906 court registers were sent to Dakar for close evaluation. Chapters 4 through 8 examine the most "troubled" areas of domestic life as revealed by the incidence of disputing. It also explores how Africans negotiated and traversed the "landscapes of power" to bring their disputes before these native courts. The first part of this book examines the struggles over these native courts as part of a wider project on establishing a colonial legal system. As I discuss in Chapters 2 and 3, these struggles involved different models of colonialism and different groups of French colonial officials who were pursuing their own intellectual and bureaucratic agendas. These agendas had to do with the structure of the native courts, oversight over them, the authority of custom, and the interpretation of African societies. I return to some of these debates in my analysis of the "trouble spots" in Part II, because the debates about custom and African societies formed part of the "landscapes of power." Knowing the struggles that led to the structures and procedures in the colonial legal system is essential to understanding how Africans traversed the landscapes of power in early twentieth-century French Soudan of which the colonial courts were a central part.

As part of the competition among different models of colonialism, the governor-general of the French West Africa Federation, established in 1895, created a colonial legal system in 1903. The first courts were up and running in 1905. Native courts applying "custom" were a central part of this new legal system. The 1903 decree mandated the formation of three levels of native courts—the village tribunal, the provincial tribunal, and the district tribunal. The village tribunal was in the hands of the village chief and designed to promote the reconciliation of disputants. No records were to be kept and these courts operated with little if any supervision by the district officer. Africans often bypassed the village tribunal in order to bring their disputes directly to the provincial tribunal.

The provincial tribunal was for all intents and purposes the formal entry point in the colonial legal system. African magistrates nominated by the district officer and approved by the lieutenant-governor presided over these proceedings. The 1903 legislation required that records of the proceedings be kept in French, and with few Africans sufficiently literate to staff all these courts, the French district officer or his French assistant found themselves in these courts maintaining the registers and overseeing the practices of these new courts and the new magistrates. The 1903 legislation permitted appeals to the district tribunal, over which the French district officer presided. Two African assessors, formally selected because of their knowledge of custom, assisted the district officer in reaching his decision regarding the judgment of the provincial tribunal when litigants appealed their cases. Although the district tribunal's decisions on judgments from the provincial tribunal were, according to the 1903 legislation, to have a "salubrious effect" on the jurisprudence of the lower court, very few judgments were actually appealed. The 1903 decree included a very stiff penalty for what the framers considered "frivolous appeals." In 1910 and 1911, for example, the overall appeals rate from the provincial to the district courts was 1 percent.[4]

The village and provincial tribunals heard all matters of disputes involving family and property as well as defined categories of misdemeanors. The district tribunal heard appeals from the provincial level and more serious criminal matters. The native court system in French West Africa was modeled on the metropolitan system in both the architecture of the system and the role of judges. In the French civil law tradition upon which the native court system was established, the appeals court judges do not "make" law, but merely uphold the judgment of the lower court or return the case to the lower court because of procedural or code application irregularities. The function of judges in the civil tradition is to interpret and apply the law as it is technically defined within his jurisdiction.[5] Of course, this model assumes the existence of a "code." Although there were recurrent pressures on both the senior administrators in Dakar and lower level officials in the bush to produce a code, codification in French West Africa was never fully attempted nor was native "custom" ever legislated. In contrast, the corpus of metropolitan law and procedure was received in Senegal and applied to the law affecting Frenchmen and those with French legal status.[6] The lack of a code or clear body of legislation regarding custom made the roles of African magistrates and French district officers in the native courts more complicated. I discuss some of the debates surrounding codification, the definition of custom, and the relationship between custom and society in Chapter 3. Because of the small case load of ordinary disputes that reached the district tribunal and because judges in the French civil law tradition did not have a strong law-making capacity (as their counterparts under Anglo-American and its colonial variants have[7]), the cases heard at the provincial level are most revealing of what these court records can tell us about African social history.

Chapters 4 through 8 of this book examine 2,062 cases from the districts of Bamako, Bouguni, Gumbu, and Segu. This corpus of cases constitutes the complete run of existing court records from these four districts between 1905, when the first of the new courts started hearing disputes, and 1912, when the records for these courts end.[8] In 1913, the governor-general in Dakar decreed a reorganization of the native legal system and the suppression of provincial courts. The new decree introduced subdivisional courts and changed the requirements for record-keeping.[9] I have not consulted the records of these subdivisional courts.

The 1903 decree establishing the native courts contributed in no small way to the transformations set in motion beginning in the spring of 1905, when thousands of slaves began to leave their masters. The exodus of slaves began first in Banamba and then spread in increasing circles throughout the French Soudan over the next several years. The 1903 decree did not cause the slaves to leave their masters; it merely ended the legal recognition of slave status and thus ended the colonial state's formal support of masters' rights over their slaves, as in cases involving returning fugitive slaves. The decree of December 1905 further tied the hands of colonial administrators by prohibiting any future alienation of a person's liberty (i.e., enslavement) and the trade in slaves.[10] As I argue in Chapter 4, slaves left for a number of reasons, including French conquest of Babemba's warrior kingdom of Sikasso and their capture of Samori in 1898. Although enslavement remained widespread throughout the French Soudan, the two largest suppliers of slaves in the region were out of business after 1898 and the theater of their operations, which had devastated local populations and communities, became much safer. Refugees and slaves who may have remembered their homelands started to return. The acceleration of French conquest after 1890 contributed to a pronounced expansion of the regional economy. Both military excursions and peace were good for the economy, although the stimulus was not equally strong throughout all sectors of the economy. Expanding military presence and conquest required, among other things, access to vast stocks of food. Slaves around Banamba, which was a grain producing region, complained in 1904 about being overworked and underfed. Extra grain extracted from slaves probably flowed to Bamako to support the military effort.[11]

From the standpoint of this project, the end of slavery coincided with the establishment of the native courts. The Banamba provincial tribunal was not established until 1907, so the records from that court do not capture the negotiations and struggles that took place between masters and slaves between 1905 and 1906 during the height of the exodus.[12] The court records from Gumbu, however, do capture these experiences. The slaves of Gumbu began their exodus in 1908. Chapter 4 examines the ways in which struggles between masters and slaves were played out in the courts in that district. Not all slaves left their masters, but the evidence from the Gumbu provincial court provides data that contribute to the debates surrounding the meanings of the end of slavery in the French Soudan.[13] Slavery did not end in 1903 or 1905 or 1908 or even with the end of the large annual slave exodus around 1911–1912; instead, slavery persisted in many parts of the French Soudan where former masters and former slaves renegotiated their relationships and obligations. Slavery as a reproducing social system of warfare, commerce, labor, social control, and social status did end and what forms of slavery remained were profoundly modified.

The end of slavery involved far more than the struggles and negotiations among former masters and former slaves. The end of slavery contributed to the linked transformations in the society and economy of the region. Slavery had been a central part of the organization of the economy in the Middle Niger valley of the French Soudan and with the end of slavery, the ethnically bounded nature of economic niches eroded as former slaves moved into occupations that had been restricted to members of ethnic-specific groups.[14] The period after 1905 witnessed an expansion of the regional economy, clearly associated with the establishment of colonial rule, but expanding along precolonial patterns of regional and interregional trade rather than following the goals of colonial officials.[15] Among the most significant changes was the shift in the investment of capital from slaves into livestock. Tracing this shift and the disputes that were associated with the diffusion of livestock ownership among wider segments of the population is central to the argument I make in Chapter 7.

The end of slavery also added significant stresses to marriages and thus influenced patterns of household formation and dissolution. Slave ownership in the Middle Niger region had been widespread and had contributed to polygyny; increased patriarchy; more pronounced gender division of labor; cosmopolitan town life; and increased agricultural, craft, and commercial activity. The end of slavery impacted the lives men and women along the Middle Niger considerably. Chapters 4 through 8 examine disputes over household relationships and over property, the twin foundations of native life as described by Girault.

DISPUTES, COURT CASES, AND TROUBLE SPOTS

The dispute has long had a privileged position within legal anthropology. Disputes provided the raw material that scholars used to extract the substance of rules and the meaning of law in societies without formal courts or strong textual traditions. In their classic study of the Cheyenne, Karl Llewellyn and E. A. Hoebel used their informants' memories of disputes to distill both the local meanings of rules guiding correct behavior and actual instances of "hitch, dispute, grievance, trouble: and inquiry into what the trouble was and what was done about it."[16] The focus on trouble cases, the authors argued, provided a means to examine the actual operation of law in society and not merely the set of normative rules. Laura Nader and her students shifted the emphasis from the dispute as a discrete event with the objective of illuminating general principles of law and society toward the study of the process of disputing. In their hands, the dispute became a feature of the "social field" or set of wider social relationships and the process of disputing revealed forms and strategies of conflict management that took place outside of formal courts. The dispute was also understood to progress through stages. Nader argued that a dispute began as a grievance, which was the condition in which a person or group experiences an injustice that forms the grounds for resentment. This is essentially a preconflict stage that can move toward resolution by avoidance, apology, sublimation, or various forms of "off-stage" expressions of resentment. If the grievance is not resolved or displaced, it can escalate and thus enters the "conflict" stage in which the aggrieved party opts for "confrontation" with the offending party. At this point, the grievance is still contained by the relationship between the two parties and can be resolved within a broad repertoire of actions designed to resolve conflicts. If the conflict is not resolved at this level, it then enters the public domain (the dispute stage) in which some third party or adjudicating body becomes enmeshed in the procedure. The character of the third party varies according to the complexity of the society and to the strategies of the disputants.[17] Statistically very few grievances enter the dispute stage, because of significant social pressures to return the relationship to its "harmonious" level or to avoid public expressions of conflicts.[18]

Nader and her colleagues contributed to the study of disputes by emphasizing the phases and hurdles through which disputants must go before their dispute becomes public. However, a focus on the processes of conflict resolution tends to efface the often profound asymmetries of power in societies and how these asymmetries skew the options available to disputants.[19] June Starr and Jane Collier have sought to place unequal power relations at the center of their analysis of law and society. They argue that law and power are mutually reinforcing on cultural and institutional levels as well as in practice. For local courts and judicial personnel, knowing a disputant's social background is highly predictive of the legal outcome. This is especially important for closely-knit local communities, where legal decisions have long lasting implications. Bringing the dispute forward in these settings has two often contradictory outcomes: first, it flies in the face of the socially desired outcome, which is often reconciliation; and second, it illuminates the power asymmetries when these courts weigh differentially testimonies from rich men or women, for example.[20] This meant that the aggrieved person of lower status was unlikely to receive satisfaction in disputes with those of higher status. Starr and Collier also draw our attention to the historical construction of colonialism, which introduced new forms of power and often of the law. The presence of courts outside of the control of the close-knit community provided litigants with new strategies about where to take their disputes but also new risks from the choices they made. To take a dispute to colonial or national courts involved higher risks, invited retaliation, and threatened to destabilize social relations and ideologies of harmony.[21] Only those individuals who wished to disrupt or to sever their relationships (or who did not anticipate that this was a likely outcome) would go to the colonial or national courts. By introducing history and colonialism into the study of law and society, Starr and Collier also point out how people at particular times and places have "used, or avoided, the legal resources available to them."[22]

While the study of dispute processing that introduces power into the decisions disputants make is a considerable advance over those approaches that do not, the study of dispute processing still privileges the individual case. The case method has a long history within the field of Anglo-American legal anthropology. Legal anthropologists like to argue that the cases they use are representative of a wider body of courts cases. They often decide on which cases to analyze after spending long periods resident in local communities. A. L. Epstein observed that legal anthropologists have used the case method "as providing the raw material for analysis, the various strands in the skein of facts being teased out and dissected to reveal underlying principles and regularities."[23] In his view, anthropologists extract from cases observed in the field general principles, the value of which stems from the nature of the case observed. The greater its representativeness, the larger the reach of general explanation. But how are we to know that individual cases are truly representative of more general trends?

In a remarkable and self-critical assessment of his own scholarship, Max Gluckman reflected on his method for using court cases and evaluating the decision making of Lozi judges.[24]

> When I had finished the book, I felt that I had made an important contribution to the problems I had tackled, but I remained dissatisfied as a sociologist. I sensed that I was on the verge of important sociological discoveries, but was not making them. It was clear to me that though I had woven my analysis out of many cases heard in court, some quoted at great length, I had in fact used each case as an isolated incident coming before the court. Yet each case was obviously but an isolated incident in a long process of social relations, with its roots deep in the past; and often the protagonists in the case would be living together again, and their interaction would be affected by the court's decision. I had not studied that process of social life; and in my opinion here lies the next step in deepening our understanding of law and morality—the intensive study of the process of social control in a limited area of social life viewed over a period of time.[25]

Gluckman's solution to his methodological shortcoming was to understand more fully the life cycle of each case, in which the disputants had a history together before their appearance in court and whose relationships persisted after the court's judgment. Gluckman's concept of the persistence of face-to-face relations presumes a community in which there is little geographical mobility and thus does not include powerful forces of historical change.

Gluckman was right to suggest that he was at the verge of significant sociological discoveries. But he chose the wrong approach. Lloyd Fallers proposed exactly the breakthrough needed when he shifted the emphasis from the

Llewellyn and Hoebel "trouble case" to what he called "trouble spots." Llewellyn and Hoebel used trouble cases to reconstruct the principles of law and the moral universe of small-scale societies. Fallers noticed that court cases tended to congeal around certain relationships that pointed to systemic conflict stemming from social change.

> The wider social system is more than merely the moral environment of the legal process—the source of the moral norms which the legal process shapes into legal norms by means of legal concepts. It is also the matrix out of which disputes arise—the sources of "trouble case," to use Llewellyn and Hoebel's phrase. Society orders its members' behavior, but it also "disorders" it in typical ways, so that each society seems to produce its own characteristic types of dispute—its own profile of conflict. . . . Thus societies have their characteristic "trouble spots" out of which disputes sprout like weeds. In societies whose members take their trouble cases to courts of law, those trouble spots shape the docket—give pattern to the traffic of litigation that flows through the courts. Arising from such troubled areas of social life one may expect to find more frequent—and more interesting (from the point of view of an analysis of legal concepts in action)—litigation.[26]

The methodology used in this book recognizes that only a small fraction of disputes make their way to courts, especially colonial courts, but that the statistically significant concentration of cases among certain categories of dispute suggest points of social conflict within the societies studied.[27] I began by identifying the trouble spots in African societies along the Middle Niger region by assessing the aggregate data for each district and for the four districts combined. Only after I identified trends in the aggregate court data do I use individual cases to illustrate the nature of the dispute and thus the relationship in question. I use individual cases to illustrate the detail of these general patterns in troubled social relationships over time. The aggregate data on disputes point to the trouble spots in society, but they do not explain them. A central part of using court records for social history is to contextualize the trouble spots derived from the cases within wider patterns of social change. Sally Falk Moore has described this method as moving back and forth between the small-scale events documented in the court cases and the large-scale social processes that are not visible through the court records themselves.[28] Students of court records must also be attentive to how courts transform disputes into the texts we read.

For this project, I am not interested in the legal reasoning of the African magistrates who presided over the provincial tribunal. Although I have records of the judgments rendered by these courts, these are far too sparse to attempt such an inquiry. Moreover, in the French civil law tradition even as it was adapted to the native courts, judges do not make law. They merely implemented the law—or in case of the provincial tribunals, "custom." Within the limits of the litigants' decisions to take their cases to the native courts (which I discuss more fully in the next section), the corpus of court cases presented here are the complete series of all the existing cases heard in these courts and thus provide a guide to the "trouble spots" in African societies as they were undergoing a period of rapid social change. I argue that changes in social relationships interacted with institutional change to produce discernible patterns in litigation.[29] Statistically, the trouble spots in these four districts are in divorce (22% of the total cases), marriage (14%), debt and contracts (19%), bridewealth (10%), child custody (9%), property (9%), inheritance (7%), and damages (7%). These categories were ones actually used in the Bamako provincial tribunal between October 1909 and December 1911. The secretaries of the provincial tribunals—mostly Europeans during this period—sometimes included dispute categorization in the court registers and sometimes they did not. Because of the inconsistency in application of categorization, I have freshly categorized each case during the process of coding them.

Divorce was the single most significant trouble spot, but when combined with marriage, the tensions between husbands and wives constitute 36 percent of all the disputes heard at these provincial tribunals. By divorce, I understand efforts to dissolve marriages. Women brought more than 74 percent of divorce cases in this sample.[30] In contrast, marriage cases refer to

Figure 1.1 Distribution of Disputes in Bamako, Bouguni, Gumbu, and Segu, 1905–1912, n = 2,062

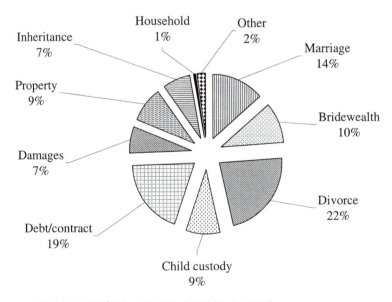

Sources: ANM 2 M 104/105, 2 M 110, 2 M 122, 2 M 143

those disputes where husbands or other male guardians sought the court's help in forcing wives to return to their husbands. Marriage cases were almost exclusively brought by males. I discuss the issues surrounding women's use of the courts to dissolve marriage they did not want and husbands' efforts to have the court force their wives to return their conjugal homes in Chapter 5. Bridewealth disputes refer to cases where return of the bridewealth or the completion of bridewealth payments are central. The records categorize these cases as *dot,* but this term is misleading. *Dot* translates as dowry, and while brides often do bring into marriage various forms of wealth and possessions, the operative concept in Malinke societies is bridewealth [Bamana: *kunafoni nafolo*].[31] Bridewealth is what husbands or their families provide to the brides' guardians or kin. Failure to provide bridewealth, failure to complete bridewealth payments, or failure to transfer the fiancée to her betrothed set in motion disputes over the marriage, the marriage contract, and over the custody of children. Similarly, if a wife sought to end her marriage without invoking mistreatment or abandonment as primary causes, bridewealth would have to be returned to her husband or her husband's kin. This created a significant barrier to divorce, as I discuss more fully in Chapter 6. Bridewealth was the central component for regularizing marriages and is thus linked to the status of rights over children should the marriage dissolve. Child custody cases usually involved proof that bridewealth was or was not provided.

Under debt/contract, I have included disputes over unfilled promises involving commerce or labor. These disputes play a crucial role in the strategies used by masters to keep their slaves on their farms in Gumbu, discussed in Chapter 4. Damage disputes usually involved compensation for losses. Damage claims tend to cluster around livestock, both in terms of livestock predations to farmers' crops and to loss of livestock themselves. As I argue in Chapter 7, livestock became a form of "new" property after the end of slavery in the sense that ownership of livestock was no longer the ethnic monopoly of the FulBe or Maures, but became a significant source of investment throughout the Middle Niger region. As livestock became a central part of the strategies for accumulation, owners of livestock had to engage herders to tend their herds. Most cases for damages or compensation involved livestock invading farmers' standing crops. Hired hands often found themselves in court, since they were responsible for the livestock they tended. And as livestock reproduced, the value of the herd increased, encouraging more kin to claim shares of the estates of "wealthy" individuals, which I examine in Chapter 8. Wealth was a highly relative term in the Middle Niger valley during the first decade or so of the twentieth century, but access to inheritance was a means of enhancing one's standing.

Focusing on disputes suggests that social conflict was ubiquitous in the Middle Niger region. Max Gluckman has argued that "The Lozi, like all Africans, appear to be very litigious. Almost every Lozi of middle age can recount dispute after dispute in which he has been involved."[32] This may also be the case in the French Soudan, but the court evidence used here suggests a substantial but not ubiquitous use of the colonial courts. Based upon population estimates collected by district administrators in 1904, before the slaves' exodus that resulted in some significant reallocation of populations, and assuming only one court appearance per inhabitant and each dispute involving two people, we can calculate that roughly 1 out of every 61 residents in Gumbu went to the provincial court sometime between 1905 and 1912, 1 of out every 96 residents in Bamako, 1 out of every 162 residents in Segu, and 1 out of every 474 residents in Bouguni went to provincial court.[33] These are very general estimates that do not take into consideration the barrier of distance to the provincial courts, which would suggest that those living further away might have been less inclined to use these courts. These rough data indicate that residents in Gumbu and Bamako were more inclined to use the provincial courts than their counterparts in Segu and Bouguni. These data also suggest that the inhabitants of Gumbu and Bamako had more troubled social relations or that they were more inclined to take their troubles to the new native courts. Gumbu, of course, was the site of a massive slave exodus and Bamako's population swelled in the period after 1890 as the French colonial presence increased. Perhaps newcomers to the region were more likely to litigate in the colonial courts than those long-time residents in villages.[34] I cannot push this analysis further because the evidence I have contains only the names and sometimes the residences of the litigants who used the native courts. Given the lack of corroborating data on individuals that European social historians have extracted from census data and church records, I cannot ascertain whether the litigants were long-term residents or newcomers.[35] I have no records on those who did not use these courts nor can I assume that they did not have disputes. But the evidence we do have points consistently to certain "troubled" areas of social life.

The aggregate data presented in Table 1.1 identifies the relative importance of the "trouble spots" among the total cases for these four districts between 1905 and 1912. But within each of these districts, certain trouble spots are more pronounced, and I have concentrated my discussions in each chapter on the incidence of these most troubling trouble spots. The following table (Table 1.1) provides a breakdown of trouble spots by districts. The percentages in bold type in the table indicate where the incidence of trouble exceeded the average for all the districts. I use the incidence of trouble to help guide my choice of evidence from these various districts. Thus, Chapter 4 draws on Gumbu data involving debt/contract disputes, which constitute 34 percent of the cases in that district. Chapter 5 uses data mostly from Bamako, where marriage and divorce cases were more pronounced than the average. Chapter 6, on bridewealth disputes, draws on evidence from both Bamako and Segu, where bridewealth cases also exceeded the average. I also draw on child custody disputes from Bouguni

Table 1.1 Trouble Spots by Districts

District/Dispute	Marriage	Divorce	Bridewealth	Child Custody	Debt/Contract	Damages/ Compensation	Property	Inheritance	Household	Other	Total
Bamako	19%	26%	11%	10%	10%	6%	6%	5%	1%	.5%	928
Bouguni	30%	22%	4%	27%	5%	4%	4%	2%	0	2%	101
Gumbu	5%	23%	8%	5%	34%	7%	10%	6%	0	2%	597
Segu	9%	16%	14%	9%	12%	7%	13%	14%	1%	5%	436
% of total	14%	22%	10%	9%	19%	7%	9%	7%	1%	2%	2062

Sources: ANM 2 M 104/105, ANM 2 M 122, ANM 2 M 143, ANM 2 M 110

and Bamako, where they were important trouble spots. Most of the property cases I discuss in Chapter 7 are also drawn from Segu, where the incidence of these disputes exceeded the average, and from Bamako, where the numbers are relatively high. Inheritance disputes, the focus of Chapter 8, are drawn from Segu, where inheritance cases were twice as frequent as the average.

These statistical considerations provide a road map toward the trouble spots, but the actual path taken in interpreting these disputes comes from time series and more fine-grained comparisons. For example, Chapter 5 on marriage and divorce plots the incidence of these two types of disputes over the period from 1905 to 1912 and this time series indicates patterns that then guide my questions. Why did divorce disputes dominate the courts from the onset of the new legal system and why did marriage cases accelerate so boldly after 1910? In Chapter 4, I plot the incidence of debt/contract disputes and the graph indicates a dramatic spike in 1908, when the slaves started their exodus in Gumbu. How were debt/contract disputes related to the end of slavery in Gumbu? I also plot divorce disputes in Gumbu over time, which reveals two seasonal spikes in incidence of divorce and an increasing incidence of divorce annually between 1908 and 1912. Because women were among the first litigants to use the new courts in 1905, I have privileged the disputes women brought and those that concerned women's wealth. This focus on women and the law provides a powerful lens into changing social relationships, changing access to resources, and agency.[36] These examples point to two important issues in the social history of trouble spots in colonial Africa: first, how and why did Africans bring their disputes to these new courts; and second, what do these disputes tell us about social change? I address the first of these issues in the section below and the second issue in the following section.

LANDSCAPES OF POWER, VENUE-SHOPPING, AND LEGAL PLURALISM

The establishment of the native courts in the French Soudan in 1905 added new complexities to the sets of formal courts and informal dispute resolution institutions available to Africans with grievances. The establishment of these new courts coincided with the exodus of the slaves and the linked sets of transformations that the end of slavery set in motion. The end of slavery contributed new challenges to authority and power and to stresses within households. People with grievances made decisions about where and how to express their concerns. This study is particularly interested in how colonial institutions—such as the new courts that come into existence in 1905—contributed to changes in the landscapes of power and authority in Africa and how Africans negotiated these new terrains. In using the new courts, women and men not only acted in their interests, but also forced subsequent changes in the landscapes of power in the French Soudan. While I do not have evidence about the prehistory of the disputes that were brought before the provincial tribunals, we do know that bringing cases to these new courts required both intentionality and agency on the part of litigants.

By using a term for a physical feature—landscape—to describe the context for studying asymmetrical social relations, I portray power as having concrete qualities. To traverse a "landscape" requires at least two actions: first, it requires intentionality. A person who seeks to move from point A to point B must prepare both physically and cognitively.[37] These preparations can be either routine, such as going to the market or the field, or strategic in the sense of anticipating new outcomes or benefits. And second, it requires action. A person must actually set out to accomplish the goals she or he has defined. Intentionality and action do not preclude unanticipated consequences. Indeed, unanticipated consequences are part of the reflective processes of human learning. Thus, linking "landscape" to the action of "traversing" provides readers with a sense that the men and women of the French Soudan actively engaged with the world in which they lived and whose actions shaped the meanings of their experiences. My concern with agency flows from this sense of active engagement with the world and, following Anthony Giddens, refers to the "capability of doing things in the first place."

> To be able to "act otherwise" means being able to intervene in the world, or to refrain from such intervention, with the effect of influencing a specific process or state of affairs. This presumes that to be an agent is to be able to deploy (chronically, in the flow of daily life) a range of causal powers, including that of influencing those deployed by others.[38]

The term "landscapes of power" also suggests the uneven nature of the terrain that men and women traversed in order to accomplish their goals. A landscape of power differs from its physical counterpart in terms of historical change. Historians can "measure" changes to the landscapes of power in eventful time and not merely according to natural or geological time.[39] The landscapes of power during the three or four decades of transition from the late precolonial to early colonial Africa changed unevenly. Established forms of power and authority were often eroded only to be replaced by new or reconstituted forms established first by Africans responding to the crises associated with the end of the transatlantic slave trade and then by the practices and policies of colonial officials.[40] During this period, Africans also tested the limits of power, sometimes unleashing ferocious efforts to reassert the power of those being challenged, often eroding power in the process, and sometimes merely slipping through the cracks opened in the landscapes of power in the aftermath of colonial conquest.[41] The end of slavery and the linked transformations set in motion by slaves' actions and the establishment of new courts altered the landscapes of power in the French Soudan and structured power in new ways. Landscapes of power thus contain physical institutions such as chieftaincy, heads of households, and courts as well as social and cultural practices such as kinship, marriage, gender, slavery, labor, religion, leisure, wealth, and authority.

These institutions and practices contributed to the structures of everyday life, which are the product of recursive human engagement with the world that establish both "sets of rules and resources."[42] To engage with the world requires cognition and reflection. People produce history through both words and deeds.[43] Representations of landscapes of power thus have at least two qualities central to the argument presented here. First, representations are intellectual constructions, products of perception and cognition. Perceptions and cognition are unstable in time and over time, reflecting ongoing struggles to shape meaning and experiences. And second, as social constructions, representations have significant institutional consequences. They actually influence the structure and performance of institutions and the ways people use them.[44] As I argue in Chapters 5 through 8, representations have distinctive histories, but without attention to how humans act on them or in spite of them, representations are hollow explanations for historical change.

The new courts altered the landscapes of power in the French Soudan, and Africans assessed the risks and rewards of using them. Within two years, some patterns of African use of the new legal system were identifiable. In the Bouguni district, where the new courts started operating in September 1905, the district administrator wrote that "natives present themselves before the courts for grievances of little importance: tensions within households, incompletely paid bridewealth, and so forth. Others come to complain of acts committed before our occupation, and especially during the time of Samory." By the end of the year, the administrator noted a further narrowing of the range of cases brought before the courts. "All the affairs presented deal with household quarrels: husbands abandoned by their wives; wives abandoned by their husbands; or bridewealth incompletely paid."[45] More striking was how quickly African litigants began to use the legal system because they wanted certain kinds of judgments. Already by 1906, Africans were bypassing the village tribunal in favor of bringing their cases directly before the French administrator—most likely the provincial court, where the district officer was present as secretary. During the first years of their operation, French administrators directly supervised the provincial courts' deliberations. "The natives prefer to come to the district headquarters and each day the administrator must listen to numerous litigants who talk at length about their domestic quarrels."[46]

This strategic use of the new courts took place throughout the French Soudan. From Jenne district, the administrator wrote that in 1907 the number of cases brought before the village courts were surprisingly small. Instead of seeking the assistance of the village chief in reconciling their differences, "the parties prefer to submit their grievances before the provincial court, thinking that at the district headquarters, they will find a more impartial jurisdiction. Instead, they find that they are sent back to the village courts, which are competent to hear their cases." Nonetheless, he noted that the provincial court "heard a great number of cases, many more civil cases than criminal ones."[47]

That African litigants wanted to avoid the "reconciliation" of the village chief's court and sought instead a more "impartial" judgment hint at two important aspects of their strategies in these early years of the new legal system: first, African litigants calculated the outcomes they were likely to receive at different courts. The women who brought their grievances to the provincial court were not interested in the chief's efforts to reconcile them to their husbands. The village chief was, after all, one of the elderly males of the community. Second, they sought not just "impartial" judgments, but decisive ones. An indication of this second point is presented in the 1909 remark by the Bamako district administrator. He noted, 17 disputes were brought by "parties soliciting from the court an arbitrary sentence as well as a condemning one."[48]

These patterns are reminiscent of those described by Bernard Cohn and Robert Kidder when the British imposed courts applying Western legal practices in colonial India. Cohn and Kidder identified several features of Indian colonial courts and their legal procedures that altered the way grievances were handled and expressed. Because colonial courts in India sought to resolve cases based on clearly defined rights, these courts rewarded winners and punished losers. By creating an arena in which judgments were "decisive," the new courts developed a "speculative air" especially for those with the least to lose and the most to gain.[49] Jane Collier described a similar phenomenon in Zinacantan, when Indians with "little to lose and much to gain" would take their disputes to the national courts at some distance from their hamlets.[50]

The administrators in the French Soudan noted exactly this kind of "speculative air" in cases brought by those with the least to lose and the most to gain. Moreover, this search for "decisive" judgments, suggesting that the litigants did not wish to be reconciled, was even more pronounced in the case of women seeking divorce. Already in 1908, the Bamako administrator saw this as a trend. "Most of the cases submitted to the provincial court in civil and commercial matters are concerned with divorce or the repayment of bridewealth. It is to be remarked that in this regard, it is almost always the women who demand the dissolution of the marriage."[51] Just as my focus on court cases tends to exacerbate the view of conflict in society, I do not want to suggest that all litigants using the new courts did so for purely instrumental interests. Litigants may not have known that the courts would render decisive judgments, often rupturing relationships rather than rebuilding them. Some may have come to these courts with the intention of shaming the defendant in order to reform his or her behavior and may have been surprised by the outcome. We have no way of knowing the attitudes of plaintiffs, but after the first few years of the courts' existence, disputants would have had a better sense of what kinds of outcomes to expect.[52]

Elizabeth Colson found similar patterns occurring among the Tonga of the Gwenbe Valley during the 36 years she has worked in the region. Colson has noted that while the nature of the disputes (the trouble spots) have been more or less constant, the disputants' have increasingly chosen to avoid the reconciliation of the village moots in favor of bringing their disputes before the headman's or chief's court, established by the British colonial native policy. Colson attributed these changes to the tendency for individuals to act on their own initiatives for their own gain and to the impact of the relocation of villages due to the Kariba Dam project, which contributed to the erosion of village elders' authority. Colson also noted that litigants understood that the chief's courts were under the authority of the larger colonial state and thus anticipated that the court's decisions would be enforced.[53]

Cohn and Kidder recognized several other features of the colonial court in India that contributed to the assessment of risks and rewards as litigants decided which venue to use. Two of the primary tenets of British law as applied to the colonial courts were that all persons should be treated equally before the law and that justice should be blind. Status differences were not to influence the judgment. The 1903 decree in French West Africa prohibited the recognition of status among the litigants, such that masters could not claim rights to their slaves. The 1903 decree was silent on the issue of gender, but prevailing metropolitan rights allowing women to sue for divorce (discussed more fully in Chapter 5) contributed to an environment in the native courts that encouraged African wives to end marriages they did not want and African magistrates to grant their requests. In addition, the legal mandate of new courts did not easily acknowledge grievances with long histories. This is what the Bouguni administrator complained about in 1905 when he noted that litigants were bringing disputes whose origins preceded the time of Samory, some quarter century before. Instead, the colonial courts dealt with isolated cases of dispute in which clear-cut rights and duties could be established by investigation of only those events that were deemed relevant to the pending case.

Such practices were diametrically opposed to local practices. Equality before the law, Kidder argued, violated principles of status imbedded in the caste system. The notion of a dispute isolated from the dense body of relationships that both preceded the case and then followed it simplified the complexities of social relationships as Gluckman had argued. By creating an arena in which decisions rewarded winners and punished losers, litigation appealed to those least enmeshed in dense webs of local relationships. In her recent study of colonial law in world history, Lauren Benton noted exactly this trend. "It is the case everywhere that indigenous actors were quick to perceive opportunity in this legal landscape."[54]

Venue-shopping had far more social consequences than the outcome of any individual case. Richard Abel has argued that the disputants' choice of legal venue has immediate consequences because each forum has its own substantive and procedural rules that affected the outcome of the dispute and the relationships of the parties to each other. Taken together, however, the cumulative effect of venue-shopping has "long-term, large-scale significance for society" by which he means not only institutional change—empowering this or that form of legal action—but changes in social relations as well.[55] The creation of multiple legal spheres structured by colonialism and involving the seepage of metropolitan legal concepts and procedures into native law and practice, which colonial officials conceived as separate, often led to changes in the legal character and the legal capacity of individuals. This enabled women, younger adults, and low status individuals to confront men and higher status individuals even in courts designed to uphold custom.

Venue-shopping certainly predated colonialism. The long history of cultural and social change and contact introduced new ideas and forums of dispute settlement in societies throughout the world. Except for the most isolated ones, all societies have some form of legal pluralism in which more than one system of normative beliefs and practices coexisted. Colonialism, however, generated what John Griffiths has termed juristic legal pluralism, in which several formal legal systems were more or less formally structured.[56] The classic example of colonial legal pluralism was the dual legal system that recognized and separated preexisting "native" law from the received law of the metropole.[57] Mahmoud Mamdani applies this concept of separate legal spheres as a central component of his argument for the development of decentralized rural despotism in colonial Africa and the thwarted emergence of civil society due to the practice of delegating political and legal authority to "native rulers."[58] Mamdani's book is concerned with the historical roots of independent Africa's tendency toward political autocracy, but his reconstruction of the colonial era overstates the autonomy of these two legal, political, and cultural regimes. Plural legal systems in colonial contexts were parts of a single, but complexly articulated colonial system. Neither colonial states nor Mamdani's rural despots were powerful enough to establish, let alone maintain, separate legal regimes. Africans crossed these boundaries continuously and challenged them by selecting which courts to use, by the kinds of grievances they brought forward, and by introducing new concepts of social relationships.

The impact of colonialism on the articulation of legal pluralism itself has a history, and Mamdani's focus on dual legal systems reflected a mature phase of European colonialism and not the messier, formative phase. It also reflects an earlier, binary conception of legal pluralism. Lauren Benton's study of colonial legal regimes is concerned with the institutional character of the legal encounter between Europeans moving overseas from the fifteenth through the end of the nineteenth centuries. During the early phase, Europeans negotiated or imposed their legal regimes in contexts where other legal regimes coexisted more or less equally. In these multicentric legal systems, individuals engaged in "rampant boundary crossing" and collective groups engaged in "jurisdictional jockeying" for legal advantage. Increased interaction between groups led to shared assumptions about the outcomes of transactions and thus cultural convergence around shared legal concepts and practices. The colonial state was not yet strong enough or sufficiently interested to structure the various legal spheres hierarchically. British practice in India bridged the early and later forms of colonialism and led to the more pronounced form of state-centered legal pluralism of the late nineteenth century in which the colonial state at least claimed dominance over other legal regimes. Benton calls for a close analysis and comparison of transformative moments during what she calls the "long nineteenth century" in an effort to identify important shifts in the definition of colonial state law and its relationships to other law.[59]

In contrast to Mamdani, Benton recognizes the imprecision of jurisdictional boundaries in the actual operation of colonial legal pluralism. Benton draws on case studies that demonstrate how plaintiffs "quickly learned legal strategies that pitted one court against another." Benton argues that despite the colonial state's greater attention to elaborate rules governing legal jurisdictions and procedures of the state-centered form of legal pluralism, indigenous actors used the rules "to manipulate strategically through the legal order" to serve their interests and in the process revealed to colonial architects the flaws in their system.[60] The colonial architects of the legal system never managed to "fix" the system because native actors struggled constantly among themselves and with the colonial state's institutions about the meanings of their social relations and access to resources. More useful than focusing on the institutions of colonial legal orders is what Sally Engle Merry calls "the dynamics of change and transformation" within plural legal systems.[61]

Recent research on legal pluralism underscores the need to focus not only on the establishment of formal legal institutions, but also on the litigants' practices in using the multiple arenas created by overlapping systems of dispute settlement. This research indicates that multiple forums, including various forms of mediation and arbitration, exist even in advanced industrial societies that have seemingly unitary legal systems. Similar types of informal dispute forums existed in colonial settings side by side with the structured hierarchies of native and metropolitan law and courts. These multiple venues provided considerable opportunities for litigants to pursue their grievances in a serial fashion through different forums. Using colonial court records, however, we rarely get a chance to see what these multiple strategies were before the case arrived in the courts. The most useful way of thinking of legal pluralism is as a form of encounter between dynamic, local processes of change in indigenous societies that predated colonial conquest and continued after conquest, and dynamic and changing forms of colonialism. The intensity of the encounter changed over time in response to the waxing and waning of empire and globalization and in response to prevailing ideas about development and modernization.[62] This encounter created new landscapes of power, which also changed over time, and thus provided new opportunities for Africans even as it engendered new conflicts among Africans.

FROM TALKING TROUBLE TO READING DISPUTES: AFRICAN SOCIAL HISTORY AND COLONIAL COURT RECORDS

This project explores the use of court records for social history during a period of social transformation at the beginning of the twentieth century in the French Soudan. This project is linked also to another period of transformation, one that is occurring now. It is one that makes this assessment of court records for social history especially important. Historians of Africa are finding themselves in the midst of the period of epistemological and methodological transformation regarding oral history as we confront the viability of many of the foundational commitments we have made to the field. To understand how we have arrived at this watershed, we need to remember the conditions in which the field of African history emerged.

African history emerged 50 years ago out of a still robust history of empire. Empire was under attack throughout many parts of the world. As the pace of nationalism and decolonization in the 1950s quickened, so too did the pressures to develop new and different kinds of histories.[63] African history emerged coincidently with the end of empire, and its emergence indicated a major paradigmatic shift in the units of analysis and methodology.[64] First with the decolonization of the Sudan in 1956, but especially with independence of

Ghana in 1957 and then that of French West Africa in 1960, decolonization spread rapidly throughout the continent with several exceptions, including the British colonies of white settlement and the Portuguese colonies.

For our purposes, political independence boosted the demand for histories of Africa and Africans that demonstrated that Africans had their own history and that it was a history that had existed well before the arrival of Europeans. This gave rise to the twin foundations of the discipline of African history: (1) to prove that Africans had agency in their own history and that Africans were not merely passive recipients of change from outside the continent; and (2) to provide an African perspective to this history, in other words, to seek out African voices or sources produced by Africans.[65] To give voice to Africans in their own history confronted a major methodological problem: most African societies were preliterate and therefore did not leave written accounts of their past. To be without writing, however, did not mean to be without history, for all societies need history and all societies produce histories to help explain their identity and to justify their institutions. Most of the early 1950s histories of Africa used European sources to squeeze out African perspectives. It fell to Jan Vansina in 1961, trained as a European medievalist and ethnographer to develop a rigorous methodology for using African oral traditions as reliable historical sources.[66]

Armed with Vansina's methodology, a whole generation of historians of Africa went to the field and asked Africans to tell them about their histories. The 1960s and early 1970s was the era of the great enthusiasm for precolonial history. This was also a period of intensive debates over methods. Oral historians debated their methods and scrutinized various forms of oral traditions, many preferring to use less formal oral traditions in order to tap into economic, cultural, and social history and to tap into the histories of acephalous societies, those without formal rulership. This is exactly what I did when I went to the field to do research in 1976. I interviewed old men and women, former slaves and former masters, nobles, marabouts, and those belonging to lower status artisanal castes. Using both more formal oral traditions and less formal oral histories, I was able to reconstruct the political history of the Middle Niger valley from the mid-eighteenth century and social and economic history from the late nineteenth century.

I went back to the field every 2 or 3 years, but by the early 1990s, I realized that I was facing a very different social, political, and generational universe than I had 15 to 20 years earlier. The ubiquity of transistor radios, cassette players, national broadcasting stations, television, rapid urbanization, economic decline, droughts, and civil wars were changing the forms of transmission of oral histories. I found that when the cohort of elders I interviewed in 1976 and 1977 died, the new cohort of elders was not able to provide me with the quality of detail on social life that I had come to expect. I am now finding that I cannot consistently get good oral evidence from the late precolonial and early colonial periods. I can still mine my informants for details on social and economic change, but not earlier than the interwar period. In other words, the temporal boundary for recovering social and economic history continues to move forward with the passing of each generation.[67] I am not alone in this discovery. Barbara Cooper's splendid study of marriage in a district of Niger has been able to tap into women's oral histories that barely push beyond the Second World War.[68]

The wrenching social dislocations that affected the world in which Africans live and in which they transmit histories between generations include protracted civil wars, involuting national economies, refugee relocations, famines, and the AIDS epidemic. Liisa Malkki's analysis of the profound reworking of identity and history undertaken by Hutu refugees living in camps in Tanzania is an example of how transformative events have changed how history is remembered.[69] Historians of Africa are increasingly tempted to write the histories of the postcolonial period.[70]

But, what about those of us still committed to writing the social histories of the transformations attendant upon conquest and the creation of colonial societies in the early twentieth century and now seemingly beyond the range of oral historical research? I have asked informants about the beginning of the native courts, but their answers have been framed as generalizations. For example, in the interview I had with Idrissa Diakite, who was in his mid-70s, he provided keen insights to the general issues of who used the colonial courts, but could not provide details.

Q: Why did women bring so many cases before the new colonial tribunals?

A: Because of their weak position in terms of culture. The same applied also to the men who brought cases to the new tribunals, because when slavery was ending, it was the weak who came forward.

Q: Why did the weak bring forward their cases to the new tribunals and not take them to the village chief or elders?

A: All reconciliation at the village level favored the most powerful, the husband over the wife, the eldest over the youngest.[71]

These are keen insights indeed, but they were in a sense timeless. Although Diakite mentioned slavery, his comments were not anchored in any particular historical period. This interview certainly directed my attention toward power asymmetries in the courts and supported some of my findings from reading court records. When my informants referred to specific knowledge of the courts, it was encounters they had and thus limited to the late colonial period. When asked whether their parents had been to court, most avoided the question. When pressed, they invoked the Bamana adage that children should not speak badly of their elders. Going to court to resolve domestic problems was not considered respectable.

In the absence of African oral sources, how well do colonial court records fulfill the twin obligations of proving that Africans had agency in their own history and providing an African perspective to this history? My discussion of agency in the preceding section should have convinced my readers that Africans actively used the colonial courts to pursue their own ends. But the answer to whether these court records provide an African "voice" is not quite as evident.

The transcripts of cases heard at the provincial tribunals do contain testimony about wrongs, claims for damages, strained or broken relationships, and requests to the court to act upon those claims. But the grievance we hear has been altered by the process of transforming the dispute into a case that the court hears, by the procedures in the court, by translating the testimony from Bamana into French and into French categories of dispute, and by the act of committing the claims to writing. I have described above Nader's three-stage model of dispute resolution, which traces the dispute as it moves through mediation to litigation. In the early 1980s, Felstiner, Abel, and Sarat proposed a different three-stage model for examining the transformation of a perceived injury into a legally recognizable claim.[72] The Felstiner-Abel-Sarat model proposes that as the grievance moves through the naming, blaming, and claiming phases, it is transformed from an injurious act that may or may not be acted upon to an articulated claim that can be understood and acted upon by an adjudicating body. Of all the potential injurious acts that people experience in the course of their daily lives, only those that are named as such begin the process of articulating the injury. Most injurious acts are not recognized as such (they are "unperceived injurious experiences") and thus not articulated. They never become disputes, per se. They remain inchoate. If the injury is named—recognized as such by the injured party—it may move to the next phase, in which the injured individual identifies and attributes to another party his or her injury. Cultures of disputing and cultures of persevering deeply influence these transformations. This blaming phase is crucial to the life cycle of a dispute; this is when an inchoate injury becomes a grievance, but the grievance has not yet been expressed publicly.

The third phase is reached when a claim is articulated publicly. The claim is made when the injured party expresses the injury to the person being held responsible and asks for a remedy. As the injury is being claimed, the injured party invokes the set of normative behavior that she or he perceives to have been broken and thus expresses the claim in terms of rights and wrongs. In the claiming phase, the dispute has not yet been taken to a third party for mediation or adjudication. If this does occur, then the injury may undergo yet another phase in transformation as it conforms to the categories that the mediating or adjudicating body recognizes. As John Conley and William O'Barr and Merry have discussed in their studies of small claims' courts and various forms of mediation in the United States, litigants expressing their disputes in everyday speech are often frustrated that their speech is often not recognized by judges or interrupted by lawyers or judges pressing for different information.[73]

The Felstiner-Abel-Sarat model points to the importance of recognizing how narrating trouble changes through the process of articulating a claim. Susan Hirsch has applied linguistic and discourse analysis to Swahili women's disputes brought before the qadi's courts in Mombassa. Hirsch uses records from the court and her own observations of disputes. By bringing disputes before the qadi's court, Swahili women both negotiated marital disputes and refashioned gender in the process. Given the gender norms in Swahili society, women were supposed to be persevering and subordinate, but by taking their disputes before the qadi and narrating their troubles, they were transforming gender through speech and attempting to transform their lives through their actions. Because speech and narration are gendered, Hirsch argues that "gender is constituted in legal contexts that reproduce and also undermine dominant cultural configurations of gendered subject and gender relations." These courts thus became "sites of resistance" not only because women challenged gendered norms, but because the judgments tended to favor women.[74] This was also the case in the native courts of the French Soudan during the first five or six years of their operation.

What Hirsch analyzed in the qadi's courts is part of what Conley and O'Barr term as "the transformative work of the law."[75] Conley and O'Barr argue that what individuals understand as a dispute changes through the life cycle of the grievance and by the contexts in which the dispute is expressed. By the time a dispute gets to court, it has been transformed through the phases of its articulation and through sets of interactions the disputant has with the opposing parties, the normative requirements of the law, the procedures of the court, and with the clerks and judges of the court.[76] For those of us interested in understanding how trouble is understood and articulated in the past, we are confronted with yet another transformation: how trouble spoken in the court is transformed into what we read as transcripts.

The transformation of spoken word into written text is especially dramatic in oral societies as Jack Goody, William Ong, and Isabel Hofmeyr have discussed.[77] That this transition took place under colonialism is also politically significant. Sean Hawkins has recently challenged historians to put writing at the center of the colonial encounter. He argues that writing was central to governmentality and to the production of knowledge. Writing shaped the way knowledge was recognized and disciplined its applicability. Because writing was central to the expression of colonial authority, writing also structured (in texts and in cognitive categories) indigenous knowledge and forms of interaction.[78] The written record also leaves out many things, which has significant implications for social historians' use of court records.

Figure 1.2 Register of Court Cases, Gumbu, 3rd Quarter 1907

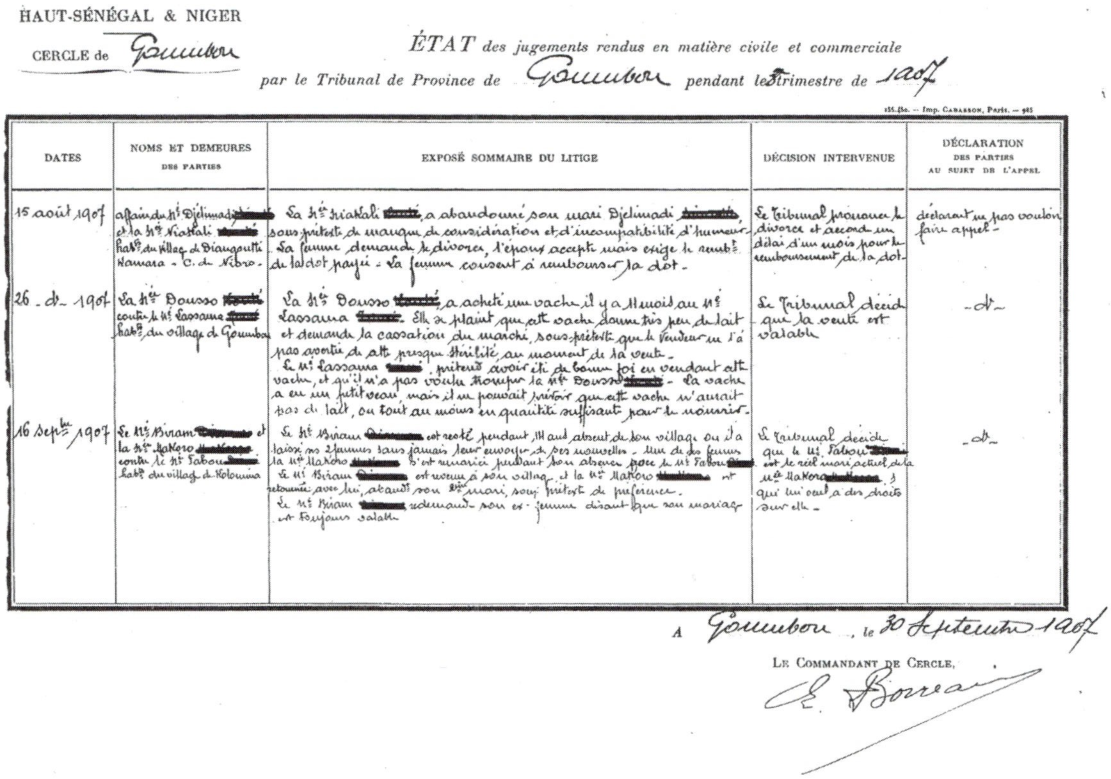

HAUT-SÉNÉGAL & NIGER

CERCLE de _Goumbou_

ÉTAT des jugements rendus en matière civile et commerciale par le Tribunal de Province de _Goumbou_ pendant le 3e trimestre de 1907

DATES	NOMS ET DEMEURES DES PARTIES	EXPOSÉ SOMMAIRE DU LITIGE	DÉCISION INTERVENUE	DÉCLARATION DES PARTIES AU SUJET DE L'APPEL

À _Goumbou_, le 30 septembre 1907

LE COMMANDANT DE CERCLE,

The transcript of the court appearance is but a shadow of the complex set of interactions that actually took place in the courtroom. Different courts have different traditions for recording the courtroom encounter. At best, court records generated by professional stenographers provide "a precise but not infallible technique [of] the meaningful, spoken words of the trial." James Clifford has reflected on the differences between this stenographic record and what he remembered and noted during the 1976 Massachusetts Mashpee Indian land claims case. He notes that the trial records omit "gestures, hesitations, clothing, tone of voice, laughter, irony ... sometimes devastating silences."[79] These omissions are potentially significant because these signs and gestures are often central to the overall effect litigants, witnesses, and lawyers have on the outcome of the trial. Hirsch also acknowledges the loss of texture and detail in the transcription process. Even though Hirsch sought to transcribe the entire dispute or lengthy segments of trials in order to use it in her own analysis, "the transcription process fails to capture so much of what made these narratives meaningful to the participants at the time and, later, to me as analyst. Tiny yet meaningful details fall out. . . ."[80] As a rule, historians cannot watch and listen to past courtroom encounters.[81] Those of us working with African colonial court records will rarely have access to even the stenographically recorded versions Clifford found so faulty. Most of our records are even more imperfect. Most colonial court records are at best summaries of the dispute that were produced by some intermediary, who presents but a single perspective on what went on in the court. The court's procedures and the act of recording the case filtered the sets of interactions, speech, silences, and gestures of all the actors present in the court.[82] I discuss some of the requirements for record keeping in the native courts of the French West Africa in Chapter 3, but let me present here three cases taken from one page of the Gumbu provincial tribunal registers between 15 August and 16 September 1907. I have selected Figure 1.2 not because the cases are particularly revealing, but because they are especially legible. Following the 1903 decree and Governor-general Ernest Roume's instructions to district officers, the court register was to contain five columns: the date of the court appearance, the names and residences of the disputants, a summary of the dispute, a summary of the court's judgment, and a declaration of whether or not the litigants wished to appeal the judgment. The second column, names and residences of the disputants, was also supposed to identify whether the litigants claimed "customary" or Muslim legal status. In the event of an appeal or judicial review by the attorney-general, this information would be central to the assessment of the case and its judgment. As I discuss more fully in Chapter 3, few registers actually recorded this information. Following the requirements of the decree, the district officer was to approve the court register and thus the procedures applied by signing the registers.[83] The 1903 decree required a written register of the cases, which permitted a double surveillance over the procedures in the courts and over the district officer in the pursuit of his authorized duties. From the standpoint of this section, I am most interested in the transformation of the talk of trouble into a text we read. I have included in

Table 1.2 Record of Three Cases in Gumbu, 1907

Dates	Names and Residences of the Parties	Summary of the Dispute	Decision Taken	Declaration of Intention to Appeal
15 Aug 1907	The case of the named (male) Djelimadi Soumare and the named (female) Niakali Doukara, habitants of the village of Diangoutti-Kamara, district of Nioro.	The named Niakali Doukara has abandoned her husband Djelimadi Soumare because of alleged lack of consideration and incompatibility. The wife requests a divorce; the husband accepts, but insists on the reimbursement of the bridewealth paid. The wife agrees to the reimbursement of the bridewealth.	The tribunal pronounces the divorce and agrees to a one month delay for the reimbursement of the bridewealth.	The parties have declared that they will not appeal.
26 Aug 1907	The named (female) Dousso Konare vs. the named (male) Lassane Toure, residents of Gumbu.	The named Dousso Konare bought a cow from the named Lassane Toure. She complains that the cow gives only very little milk and requests the annulment of the purchase agreement. She alleges that the seller did not reveal this condition of almost sterility at the time of sale. The named Lassane Toure alleges to have had only good intentions in selling this cow and that he had no intention of deceiving the buyer. The cow has a little calf, but he did not know that the cow did not have milk, or that the quantity of milk was insufficient to nourish the calf.	The tribunal decides that the sale is valid.	Ditto. [The parties have declared that they will not appeal.]
15 Sept 1907	The named (male) Birama Taraore and the named (female) Makoro Boudy vs the named (male) Fabou Daillo, residents of Kolomina village.	The named Birama Taraore has been absent from the village for 14 years and has left his two wives without ever sending any news. One of his wives, the named Makoro Boudy remarried during his absence with the named Fabou Daillo. The named Birama Taraore returned to his village and the named Makoro Makessa returned to him and abandoned her second husband alleging that this was her preference. The named Birama Taraore reclaimed his wife by claiming that his marriage has remained valid.	The tribunal decided that the named Fabou Daillo is the real, current husband of Makoro Boudy and that he alone has right to her.	Ditto. [The parties have declared that they will not appeal.]

Source: ANM 2 M 122

parentheses in the names and residences column the gender of the disputants, which is evident in the French, but not in the English translations. The first observation should be how sparse these summaries are. Given how sparse these records are, we could assume that the dispute only took moments in court. However, each dispute may have taken much longer. District officers regularly complained of the tedious and unending palavers they participated in as they adjudicated ordinary disputes.

In examining the summary of the cases, the reader has no sense of how long, for example, Niakali Doukara and her husband, Djelimadi Soumare, have been married nor how long they have been struggling with their marriage. All we hear is that Doukara has accused her husband of lacking in consideration and that they have incompatible personalities. We do not know what Doukara meant by lack of consideration. Her husband does not appear to contradict these assertions, nor does he challenge his wife's request for a divorce. He only demands the return of the bridewealth he had provided upon marriage. Doukara agrees to return the bridewealth, although as we shall see in Chapter 7, brides rarely received the bridewealth in the first place. Their fathers or other male guardians did. Only from the judgment column do we hear of Doukara's request for a month delay in order to raise the funds needed to repay the bridewealth. That fact that Doukara was able to raise the funds needed indicates that she may have had her own property to draw from. But we cannot be sure from the evidence presented in the court register. It could be that Doukara has already located another suitor, who would funnel the bridewealth to Soumare. We cannot consider this interpretation because there is nothing in the record to suggest that Doukara had another suitor or lover. More intriguing is the claim for incompatibility that Doukara raised. I am not sure that incompatibility in marriage was a common Malinke category at the turn of the twentieth century, although divorce and serial marriages were common in West Africa.[84]

The second case provides a clue to the source of Doukara's property that she might have had to liquidate to repay the bridewealth to Soumare. In this case, Dousso Konare bought a cow from Lassane Toure, but found that cow was not producing the volume of milk that she expected. The fact that Konare was buying a cow as her own property provides some proof for the proposition that Doukara in the previous case had also her own property, which she could use to end her marriage to Soumare. I discuss the issues of women's property and especially women's investment in livestock more fully in Chapter 7.

The second case, perhaps because it deals with a specific commercial transaction, provides a smoother transition of trouble talk into text. The cause of the dispute surrounds the full disclosure of the condition of a cow upon its sale. We also know from the structure of the summary that the buyer was the plaintiff in this case. The buyer alleges that the seller did not fully reveal the faults in his property and that only upon some time after the sale, did she notice that the cow did not produce sufficient milk. The seller responded that he was not aware of this deficit in his property, which had recently bore a calf. From the record, we do not know whether the judges cross-examined the defendant or the plaintiff, although the evidence that the cow had recently born a calf appears in the summary as an afterthought, suggesting that this datum emerged from the give-and-take of testimony. We also do not know whether or not the judges pressed Toure, the seller, for proof that he did or did not know about the cow's poor milk production. We can assume that the judges were satisfied with Toure's veracity because they rejected the plaintiff's claim. Although I do not deal extensively with contracts and commercial transactions in this book, Chapter 7 on property explores the principle of *caveat emptor* as it was revealed by the court cases.

The third case is the most interesting of the three. It hints at the logic behind African judges' decisions in this case even though the summary of the judgment does not provide a transcript of their decisions. It shows the vulnerability married women faced and suggests some of the ways women sought to reduce their vulnerabilities. This case also reveals some of the problems in the linguistic construction of the summary because it does not clearly indicate who the plaintiff was. I discuss the use of passive voice in the judgments in Chapter 6 on bridewealth disputes, but in this case, the actual construction of the summary of the case does not indicate that it was Fabou Diallo who was bringing the case against Birama Taraore and Makoro Boudy. I doubt that this case would have come to court if Diallo had not wanted to have the court force wife, Boudy, to return to him.

Sociologically the case is fascinating in what it tells us about Makoro Boudy. How long she was married to Birama Taraore is not clear, but sometime around 1893, Taraore left his two wives and did not return. Being abandoned for a year or longer and without news of his whereabouts, Boudy and her co-wife could have requested a divorce from the native courts and it would have been granted, because abandonment was one of the recognized causes of divorce. Boudy did not request a divorce, but sought out another man to support her. Assuming that her husband was dead, Boudy married Fabou Diallo, although the court record does not tell us when. We do not know from this record what her co-wife did to survive. She does not enter the trouble talk or its text. When her first husband reappeared after 14 years, Boudy embraced him and returned to live with him. Diallo was in court seeking to have the court force Boudy to return to his house as her rightful wife. Boudy demurred, alleging that she preferred to live with her first husband, Taraore. We are offered no more information than these statements of fact.

The court ruled in Diallo's favor and demanded that Boudy return to her second husband, whom the court declared as her rightful husband. The court moved to this decision most likely by upholding Boudy's original action in thinking her marriage was over because Taraore had abandoned her and her co-wife, although we do not know for how long. That Diallo formally married

Boudy and most likely provided bridewealth to regularize the marriage is indicated in the court's claim that he was the rightful husband and he alone had rights to her, which could only be acquired by formal marriage. In comparison with the *Doukara v. Soumare* case of 15 August 1907, the court did not accept or recognize Boudy's wishes. It could be, although we have no way of knowing, the judges so ruled despite Boudy's wishes, because Taraore's 14-year abandonment had ruptured what they understood as the moral economy of his marriage.

I included these three cases as examples of what we have in the court records and also what we do not know from these records. The cases all point to the expression of injuries, although we cannot trace the transformation of the talk of trouble into the summary of the disputants' interactions in the court. We have no way of knowing whether or not the disputants sought to reconcile their differences before they arrived in court, although we can assume that they tried. Thus, we have no way of knowing what may have been lost in the transformation of the more expansive discussion of the trouble between the parties into the sparse summary of the dispute that we read in the records. Nonetheless, the court records provide some indication of Africans expressing trouble and of their actions to resolve it, if only in the court session being described.

SUMMARY

This book is organized into two parts. The first part provides a history of the making of the colonial legal system in the French Soudan. In Chapter 2, I reconstruct the history of the forces shaping the French colonial legal experience in West Africa and link these to the French Revolution and especially to Napoléon's Egyptian experience, which sets an important precedent for the development of colonial plural legal systems. I link the brief Egyptian and the formative Algerian experience to the development of the colonial legal concept of the protectorate. I explore the pressures on policy and practice as the French expanded their conquests in West Africa. These forces of conquest and administration led to the articulation of new forms of legal pluralism. The second half of Chapter 2 picks up the story about the competing models of colonialism during a period of increased territorial conquest and the establishment of colonial institutions. I compare the colonialism of indirect rule applied by the senior military leader Colonel Louis Archinard with the more centralized colonialism of the newly created government-general in 1895. As military leaders became district officers during the routinization of colonial rule, they became engaged in adjudicating ordinary civil disputes as well as more serious crimes. The tensions between these two models of colonialism were played out in terms of the issues of proportionality between crimes and punishments, the regularization of punishments, the surveillance of the legal authority wielded by French district officers, and issues of legal jurisdiction.

The colonialism of the government-general eventually prevailed. Chapter 3 examines the making of the 1903 legal system and probes some of the procedural innovations it introduced, which had significant impact of the production of the court records I use in this book. In this chapter, I also examine some of the debates over how to understand and apply customs and the place of codification within the native court system. Part 2 of this book begins as the new courts are created in 1905 and how these courts then become part of the landscapes of power along the Niger River as the slaves began to leave their masters. Chapter 4 uses Gumbu court data as a case study to see the interrelationship between the new courts and the social processes of change linked to the end of slavery. Chapters 5 through 8 examine marriage and divorce (Chapter 5), bridewealth (Chapter 6), new forms of property (Chapter 7), and inheritance (Chapter 8) through the lens of the court cases for the period 1905 to 1912.

There is a logic to the order of the presentation in Part 2. I begin with a discussion of divorce and marriage precisely because women seeking divorce were the ones who forced the French to think more fully about African households and women's choices in marriage. If this project were a historically grounded ethnography, I would have begun with a discussion of bridewealth and then pursued a discussion of marriage and divorce, because the transfer of bridewealth permitted marriage. However, I am writing a social history whose evidential core comes from court cases. Thus, reading divorce cases led me to think about bridewealth because marital rupture ending in divorce confronted one of the central barriers to divorce, namely the return of bridewealth from the wife's kin back to the husband's kin. While I explore a range of disputes surrounding bridewealth in Chapter 6, the central insight emerges from an analysis of how women overcame the barrier of returning bridewealth in order to secure divorce. The key here is that women had rights to their own property independent from their husbands. While the court records often do not identify who was responsible for returning bridewealth, we can assume that given the barriers her kin faced in this regard, women likely used their own property to return the value of the bridewealth. We can also identify cases where newly divorced women funneled bridewealth from their new marriages back to their former husbands. Tracing women's property through court disputes thus forms the central theme in Chapter 7. I am particularly interested in women's investment in "new" forms of property, especially in livestock and use court records to trace some of the complexities of women's separate property within their husbands' households. Tracing the complexities of women's property within their husbands' households becomes visible in inheritance disputes. Chapter 8 focuses on inheritance disputes as a means of examining the complex set of linked and separate spheres of property within households. This study ends in 1912 when the native court system underwent the first of a long series of periodic reorganizations that lasted until independence.

Part I

Colonial Courts

2

THE FOUNDATIONS OF THE FRENCH COLONIAL LEGAL SYSTEM IN WEST AFRICA, 1673–1903

Colonial legal systems do not emerge fully formed, but adapt over time to the changing character of colonial and imperial rule and to the forms and nature of indigenous responses to colonial conquest. Changes in colonial legal systems reflect the encounter between metropolitan pressures and local processes of change. In order to examine how African litigants used the native courts, we need to understand the institutions and practices of colonial law and the historical processes that led to their establishment. This chapter examines the pivotal moments in the development of legal institutions in French West Africa from the early phase of the French chartered commercial companies through the commission charged with developing a comprehensive colonial legal system in 1903. The bulk of this chapter focuses on the period from 1893–1903, which witnessed a struggle over very different conceptions of colonialism.

Between 1673, when the first of a series of French chartered companies laid claim to the tiny entrepôts on the West African coast, and 1893, four pivotal events defined the arena in which colonial officials struggled over the place of law within French colonialism. The first was Napoléon's Egyptian expedition of 1798, which established the principle of the protectorate, in which a conquering power agreed to respect the legal authority of "customs" as part of ceding authority over the internal affairs of the society to designated indigenous authorities. The French first formally proclaimed the protectorate in their claim over Tahiti in 1842, although they had experimented with the protectorate in Algeria. The second event was the commission charged with producing a unified legal code for metropolitan France, which resulted in the Napoléonic Code in 1804. The idea of a code as a legislated body of laws and procedures applied uniformly throughout the land stood in sharp contrast with practice of a protectorate, which protected indigenous custom. The third was France's colonial experience in Algeria, which became a laboratory to test out France's thinking about what nineteenth-century colonialism was to be. Many of France's experiences in Algeria, especially those dealing with France's relations with Muslims and Berbers, informed colonial practices in Senegal under Faidherbe from 1854–1860 and 1863–1865. And the fourth was the conquest of the Western Sudan, which opened up a vast area of the interior of West Africa to French colonial rule and set the stage for a major struggle over what colonialism meant. In that struggle, the place of law was central. This chapter ends with the promulgation of a unified colonial legal system for French West Africa in 1903. As I shall argue, despite the plans elaborated in Paris, the shape of the colonial legal system in French West Africa reflected the encounter between metropolitan ideas and goals and local practices of Africans and French administrators on the ground.

CONSTRUCTING A COLONIAL LEGAL SYSTEM, 1673–1893

Under the *ancien régime,* the colonies of Senegal and those of the southern coast of India differed from those of the Antilles and New France in that they were primarily commercial outposts and not colonies of settlement or plantations. All three types of colonial endeavor were pursued under a mix of direct royal initiative or indirectly through chartered companies. In all cases, the mercantilist goals were the same: colonies were for the benefit of mother country and the colonizing agency. Realizing the benefits of colonization most often required establishing some degree of control over the new spaces and some forms of collaboration with local inhabitants. Control over territory, however fragile, rested upon assumptions about the "rights" of possession.[1] Extracting the benefits of territorial control rested upon a combination of force, collaboration with local inhabitants often through cross-cultural brokers, and through control over labor.

Interactions between local inhabitants and Frenchmen were often conducted by a sense of mutual benefit. Not all transactions, however, were mutually beneficial and thus some recourse to adjudication was required. Sometimes adjudication was done according to local customs; sometimes by hybrid European institutions.[2] Where European control over territory was proclaimed, Europeans imported their own legal institutions. These institutions were far from uniform. "Each tribunal, each judge," wrote Emilien Petit in 1771, "has its own system for the observation of royal laws even within the same colony."[3]

The "anarchy" of colonial legal space reflected metropolitan realities. Metropolitan law in eighteenth-century France consisted of an overlapping patchwork of divergent jurisdictions of customs drawn from feudal practices, canon law, seignorial rights, and royal intrusions. By the middle of the eighteenth century, France had a bewildering array of civil and criminal tribunals, church courts, tribunals charged with surveillance of currency, those controlling the hunt, military courts, and commercial courts. Every corporate entity, it seemed, had its own jurisdiction and its representative court. Each dispensed justice according to its "customary" practices. Plaintiffs and defendants alike faced a legal system that was complex, often venal, and fraught by conflicting jurisdictions.[4] The royal edicts of 1664 and 1671 provided the earliest reception of French law into the newly founded colonies. Those edicts reiterated that the colonies will "follow the rules of custom of Paris for the justice rendered to the inhabitants of the colonies."[5]

Notwithstanding these initial centralizing efforts, the king and his court could not impose legal uniformity on distant colonies and each developed practices reflecting local necessity. During a visit to Senegal just before the French Revolution, Dominique Lamiral, a former agent of the chartered Compagnie de Guyane, described Saint Louis as a "village inhabited by some three hundred freemen, blacks and mulattoes, and around five or six thousand slaves or foreigners from diverse neighboring nations." Lamiral further noted that authority, such as it was, was administered by "the garrison composed of a battalion. . . , which is commanded by an officer, who also rules the colony. The single public official who is in the colony is the *greffier garde*. There is hardly any regular justice."[6] During the course of the Napoléonic wars in Europe, Britain seized France's Senegalese territories and returned them in 1817. In the meantime, the first of two foundational experiences in the making of a colonial legal system had occurred.

In May 1798, a large flotilla carrying a substantial army left the French port of Toulon for Alexandria. Under the command of Napoléon Bonaparte, French troops conquered Egypt in six weeks. Napoléon's Egyptian policy was part of his larger geo-political strategy of war in Europe and was designed particularly against the British. In response, the British promptly sunk the French fleet outside of Alexandria and Napoléon secretly left Egypt in August 1799 to return to France. By 1800, revolt, disease, and military setbacks demoralized the French army and by August 1801, the French retreated from Egypt.[7]

Despite its short duration, Napoléon's Egyptian expedition marked a significant break in French colonial history, although it was clearly consistent with French revolutionary zeal to remake conquered territories in Europe in its own image. Throughout their territorial conquests in continental Europe, the French sought to impose their bureaucratic models of government, their concepts of equality in the face of privilege, and their sense of the unity of law. But in Egypt, which was France's first effort to control new overseas territories since the French Revolution, French rule was conceived differently. Keenly aware that Islam was a central part of the political and cultural expression of Egypt, Napoléon sought to establish an "enlightened" protectorate, which at once respected cultural difference, but nonetheless sought to "regenerate" Egypt into the glorious kingdom it once was.[8] He sought to establish an administration that associated French military leaders with local Muslim notables and brought with him not merely soldiers, but also scholars, whose task it was to understand the civilization of the conquered lands. These scholars established the Institut d'Egypte, which was modeled directly on the Institut de France and was thus a self-conscious Enlightenment project. There was, of course, an audacity to Napoléon's colonialism of scholars: part of colonialism's civilizing mission was, in Edward Said's terms, to "render [Egypt] completely open, to make it totally accessible to European scrutiny" and to return Egypt to its former glory, which only the French savants, using modern science, could accomplish.[9]

Napoléon's Egyptian expedition failed. But the expedition set in motion a profoundly different conceptualization of colonialism. Jean-Loup Amselle has described this new colonialism as a form of "cultural administration." Napoléon's cultural administration was based upon respect, more or less grudgingly, for local Islamic culture within a broader ethnocentric conceptualization of civilization and the incorporation of local notables into a colonial administration. This did not mean that the French were not prepared to intervene aggressively to transform institutions and practices that they assumed were the bases of "the degenerative oriental despotism." Respecting custom yet transforming barbarous and corrupt practices made the fiscal and judicial systems of Egypt sites for colonial social engineering.[10] French troops fled Egypt before such reforms could be sustained, but the principles of cultural administration were to become part of French colonial practice. Napoléon was, however, preoccupied with war in Europe and had no further opportunity to advance his colonial projects. However, immediately upon his return to France, Napoléon took charge of the commission designed to create a uniformed legal system and pushed it to completion.

The idea of a single code for all of France had its roots in the Parliaments of the mid-eighteenth century and its direct antecedents in the Constitution of 1791 as well as in the reforms projects of 1793 and 1794.[11] In many ways, the Code of 1804 came to epitomize a commitment to rationality within the diverse body of eighteenth-century Enlightenment thought. By eliminating the juridical diversity of the *ancien régime,* which was so tied to "particularisms and privileges," François Furet argues that the Revolution "flung open the door to the French passion for laws, in which the rationalist universalism which is one of its dominant characteristics finds its finest expression." He sees a "causal chain" directly linking Enlightenment ideas to reforms in civil legislation and to the rationalist assumptions of a state-centered source of all civil authority.[12] The code was also a fundamental rupture with the authority and sources of preexisting bodies of law. In describing the development of the civil code system, Edward McWhinney states that

An act of codification is always something of a revolutionary step in the sense that it represents a certain intellectual break with the past. Although all the codes purport to be merely a restatement of the old, pre-existing law, most of the great codifying commissions have used the opportunity to make innovations and changes in the old law: and the act of codification itself, in the sense that it involves reducing a large and hitherto unorganized mass of materials to comprehensive form, necessarily involves a certain clarification and streamlining of the existing law.[13]

The shift from the patchwork jurisdictions of the *ancien régime* to the Napoléonic Code was much more than the "streamlining and clarification of existing law." Most of the authority of law in the *ancien régime* flowed from the assumptions of status and privilege. The Code enshrined the idea of natural rights of individuals—all individuals regardless of rank, but not of gender— and shifted the authority of law to the collective will of the nation as expressed by the National Assembly.[14] The Enlightenment concept of the perfectibility of all men was linked directly to the natural "rights of man." The perfectibility of all men and their natural rights were framed in universal terms, but had, as we shall see, a profoundly ethnocentric caste, which confronted the protection of "customs" in the practice of the protectorate. These tensions emerged early in Algeria.

The French slid into colonialism in Algeria. The immediate antecedent to French military conquest was a silly diplomatic affront occasioned when the Dey of Algers smacked the French consul with a fly whisk in 1827 for allegedly maligning Muslim respectability. For reasons having more to do with internal French politics and the growing weakness of the Bourbon restoration, Charles X ordered first a blockade of Algers in 1827 and subsequently the occupation of the city in 1830. The French conquest of Algeria that followed was driven by both internal French politics—propelled by the fall of the Bourbons and the rise of the July Monarchy under Louis-Philippe in 1830—and the press of military events than from any plan or vision of what colonialism in the Maghreb was to mean.[15] By the time Louis-Philippe claimed French possession of North Africa in 1834, three distinctive trajectories of French colonialism were already evident in the tiny footholds France had secured along the coast. Almost immediately, the French military faced significant resistance, which served to promote the military model of colonialism as well as a grudging respect for Islam and the resiliency of Muslim institutions. These conquered footholds also gave rise to a frenzy of land speculation, which in turn stimulated European immigration.[16] Hence, the colonialism of the military barracks confronted the colonialism of settlement and both confronted the colonialism of the protectorate or some ill-defined model of indirect rule in which Berber and Arab tribal leaders ruled. All three models of colonialism, however, faltered in the face of the stiff resistance of Abd al-Qadir and by regional confederations of Berbers and Arabs.[17]

Indirect rule in Algeria rested upon the development of a class of cross-cultural brokers, a kind of military in ethnographers' clothes. Many of the soldiers who populated the Bureaux Arabes were mid-level officers, veterans of the conquest, who had intellectual interests in languages, histories, and cultures. They were required to know Arabic and through their linguistic abilities, they became crucial intermediaries between the military administration and the notables charged with running local communities. The members of the Bureaux Arabes were charged with collecting intelligence and overseeing the activities of the local administration in the hands of the shayhks, including the operation of the Muslim courts.[18] The foundation of the French program of indirect rule necessitated an ethnographic imperative of "scientific description and analysis of indigenous institutions."[19]

French respect for Islam within the societies and polities of North Africa came not from an appreciation of the cultural genius of Muslim civilizations, but from a fear of the passions that bound the faithful to their rightful leaders. The French believed that the Arab and Berber inhabitants profoundly disliked their despotic and corrupt Ottoman rulers and that if the French respected the Algerians' religion, their women, and their property, they would easily win control over the region.[20] The French committed themselves to the free exercise of the "Mahomatan religion" in the treaty of Algers of 5 July 1830. Respect for Islam also demanded respect for Muslim law, because Muslim law had its source in the Koran and was therefore inseparable from Islamic faith. To force Muslims to bring their legal cases regarding their personal status (marriage, divorce, orphans, inheritance, etc.) before French magistrates or French military officers administering French civil law could be perceived as a step toward the desacrilization of Muslim law and toward forced conversion. Thus, both expediency and cultural awareness led to the incorporation of Muslim courts into the colonial administration of French possessions in North Africa.

The incorporation of Muslim courts into the administration of colonial Algeria proceeded unevenly and was subject to broad, often contradictory shifts in France's native policy for Algeria. Even at its most pragmatic, French efforts to incorporate qadi justice into the colonial order resulted in fundamental tensions and profound shifts in the nature of legal jurisdiction and practice.[21] According to Allen Christelow's study of qadi courts in the mid-nineteenth-century Algeria, the French thought that their policy of permitting Muslims to retain their civil status and bring their disputes to their own judges represented a benevolent attitude toward Islam and thus provided a means to draw religious leaders into an alliance with the colonial state. The French underestimated the transformations that they set in motion by conquest and by their subsequent efforts to control the activities of qadis. To assist the French officers of the Bureaux Arabes in their efforts to control the legal work of the qadis, the Malikite legal code was translated into French into a multivolume edition in 1854 and later condensed in a new one-volume translation focusing on the Malikite code dealing property and inheritance. The new translation, published in 1878, was produced by N. Seignette, an officer of the Bureaux Arabes.[22] Qadi's courts were not the only courts in Algeria, nor the shari'a the only source of law. French law prevailed where there were dense populations of Europeans; and among the Berbers of Kabyle, village chiefs administered a form of customary law.[23]

The Second Republic pursued a more aggressive approach toward the principles of universal human rights and assimilation of indigenous people into colonial civil society. In 1848, the constituent assembly abolished slavery in all French possessions and extended the rights of French citizenship to selected inhabitants of those territories. The Second Republic declared Algeria to be French territory and transformed its provinces into *départements* along the metropolitan model. During its short-lived existence, some administrative services were actually assimilated into metropolitan ministries, but critical functions of colonial administration remained with the War Ministry. With the rise of Louis Napoléon and the Second Empire, the trend toward civilian dominance of colonial administration was reversed and the military were again ascendant in Algerian affairs. The military also confronted a series of revolts in the 1860s and 1870s, redoubling its sense of its own crucial role. During this period Louis Napoléon introduced legislation that articulated a more generally held view that there were three Algerias: a military territory, a colony of settlement, and an Arab kingdom.

The path toward the construction of a colonial legal system differed in Senegal precisely because the colony lacked both the powerful influence of settlers and an unconstrained military. In 1822, a tribunal was established in Gorée, which heard cases involving French citizens of metropolitan origin. In 1830, a local decree "received" the French civil code in effect in France and expanded the rights of citizenship, which Napoléon Bonaparte had suspended in 1794.[24] According to the principles of the 1830 decree, all "persons born free and living in Senegal or its dependencies will have the rights of a French citizen as guaranteed by the Civil Code."[25]

Extending the French civil code to the free inhabitants of Saint Louis and Gorée confronted the fact that the majority of the Senegalese inhabitants of these towns were Muslim. For them, marriage and the organization of the family were founded in religion and in religiously sanctioned law. As such, Muslim law lay outside the purview of the civil legislator, whose jurisdiction was defined by legal separation of church and state.[26] At its very foundation, then, Muslim law was incompatible with the French civil law tradition. Bowing to the sustained pressures of the Muslim inhabitants to recognize the jurisdiction of Muslim family law, Governor Baudin convened a consultative committee in December 1847, which was charged with advising the French tribunal on issues of Muslim law submitted to the courts. In 1848, a Muslim tribunal was given legal standing within Senegal, but it was overtaken by the revolutionary events of 1848 and never convened.[27]

Governor Faidherbe launched a more aggressive policy toward neighboring African polities in the 1850s, increased the size of the colony, and forced it to confront some of the legal ambiguities surrounding the place of law in the day-to-day administration of the colony. Part of Faidherbe's strategy for the expansion and consolidation of French control lay in building the core of an army around African recruits and in encouraging Muslim collaboration. To encourage Muslim collaboration he included prominent Muslims in his political affairs bureau, built mosques, sponsored Arabic education for interpreters, subsidized the pilgrimage of loyal Muslim notables, and recognized Muslim legal jurisdiction.[28] In 1857, Faidherbe established a Muslim tribunal in Saint Louis, which had jurisdiction over matters of family law, inheritance, and related civil matters.[29]

The establishment of the Muslim tribunal was part of a set of administrative acts that had significant implications for the establishment of a colonial legal system in Senegal. The other administrative act with significant legal implications was Faidherbe's policy of selectively applying the 1848 abolition decree. Slaves were actually freed in the three core territories France controlled along Senegal's coast, but Faidherbe's governorship had included a more aggressive military policy, which resulted in newly conquered territories. Fearing that the wholesale abolition of slaves within these newly conquered territories would undercut African slave owners' loyalty to France at the same time as the militant Islamic leader al hajj Umar was preaching for a religious struggle against the French, Faidherbe conveniently adopted the distinction made by Carrère, the head of the judicial service in Senegal, between citizens and subjects. Citizens were bound by the abolition decree, but not subjects. Faidherbe forestalled legal challenges to his policy by disannexing territory and creating protectorates. Hence, Faidherbe could minimize the consequences of the abolition decree by limiting the physical space where French law prevailed.[30]

In acting as he did, Faidherbe drew upon the concept of the protectorate, which the French had applied in Algeria and Tahiti. The practice of protectorates, however, was legally messy. Paul Dislère, one of the leading scholars of colonial legislation, argued that "[o]nce a state is placed under the protectorate of another power, it abdicates completely its external sovereignty and abandons entirely its foreign policy. But, in terms of its administration of its internal affairs, the protected state in general reserves more or less full independence to run its local government. . . . This regime varies from country to country and it is impossible to establish a precise formula for the operation of the protectorate."[31] Frantz Despagnet agreed with Dislère on the legal complexity of the protectorate but shifted the emphasis between old and new protectorates, which differed in the degree of internal sovereignty practiced by traditional rulers.

With the "modern" establishment of protectorates, Despagnet wrote, "the protector nation is required to assist the protected on the road towards civilization." At its base, however, the protectorate has its origins in the circumstances that obliged the second party to submit to the protection of the first, most often through force or the threat of force.[32] In this regard, the modern protectorate shared many of the same ambiguities regarding the place of law with the colonization practiced in the seventeenth and eighteenth centuries.

Faidherbe's administrative acts of distinguishing citizen from subject and in establishing a separate legal jurisdiction for Muslim personal law within the colony had the unintended consequence of creating ambiguities concerning legal jurisdictions. The net result was the persistence of tensions between judicial officials and colonial administrators each competing to preserve or to restrict the jurisdiction of Muslim and indigenous law. When the administrators prevailed, the legal order of metropolitan origin cohabitated with the legal order based upon Muslim institutions and local customs. In contrast, when the magistrates prevailed, Muslim law and local customs were restricted and qadis were reduced to advising French tribunals of Muslim legal traditions. Both magistrates and military leaders faced very different circumstances as the French embarked on the conquest of the Western Sudan, the majority of which became the French Soudan.

CONQUEST, COLONIALISM, AND THE ORIGINS OF COLONIAL LAW IN THE FRENCH SOUDAN

The period from 1879 to 1893 marked the ascendancy of the military in colonial expansion in the Western Sudan. During this relatively brief period, the French laid claim to the vast interior of West Africa. With the exception of the command of Louis Archinard from 1888–1891 and 1892–1893, most military leaders probably gave little thought to the architecture of colonial rule.[33] Nonetheless, this period is central to the establishment of a colonial legal system during which the practice of indirect rule through the model of the protectorate was implemented. The expansion of colonial conquest in the Soudan dates back to the Governorship of Brière de l'Isle in Senegal in 1876, when he led his army into the zone of expanding peanut cultivation in Siin and Saalum. The actual march into the Western Sudan occurred first under the military command of Colonel Borgnis-Desbordes in 1881. In February 1883, notwithstanding his orders to the contrary, Desbordes reached the banks of the Niger at Bamako and established a post. The forward march of French conquest along the Niger was halted until the appointment of Louis Archinard as supreme military commander in 1888. Between 1883 and 1890, the French sought to consolidate their control over the southern flank of the Umarian state, to fortify their presence in Bamako, to secure the supply route from Kayes, and to prepare for the inevitable battle with the Umarians.[34]

At the head of a motley force of 720 mostly African soldiers, 32 French officers, and more than 1,500 African auxiliaries, Archinard marched against the Umarian fortress of Segu in the spring of 1890. In less than a day of fighting, Segu belonged to the French. Already well before his conquest of Segu, Archinard had opened negotiations with the leader of one of the main factions of the rebellious Bambara, first with Karamoko Jara and following his death in 1887 with his brother Mari Jara, concerning the restoration of Bambara rule at Segu following what he anticipated would be the speedy demise of the 30-year-old Umarian regime. As the French were to discover, conquering Africa militarily and building colonial rule were quite different endeavors.

Archinard's model of indirect rule was framed by two related pressures. As supreme military commander, Archinard was keenly aware of the pressures exerted by Paris to contain the rapidly accelerating costs of conquest. But as an ambitious military man, he was anxious to move the military agenda forward. In his correspondence with the governor of Senegal on the eve of his march on Segu, Archinard explained how the capture of Segu would, in fact, reduce costs because a whole series of French garrisons and forts could be withdrawn. He also made clear that while he had no intention of marching on Segu, he nonetheless demanded the freedom to respond to Umarian aggression against the French or her allies, which he later used to justify his march against Segu in April 1890.[35] The other pressure was to relieve both the budget and the military officers of the task of administering directly the newly conquered lands. In thinking about the post conquest control over the Middle Niger region, Archinard probably drew on the concept of protectorate.

Did Archinard have a plan for what the subsequent model of administration would actually be? Archinard probably did not have a "plan" as much as he had a set of inclinations. His first inclination was to keep his military officers as free as possible from direct administrative burdens. Second, he wanted to insure the security of his troops and the maintenance of order, because disorder required redirecting resources and distracting the military from the bigger battles still ahead. To insure order while simultaneously keeping his officers free from the burdens of direct administration meant that Archinard had to rely on African intermediaries. In what Kanya-Forstner has termed "merely a temporary expedient," Archinard set about reestablishing African kingdoms in newly conquered regions.[36]

In correspondence with the Jara descendants of the Bambara state, Archinard promised to return them to their "rightful" position as "kings" of Segu.[37] This sentiment is clear from the minutes of Archinard's meeting with Mari Jara and other Bambara notables and officers following the French capture of Segu on 11 April 1890 where the structure of the newly reconstituted political order was outlined. Archinard opened the meeting as follows:

> The French have come to take this land of Segu not to governor it them-
> selves, but to return it to the Bambara, the former owners. . . . In returning
> the land to Mari Jara, the *faama* [Bamana: king] of the Bambara, the com-
> mandant supérieur does so in order to promote the prosperity of the land
> and the development of commerce and not to permit the Bambara of the
> right bank of the Niger to resume their raids on the left bank. To that end, I
> am installing here at Segu a military unit. The French commandant will not
> concern himself with the affairs of administration of the *faama* and his vil-
> lages. The *faama* may do as he wishes, but he must keep the commandant
> informed.

Archinard concluded by arguing that he was convinced that "these dispositions will assure the good relations between the *faama* and the French, but if
they fail to assure these good terms, the French will return. We hope not to
return as enemies after having arrived in order to protect."[38]

Even more revealing of Archinard's conception of the Soudanese kingdom
he sought to reestablish at Segu was contained in a telegram he sent to the
governor of Senegal the day after the fall of Segu.

> I have received the submission of all the land and all give us thanks for end-
> ing the tyranny of the Toucouleur and for returning their liberty. I will stay
> here for a few days in order to reorganize the column and to organize the
> land. I will install next to the Faama of the Bambara of Segu, who I have re-
> established in his position, a resident who will be the real king (*le vrai roi*)
> and who will sign all the treaties that I have authorized with Macina, Tim-
> buktu, and neighboring areas.[39]

Within a week, Archinard actually did "organize the land" as he promised and
he appointed Captain Underberg as the resident. That Archinard felt he could
organize the land in such a short period of time indicated that he fully
believed that the Jara dynasty could be reestablished after three decades in the
bush waging on-again, off-again war with the Umarians. On the other hand,
he may have believed that the organization of African kingdoms did not
require much "planning." Calling the resident the "real king" was also indicative of what Archinard meant by protectorate. The resident was charged with
all foreign relations, such as signing treaties, but he was not to meddle in the
internal affairs of the kingdom. In a report written at the end of the 1890 campaign, Archinard admitted that when he installed Mari Jara as *faama,* he did
not have a great deal of confidence in Jara's abilities to rule in the manner the
French anticipated. Within two months, Captain Underberg executed Mari
Jara and the leading Jara notables, allegedly for conspiring to murder the
French resident and his garrison. The fact that the French could execute the
"legitimate" rule of the Segu state surely indicates where the real power

resided. Moreover, the execution of Mari Jara did not seem to undermine Archinard's concept of African kingship under French protection, for he promptly appointed Bojan, a minor royal from the rival Massassi dynasty of Kaarta, as *faama* of Segu. Archinard termed this a "palace coup that led the Massassi to the throne and assures definitively the future of the kingdom of Segu."[40] The appointment of Bojan as *faama* of Segu indicates just how instrumental Archinard's model of the restored African kingdom was. These were to be polities, but not necessarily polities that had precolonial antecedents.

Archinard's disinterest in precolonial antecedents was especially pronounced in 1891, when he appointed Mademba, a loyal African employee of the post and telegraph service who had also served closely with the chief military officers Gallieni and Archinard.[41] In 1893, Archinard appointed Aguibou, a dissident son of the Futanke "royal" family, who had broken with his half-brother Amadu Sheku and formed an alliance with the French, *faama* of Bandiagara. Widespread revolts against the French and French-appointed rulers severely tested Archinard's model. In March 1893, Archinard retired Bojan and established a direct colonial administration at Segu under the authority of a French *commandant de cercle*. Archinard further delimited the powers of Mademba and Aguibou, the two remaining indigenous rulers of Archinard's system. At Segu, the commandant took over the political, magisterial, and police functions normally assumed by African kings.[42]

As the political economy of conquest and colonialism altered the social, cultural, and economic landscape of the Middle Niger valley, the place of law within those transformations also underwent a sea change. Law, after all, was intimately associated with power. Eight months after the relatively easy conquest of Segu in 1890, Archinard reassured Captain Underberg, whom he had left in charge of overseeing the Segu protectorate and who was faced with widespread Bambara revolt, that transforming men of arms into agents of administration was probably not as difficult as it seemed. Military success on the battlefield, after all, depended upon organizing an army of services as the conquest of Segu had demonstrated. Archinard felt obliged to help Underberg prioritize his functions, lest the latter lose sight of the most important tasks at hand. But even the lower priority of administering justice could serve to bolster the authority of colonial rule.

> Knowing how to administer a province is not always the same thing as knowing how to command one's troops, even if the officers' experiences of authority will be the most important guarantee that they will be good administrators of provinces. . . . Rendering justice is not the first preoccupation to have. It is necessary first to make clear our authority, even if that authority is not widespread. It goes without saying that while rendering justice is a means of affirming authority, it is necessary to render

justice in such a way as to give the Blacks a good idea of our disinterest-
edness [of our justice], our superiority, and [the fact that rendering justice
is] a consequence of our right to command.[43]

Archinard's concept of justice was functional, designed to support the authority of the new colonial order. The power of military officers turned district
administrators must be uncontested and unambiguous. Among the most
unambiguous expressions of power was capital punishment. The authority to
execute was reserved for the chief military officer. Military officers continued
to harbor the belief that justice should be swift, harsh, and public, especially
when it dealt with crimes. As late as 1895, the administrator of Segu urged the
governor to implement what he considered to be an "Algerian institution" of
criminal justice, based upon a military tribunal of three French officers. This
tribunal, the administrator argued, has "rendered large service" to the establishment of colonial authority.[44]

The model of the protectorate, even with the direct administration of the
French military officer, guided the practice of rendering justice in these newly
conquered spaces of the Soudan. Etienne, the undersecretary for colonies,
instructed Archinard to quickly implement the organization of the Soudan
along the lines of administrative districts (*cercles*), in which French administrators would play more prominent roles. Etienne also reiterated what he considered to be the policy of "respect for native customs."

> In maintaining and supporting this organization of districts, you will be
> directly in contact with the natives for whom you have become their pro-
> tectors, and in relationship to whom you must constantly practice a policy
> of humanity, generosity, and justice. This will take the form both of respect-
> ing their traditions and customs and in presenting ourselves as their libera-
> tors, especially those conquered populations.
>   These thoughts should order all the relations between our administration
> and the natives, especially in the organization of justice as well as in the
> development of native schools and the system of taxation.[45]

In 1893, Archinard summarized his instructions to the newly appointed district officers regarding the application of justice. "Whenever possible," he
wrote in his final report for the Minister of Colonies, "leave the application of
justice for natives to their natural judges. The personnel we have to administer the colony do not permit us to participate in the solution of all conflicts. In
addition, our ideas of justice may often be in contradiction with those admitted by the blacks." Archinard permitted his administrators the participation in
the adjudication of local disputes only when they felt that "native justice was
insufficient or overly venal." They could, however, adjudicate cases when
disputants were from different "races," different religions, or claimed different customs.[46]

By 1893, the practice of administration in the Soudan was founded upon a broad and fairly loose application of the concept of protectorate. In Archinard's hands, the day-to-day activities of rule were to be left to Africans operating within reconstituted African kingdoms, chosen more for their loyalty to France than for their intrinsic legitimacy. French officers were to spend their time winning battles and gaining glory. However, as Archinard tried hard to deflect Paris's efforts to establish civilian authority, he put French officers in a position where they were obliged to spend more of their time with the ordinary business of empire than with the exciting prospects of conquest. Paradoxically, Archinard's model of the reconstituted African kingdom in which the *faama* had little legitimacy served only to increase the burden of the French officers' daily activities in adjudicating disputes among Africans who chose not to bring their grievances before African judges they did not respect or who chose to subject themselves to Frenchmen who did not fully understand African distinctions of status and gender.

Archinard's model of colonial rule did not long remain unchallenged. Despite the rapid forward march of conquest, the French National Assembly was running out of patience with the military rule in West Africa. No longer willing to accept the autonomy of the military command in the Soudan, Minister of Colonies Delcassé dismissed Archinard, the military commander in the Soudan who was both popular among the French officers eager for combat opportunities and among the French masses eager for stories of conquests.[47] Declassé appointed Louis Alphonse Grodet as governor in 1893. Grodet was a strong-willed administrator with experience in the Antilles and French Guyana, but he had pronounced antimilitary sentiments. Grodet was probably not the best choice for the task of taming the military. The military officers in the field resented his intrusion into their freedom of action and resisted his policies. Grodet could never be sure whether his orders would be implemented. Colonel Louis Edgar de Trentinian replaced Grodet as governor in 1895.

LAWYERS AND THE THIRD REPUBLIC'S ANTIMILITARISM

Realizing that far stronger measures were needed to tame the military in the Soudan, Minister of Colonies Chautemps established the French West African Federation in 1895 and appointed Jean-Baptiste Chaudié as governor-general. The establishment of the French West African Federation was but the first stage in what I describe in this chapter as the conflict over colonialisms, which pitted Archinard's model of indirect rule against the centralized, uniform, and regularized program of the republican civilizing mission.[48] It was not until 1899, at the end of Trentinian's appointment, that the Minister of Colonies again sought to impose a civilian order on the Soudan.[49] In 1899, William Ponty, born Amédée William Merlaud-Ponty but preferring the shortened version of his name, was appointed the permanent delegate of the governor-general in the Soudan. This was effectively the governorship, and his title was so changed in 1904. Ponty had been a civilian appointee to the administrative office of the commandant superieur since 1890, interrupted only briefly by a tour of duty in Madagascar. As a civilian, Ponty had a considerable combat experience—he was actually wounded in action against Samory's forces—and both understood and respected the military agenda in the Soudan. This helps to account for his success as governor. His tenure in office was central to the elaboration of both the administrative structure of the colony and many of its economic, political, and social policies. He remained in office until 1908, when he became governor-general.[50]

The Third Republic's willingness to tame the military had its roots in the general antimilitarism of the 1880s. Throughout the nineteenth century the republican tradition viewed the military as a monarchist and royalist bastion of privilege, power, and patronage. Republicans saw the military as opposed to their concepts of civil society. Antimilitary tendencies were enflamed by the Boulanger affair from 1886–1889. General Georges Boulanger had been a highly popular minister of war in one of Georges Clemenceau's short-lived ministries. Although he was in office a mere 18 months, General Boulanger quickly rose to be a commanding political figure with a belligerent anti-German nationalist message. His political ideology was inconsistent, which made him simultaneously attractive to both centrist Republicans and Royalists. After he left Clemenceau's ministry, Boulanger became increasingly demagogic and rightist. Boulanger's pretensions to authoritarian political role frightened republican sentiment in France, which associated Boulanger with the old fears of military power and privilege. The Boulanger affair contributed to the Third Republic's increasing intolerance of the military's insubordination in the Soudan.[51]

Third Republic's attack on the military's autonomy in the Soudan also had its roots in the predominance of lawyers as both deputies in the National Assembly and in the civil service. By the mid-nineteenth century, the study of the law had become one of the most popular choices for a liberal education. The legal profession became overcrowded, leading to the situation in which, according to Theodore Zeldin, "young barristers without clients, living from hand to mouth by private tutoring or literary hack work, were a principal ingredient of the intellectual proletariat of most towns. They were the natural champions of the underdog. Rhetoric was the common language of the Bar and politics. . . . It was not accident that when the republic was at last established, they should have occupied so prominent a role in it."[52] Lawyers played an important role in the formation of the Third Republic. They were generally skilled in the arts of compromise, they could mediate between classes and cliques, and often had the ability to administer well, or at least to help bring about "order." In 1881, 41 percent of the chamber of deputies were practicing lawyers. Lawyers constituted 52 percent of all ministers between 1873 and 1920 and they also predominated in the civil service middle management. Philip Nord has aptly termed the late nineteenth century the "republic of lawyers." These newly empowered lawyers also engaged in a major assault upon the metropolitan judiciary. Between 1879–1883, hundreds of judgeships dating from the Second Empire were abolished, well over a thousand justices quit or were forced to leave office in what has been termed a "judicial revolution." The new organization of justice in France was to be founded upon the new commitment to republican principles of increased attention to personal and public freedoms and increased involvement of the citizenry in its operations. Jury trials became more common.[53] Civil servants and elected officials with legal backgrounds who were willing to reform existing institutions in order to bring them more in line with contemporary policy and republican ideals were also eager to reach deeply into the colonies.

French republicanism was neither internally consistent nor was it consistently applied to colonial policy. Indeed, the marked antimilitarism of the 1890s gave way at the turn of the century to what Wesley Johnson has termed "republican paternalism." In thinking about the meaning of policy, we also need to differentiate between the rhetoric of colonial policy and what was actually implemented on the ground. Here, of course, the question of vantage point comes into play. The view from Paris differed considerably from that of the government-general. Ministers and bureaucrats in Paris were far removed from French West Africa and rarely understood the realities on the ground. In a similar manner, the policy adumbrated by the government-general may have been designed as policy for district officers; or it could have been designed for consumption in Paris.

What is of consequence for our story is that the French military officers in the field experienced the pressures of antimilitarism and institutional reform. Some of these pressures were felt through efforts to directly change the order of command by placing a civilian at the head of the newly conquered regions of the Soudan in 1893. But they were also felt by the increasing pressures to regularize administrative actions. Such regularization played itself out clearly in the application of justice in the Soudan.

THE RULE OF LAW AND THE ASSAULT ON ARCHINARD'S MODEL OF INDIRECT RULE

From among a variety of administrative tasks facing the new colonial order in 1890, the execution of justice in the French Soudan was to emerge as the single clearest reflection of the cultural program of colonialism in the decade between 1893 and 1903. Changes in the place of law within the program of colonialism reflected the struggles among the French over competing models of colonialism. Shifting administrative practice therefore reflected debates about the meaning of colonialism. Grodet, appointed governor of the Soudan in November 1893, was quick to feel the military's resentment against his efforts to constrain their agenda of combat and conquest. French officers tried hard to disregard or circumvent Grodet's orders, particularly those orders that seemed to countermand the new district officers' expression of authority. The application of justice quickly became a site for the struggle between Grodet's vision (supported by the civilian politicians of the Third Republic) of a society ruled by law and by a commitment to basic human rights and the military's commitment to its autonomy, its authority, and its understanding of its mission. In January 1894, Grodet wrote to Colonel Etienne Bonnier, the supreme military commander, regarding the issue of corporal punishment. "I am absolutely opposed to this type of repression of natives. In my opinion, it undermines [our] prestige in the eyes of the Blacks." Corporal punishment, the military countered, was the logical expression of French officers' replacing African kings as commanders of districts. To prohibit corporal punishment would result in the loss of face. Grodet persisted:

> In regard to the weak nature of our authority, I believe that using brutal coercion will have no success. It will reduce our authority to their level of morality. It is necessary to treat the native with firm resolve, but also with humanity. In a word, do not confuse resolve with rudeness, energy with brutality.[54]

In a circular of 26 February 1894 Grodet formally prohibited the use of corporal punishment in the Soudan. There was thus undisguised frustration in Grodet's letter of 19 July 1894, when he wrote to the senior military commander of the Eastern region that "I have prohibited (corporal punishment) in the most formal and absolute manner. . . . I prohibit yet again in the most absolute fashion this type of punishment, which is unworthy of our civilization. Please make certain to bring this letter to the attention of all the district commanders in your region."[55]

Grodet used the struggle over corporal punishment as a lever to try to impose a greater administrative order over the activities of the district officers. To provide a more coherent picture of the administration of justice—and to control better against the abuses—Grodet ordered each district officer to report on the application of justice in his district. "There does not exist in the Soudan a code of administrative justice applicable to the lands placed in our dependence. At this time, I believe, one renders justice by inspiration to prevailing customs whenever possible." While Grodet recognized that in a land populated by different "races" it would be wrong to impose uniformity in judgments, he was concerned that "for identical misdemeanors, the punishment varies according to the temperament of the one who imposes the verdict." Grodet wanted a "guide to the principle offenses" in order to assist the commandants when rendering justice.[56] The reports written in 1894 are of uneven quality, but they are the first of a successive series of questionnaires about the administration of justice and about customs. The very effort of collection of information lay at the heart of the colonial effort to control; control over both administrators and Africans.[57]

The Segu administrator's report, written by Lieutenant Quiquandon, is particularly thoughtful. It also reveals both the haphazard dispensation of colonial justice and the underlying struggles over law.

> At the post of Segu, an officer, usually one of the commandant's assistants, is designated to render justice. The natives of the district present themselves successively at the office of that officer without fear and expose freely their complaints or their requests.
>
> Everyone has access to the post and is presented in his turn by an old African chief, who is an aged native of the land and admirably knowledgeable about justice. He is an excellent auxiliary to the officer, who consults him. Many of the cases presented are absolutely local in the land and often quite obscure; it would be very difficult to define a wrong in this or that sense, if one did not have recourse to an ancient of the country. Judgment is always rendered in the presence of the two parties. In effect, the natives who have a dispute, explain each in his turn and as fully as he wishes, and when the officer is assured that the two have nothing more to add, he pronounces the sentence, which is usually perfectly accepted.[58]

Despite the seemingly transparent nature of the administration of justice characterized by this report, three aspects are worth noting. First, the French administrator depended upon a knowledgeable native for advice on disputes that he did not understand. Second, he rendered judgments quickly and definitively. And third, Africans voluntarily came forward to have their disputes resolved by the French administrator. While we only hear the French administrator's voice when he notes that the litigants "usually perfectly accepted" the judgments, these attributes are analogous to Robert Kidder's descriptions of colonial justice in India. Kidder speaks of the "speculative" air of the colonial courts and of definitive judgments, which unambiguously rewarded winners and punished losers.[59]

Later in this report, Quiquandon raised two additional points. The first is that there was no uniformity to punishments, such that when "two natives commit the same fault, they will likely see two different punishments applied." This was the case because "custom" varied from region to region, among the different "races,"[60] and according to extenuating circumstances. Quiquandon was certainly neither the first nor the only one to articulate a concern about the "regularity" of justice. Although it was not at all his objective, this concern with regularity lay at the heart of the tensions between the two models of colonialism jostling for prominence in the Soudan.

In his second point, Quiquandon took a forceful stand against Grodet's prohibition against corporal punishment.

> It is regrettable that we can not apply the usages of the land in all the range of punishments which we inflict, because our humanity opposes some. I speak primarily of corporal punishments. These are the only ones in certain instances which produce the desired effect in the Blacks: corporal punishment is widely used among the natives and they accept it completely. It is part of their morals.[61]

Despite the linkages of corporal punishment with authority, which he did not articulate, Quiquandon raised an important issue regarding inconsistency in French colonial justice policy. How was it possible on the one hand to respect custom (no matter how arcane and difficult it was to interpret) and not to respect customary punishment?[62] A similar situation prevailed in British Central Africa. Martin Chanock has argued that the terror of precolonial punishments were deeply enmeshed with the maintenance of political authority. Once the ordeal, for example, was removed, the authority of the indigenous rulers, which the British were attempting to foster, weakened. In place of the terror of punishment, Chanock writes, came a "routine oppression."[63]

Already in 1891, Archinard had feared that in establishing French authority, he was inviting Africans to turn to his French officers as judges for their ordinary disputes. "The district officers should not judge disputes except in very exceptional cases and particularly when there are disputes between different villages or cantons or in cases dealing with strangers."[64] It was abundantly clear to Captain Porion in 1894, commandant of Bamako, that he was spending a considerable amount of his time adjudicating local disputes. "Justice," he wrote to Grodet, "is rendered in the headquarters of the district every Monday, Wednesday, and Friday. After listening to the contradictory statement of the parties, translated by the official interpreter, the commandant gives his verdict." From this passage it would seem that Porion moved fairly expeditiously through the disputes, but later in his report he stressed that he consulted with individual notables of the three leading families of the district in his efforts to rendering justice "conforming to the custom of the Bambara and the Maures." Porion also noted that he had charged a group of 10 notables to assemble a compendium of the district's customs. This group spent six hours per week on the task and had already distilled the customs relating to marriage, property, and inheritance. This compendium, Porion stated, will shortly serve as a guide for officers charged with rendering justice in the district.[65]

In response to Grodet's suggestion to staff the local tribunals with three French officers, Porion argued that such a plan was impossible and impractical. Some districts, he reminded Grodet, did not even have three French officers; those that did, the burden of participating in the thrice-weekly court would overwhelm the already overburdened administrators. Porion stressed that the power and authority of the commandant was intimately tied to rendering judgments. "Judgments are pronounced by the commandant alone, and to alter that practice would result in the complete destruction of the prestige of the commandant. From the point of view of Bambara law, the commandant replaces the former *faama* and exercises an absolute power."[66] Although Porion had not followed Archinard's advice to avoid entanglement in local disputes, he nonetheless clearly articulated Archinard's instrumentalist position that rendering justice was a clear expression of authority. Porion's statements also provide evidence that the district officers were already becoming what Robert Delavignette has described as the *"vrais chefs d'empire."*[67] Porion saw himself as the unquestioned ruler of his district. This is exactly what Grodet was worried about. For Grodet, the power and authority of the French district officers should flow from their prestige as representatives of France and from their reputation for humanity and evenhandedness.

Captain Froment's report from Kita echoed many of the sentiments presented by his counterpart in Bamako, particularly those regarding the authority of the commandant and the messy process of consultation.

> In countries like the Soudan, where the *commandant de cercle* is considered the sole intermediary between the people and the ruler of the colony, that is to say, the competent authority, the inhabitants do not hesitate to bring their disputes before the commandant. . . . At Kita justice is rendered by the *commandant de cercle* assisted by the disputants' village chief and numerous notables of the region.

Froment added, however, a crucially important datum to the explanation of the volume of ordinary disputes brought before the district officer. In bringing forward to the commandant their disputes and their complaints, the inhabitants also "requested the suppression of certain abuses committed against them by their direct chiefs."[68] Froment's insight will be a central component to the argument advanced in this book about disputants' strategies in using the colonial legal system to achieve outcomes that they anticipated that they would not receive under indigenous law and legal authority.

In April 1895 Grodet was forced from office by the military he could not control and by his own failure to adapt to the peculiar pressures of building a new colony in the heart of the West African interior. He was succeeded by Colonel Louis de Trentinian, an old military hand, but astute enough to recognize the waning era of military rule in the Soudan. Trentinian pushed for the establishment of a more formal native tribunal system in order to remove the bulk of "little affairs" from the shoulders of the French commandants. Early in 1896 he sent a circular to all administrators.

The task of rendering justice has become a heavier burden for the district officers because of their increased administrative duties and above all because the numbers of legal affairs brought to their attention increases without stopping. The natives have become accustomed to bring even their smallest dispute before the jurisdiction of the commandant, who is reduced to the role of a simple justice of the peace.[69]

It was probably painful enough for the brave French soldiers to be saddled with desk jobs, especially at the time when the job of conquest was not yet finished. But to be transformed into "simple justices of the peace" was just too much. "Do not," Trentinian cautioned his administrators, "get mixed up in the many disputes without significance, which demand understanding of the morals and traditions of the population. Give instead additional prestige and authority to the native leaders, who are our indispensable intermediaries." Depending upon the status of the litigants, the task of rendering justice should fall upon the elders, the notables, the village chiefs, and the marabouts. Commandants were to judge only in cases involving disputes between villages, those involving strangers, and cases of serious offenses. The intent of Trentinian's instructions was to relieve the commandants of the burden of resolving ordinary disputes, which "increased without stopping." In so doing, Trentinian began to articulate a structure for the administration of native justice and to regularize it. Regularization flowed logically from the desire to spare the commandants these tasks, but also to provide a means of controlling for abuses. Regularization led inexorably toward codification and inevitably toward a resolution of the struggle between the two colonialisms of the Soudan. Trentinian's governorship coincided with the formation and formative years of the French West African Federation.

THE FORMATION OF THE FRENCH WEST AFRICA FEDERATION: DECENTRALIZED REGULARIZATION

The France that entered the nineteenth century virtually bereft of its old colonies ended the same century with a huge overseas empire. By the end of the century, France had territorial claims over vast areas of the Pacific Ocean, Indochina, Madagascar and the Macarennes, coastal establishments on the Indian subcontinent, the Horn of Africa, equatorial Africa, West Africa, the Maghreb, and the remnants of France's colonial possessions in the Western Hemisphere. Colonial rule was established throughout France's overseas empire in a haphazard manner, reflecting the rush to claim territory. Direct control was established in some regions, while neighboring lands were held under protectorates. Communication within this far-flung empire was difficult at best. Notwithstanding their efforts, Paris could not effectively control these regions or the men who ran them. In 1887, Paris formally recognized the need to establish regional centers of authority by delegating administrative oversight to the office of a governor-general. The government-general of Indochina was established to provide regional supervision over the five territories of Indochina (Cochinchine, Annam, Tonkin, Cambodia, and Laos). The model of the government-general of Indochina allowed each governor (or residents-general of the protectorates) of these five colonies considerable autonomy. They, however, were transformed into lieutenant-governors and obliged to report to the governor-general. The governor-general alone had the authority to contact the minister in charge of colonies in Paris. The governor-general, as was later determined by judicial decisions, was the "sole holder of the powers of the Republic" in their various federations. Girault described the creation of the Indochinese government-general as the "vertible abdication of metropolitan power to the governor-general, who was invested with the authority of French policy."[70] It took fully 10 years of relatively short-tenure and indecisive governor-generals of Indochina before the forceful Paul Doumer realized the full extent of the authority delegated to the position of governor-general.[71] The Indochina model was imported into French West Africa in 1895.

The delegation of authority to a man who could be trusted to follow the wishes of Paris must have been especially appealing to Minister of Colonies Delcassé after Grodet's failure to curb the military in the Soudan. Two additional incidents in 1894 raised further concerns about civilian-military relations in French West Africa and about intercolonial authority. Governor Lamothe of Senegal ordered his troops to raid deep into Fouta Jallon in reprisal against cross-border incursions. Lamothe's actions irritated Governor Noël-Victor Ballay of Guinea, who was pursuing a quite different strategy in Fouta Jallon. Later that year in eastern Guinea, Governor Grodet refused to order his troops to support the small military column led by Lieutenant-colonel Monteil when it ran into difficulties in skirmishes against Samory. Monteil was forced to retreat hastily.[72]

The creation of a separate Ministry of Colonies out of the combined Ministry of Navy and Colonies in 1894 further strengthened the hand of those wishing to impose the civilian agenda over that of the soldiers in French West Africa. In June 1895, Minister of Colonies Chautemps drew up the constitution of the French West African government-general. Despite its little success until 1897, the Indochinese model lay at the heart of the efforts to establish the government-general of French West Africa.[73] The weaknesses of the Indochina model also plagued the French West African Federation.

In appointing Jean-Baptiste Chaudié governor-general of French West Africa, Chautemps hoped to impose an order of command over the newly created colonies of French West Africa and to insure that the minister's program would prevail.

In appointing you to the high functions that are invested in your office, the government of the Republic does not under-estimate the difficulty nor the importance of the tasks delegated to you. You are to be the artisan of a program whose success will bring prosperity to the lands united under your command. Thanks to the powers you have, the government expects you to imbue our colonial policies in these regions with a method and a spirit that they have been all too often lacking.[74]

Chautemps chose Chaudié as governor-general because of the latter's proven record as an inspector within the Ministry of Navy and Colonies. The role of the inspection division within the Ministry of Navy had its roots in the *ancien régime,* when Paris appointed spies to insure that their colonial officials were actually doing their jobs. The modern system of colonial inspection has its roots in 1825, when Charles X established the position of *contrôleur colonial.* Although attached to the Ministry of Navy and Colonies, the *contrôleur colonial* was the official watchdog of the ministry and reported to the private council of the minister and the king. However, the appointment of a controller from within the ministry to be inspected always suggests limited independence and potential conflicts of interest. The role of the colonial inspector changed over the course of the nineteenth century, but the position gained greater authority only in the 1890s. With the creation of a separate Ministry of Colonies, the corps of colonial inspectors was given a fuller mandate and a higher degree of autonomy.[75] Chaudié, who had been a naval commissioner and inspector in the Ministry of Navy, was promoted to the senior position of inspector-general in the Ministry of Colonies. Chautemps thus expected Chaudié to impose a greater regularization of colonial rule.

This may have been Chautemps's expectation, but the organization of the government-general did not serve the expected results. The governor-general was simultaneously the head of the newly federated colonies and the governor of Senegal. Nor did the governor-general have the authority to impose his will on the lieutenant-governors, who, much like their counterparts in Indochina, retained a wide degree of autonomy. This was especially true in terms of financial autonomy. Colonial budgets were approved by the Minister of Colonies; Côte d'Ivoire and Dahomey retained an even more tenuous relationship to the government-general. The only direct control the governor-general actually had was over Senegalese affairs and over military operations in the Soudan. Without the power of the purse or clear authority over decisions in each colony, the government-general of French West Africa was, in Girault's terms, "a useless facade."[76]

The year 1898 marked the watershed in the organizational history of the Soudan and the French West African Federation. The military had achieved their goals of conquest: both Babemba, ruler of Kenedugu, and Samory were defeated. The military continued to face small-scale challenges, but there was little glory to be earned.[77] The commercial house of Dèves and Chaumet wrote to the Minister of Colonies in Paris that the capture of Samory marked the "beginning of a new era. The era of the sword has ended." Merchants, they argued, were now poised to "nationalize the fruits of conquest."[78] The Minister of Colonies also understood the conquest of Samory and Tieba to signal the end of "military occupation, which should not continue indefinitely."[79]

Chaudié's failure to restrain the military should not obscure his other efforts to regularize colonialism. While not wholly successful, Chaudié used the regularization of justice as an instrument for grafting the "spirit" of civilian rule onto the colonialism of Archinard as mandated by the Minister of Colonies in 1895. This had probably also been the intention of Minister Chautemps when he placed the head of the judicial service, the attorney-general, on par with the commander-in-chief of the military and with the lieutenant-governors as members of the *conseil supérieur* of the French West African Federation.[80] Chaudié continued the attack on corporal punishment and on the lack of proportionality in judgments that Grodet had initiated.

Evidence of corporal punishment may have disappeared from the archival record after Grodet's instructions in 1894, but it certainly did not disappear from the district officers' tool kit of powers.[81] Early in 1900, Governor-general Chaudié wrote an angry letter to the Minister of Colonies following another tour of the Soudan. "Regarding the administration of justice, my tour revealed an unacceptable situation. . . . The fundamental principles upon which rests the entire judicial edifice of the land where civilization exerts its influence is often not understood by district administrators." Chaudié was especially concerned with widespread "irregularities," which he did not explain, and with the lack of "proportionality." Chaudié railed against district officers who inflicted punishments wholly out of character with the offense, such that even minor offenses resulted in long prison sentences; in some cases even life imprisonment. Too often, Chaudié argued, the commandants continued to render justice themselves, without recourse to local elders and thus without a sense of local customs. Too often, Chaudié wrote, "commandants have a disdain for the life and liberty [of the natives], which I believe must characterize justice in regard to the natives." In closing this letter, Chaudié committed the office of the government-general to assuring the proper functioning of native justice.[82] For Chaudié, the regularization of the native legal system was an unambiguous effort to control the French military officers.

The period between 1898 and 1899 actually marked the transition from military dominance to civilian rule. In 1899, both Chaudié and Trentinian were summoned to Paris to discuss the proposed restructuring of the government-general and the Soudan. Chaudié wanted, among other changes, military officers replaced by civilian administrators. The minister appeared to want to punish the military by dismembering the Soudan and attaching its parts to the coastal colonies with better prospects for raising local revenue to support the costs of colonialism. The dismembering of the Soudan was based upon the argument currently circulating among the leadership of the French West Africa Federation that as a colony, the Soudan had no inherent logic. Commandant Destanve argued that the "Soudan is formed by the juxtaposition of territories without connections between them, without unity, without cohesion, composed of many different groups and languages, which the necessity of conquest alone united."[83] Trentinian argued against the breakup of the Soudan and reminded the Minister of Colonies that French claim over the vast interior of West Africa was due to the "courage, bravery, and talent of our officers, the discipline of our troops, and the superiority of our weapons." It was the prestige of the French, he continued, that kept the whole colony together. Prestige was in Trentinian's mind directly linked to military prowess and conquest. The government-general should exert its influence over policy, Trentinian argued, but it should leave to the leadership of the separate colonies considerable autonomy.[84] The minister was not persuaded and recommended dismemberment. Trentinian, who had become general, resigned. He continued to exert a strong influence in Paris among the colonial lobby. Trentinian was replaced by William Ponty, the civilian governor with long Soudanese experience.

The government-general emerged only slightly strengthened. In 1900 Chaudié was replaced by Ballay, who had served as governor of Guinea. Ballay in turn was replaced by Ernest Roume as governor-general in 1902. Roume emerged as the strong-willed governor-general capable of building the central authority of the government-general. In 1902, the government-general was reorganized yet again and much of the old Soudan was reassembled as Haut-Sénégal Moyen-Niger.[85]

THE EMPIRE OF THE LAW: REGULARIZATION OF JUSTICE AND THE ROOTS OF THE 1903 NATIVE LEGAL SYSTEM

The very success of the military in achieving its goals of conquest in 1898 undercut its claim to unfettered rule in French West Africa. French merchants' efforts to "nationalize the fruits of conquest" led to the rapid movement of French commercial houses and activities deep into the interior. "Today," wrote Lieutenant-governor Marie François Joseph Clozel of the Côte d'Ivoire in 1901, "the pioneers of commerce and industry have settled in regions where our military columns and our explorers had not even penetrated in 1890."[86] The coincidence of military victory and the expansion of French citizens deep into the interior of the new French West African colonies provided the protagonists of the civilian model and judicial activists with further opportunity to impose an alternative model of colonialism under the banner of regularization of justice. The Soudan continued to be at the center of the struggle, but efforts to regularize colonialism were also taking place in three southern colonies: Dahomey, Côte d'Ivoire, and Guinea.

Well into the waning days of his tenure as governor-general, Chaudié continued to press for means to tame the military officers of the Soudan. Chaudié voiced his concern to both the lieutenant-governors of the federation and Minister of Colonies over the "irregularities" in the administration of justice, particularly when district officers "exercise a role as direct judges without including the indigenous element, which, by its knowledge of local customs, should have been qualified to intervene" in judicial decision. Chaudié admitted that a certain "tolerance" has to be shown on behalf of these district officers during this formative era of establishing colonial rule, but not if the authority of the position "is constantly violated."

> During my recent tour of the territories of the former Soudan, I unfortunately must testify that in terms of the administration of justice to natives, the district commandants are not always inspired by principles which should preside over the exercise of such significant power and the abuse of which engenders the most serious consequences. In all cases [of judgments], the most elementary forms of investigation and sentencing have not been observed. . . . The rule of proportionality between the crime and the punishment has not been respected. Especially harsh sentences have been issued in circumstances that do not appear exceptional nor under conditions of imminent threat, which may justify them.[87]

Chaudié was particularly concerned with the "excessively severe punishments" out of proportion to the damage or crime committed.[88]

Chaudié went so far as to request that the president of France grant a general clemency to all Africans subjected to these excessive prison sentences. The Ministry of Colonies in turn voiced its deep concern about the "abuses of power" and the "arbitrary sentences and for the most part illegally taken by the administrators in the Soudan." The Ministry of Colonies reminded the governor-general that the 30 September 1887 decree establishing the *indigénat* provided effective disciplinary powers for district officers.[89] The *indigénat,* often translated as administrative police powers, was designed to provide colonial administrators with powers to impose fines and prison sentences without recourse to the courts or approval from superiors on a set of defined offenses dealing mostly with acts of disrespect or disorder toward colonial officials and official regulations. Administrators could summarily punish Africans for their failure to pay taxes or their failure to show respect to administrators. Originally limited to 16 identified offenses, the scope of these infractions increased over time. Each colony revised its own list of scheduled offenses. By 1907, the French Soudan listed 24 acts that were subject to the *indigénat* and by 1918 the Côte d'Ivoire had 54. The fact that the *indigénat* was an arbitrary system of punishments against which no appeal was permitted and that it was only extended to African subjects (French citizens and assimilated Africans were excluded) increased African resentments toward this domain of the colonial legal system.[90]

Despite the abuses of the *indigénat* in the Soudan, the senior official in the Ministry of Colonies would not forward Chaudié's request for clemency higher. This decision should be made, he argued, by the governor-general, who has the authority to order the immediate release of prisoners.[91] Concerned that even the issue of clemency would only be an "insufficient palliative that would not prevent the recurrence of these deplorable acts," the Ministry of Colonies ordered Chaudié to "develop proposals for the reorganization of justice at once complete yet economical to implement in our possessions in the Soudan."[92]

Ponty, effectively the governor of the Soudan, took up the call for greater supervision of punishments. Throughout 1900 and 1901, Ponty reviewed the district reports on punishments.[93] He consistently reminded his district officers of the need to make the punishment fit the crime. "Attempted kidnapping of a child with the intention to sell it and the lack of respect to the officer of the spahis are far from being faults of the same gravity, yet in both cases the perpetrator was subject to 15 days in prison." Ponty chastised the district officer of Segu for sentencing a native to eight days in prison for traveling without a permit. "I find that an exaggerated punishment is ordered for the fault committed." Ponty also lectured the administrator in Bouguni about the sentence he imposed on Samba Sidibe of 15 days prison for attempted murder, arson, and refusal to obey his canton chief. This sentence was equally out of proportion to the crimes committed. In another letter to the Segu administrator, Ponty wrote that "we must take into consideration the current social condition of native society if we are to appreciate fully their acts. Stealing a cow and beating one's wife are two very different faults; they should not be punished with the same sentence in prison." Ponty failed, however, to instruct his administrator as to which of these faults was more serious. Ponty kept reminding his administrators that the *indigénat* was for punishments relating to administrative matters and that the native tribunals "are invested with powers to pronounce punishments in proportion to the crimes."[94] Ponty was clearly concerned that by imposing the *indigénat* on misdemeanors and crimes among Africans rather than sending these cases to the native courts, the administrators were acting outside of the mandate of their legislated powers.

Abuses of sentences and long incarcerations continued to trouble the colonial administration. Minister of Colonies Gaston Doumergue strongly condemned the practice of incarcerating Africans alleged to have committed either misdemeanors or crimes. Some Africans remained in prison for "a more or less long period" awaiting their hearing before the native tribunals. Doumergue argued that this practice "does not conform to our legislation" and that it was patently in conflict with "the ideas of civilization and the good name of France." He required that no native be incarcerated for longer than eight days before his trial.[95] Despite this requirement for a speedy trial, there was no adequate control against abuses if there were no prison registration records. Ponty reminded his administrators yet again that they were required to keep prison registers. "I have on many previous occasions urged you to maintain scrupulous records for each district." To control against abuses in sentencing, prison records should provide detailed information concerning the identity of the prisoners, the type and causes of their sentences, the jurisdiction that rendered judgment, and the dates of entry and discharge from prison.[96] Ponty's concern with records was reproduced in the 1903 legislation creating the French West African legal system. Records were clearly the means to control for abuses of power.

Pressure on the government-general to reform the practice of justice in French West Africa received a significant boost in 1900–1901 from two events dealing with legal issues. On 24 November 1900, the superior court of Senegal (*cour de cassation*) overturned the ruling of the lower court (*cour d'assise*) regarding its competence to hear a criminal case against an African from Cayor, a region held under protectorate status. The lower court had ruled on 31 May 1899 that it had absolute jurisdiction to try all cases regarding crimes committed throughout the territories of Senegal, including those areas directly administered and those indirectly through a protectorate. Governor-general Ballay railed against the judicial activism of the superior court, which he accused of "intentionally establishing a new jurisprudence." The superior court's ruling essentially required that the colony establish a series of separate legal jurisdictions based upon the well-established distinctions in Senegal between citizens and subjects. Ballay's interpretation of the ruling suggests that he understood the intention of the court to require a consistent rule of law in which all inhabitants were subject to the same laws. He called it "premature and dangerous to submit natives to French jurisdictions" but also "ambiguous." In 1901 Ballay wrote to the Minister of Colonies that

> In their actions, the magistrature has moved in a direction that poses serious danger [to the colony] and to which I draw your attention. We should not be surprised if this [ruling] results in complications, because the judgments of our tribunals will not be accepted by all the natives and the solution to this conflict of jurisdictions will not be simple or easy to resolve as in France.[97]

Two aspects of the superior court's rulings are important for our story. First, the governor-general wrote to the Minister of Colonies stating that a special commission on the reorganization of justice was already operating.

Indeed, this commission, which completed its task in 1903, laid the foundation for the major legislation on the colonial justice system promulgated that year. This special commission had been called for by the Ministry of Colonies in April 1900. And second, in their ruling the magistrates manifested a degree of autonomy from the governor-general. The Republic of Lawyers in France was clearly finding a home in French West Africa. On the other hand, the judicial activism of the court was directed only at clarifying the jurisdictional reach of various systems of law. The magistrates were no longer willing to accept the irregularities in the administration of justice that had characterized the formative era of colonialism in French West Africa. This concern with jurisdiction and with the regularity of justice was clearly linked with another judicial initiative coming from the southern colonies of the French West African Federation.

In May 1900, Justice Liontel, the president of the Court of Appeals of Dahomey, was sent on a mission by the Ministry of Colonies to evaluate the judicial situation in Dahomey, Côte d'Ivoire, and Guinée. Before he left Dahomey at the beginning of 1901, however, Liontel had assembled evidence of a series of administrative abuses in that colony including unfounded capital punishments and a conspiracy by colonial officials (including former Governor Pascal) and French merchant houses to defraud African porters of their salaries. Liontel also accused several colonial officials of withholding crucial information he needed to assure the regularization of justice. Among his several concerns, Liontel raised questions about the lack of qualified magistrates to administer the law to French citizens deep in the bush in Dahomey. Whatever justice was administered was done by district officers often with little knowledge of the law. Liontel sent a formal complaint to the Minister of Colonies in January 1901. In a letter accompanying the complaint, acting Governor Liotard closed ranks around his administrators. Liontel, the governor argued, had been well received by the administrators in the colony, all of whom wanted to facilitate his tasks. If there was any problem, the governor added, it was that Liontel had "disdain" for certain functionaries.[98]

Liontel's experiences were quite different in the Côte d'Ivoire, where administrators opened "their doors and put all their archives at my disposition, which helped me formulate my project on judicial reorganization." Liontel reported to the Minister of Colonies that he and Lieutenant-governor Clozel were in complete agreement not only on the subject of the organization of French tribunals, but also on the organization of native justice. Liontel could not resist yet another swipe at the colonial regime in Dahomey: "It is truly remarkable that in everything that deals with the administration of justice is much better understood here than in Dahomey." Among the proposals Liontel advanced were a more professional magistrature for the administration of French justice, a special court to hear criminal cases drawn from all over the colony, and a program to learn more about African customs. Liontel

urged that customs be "codified or more exactly studied and widely published
so that the law that is applicable will be known by both the defendant and the
judge." Clozel agreed to this idea and together with a justice of the peace,
Liontel hammered out a questionnaire on customs to be sent to all district
officers in the colony.[99] Clozel was obviously serious about this task because
some of these studies were typeset and published.[100]

Minister of Colonies Degrais was equally serious about reforming the judicial system in the three southern colonies system because he promulgated two
decrees (6 August 1901 and 15 April 1902) that mandated the regularization
of justice especially for Europeans, but also for African subjects. Regarding
African defendants, the decree was concerned primarily with criminal matters. Taken together, these decrees called for the appointment of career magistrates to staff the tribunals of the first instance in the major centers of Porto
Novo, Bingerville, and Conakry. Most importantly, the 1902 decree created a
new, superior court—a court of "homologation"—designed to regularize
judgments, especially sentences involving more than one-year incarceration.
The 1902 decree also created a new administrative position equivalent to that
of attorney general, to be established in Conakry, in order to avoid sending all
appeals to Saint Louis. The decrees also clarified the jurisdiction over criminal cases, particularly in providing assimilated African defendants with rights
to determine whether they wished to be held accountable to native customs or
to the "empire of French law."[101] Clozel described these acts as providing
"Europeans with all the guarantees involved in the functioning of justice in
civilized lands."[102]

In calling for a professional magistrature and in clarifying legal jurisdictions in some criminal cases, these decrees were important not only in regularizing the courts in these new colonies, but also in promoting the separation
of powers. Roger Villamur and Léon Richaud lauded these decrees for ending
the "confusing situation of putting both administrative and judicial authority
in the same hands, which during the first phase of colonial occupation is natural, but which subjects the sentences of judges to serious criticism."[103]
Clozel, in the Preface to Villamur's 1902 study of the juridical authority of
administrators in the Côte d'Ivoire, signaled that the regularization of justice
was an important step in the professionalization of colonial administration.
"In regard to the administration of justice, good sense and natural justice, if
they are not conjoined to the strict observation of legal forms required for the
validity of judicial decisions, are just not sufficient."[104] At the same time,
other administrators were strongly opposed to the new court in Conakry,
arguing that its location there created a huge spatial gulf between the judicial
and political consequences of its legal decisions. These administrators also
argued that the assessors on the new court would not be conversant with customs from the other southern colonies and the time it would take to send the
dossiers of cases to the new court would delay judgments.[105] Many adminis-

trators also did not like the idea that professional magistrates would oversee the administration of justice.

The 1901–1902 ministerial interventions into colonial justice left unclarified the potentially much bigger issue of what to do with disputes and crimes among African subjects. Native justice remained a residual category. Villamur and Richaud argued in their 1903 volume, that "in that which concerns the natives, their disputes are overseen by the exercise of justice rendered by local tribunals. These tribunals apply procedures and customs drawn from palabres as long as they are not in flagrant opposition to the principles of humanity and the teachings of natural justice."[106]

Villamur and Richaud's depiction of the operation of the native tribunals naturalized what was a far more complex and contentious institution. The native tribunals in the Soudan were the sites of significant pressures, which pushed the tribunals and colonial officials in different directions. Nor was there any uniformity to the composition of these tribunals. Already in 1896, Governor Trentinian worried that his district officers were already drowning in a sea of petty disputes brought before them.[107] Trentinian warned his administrators not "to meddle in conflicts without importance." Africans should instead take their disputes to the native authorities. Trentinian reminded them that Archinard had already in 1891 established the principles of native tribunals "in which the task of rendering justice is confided to certain natives, elders, notables, village chiefs, and marabouts whose authority is respected."[108]

Trentinian realized that Archinard's mandate for native tribunals was not adequately proscriptive. At the end of 1896, he issued another circular further qualifying the role of district officers in legal matters. The district officer was, in principle, the recognized authority for dealing with all political misdemeanors and threats to public order, all conflicts between villages, and all crimes committed within the district. Although Trentinian recognized that the "natives have great confidence in our justice and that adjudicating their conflicts would affirm our authority," he ordered each administrator to establish a tribunal of notables at the district headquarters. Elders, recognized chiefs, and qadis should be recruited to the staff of the tribunals. The district officer should only "ratify the judgments and intervene when there are issues remaining in dispute."[109] Far from reducing the role of district officers in justice, Trentinian's order maintained the district officer at the center of native justice.

Notwithstanding Trentinian's description of elders and chiefs as indispensable intermediaries, finding elders and chiefs who actually commanded respect turned out to be more difficult than he had anticipated. Lieutenant Sargols, the Segu administrator, wrote to Trentinian in 1897 that "the native's search for justice is constrained by his chief, often incapable and venal." Sargols urged in strong terms that the *chefs de canton,* the French appointed chiefs—obviously their most "indispensable of intermediaries"—be prevented from serving as judges because of their "little influence and their complete lack of morality."[110] All candidates considered as judges should be subject to "a scrupulous inspection of their character," he argued in a different report. To compound the difficulties of organizing a tribunal in a district such as Segu, where the majority of the population were animists, the authority of the qadi "will not always be accepted by certain groups, especially the Bambara."[111] In contrast, the qadi of Segu was highly respected by the Muslims of the district. For Muslims, Sargols wrote, the qadi was empowered to render justice by the Koran and Muslims readily submitted to his judgments. But, Sargols warned, for the French to elevate the authority of the qadi was to constrain the "propagation of our ideas among the practitioners of a religion that is in principle hostile to us."[112] Lieutenant Perignon was not quite as sanguine about qadi justice as was his predecessor. Perignon wanted qadis to hold court at the district headquarters rather than in their own compounds. Such supervision was necessary, he argued, because "qadis generally render their decision based upon the wealth of the defendants."[113]

The difficulty of finding native judges willing to rule equitably among disputants was compounded by the choices the disputants actually made about where to bring their grievances. Sargols penned a remarkable report explaining why Africans sought out the French district officer to resolve their disputes.

> The Bambara, mostly farmers whose labor constitutes the major part of the wealth of this region, have docily accepted us as the successors to the black conquerors, al hajj Amadou (sic), or their former kings, the Jara. They consider themselves the slaves of their new masters, just as they considered themselves the slaves of their former rulers. They appreciate the results of an occupation that has opened for them an era of tranquility and justice from which they were long deprived. As a consequence of an administration that has made them free in a land that they consider their own, they have chosen not to accept any authority but our own in order to regulate all their affairs, even the most inconsequential.[114]

Despite Trentinian's warnings to administrators not to get involved in those "small affairs that increase incessantly," African litigants brought their grievances before the district officers because they wanted to avoid the justice of the elders and chiefs.

In 1902, the native tribunal system in the Soudan was modified once again to permit regions with significant Muslim populations to establish separate tribunals for animists and Muslims. Appeals against the judgments rendered were possible and were to be presented directly to the district officer. The Segu commandant wrote with considerable pride that "the tribunals established have given excellent results. The natives appreciate the guarantee of impartiality and rare are the appeals before the commandant."[115] These 1902 modifications were included in the 1903 legislation creating a federation-wide legal system.

Early in 1903, fully six months before the promulgation of the new colonial legal system in Dakar, Lieutenant-governor William Ponty issued a major statement on the administration of justice. Ponty was well connected to the governor-general and had helped the transition from the military to the civilian models of colonialism in the Soudan. His statement on the administration of justice clearly was written both for his officers in the field and his superiors in Dakar. It signaled that the foundations of the new era lay upon regularization of justice and the proportionality of punishments to the crimes.

> Among the most important powers which have been conferred on you, those whose exercise requires the most wisdom and tact and which you must never apply except with zealous care because of their implications for your reputation and that of France itself, those relating to justice are without contest at the top of the first rung. Numerous and grave indeed are the responsibilities that inhere in the application of justice and one can not bring too much reflection to their daily application.[116]

Ponty's statement was still not sufficiently programmatic. That program awaited the final completion of the commission on justice in the French West African Federation.

THE 1903 COLONIAL LEGAL SYSTEM

In his struggles with the military's control over colonialism in the Soudan, Governor-general Chaudié had set the groundwork for the regularization of justice in French West Africa. By 1900, the Colonial Ministry was firmly behind his efforts to impose greater control over the administration of justice and scrutiny of criminal sentences. The Liontel Mission of 1899–1900 and the resultant modifications of legal institutions in Dahomey, Côte d'Ivoire, and Guinea in 1901 and 1902 were part of Paris's efforts to reduce judicial abuses and to extend the jurisdiction of French law. In a similar fashion, the 1900 superior court ruling regarding the jurisdiction of courts in regions held under protectorate status forced the government-general to clarify both the jurisdictions of law in a colonial setting and to provide for the network of courts necessary to jurisdictions of the law. Before Chaudié left office, he established a commission to review the situation and to propose modifications. His successor, Ballay, who became seriously ill and died in office, did not leave a rich archival trail to follow regarding the regularization of justice. Nor was Ballay's successor, Ernest Roume, particularly interested in justice upon his appointment in 1902. Although Roume brought this commission to closure, he did so as part of his efforts to strengthen the power of the government-general.

Ernest Roume was a consummate bureaucrat of the expanded state apparatus of the Third Republic. A graduate of the École Polytechnique and trained as an engineer, Roume rose through the ranks of the Ministry of Colonies. From the Indochina desk, Roume oversaw the efforts of the various governors-general to cobble together the authority of that new office. Roume must have paid careful attention to Indochina's Governor-general Paul Doumer's successful efforts, especially those to secure a separate budget for the government-general and to subordinate the authority of the governors and residents of the constituent colonies. From his vantage point as director of political and commercial affairs bureau in the Ministry of Colonies, to which he was appointed in 1895, Roume witnessed firsthand Chaudié's struggles to tame the military and to empower the newly created government-general of French West Africa. Thus, when Roume was called upon to succeed Ballay as governor-general, he was ready to orchestrate a reorganization of the government-general.

Central to the reorganization of the French West African Federation in 1902 was the establishment of a separate budget for the government-general. The government-general finally had the resources to act independently and to support its own corps of administrators. More importantly, Roume secured the authority to approve the budgets for the constituent colonies of the federation with the exception of Dahomey. Roume used his financial independence to secure additional credit, upon which he built an aggressive program of railway construction and other infrastructural development. The reorganization also called for the separation of responsibilities between the governor-general and the lieutenant-governor of Senegal. Roume moved the federation capital to Dakar. From now on, the governor-general could concentrate on the affairs of the federation exclusively.

To further strengthen the governor-general, the 1902 legislation created the office of a secretary-general. Roume appointed Marital Merlin as his secretary-general. Merlin was an able administrator and served as governor-general during Roume's absences. And finally, the 1902 reorganization reversed the dismemberment of the old Soudan. The new entity, called Territories of Senegambie and Niger, reassembled the parts of the former Soudan and included the military-administered territories of recently conquered Niger and Upper Volta. The governor-general had direct authority over this new entity, but for all intents and purposes, it remained in the hands of William Ponty, who continued his formal title as the permanent delegate of the governor-general at Kayes. Roume served from 1902–1908 and oversaw the maturation of colonialism in French West Africa.[117]

Having established the authority of his position, Roume turned his attention to completing the work of the commission charged with the reorganization of the colonial legal system. The regularization of justice was a central piece to the architecture of colonialism under the civilian model of the government-general. Under the direct authority of the attorney-general (*procureur-général*), Georges Cnapelynck, the commission was ready to present its report to the General Council of the government-general in May 1903. The General Council, was composed of roughly equal numbers of French magistrates and senior colonial officials, including the lieutenant-governor of Senegal, as well as several civilian members. Roume chaired the sessions. The Council met for three day-long sessions (two in May and one in June) during which all 96 articles of the proposed legislation were debated, modified where necessary, and approved for submission to the Minister of Colonies. Of the issues debated, three emerged central to the final version of the legislation. The first was the issue relating to the jurisdiction over crimes committed by African subjects. Gougoul, the chief of judicial services for the three southern colonies, argued that such authority should reside solely with professional magistrates. Africans, he argued, preferred French justice. Second, the lieutenant-governor of Senegal was concerned that the proposed legislation did not provide sufficient guidance on procedures to follow in the native courts. Without procedures, how could administrators and magistrates be certain that justice was properly rendered? Merlin argued that it is virtually impossible to establish procedures for native justice that is mostly custom and therefore highly variable in form. Cnapelynck, the attorney-general, weighed in with what would end the discussion: he noted that any effort to codify procedure for custom would entail significant expense. And finally, the Senegalese governor and one civilian representing Senegal pointed out that the new legal system would lead to the suppression of the Muslim tribunal of Saint Louis and thus the role of the *tasmir.* Raymond Martin, the civilian representative, noted that such a suppression would be "dangerous" because the *tasmir* of Saint Louis exerted such a powerful influence over the Muslims of the region. Roume responded by arguing that the *tasmir* or another qadi would be appointed as assessor to the *tribunal de première instance* in Saint Louis and Dakar, and thus serve the same functions on those courts. In addition, a qadi was to be appointed to the appeals court in Saint Louis and to make the change more palatable, the members of the Council agreed to rename the qadi of the appeals court the "qadi-*tasmir.*" The Council also debated the jurisdiction of the justice of the peace and the status of the métis population of Dahomey. The Council agreed to minor changes in terminology, but not with the structure of the legislation.[118]

Roume described the three principles undergirding the 1903 reorganization of the colonial justice system. First, "to unify the administration of justice" hitherto operating under many different legal regimes throughout the length and breadth of the federation. Second, "to assure our nationals and all those who are assimilated the benefit of the legislation and jurisdictions of French metropolitan laws regardless of their residence." Roume did not add, but non-

French Europeans were considered assimilated French for juridical purposes in the federation. And, third, "to guarantee to the natives under our control in all that is not contrary to our essential principles of humanity and civilization the maintenance of their customs, which are the foundation of their civil law (*droit privé*) and appropriate to their mentality and their social status."[119]

Implementing the provisions of the 1903 legislation confronted Africans pursuing their own strategies of dispute resolution at a time of accelerated social change. Chapter 3 takes up the story of actually implementing the native courts as established by the 1903 legislation. In Chapter 4 we examine the linked sets of social transformation occurring as the new native courts opened.

3

CUSTOMS AND LEGAL AUTHORITY IN THE NATIVE COURTS

The commission charged with drafting the legislation for the reform of the legal system in 1902–1903 proceeded remarkably smoothly for what was a major program of institutional change. The commission, chaired by Attorney-general Georges Cnapelynck, made progress because its reforms hinged both upon a set of strategic compromises that seemed to satisfy the claims of activist magistrates and administrators and also upon an institutional architecture that was cognitively familiar to both magistrates and administrators. There was also little dissent from the General Council, which approved the commission's proposals. The new legal system promised the regularity and accountability that the governor-general sought in transforming the colonies of conquest into those in-line with the civilian character of the Third Republic.

All 96 articles of the proposed legislation were debated, modified where necessary, and approved for submission to the Minister of Colonies. Minister Gaston Doumergue reviewed the proposed legislation, sent it to his colleagues at the Ministry of Justice and the Garde des Sceaux for their approval, and finally presented it formally to the President of the Republic for action by the National Assembly on 10 November 1903. Minister Doumergue argued in his presentation that until this moment, the "administration of justice in the colonies [of the Federation] operates under separate regimes." The time has come, he argued, for France to "unite under one system and under one common law, taking into consideration the rights of our nationals, the needs of the indigenous populations, and the higher interests of our policies, those systems of laws previously separate and independent."[1] Doumergue's description of the 1903 legislation was not completely right. While the legislation clearly created one "system" of law, it did not create "one common law." The legislation essentially established two jurisdictions within one legal system for French West Africa: one for French nationals and assimilated Africans and the other for African natives. Both jurisdictions were conjoined at the top, because of the supervisory role the attorney-general played over judgments from the lower courts and because appeals moved upward toward the superior court (*cour d'appel*). The superior court had a special chamber on homologation, designed to regularize judgments and to ensure that procedures established by the 1903 legislation were followed correctly and fully.

This chapter begins with a discussion of the design of the new courts. The 1903 legislation essentially created two legal tracks within one colonial legal system. The courts for Frenchmen or those with French citizenship applied metropolitan law and procedure; those for African subjects were to apply African custom. The strategic compromise between administrators and magistrates glossed over significant issues of procedure and jurisdiction. Nor did the 1903 legislation provide much guidance on the content of "custom." Indeed, the legislation made some fundamentally erroneous assumptions about the bounded nature of custom. It also conflated Muslim family law with custom, making Islam merely one of the many customs operating in the colonies. The core of that section examines the initial responses of African litigants to these new courts. I explore these under the rubric of "conflict of customs."

THE DESIGN OF THE COURTS

The 1903 legislation governing the colonial justice system marked the victory of the government-general's model of colonialism over that of the military conquerors. The new legal system mandated surveillance and accountability over local decisions taken in the field by district officers. The new legal system also provided guarantees for both citizens and subjects that their personal status would be respected. In respecting the personal status of citizens and subjects, the legal system also separated the two, providing metropolitan institutions for citizens and an ill-defined "regime of custom" for subjects. While the new legal system created guarantees that "custom" would be respected and that African magistrates would preside over the new courts, this was not the incorporation of indigenous courts into the colonial legal system. On the contrary, the 1903 legislation created a wholly new colonial legal system.

One of the reasons that the architecture of the new court system posed few challenges to either the magistrates or the administrators on the commission or the Grand Council was that the new courts in colonial French West Africa were essentially modeled on a French metropolitan template. Figure 3.1 captures the design of the colonial legal system. Figure 3.1 demonstrates the extraordinary parallel construction of the two tracks of the colonial legal system. In effect, Cnapelynck and his staff assimilated the metropolitan legal system into French West Africa, modifying the names and procedures, but leaving intact the structure of the courts and the flow of legal authority up the ladder of courts. Cnapelynck's task in the commission was not simply to

Figure 3.1 Architecture of the Colonial Court System, 10 November 1903

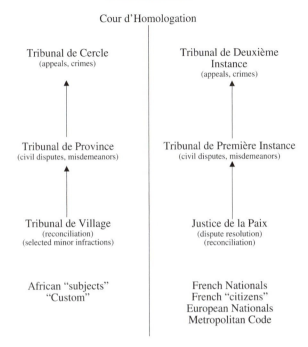

"receive" metropolitan law and procedure into the colonies, as was done in 1822 for metropolitan law into Saint Louis and Gorée, but to create a new legal system for the realities of the colonial world.

The new legal system created two discrete legal tracks. Europeans and assimilated Africans brought their legal cases before a hierarchy of tribunals that were virtually identical to those found in France and where the law and procedure were taken from metropolitan system. Under the 1903 legal system, African subjects brought their cases (if they were engaged in civil suits) or were brought before (if they were subject to criminal cases) a series of native tribunals with clearly demarcated jurisdictions. The structure of these courts imposed a French template on African litigation.

Civil litigation for African subjects in French West Africa was supposed to be channeled, as in France, up a hierarchy of courts, each applying stricter procedures in ever-wider jurisdictions and each hearing appeals from the one below. The 1903 system established three layers of native courts: the *tribunal de village*, the *tribunal de province*, and the *tribunal de cercle*, which acted as the appeals court. From the *tribunal de cercle*, a case could be forwarded to the highest appeals court in the federation, the *Chambre spéciale d'homologation*.[2] The court of homologation—the court of confirmation—was a division of the French West African court of appeals, the highest court in the federation and the point of convergence between the two legal tracks.

At the lowest level, the court was instructed to seek reconciliation between the parties; at the provincial and *cercle* (district) levels, legal judgments would reward those who prevailed in the court and punish those who lost.[3] The village chief presided over the *tribunal de village,* which was analogous to the French justice of the peace. If the litigants were not pleased with the village tribunal's efforts at reconciliation, they were instructed to bring their cases before the *tribunal de province,* where the 1903 legislation mandated the composition of the tribunal. The *chef de province,* the historic or invented indigenous ruler of the region, presided over the affairs of the tribunal, assisted by two assessors nominated by the French district officer. The *tribunal de province* was to apply "custom" and the assessors were selected from those reputed to be most knowledgeable of community custom. In Muslim regions—or if litigants were Muslim—at least one of the assessors was to be a qadi or Muslim judge. Judgments rendered were to be recorded either in Arabic or in French and the litigants were to be instructed to proceed to the *tribunal de cercle,* if they wished to pursue their appeal. To insure that the *tribunal de cercle* was not inundated with unwarranted appeals, a steep fine of 100 francs was imposed in cases of frivolous litigation.

While the architecture of the new courts was cognitively familiar to members of the commission and therefore elicited no serious dissent, the set of strategic compromises between magistrates and administrators shaped the nature of legal authority within these new courts. The magistrates wanted the colonial legal system to be as similar as possible to the metropolitan one with the same rigorous procedures and controls over lower courts. Administrators wanted the greatest flexibility in delegating judicial authority to their African collaborators even as they retained oversight over the operation of the local courts. The compromises agreed to in the draft legislation seemed to satisfy both parties, because each secured the core of their demands. Administrators could accept the plan because the district officers would be relieved of the heavy burdens of adjudicating African disputes. The model of the protectorate, which guaranteed the legitimacy of the domain of custom, demanded that the institutions of local authority be retained and that natives continue to adjudicate their own disputes. As we shall see, however, the colonial state retained its authority to determine whether or not customs were "contrary to French civilization."

Magistrates, especially those committed to judicial activism, held out for the greatest amount of control over legal decisions and for the most rigorous procedures. In the end, the magistrates won on the rigorous application of metropolitan law and procedure for French citizens, European nationals, and assimilated Africans and they compromised by accepting less on procedures but received more legal control in the native court system. Indeed, the magistrates secured for themselves final authority in the native courts because all judgments could in principle be appealed to the court of homologation. Quoting Girault's classic compendium on the principles of colonization, Pierre Meunier has argued that the debates over jurisdiction over legal supervision in the 1903 legislation were driven by magistrates' concern to exert control over criminal procedures and penalties: "The right to punish gives those who exercise it enormous prestige." Magistrates were prepared to grant judicial authority over civil disputes to African judges and colonial administrators as long as they retained control over punishments.[4] In practice, the 1903 legislation mandated that the court of homologation review only criminal cases in which sentences exceeded five years.[5]

Where the magistrates secured their most significant victory was in terms of the multiple layers of oversight exerted over the operation of the native courts at the provincial level. Here the magistrates' agenda and that of the governor-general overlapped. Both wanted the means to control the actions of administrators and native judges in the field. Such control was exerted by the requirements that records of all judgments be kept in a register, that the district officer approve the register of judgments regularly, and that all litigants be offered the opportunity to appeal their cases. Indeed, the magistrates' decisions to accept less clarity on procedures stemmed from two assumptions: first, that African customs were fluid and highly variable from group to group and even from village to village; and second, that the *tribunal de cercle,* which was presided over by the district officer, would exert considerable backside pressure on procedures in the *tribunaux de province* through their decisions on appeals. "The appeal," wrote Meunier, "will of necessity force native judges to conform to the jurisprudence of the *tribunal de cercle;* fear of appealed decisions exerts a salubrious pressure on native judges."[6] Lieutenant-governor Ponty understood the role of appeals at the level of the district court in the same way. "Above the village and provincial tribunals, the administrator of each district, assisted by two indigenous notables, constitutes the appeals court. Judgments from these courts are regularly transmitted by the authority of the local administration to the chief of the judicial service."[7]

Additional control over the operation of the native courts took place at the level at which native judges and assessors were selected and at the location in which the courts were held. District officers nominated African assessors to the lieutenant-governor, who then sent a final list to the governor-general for approval. District officers selected assessors from those African notables who had reputations for their local knowledge and who had proven themselves loyal to the French colonial project. Sessions of the provincial tribunal were almost always held right next to the headquarters of the district officer, thus representing the intimate relationship between native justice and French administration. Because of the importance given the operation of the native courts by the senior administration, district administrators found themselves directly involved in the activities of the courts during the early years of their operation. Some attended the court sessions because they were the only ones capable of maintaining the court registers in French; others, who had able Francophone assistants, hovered nearby to ensure that the native courts operated according to the principles inherent in the 1903 legislation.

Governor-general Ernest Roume's 1905 instructions to district administrators charged with implementing these new tribunals underscored the importance of colonial control over the native courts. "It deals with my highest concern that all decisions rendered by native justice will be controlled by the higher colonial administration and by the head of the judicial service."[8] Roume had in mind the control both over African "magistrates" and colonial officers and provided in the appendix to his instructions a model of what a native court's register should contain. Not all judgments were to be recorded and forwarded to the lieutenant-governors and the French West African judicial service. Decisions taken at the village tribunals were "in general, not to be communicated, because of their large number and little importance." But this did not, Roume warned, suggest that administrators need not concern themselves with village level disputes and cases. On the contrary, Roume instructed the district officers to control carefully the proceedings at the village level and report all irregularities immediately.

For civil and criminal cases brought before the provincial tribunal, separate registers were to be maintained and submitted quarterly. Regarding civil cases, these registers were to contain a "summary" description of the grievance; the names, domiciles, and "customary status" of the litigants; a description of the judgment rendered; and an indication whether or not the litigants were prepared to pursue an appeal. If they wished, litigants could appeal to the district tribunal, which was presided by the *commandant de cercle,* the senior French colonial official in the district. He was assisted by two assessors, chosen according to the same criteria as the assessors for the provincial tribunals. The provincial tribunal and the district tribunal were analogous to the *tribunal de première instance* and the *tribunal de deuxième instance* in France.

Criminal cases followed paths determined by the severity of the alleged acts. The French distinguish between *délits* and *crimes,* which are roughly parallel to misdemeanors and felonies. In French West Africa a simpler distinction was applied. In 1905 Roume wrote that "this division does not conform to contemporary criminology. Instead, it reflects, in its simplicity, the actual state of morals in the land [i.e., this colony]." According to Roume, only attempts against human life and acts involving the traffic in people (the slave trade) were considered serious enough to warrant the term "crimes." Less serious acts against people and those against goods, "generally of little importance in the state of native property," may be defined as misdemeanors.[9] The village court had authority over a very small set of infractions; the court of the province heard most misdemeanors. Felonies were heard only by the district court, subject to review by the *chambre d'homologation.* All cases could be appealed up the tribunal ladder. Criminal cases were also referred to as "correctional" because they were subject to penal and capital sentences.

Although the native legal system was designed to channel civil litigation along a path the French seemed to understand well enough, it was not the intention of the French architects of the colonial legal system to require that Africans conform exactly to French metropolitan legal procedure. "Procedure," Roume wrote in 1905

> should not be taken in the same sense as it has in the judicial language of the Metropole, where the term evokes the feelings of difficulties, complications, delays, delaying tactics, nullities, and costs incompatible with the simplicity of native justice. Procedure, in this case, is limited to verbal or written formalities strictly indispensable for the rapid and free solution of grievances and appropriate to the state of rudimentary social conditions [in the colony] without prejudicing the interests of the litigants. No special form is prescribed for appearing before competent tribunal.[10]

Moreover, Roume reiterated that all legal proceedings were to be open to the public unless the publicity surrounding a case might endanger public order and morals.

Roume wanted the native courts to be as free as possible from the technical burdens facing litigants in France. Justice rendered in the native courts should be free, simple, fair, and public. The magistrates held out for surveillance and control. Surveillance and control took the form of procedural interventions in the new native courts. The most important of these included maintaining a written register for all judgments, the central presence of French district administrators in the courts, and the possibility to appeal judgments.

The 1903 legislation establishing the new legal system incorporated earlier administrative practices, but gave them greater authority. This was the case with the obligation to maintain written registers of judgments. District officers were required to maintain such registers from 1889, although few actually did. In 1894, Lieutenant Quiquandon reported that "all judgments are inscribed in an a hoc register, which contain the complaint, explications of the parties in dispute, causes of their complaints, plus the names of the villages from which the parties come, and finally the judgment."[11] Lieutenant-governor Trentinian reminded all his district administrators in 1896 that they were "obliged" to maintain a register of the legal cases in their districts and "to inscribe in it the judgments and punishments pronounced."[12] The corporal punishment controversy discussed in Chapter 2 put increasing pressure on the administration to record and regularize punishments. Surveillance over punishments, however, was not resolved to the satisfaction of the Minister of Colonies, Gaston

Doumergue, who in 1902 reiterated his concern that no guarantees of justice can be given to natives without maintaining a register of arrests and punishments.[13] Pressure on Governor-general Roume to bring greater control and accountability over the actions of district officers and greater transparency in judgments resulted in the inclusion of registers in several articles of the 1903 legislation. Article 54 required the provincial tribunal to maintain a register for all correctional cases brought before it. Articles 70 and 71 laid out the method for maintaining the records of disputes: in all cases—civil and correctional—a summary of the case including the statements of the parties and the witnesses, the names of the judges, and the judgments must be kept. Article 71 placed this burden directly on the district officer: "these judgments will be transcribed at the time [of the case] in a special register, classified and signed by the administrator of the district." According to article 74, neither civilian nor penal judgments rendered in the native courts had validity until the administrator approved the register by signing it.[14] By signing the court register, the district administrator lent the judgments the full authority of the colonial state. This premise is evident in the report from Sikasso in 1905 stating that the "court registers are open," carrying the double meaning of open for business and public for all to see.[15]

Colonial justice was designed to be public. Its public character gave it accountability and thus marked it differently than precolonial justice. In precolonial Sikasso, "justice was that of the prince. The faama considered his subjects his personal property . . . and he received payments for fines and as substitutes for corporal punishments and death sentences." The new legal system, the administrator wrote, will "spare the population from the exactions and abuses of power to which they were subject."[16] Even the application of Muslim family law, in principle derived from written codes, would be public and thus different from the precolonial period when "justice was rendered by the qadi in his home. But it is preferable to have the qadi render justice at the post of the commandant in order to provide more surveillance because, in general, the qadi renders decisions according to the wealth of the plaintiffs."[17] As late as 1910, the qadis of Sokolo remained the "docile instruments of the old chiefs and their clandestine jurisdiction escapes all control and surveillance."[18]

The public, written court register defined colonial justice differently from its precolonial counterpart and from the qadi's justice. The written court register also gave the new courts a "textual" quality, permitting a much higher degree of accountability and transparency.[19] The obligation to maintain a written court register also inserted a colonial presence at the heart of the proceedings of the native courts. Even for the provincial courts, which were to be manned by African magistrates, the need to maintain a written record of the disputes and the judgments transformed the application of custom and the rendering of judgments. Article 73 called for the appointment of a secretary to each provincial tribunal in order to maintain the court registers mandated by article 71. Ponty anticipated that the secretary would not ordinarily be a native. "These requirements, although quite simple, will not be satisfied for the most part by native judges." Instead, he assigned the responsibility to the commandants to ensure that the tasks were done correctly.[20] The commandant of Koutiala wrote that the "presence of the district officer in the provincial tribunal will be indispensable for a long time to come in order to instruct the judges in making precise recordings of the dates, the facts, and the attenuating or aggravating circumstances in each case."[21] In some districts, the commandants were able to delegate the registers to a lower-level official, usually a European *commis* or clerk. Sometimes, African clerks were available, as in the case of Sikasso, where Paul Dembele, interpreter for the district, served as secretary to the tribunal.[22] Literate African clerks were still few and far between in the first years of the twentieth century.

The European presence in the native courts lent those courts the authority of the colonial state. The Sikasso administrator captured this sense when he noted that the African plaintiffs come to the new courts because they are convinced that "the proper administration of justice depends upon the conscience of the African magistrates, who are under the control of the district commandant."[23] Beurdeley captured the paradox of applying custom under the authority of the colonial state when he noted that "I have assisted in many court sessions and I can attest to the fact that the presiding [African] magistrate is frequently embarrassed in having to seek advice from the European secretary." While Beurdeley's observation points to the power dynamics within the native court, he worried about the perception of those attending the court session that the European was "subordinate to the presiding magistrate."[24] In noting that the European officer served as the secretary of the Banamba provincial tribunal, Inspector Saurin argued that the European presence in the native courts was contrary to the spirit of the 1903 decree. The European officer's role should be limited to exercising control over judgments as manifested in his approval of the register.[25] Lieutenant-governor Clozel disagreed. He thought that the value of the European presence in the native courts outweighed any disadvantage in that his presence alone would "guarantee the respect for defendant's individual status."[26]

The presence of Europeans in the native courts did much more than simply insure that the registers were correctly kept. Europeans subtly directed African judges toward decisions that fit their conceptions of natural rights. Colonial administrators liked to claim credit for the "progress" in the administration of native justice. But they often only saw part of a much more radical transformation. I am not sure how much of this more radical transformation the French actually understood, but let me quote at length this 1906 passage from Sikasso regarding the "education" of African magistrates who sat on the provincial tribunal.

The judges are chosen from among the members of the old native tribunal, who are regularly re-elected because of the care they bring to their duties and of their detailed understanding of the mores and customs of the different people in the district. Their prestige among the populations is still considerable. They have shown themselves to be curious about our formal institutions [of justice] and respectful of the counsels given them. Little by little and without violence [i.e., radical change] the blacks adapt certain essential modifications to their personal status and to the system of sanctions against misdemeanors. . . . Our task of education is much more delicate in the area of civil disputes, which also see undeniable amelioration. Thus, in the cases of marriage and divorce, we have brought the judges to the point where they take into consideration the personal wishes of the women, whom one rarely consulted during the previous state of things. . . . The results we have obtained in such little time are much appreciated, and the manner in which we understand justice will contribute significantly to our ability to win over the populations [of the colony].[27]

The presence of Europeans in the courts was only part of the transformations in indigenous justice and the application of custom. I develop the debate over custom more fully in the following section and as they relate to the issues of women and marriage in Chapter 5. The effectiveness of Europeans in the court depended upon Africans who interpreted for them. Colonial administrative policy tended to limit French administrators to fairly short tours of duty in any one district, thus effectively limiting their abilities and willingness to learn local languages and cultures.[28]

The only other procedural transformation I will discuss in this section is the appeal. The designers of the 1903 legal system were keenly aware of the power of the appeal in controlling for abuses and inconsistencies in judgments and procedures. The designers of the new system knew that some Africans were eager to bring their disputes before French officials, because the lieutenant-governors of the Soudan had often complained about this very situation. What the architects of the new system could not know was whether or not African litigants would pursue appeals if they were merely unsatisfied with the decision of the lower court, but did not have the grounds that a procedural wrong had occurred. In their design of the native court system, the magistrates and administrators drew on metropolitan practices in which appeals were a central part of civil procedure. These architects wanted appeals from the provincial court to the district court to provide backside pressure on procedures and to clarify disagreements over custom at the lower court. Indeed, a central part of the court register was a column for indicating whether or not the litigants wished to pursue an appeal (article 52). But they were worried about inundating the district court with "frivolous appeals" (*fol-appel*). A frivolous appeal was an appeal without legal or procedural substance and launched for vindictive or entrepreneurial reasons.

Thus, the architects borrowed from metropolitan civil procedure a fine for frivolous appeal. Whereas the fine in France was a token five francs for a frivolous appeal of a judgment delivered at the justice of the peace and ten francs at the tribunal of the first instance, it was up to 100 francs for a frivolous appeal of judgments rendered at the provincial court. This was, in Meunier's terms, "an intimidating penalty."[29] As a result, few African litigants were willing to pursue an appeal. Indeed, the appeal rate in the native court system throughout the Soudan was miniscule: in 1910, there were 63 appeals out of 4,373 judgments (1.4%); and in 1911, there were only 31 appeals out of 4,304 judgments (0.7%).[30] It could be, as Lieutenant-governor Clozel interpreted, these statistics that they "demonstrate the ever increasing confidence that the Africans have in their native judges and it attests to the judges' moral authority and spirit of equity." Or, it could be that African litigants were fearful of the crushing fine attached to a ruling of frivolous appeal. In any case, the assumption built into the design of the legal system that appeals would have a salubrious effect on procedure in the native courts obviously did not come to pass. Instead, the only pressure exerted on the operation of the native courts came from the district officer who was obliged to sign off on the court registers and from the occasional scrutiny by the attorney-general in Dakar. Following the attorney-general's examination of the 1906 court registers, he wrote

> The form of the registers is not always perfect. Regrettable lacunae creep into these records. . . . However that may be, despite local difficulties, the enormous distance within districts, the continued little evolved civilization of the hinterland of our African Republic, native justice seems to me to be functioning adequately in Haut-Sénégal-Niger and the judgments rendered are, in general, acceptable in civil cases as well as in misdemeanor and felony cases. The praise belongs in large measure to the district commandants, who have understood the spirit and the letter of the organic acts [of the legal system] and have instructed usefully the native judges.[31]

The very structure of the native legal system, the presence of written registers, the possibility of appeals, the categorization of cases into separable civil, commercial, and criminal issues, and even the modification of legal procedure to "fit" African conditions nonetheless reflected the imposition of a grid of Western legal institutions on African grievances. This program of creating a colonial legal order in French West Africa was further complicated because of the privileged place "custom" was to play in the decisions taken by the native tribunals. The program for implementing this colonial legal system, which at once "respected" custom but also sought to channel African grievances into Western legal categories and legal assumptions had unforeseen consequences.

Although promulgated on 10 November 1903, the new courts were not up and running in the Soudan until early in 1905. Courts in some districts opened even later. The delay was warranted, Lieutenant-governor Ponty argued, because the decree "constitutes a most important reform and its strict application will contribute significantly to the moral development of our natives." The installation of new and regular courts as part of a new organization of justice will be, Ponty believed, a major step towards the "cause of civilization."[32] The cause of civilization demanded the utmost care and preparation. Special instructions regarding the new courts were compiled in 1904 by the governor-general and sent to district administrators. The period between promulgation and operation of the new courts was one of "elaboration" and transition from the former legal system to the new one.

CONFLICTS OVER CUSTOMS

The 1903 legislation establishing the new colonial legal system was the result of intense debate and strategic compromise within the commission regarding the domain of French and "customary" law.[33] Those promoting judicial assimilation were persuaded that with the expansion of French colonial control over huge parts of the West African interior the mass of rural Africans were not yet ready for inclusion in the French civil tradition. Article 46 defined the domain of the customary in negative terms: "In the territories that do not fall under the purview of the court of the first instance (*tribunal de première instance*) or the justice of the peace with expanded competence at Kayes (*justice de paix à compétence étendue*), native justice is administered in regard to individuals not under the jurisdiction of the French courts by the village courts, the provincial courts, and the district courts." What form of justice was to prevail for those who were not French citizens or subject to French metropolitan law? Again framed in negative terms, article 75 stated that "native justice applies in all matters of local customs, insofar as they are not contrary to the principles of French civilization." Defined as everything that was not French metropolitan law and that was not "repugnant" to French civilization, the domain of the custom in the colonial legal system lumped together all varieties of local customs and Muslim law. The only section of the 1903 legislation that addressed Muslim law was article 49, which mandated the structure of the provincial court. "At the headquarters of each province, a tribunal will be established and composed of the provincial chief or canton chief assisted by two notables designated by the governor of the colony in a proposal to the attorney-general. In regions where Muslim personal status prevails, one of the two notables will be the qadi if one exists."[34]

Article 75 of the 1903 decree shaped the way in which the French expected their new courts to run. Already in 1904, Roume drew the attention of the lieutenant-governors of the federation to the provisions of this article, which was later used verbatim in his 1905 *Justice indigène: Instructions aux administrateurs sur l'application du décret du 10 Novembre 1903 portant réorganisation du Service de la Justice.*[35] I want to quote this at length, because it reveals the administration's naiveté in regard to complexities of implementing a native court system in a plural legal environment. Roume wrote to his local administrators,

> I draw your particular attention to the dispositions of article 75 and to the terms under which native justice applies in all areas of local custom, in so far as it is not contrary to the principles of French civilization.
>
> Native courts will judge applying either Malikite rites, which are accepted in a large portion of our territories and are more or less modifications of Koranic law by local practice, or by applying local traditions in regions where Muslim influence is not yet strong. Such application will be mostly in civil matters, property, obligations, contracts, marriage, affiliation, child custody, inheritance, in which the judges will conform to these written records or oral traditions.
>
> We shall not, in effect, impose on our subjects the disposition of our French law, which is manifestly incompatible with their social status. But we shall not tolerate the maintenance, under our authority, of certain customs that are contrary to our principles of humanity and natural rights. It is in this order of ideas that the native courts can not recognize disputes relative to the condition of captivity, which we do not legally recognize. . . .
>
> In regard to civil [law], customs are not the same throughout the full extent of our territory. Variable by regions and by native group, it is not uncommon for customs to be different from village to village. Within this very great diversity, it may become difficult to supervise the practices of the native courts without imposing arbitrary conclusions.
>
> It is nonetheless our firm intention to respect customs without restraining progress towards the regularization and amelioration of customs. With the approval of the native courts themselves, it will be possible gradually to establish a rational classification of customs leading to a generalization of practices compatible with the social condition of our subjects while rendering these practices more and more in conformity, not necessarily with our metropolitan legal doctrines, but with natural rights, the foundation of all legislation.
>
> In the exercise of your judicial powers, you shall study with particular care the application of native customs. Towards this end, you shall compare diverse practices with the intention of yielding the general character of common practices. You shall group common customs together in a methodical manner, formulate them with precision, and offer them a clarity that they too often lack. This labor will eventuate in a codification of customs (*rédaction coutumier général*), which shall become the code for the native courts dealing with civil disputes. A detailed questionnaire will eventually

be sent to you to guide your methodical and rational classification of your observations.[36]

Roume never sent out that detailed questionnaire on customs that he had indicated. Instead, that fell to Roume's successor as governor-general, William Ponty, who passed this burden on to his lieutenant-governors in 1908–1909. Lieutenant-governor Clozel ordered his administrators to complete these questionnaires and assigned to Maurice Delafosse the task of compiling these surveys into a coherent statement, which he published in 1912.[37] Delafosse distilled a generic "Soudanese" model, defined in profound ways by its opposition to what he described as "Soudanese Islam." I shall return to Delafosse's project in Chapter 5.

Until 1912, there was considerable debate within the administration over what Roume had called a *coutumier.* On the one hand, to apply custom required knowing what it was. On the other, committing custom to paper had the effect of freezing it in time. Elements of this debate appeared already in the June 1903 meeting of the Grand Council as it voted on the draft of the 1903 legislation. The lieutenant-governor of Senegal had criticized the text for its lack of precision on the application of custom in the new courts. The draft legislation was virtually silent on this issue. Secretary-general Merlin responded that it would be difficult to establish fixed procedure and thus codify custom, which is "following its form highly variable." Merlin quashed further discussion on this issue when he added that codification would entail significantly added costs. Merlin left unstated the issue for whom codification would add costs, but it was clear that he meant the government-general although he may also have implied added costs to African litigants, who, if faced with complex procedure, would of necessity have to turn to professional attorneys.[38] But the pressures on administrators and magistrates for regularity in judgments had already resulted in a creeping movement toward codification. Already in 1901, Lieutenant-governor Clozel in the Côte d'Ivoire had authorized a commission to begin the codification of the customs of major ethnic groups. Roger Villamur, an attorney with legal experience at the *cour d'appel* in Paris and an administrator of Grand Bassam, chaired this commission. Villamur described the basic conundrum for administrators and magistrates newly arrived in the colony who were faced with rendering legal decisions brought forward by their African subjects.

> In effect, these customs are not the same throughout the length and breadth of the land. Similar to our ancient France where the law was drawn from use, law throughout the colony varies. The law varies from village to village, even among groups united politically, which claim the same community of origin and the same traditions. This is similar to seigneurial France, where the usage modified the law in adapting to primitive environments,

such that a voyager traveling through our region would change customs as often as he changed localities.[39]

Villamur's commission recommended codification as a means to ease the tasks of the administrator and Clozel committed his staff to this end. Starting in 1902, the first of the *coutumiers* began to appear in the official government journal.[40] The Sikasso administrator in 1905 lent support to Villamur's project when he noted that civil and commercial customs as well as a table of corresponding criminal punishments should be organized into a "type of code" available at the *tribunal de cercle,* where the administrator actually presided.[41]

Discovering what custom prevailed was not as transparent as the Sikasso administrator suggested. The administrator of Segu in 1897 noted that before district officers could exercise their judicial functions, a detailed study of community and customs in his district should be undertaken. He warned, however, that the administrator should be prepared "to submit patiently to numerous and long palabres with natives . . . over many seemingly insignificant subjects."[42] That was exactly Captain Porion's experience when he assembled 10 notables in Bamako for six hours of deliberations each week with the goal of producing a guide to help officers render justice.[43] Correnson, the Segu administrator in 1907, captured the sense of debate over custom that continued well into the next decade.

> The institution of native courts corresponds to a genuine need by the population: this entailed a substitution of the ancient justice of the chiefs, which was unsatisfactory and partial, where the influence of family status and family fortune constituted the principle element of procedure and where there were interminable palabres between elderly men over the resolution of legal questions. This was only possible because it conformed to the black's ignorance of the value of time.[44]

While Correnson disparaged these interminable palabres because they seemed like such a waste of his time, what he missed was the fact that these elders were actually debating what custom was in any given dispute. In invoking custom in the new native courts, the French failed to realize that there was no agreement as to what custom and whose custom was to be applied in any given dispute.[45]

A fascinating case heard in Kita in 1910 demonstrates how custom was "discovered." The elderly chief of Komakana village brought a suit against his eldest son, Famoussa Konate, for failure to perform labor on his fields "for a long time." In the course of its investigations into this complaint, the provincial court discovered that according to custom, sons should devote at least four days per week to cultivate their father's fields. During this period, the children, regardless of age, are considered the "employees of their father and are obliged to execute all his orders." The court ruled in favor of the elderly Konate and ordered his son to work on his father's fields.[46] The report is not detailed enough to see clearly how custom was discovered, but the case speaks to the issue of competing interpretations of custom and challenges to the authority of the household head. Competing interpretations of custom lay at the heart of the Sokolo administrator's remark in 1908 that "without wanting to make ignorance a legitimate excuse [against a complaint], it is necessary to note that local customs are very often confused."[47]

Most administrators seeking to discover what custom was did not likely relish participating in the "interminable" palabres of the elderly men as they debated custom. They were under considerable pressure to accomplish the enormous range of tasks they were assigned. Most probably turned to one or two trusted African interlocutors, as Charles Monteil did when he was compiling his studies of Bambara custom and history.[48]

Not all administrators or even magistrates wanted custom to be codified. Secretary-general Merlin captured the ambiguities of applying custom when he sent instructions to the district officers of the Soudan in 1904. "Guarantee to the natives under our control and under our authority, in all which is not contrary to our essential principles of humanity and civilization, the maintenance of their customs, the foundation of private law appropriate to their mentality and to their social state." Merlin further complicated the task of implementing a colonial legal system because he assumed that "custom," like metropolitan code-law, was continuously evolving.

> Our firm intention to respect customs does not establish an obligation to restrain progress, nor the regularization and amelioration of custom. With the assistance of the native tribunals themselves, it will be possible to bring to them, little by little, a rational classification, a generalization of compatible practices [increasingly in line with] not our metropolitan judicial doctrines, but the fundamental principles of natural rights, the fount of all legislation.[49]

Meunier argued strongly against codification lest codes fix customs, which were often "abstruse and confused." The very uncertainty of customs was an advantage, Meunier argued, to their transformation. "Exposure to new ways of living, resulting from contact with French civilization, as well as the substitution of barbarous practices based upon coarse superstitions for more equitable, more rational rules, are facilitated by the absence of a corpus of codified customs which would bar assimilation or more exactly evolution."[50]

The debate on codification reflected the unresolved tensions between the respect for difference and the social project of advancing civilization inherent in the legal construction of the protectorate. The protectorate bequeathed to native authorities internal autonomy within the limits of the repugnancy clause.[51] But the social project of advancing civilization also entailed making progress, which in administrative terms translated as bureaucratic efficiencies. This was not only a debate within the French colonial establishment; Africans were forcing the hands of the administration. Already in 1896, Lieutenant-governor Trentinian had argued that African litigants had become used to bringing even their most insignificant disputes before the French district officer, thus deflecting his effort from his other important tasks. Trentinian argued that with the exception of "serious" crimes, cases involving "strangers," or disputes between villages or cantons, resolution of civil disputes should be left to the notables and village chiefs.[52] But the Africans kept coming to French officials to have them resolve their disputes. By the end of 1896, Trentinian let his exasperation creep into his reports. "District officers have too many tasks that are too important to have all their time taken up with resolving disputes." Trentinian ordered his officers to establish at the headquarters of each district a native court composed of notables or qadis to serve the needs of African subjects and to maintain a "register" of judgments.[53] Trentinian followed this order with another outlining the district officers' obligations to complete the questionnaire on customs developed by the International Union of Law and Political Economy based in Berlin. The completed questionnaire, Trentinian argued, would be immensely useful to those who served in the colony.[54] In 1897 Trentinian sent out the questionnaire to all district officers and the task of compiling the rough responses into a coherent overview fell to Native Affairs officer Barrat. Barrat's compilation of the 1897 survey was finally completed in 1899. It was the first *coutumier* for the Soudan. Barrat completed his *coutumier* at a moment of significant transition in the senior leadership of the Soudan: Ponty replaced Trentinian as lieutenant-governor. Barrat's *coutumier* seems to have been lost in the archives since none of the subsequent debate on codification refers to it.[55]

The debate on native custom and the vague wording of article 75 of the 1903 legislation forced the issue of codification into the forefront once again. The native courts were to respect and apply native custom regardless of the diversity of custom. This was not a simple assignment. It plunged the district officer back into the center of the need to discover custom. Based upon a review of the chamber for homologation's annulment of lower court decisions and the attorney-general's office's assessment of the 1906 court registers, Ponty chastised the district officers of the Soudan for their failures to conform to the particular instructions of the 1903 legislation regarding the identification of custom. The two most frequent reasons for annulling the native court's judgments was the failure to identify the personal status of the assessors and the litigants and "the most frequent and the most serious is the failure to identify which custom prevailed in the specific case."[56]

Administrators were under enormous pressure not to spend all their time discovering custom and adjudicating disputes among Africans. The pressures to move the caseload along expeditiously had the unintended consequence of favoring Muslim family law over custom in the operation of the courts. The French had long harbored ambivalent feelings toward African Muslims: they were simultaneously respectful of Islamic civilization and the authority of written texts and they were distrustful of the power of Muslims to challenge and ignore French authority. French colonial Islamic policy in West Africa has been subject of considerable research and debate.[57] While I am not concerned here with French Islamic policy per se, the pressures to adjudicate the ever-increasing caseload tended to favor Muslim judges because they were supposed to apply an already written code and thus regularity in their judgments.

Rome's 1905 instructions to district administrators had urged them to engage with African customs in order to develop a rational, general compilation of prevailing customs in order to facilitate the court's deliberations. When assessors and native judges did not agree on what custom prevailed, the execution of justice would be delayed and thus subverted. Codification of custom never materialized, although many efforts were made to synthesize the diversity of custom into a more ordered, but highly reductionist form. Above all, administrators wanted to avoid the "interminable palabres" over custom that took place in the native courts. In contrast, Muslim law was already codified and even if there was recognition of the ways in which practice shaped application, Muslim law provided administrators and judges with ready-made templates to apply to individual cases. The Segu administrator in 1906 wrote to Lieutenant-governor Clozel requesting that his and all district headquarters be supplied with copies of Muslim legal compendia. "Each district and each site for a provincial tribunal should possess the *Traite de droit musulmane ou zohfait d'Ibn Acem,* translated by Houdas and Martel, as well as the *Précis de législation musulmane de Sidi Khalil,* in the Seignette translation edited by Challamal. These books will permit administrators a rapid control over the interpretations of Muslim law provided by the qadi."[58] The Seignette translation was published with the express purpose of providing an easy guide to French colonial administrators.

Given the efficiencies of applying and controlling Muslim law, it should not be surprising that Muslim judges would play a significant role in the operation of the native courts. Lieutenant-governor Clozel noted exactly this tendency throughout the Soudan and especially in regions where Muslims were numerically insignificant. "As a result of a common tendency among many administrators, they have chosen Muslims as their legal counselors, even in animist regions. In Bobo-Dioulasso, where the number of animists is 440,950 and the number of Muslims is only 15,112, there are only Muslims [judges] on the native tribunals. In the Sokolo district, the 11,304 animists have no judicial representation." This was a situation, Clozel argued, that was in direct violation of the principles of the 1903 decree and undermined the "assurances of respect for the individual status of the litigants."[59]

Not all Muslim assessors or judges performed their duties as the French expected. The 1903 decree provided for a formal mechanism in which lieutenant-governors nominated assessors for the district courts and judges for the provincial courts. Lieutenant-governors, in turn, relied upon their district administrators to recommend assessors and judges. There was, therefore, a filtering process that selected Muslims who were willing to aid the French and knowledgeable in Muslim law. Demands, however, on the disposition of judge's favor were commonplace and in 1906, De la Bretesche, the Segu district administrator, wrote to the lieutenant-governor requesting that Seidou Haidera replace Omar Ba as Muslim judge and Arabic translator at the district's provincial court. "I wish to propose replacing Omar Ba because he lacks independence in regard to the parties concerned [in disputes] and provided dangerously specious interpretations of texts. Moreover, he has participated in resolving affairs in which he was an interested party. The reasons for seeking his replacement is also due to questions regarding the fidelity of his translations."[60]

The deep ambivalence many administrators harbored toward Islam sometimes expressed itself in a nuanced assessment of the treatment of the individual under Muslim family law. Charles Correnson, administrator of Segu, captured exactly this sentiment in his discussion of the condition of women under custom and Muslim family law. Correnson's thoughts coincided with a significant debate among administrators about how to explain and what to do about the wave of women coming before the native courts seeking divorce. Many administrators in the period up to 1910 or so were sympathetic to women seeking divorce. They contributed to a debate about the condition of women and the nature of marriage in the Soudan. Correnson echoed much of the critique of custom in which it appeared that women were "sold" into marriage through bridewealth payments and inherited by brothers upon the death of their husbands. Correnson picked up on this debate as he compared women under custom to women under Muslim family law.

> My previous discussion of custom among the Bambara has indicated that custom is evolving. It is, nonetheless, still oriented harshly against individuals. Custom is changing slowing under the combined pressure of our influence and the machinations of the marabouts. The Koran, if interpreted apart from its political persuasion, is a religion of kindness and charity and the marabouts are its principle propagators.
>
> Women are the ones who benefit the most. They are incontestably moving towards the improvements of their social condition. For example, the condition of women has improved particularly among the Somono, who were previously animists and ruled by custom, and are today Muslims.

The organization of justice, the repression of misdemeanors and crimes against individuals is developing among our subjects and implanting the concept of a society. Although this idea remains imprecise among them, it is nonetheless being anchored among them through their experience in seeing how justice is being rendered [in the new courts]. The Muslim conception of justice strongly aids us in this task.[61]

Despite the pledge to respect custom, the practice of the native courts favored Muslim law and Muslims even if Muslims were originally reluctant to bring their disputes before these courts because the judges often included animists. French administrators found in Muslim qadis allies in their efforts to provide expedient resolutions to disputes and consistent judgments. Notables knowledgeable about custom often argued with other notables about the meanings of custom and the appropriate remedies. The need to provide efficiencies in the administration of justice led administrators to favor Muslims assessors and judges despite the 1903 decree requiring equality of custom and Muslim family law in the construction of the native courts.

As I will discuss in Chapters 5, 6, and 7, judgments in favor of women seeking divorce—even those that appear to apply custom—in the native courts bear a striking resemblance to Islamic norms on divorce. Shari'a and its Malikite interpretation, that was widely practiced in French West Africa, recognizes several avenues for women to seek divorce, including mutual release of the marriage contract by the spouses (*mubara'a*) and the dissolution of the marriage, initiated by the wife and sanctioned by the husband on the basis of the return of bridewealth or the dower (*khul'*). Shari'a also provided the qadi with the authority to pronounce divorce when the husband fails to adhere to the marriage contract and its moral counterpart through cruelty or mistreatment of his wife, desertion or failure to maintain (i.e., provide subsistence for) his wife, or if the husband has a serious disease or ailment. When thinking about Muslim law in precolonial and colonial Africa, we need to bear in mind that shari'a was both a "fixed" body of laws and practices and a flexible practice that was adapted to the larger social and cultural environment. The influence of shari'a on African custom is an important area of research.[62]

The senior administration was not pleased with this outcome. Ponty, now serving as governor-general, wrote to the lieutenant-governor of the Soudan that while Muslim family law occasionally modified custom, "it was never the intention of our native policy to favor Muslim influence [over customary law]. . . . Do not lose sight that only local custom should prevail in native justice."[63] Ponty's letter to Clozel followed closely on his major September 1909 policy change that has come to be known as the *politique des races*. Ponty had long harbored deep prejudices against African "feudal potentates" (including al-hajj Umar, Samory, and Amadu) whose authority dated from the era of massive insecurity and conquest that predated the arrival of the French.

In Ponty's terms, these feudal rulers owed their authority to conquest and imposed on conquered communities an "alien" character. Ponty's *politique des races* was designed to eliminate these "alien" rulers and allow each "race" to be ruled by its own traditions and its own rulers. Evolution of customs will come from exposure to French civilization and not other "foreign" (namely Muslim) influences.[64]

This is the context in which Lieutenant-governor Clozel sent out the second questionnaire on customs in 1908–1909 and which Maurice Delafosse used to implement his new course on African customs at the École Coloniale in Paris in 1909–1910. These questionnaires formed the raw material for his distillation of Soudanese legal tradition in his *Haut-Sénégal-Niger,* which appeared in 1912. I develop this story more fully in Chapter 5, which takes up the issue of African women seeking divorce in the new native courts. Indeed, women seeking divorce were among the first clients of the new courts and their grievances sparked a significant debate over the condition of women and the nature of African marriages. I need to preview this story here, because the issue of women seeking divorce became a significant test for what the French actually meant by "the repugnancy clause," which appeared as article 75 of the 1903 legislation: "native justice applies in all matters of local customs, insofar as they are not contrary to the principles of French civilization." As I discuss in Chapter 5, many French administrators, who were overseeing the operation of the new courts, were imbued with republican spirit and familiar with metropolitan changes in marriage laws and were solicitous of African women seeking the termination of marriage in which they had no say. The same situation applied in the case of child custody where the republican ideals of "civilization" were applied even though they were clearly in conflict with African customs. The Bouguni administrator captured the tensions facing French administrators when confronted with the custom that upon the death of her husband, a mother's child should be placed with the deceased father's brother. "It would be painful for me to conform to that custom," he wrote. "Is it not in effect contrary to our sentiments to remove a child from his mother to give it to an uncle in a family the mother does not wish to remain? This is a custom I would be happy to see disappear."[65] The Bouguni administrator did not indicate how he ruled in this appeal case, but in the related cases of levirate in Sikasso, under the pressure of the French administrator, the judges of the provincial court increasingly gave widows their freedom to remarry whomever they wished.[66] I develop disputes over child custody and levirate more fully in Chapter 7, but I allude to them here only to indicate the pressures on the application of custom due to the particular sensibilities of French administrators in shaping the outcomes of cases brought before the native courts.

Adultery was another site in which French sensibility intruded into the practice of custom. In France, adultery was criminalized, although it had a significant gendered component. Designed primarily to protect the sanctity of marriage and the honor the husband, the husband had the right to kill his wife if caught in the act. More often, adulterous wives were subject to prison sentences ranging from three months to two years. Adulterous husbands were simply fined between one hundred and two thousand francs. These fines were assessed for criminal acts and thus were retained by the state. The meaning of adultery shifted in the late nineteenth century in response to wide-ranging changes regarding the legal character of women and in response to increased popular discussion of sexuality. By the 1880s, prison terms for women were sharply reduced and between 1895 and 1910, fines replaced prison, although adultery remained a criminal act. Adultery had a civil law dimension in that it was admitted as evidence in metropolitan divorce proceedings, but adulterers were not subject to damage claims.[67]

While the custom regarding adultery in the Soudan varied, it usually had simultaneously a criminal and a civil character. Under custom, adulterers were subject to corporal punishment—usually a whipping, sometimes the shearing of the culprit's hair—and to damages. The cuckolded husband usually received compensation from the adulterer in the form of cash or cattle. In Sokolo, the prevailing compensation in 1909 was 2,500 cowries although it was as high as 50,000 cowries in neighboring Gumbu. Corporal punishment, as we have seen in Chapter 2, was considered incompatible with French civilization and prohibited. In place of whipping, adulterers were sentenced to imprisonment. Two to four months prison sentences were common toward the end of the decade.[68] But more importantly for assessing the influence of French sensibilities on custom was the change in the nature of adultery from a criminal and civil case to one that was solely criminal in nature. The Gumbu administrator captured the consequences of these subtle changes in the jurisdiction of adultery.

> Accusations of adultery had been very frequently presented to the provincial court, especially by animist Bamabara, who viewed adultery as a source of profits since their customs obliged the accessory to indemnify the husband. Before our arrival, the indemnity consisted of the confiscation of all the adulterer's goods, but since then it has been limited to 50,000 cowries (Fr 50). Little by little, we have transformed adultery from a civil action into a penal one. . . . This has resulted in a nearly complete disappearance of charges of adultery, because there is no longer anything to be earned from the suit.[69]

This is a cynical interpretation of Bambara practice, but it does indicate the changes set in motion when a French metropolitan grid over jurisdiction was imposed over African practices.[70]

Jurisdictional issues also lay at the heart of the conflict over customs generally. In invoking custom in the new native courts, the French failed to realize that there was no agreement as to what custom and whose custom was to be applied in any given dispute.[71] What is certain is that the new native courts were erected on profoundly unstable foundations of "custom." Nor did the 1903 decree or Roume's 1905 instructions help administrators who were faced with litigants demanding the application of different customs.

As we can expect, the first conflict of customs in the new native courts appeared just after the tribunals started operating. This involved a homicide in Bandigara, in which the two defendants each claimed different personal statuses: one claimed Muslim personal status and the other Habe custom. The Bandiagara administrator did not know how to proceed with a case against these two defendants. He bounced the case up the ladder to the lieutenant-governor, who in turn bounced the case up to the governor-general. In his covering letter, the lieutenant-governor of the Soudan mused about the options in this case, none of which seemed satisfactory. On the one hand, it was clearly against article 75 of the 1903 decree to impose either Muslim law or custom on both of the defendants. Nor was it reasonable to proceed with two separate cases, each invoking different regimes of law, because the judgment of the two courts might be different. This would be unacceptable, he argued, because both men cooperated in the execution of the same crime. The lieutenant-governor suggested that only one law should prevail in such a case regardless of the different statuses claimed by the defendants, although he was agnostic as to whether it should be French law, Muslim law, or Habe custom.[72]

Governor-general Roume, after consulting with the attorney-general of French West Africa, responded in February 1906 to the issue of conflict of customs with a major clarification of the procedure in the native courts. Roume's response reified the notion of equal domains of custom and Muslim family law, but provided a procedural mechanism for determining which regime of law prevailed in any given dispute involving litigants claiming different personal statuses.

> My attention has been recently directed to an obstacle that may sometimes occur in the native courts when one of the parties is Muslim and wishes to be judged following Koranic law and the other is non-Muslim and claims his custom. Most of these disputes concerning Muslims and non-Muslims will almost certainly involve resolving inheritance or the execution of a contract. In criminal cases, we will simultaneously pursue natives according to their different statuses.
>
> In inheritance disputes, inheritance will be adjudicated according to the personal status of the deceased without considering the prevailing law in the region in which he died nor the personal status of those claiming the inheritance. In regard to resolution of disputes over contracts, the only method for proceeding is to strictly apply the dictum *locus regit actum*, which is adopted by all legislation due to the equity principle it contains.[73]

Roume's principle, the law prevailing at the time of the agreement will prevail, did not fully satisfy the ambiguities of whose law will guide the disposition of the case in the native courts because the "ground" upon which the agreement was made was composed of multiple and overlapping regimes of custom. Further clarification to these issues awaited the outcome of the 1908–1909 survey of customs that Lieutenant-governor Clozel required his district officers to complete. The Segu administrator probably captured the emerging consensus over the continuing ambiguities over whose law was to prevail in cases where there was conflict over laws. In 1909, he wrote that "the status of the disputants determines the prevailing law; in the case of conflict, the dispute is judged according to the status of the plaintiff."[74]

The central problem in the conflict over customs was the assumption that Africans lived in neatly bounded ethnic units. The reality of the first decade of the twentieth century was considerably different. This was a period of increased social and economic transformations that I address more fully in Chapter 4. People were simply moving from place to place; many former slaves after 1905 were moving from their former masters; some made it back to their original homes; others settled in areas of expanding economic opportunities. Ponty's *politique des races* and Delafosse's *Soudanese civilization* should be understood as reactions to the messiness of the social transformations occurring on the ground.

CONCLUSION

The colonial legal system introduced in 1903 and implemented in 1905 contained within it procedural conflicts that reflected serious legal, policy, and cultural debates within the French West African colonial government. The 1903 legal system glossed over deep ambivalences that France and French administrators harbored in regard to Islam and Muslim law as well as toward African animism. Far from creating a venue where custom and Muslim family law could cohabitate equally, the colonial legal system of 1903 was built on a set of profound social changes that politicized the courts by creating new opportunities for litigants to use the native courts to pursue their grievances in new ways.

The colonial legal system was created to impose "regularity" in the application of justice within French West Africa. To some extent it did this by mandating an architecture of courts and regular forms of reporting. Governor-general Roume called for a codification of customs to facilitate the application of custom to dispute. However, the new courts did not end improvisation. The architects of the new colonial legal system did not anticipate the range of social changes that followed colonial conquest and they underestimated the high degree of variability in customs. Nor did they anticipate that litigants to the new courts would bring with them complex cultural strategies for maximizing the outcomes they wanted.

The second part of this study explores how Africans used the newly created native courts to resolve their most intimate domestic disputes. The first of the newly created native courts were up and running in the spring of 1905, which coincided with the first major phase of the slaves' exodus from their masters. This exodus began in Banamba and spread outward in time and space over the next five years. The slaves' exodus set in motion the end of slavery, which in turn set in motion linked sets of transformation in social and economic life throughout French West Africa. In Chapter 4, I trace the struggles between masters and slaves in Gumbu as the slaves began their exodus in the spring of 1908. After 1910, the court records no longer provide direct evidence on whether or not former masters and former slaves who had not departed earlier continued to struggle over work and property. However, the Gumbu records do provide a window into examining the impact of the slaves' exodus on marriages.

Entry-level civil disputes, as I have outlined in Chapter 1, provide a lens into the meanings of these changes for the men and women who actually lived them. I use the aggregate court data derived from two thousand cases to examine which areas of domestic life were the most "troubled." Following Lloyd Fallers, I trace the "trouble spots" in four districts in the French Soudan back and forth between trends indicated by the aggregate data and individual cases that can provide evidence of the meanings of these disputes. My analysis of the "trouble spots" indicates that marriage was among the most troubled areas of domestic life and a reading of the individual cases indicate that women were among the first group to use the new courts to end marriages that they did not want. To help explain how and why women used these new courts to end their marriages, I apply the concept of landscapes of power, as discussed in Chapter 1. French conquest, the end of slavery, and the establishment of the new native courts contributed to the changes in the landscapes of power that comprised both new and established institutions of social and political life as well as new ideas about rights and authority and about African women and patriarchy. I also use the concept landscape of power to highlight the conscious agency of litigants in using the courts. The evidence from the courts about women seeking divorce provided me with the first step in organizing the subsequent chapters of Part 2. Chapter 5 examines the changing landscapes women had to traverse in seeking divorce. Chapter 5 is in many ways the core chapter of this book, because all the other chapters surround the issues raised first there. Chapter 6 examines the disputes over bridewealth, and thus provides a central element of the context for examining divorce. For the native courts to grant women divorce, the woman often had to agree to return the bridewealth that her guardian had originally accepted. As I argue, few guardians were willing or able to return bridewealth on behalf of their kinswoman seeking divorce. Women, therefore, had to seek either another lover or draw on their own property to return the bridewealth. Chapter 7 examines women's property in particular as it explores how the end of slavery contributed to the articulation of new forms of property and new social relationships derived from new forms of property. Using women's property as my starting point in Chapter 8, I examine disputes over inheritance, which was one of the major trouble spots of the Segu district. In the conclusion, I reflect on the promises of using entry-level civil disputes to reconstruct African social life for an era more or less beyond the reach of the vast streams of African oral history.

Part II

African Disputes

4

THE COURTS, THE END OF SLAVERY, AND THE LANDSCAPES OF POWER

The landscapes of power in the French Soudan shifted dramatically between 1898 and 1912. In 1898, the French conquered Sikasso, Babemba's military stronghold, and captured Samory. The French emerged as the dominant military power in the region. Their monopoly of military power did not mean that French rule was unchallenged. Revolts against the French flared in isolated areas throughout the colony; most were suppressed fairly easily. French control over the sahel and Saharan region was much more tenuous, but the 1898 military victories in the southern savannas ushered in a profound change to the political and economic landscapes of the wider savanna country. What these changes meant to the men and women of the French Soudan took several years to become evident.

As the men and women of the French Soudan negotiated the changes set in motion by French military conquest, the landscapes that they had to traverse shifted yet again by the 1903 decree establishing the colonial legal system, which included a provision prohibiting the legal recognition of slave status in the courts. While the new courts were not established until the spring of 1905, the massive exodus of thousands of slaves from the French Soudan also starting in 1905 provided impetus for former masters and former slaves to test the meanings of the new landscapes of power. This chapter is a case study of linked transformations of French conquest, the end of slavery, and the operation of the new courts.

The most important result of the capture of Samory and the conquest of Sikasso in 1898 was the dramatic end to the era of insecurity. Both Samory and the rulers of Sikasso had established their political kingdoms on warfare and enslavement. Mobilization of resources for continuous warfare led to distortions in investments and commerce, and actual warfare led to endemic insecurity. The booty of war, mostly slaves, but also livestock and granaries, fed the soldiers and the circuits of commerce designed to support the military endeavor. French military preparation depended upon a line of supply linking Bamako to Kayes and through Kayes to Saint Louis. The French also drew on local sources of grain and livestock, stimulating the supply of goods and services necessary to the colonial mission. The building of the railway linking Kayes to Bamako followed the *route de ravitaillement,* and as it inched its way toward Bamako, it brought with it a new set of economic opportunities to the region.

The years immediately following 1898 saw the slow and fitful return of ordinary cycles of village life. Groups of men and women who had fled Wasulu and Sikasso in the 1880s and 1890s to the relative safety of the region west of the Niger and Milo Rivers began to trek back to their homes. Cautious villagers displaced by war and the expropriation of their harvests and livestock began to plant crops and rebuild their villages and herds. By 1901, French district administrators were reporting that the trickle of returning fugitives had taken the form of ever-larger numbers. News of the returning migrants circulated throughout the region, stimulating an increasing flow of returning fugitives. In the years leading up to 1901, most of these were free peasants who had fled the region to escape the predations of warfare and enslavement. In 1901, we have evidence of a large group of slaves trying to free themselves and to return to their homelands.[1]

The increased movements of refugees and runaway slaves in the early years of the twentieth century were stimulated by the "descent of peace."[2] Departures from settlements along the *route de ravitaillement* were also stimulated by the colonial administration's unending requisitions for goods and labor to build the infrastructure of their new colony. Originally imposed to aid the supply of the forward French military mission as it made its way to Bamako in 1883, the mobilization of local sources of labor and goods to support the development of the French presence on the Niger continued throughout the next two decades. The overland movement of goods required virtually an army of its own. Convoys of porters carrying matériel and food marched alongside colonial troops. Porters rarely came forward willingly; many were impressed from villages along the supply route. The French had strategically established a set of *villages de liberté* along the line of supply. Founded as a measure to protect freed and runaway slaves as well as refugees, the inhabitants of these villages were especially vulnerable to impressment into the supply caravans. Although porters were compensated for their labor, the work was grueling and the toll on porters high. Many were forced into the corvées exactly when they should have been in the fields, harvesting the crops, or preparing for planting.[3] Hard on the heels of the *route de ravitaillement* came the railway linking Kayes to Bamako. Building the railway in the absence of heavy machinery required massive inputs of cheap labor. Inhabitants of the liberty villages formed a ready pool of labor, sufficiently vulnerable not to resist these impressments. In 1897 Colonel Trentinian warned district officers "to avoid falling into abuse and profiting from the proximity and submission of the [inhabitants] of the liberty villages by extracting from them all sorts of corvées for all purposes."[4] Slave and free alike may have evaluated the risks of returning to Wasulu and Sikasso and compared them favorably to remaining along the supply route.

Preparations for the military campaigns of 1898 further stimulated the regional demand for African goods and services. The Bamako grain market emerged in the mid-1890s as a crucial resource to French efforts to build their center of power along the banks of the Niger.[5] The expansion of the Bamako grain market rested on both cheap transportation afforded by the Niger and the annual migrations of herds, and by the capacity of African slave owners to expand grain production by increasing the amount of labor demanded of slaves and reducing the volume of food offered to them. Commandant Brevié noted this in a set of interviews he conducted with slaves in 1904. "Slaves are poorly fed, mistreated, and poorly clothed. Masters rarely give them their two days free [which is theirs by custom]. They prefer to feed them poorly and to be assured of all their labor all the time."[6] Changes in the customary practices of slavery in response to the changes in the landscape of power in the French Soudan contributed to the exodus of the slaves beginning in 1905.

THE END OF SLAVERY AND THE EXPANSION OF COMMERCE

Colonial conquest stimulated the regional economy, but not necessarily in ways the French had anticipated. Although French colonial expansion stimulated specific economic demands for labor and goods, much of the expansion of production in the Soudan from 1890 followed the deep patterns of ecological specialization that had characterized the precolonial continental economy of West Africa. The expansion of the Bamako grain market and the role of European and African merchants in it are indicative of the nature of the colonial economy that was established in the Soudan. The colonial economy rested upon an African foundation of ecologically specialized production stimulated by the ascendance of the French military and the gradual establishment of physical security. The arrival of the railhead in Bamako in 1904 provided a new means for moving goods overland, but the size of the colonially controlled import-export economy remained insignificant to the overall increase in the movement of African goods along the long-established north-south commercial axis.[7]

Nonetheless, French conquest created the conditions in which Africans struggled over the nature of productive relationships made possible by the erosion of ethnic boundaries over economic resources and the end of slave labor. The reorganization of access to economic resources was probably the most revolutionary shift during the period under investigation but it is also the most difficult for historians to trace because it was linked to changes in identity and community.[8]

The precolonial economy had been organized largely by what Fredrick Barth has termed social boundaries over economic niches.[9] The erosion of the ethnic boundaries around access to resources was linked to changes in the regional political economy. As the regional economy started to boom, Africans began to push through what had been at best permeable social boundaries even during the precolonial period. Cracks in these ethnic boundaries over resources were already becoming evident at the beginning of the century, as demand for locally produced commodities increased. Indigo dyed cloth, for example, had been produced by the Maraka for a relatively small luxury market. As commerce expanded, so did entrants into this industry. "Manufactured even last year by the Marakas exclusively," wrote the Segu district officer in his agricultural and commercial report in 1901, "the Somonos and even the Bambaras are now imitating them. Trade in local *pagnes* (cloth) greatly increases each day; it goes without saying that cotton and indigo cultivation are also developing."[10] Conflicts over access to economic resources predated the end of slavery, but the movement of freed slaves into all sectors of the economy accelerated change. And in the case of livestock, cattle rapidly emerged as the most important form of capital investment with the end of slavery. The French administrator in Segu was among the first to notice this change.

> Trade, agriculture, and herding, all monopolies long recognized [as belonging] to this or that race, are today contested by all. Today, more common are the natives of all origins who during the dry season follow the *juulas* [Bamana: traders] of profession, who go by new routes to Bamako, San, and Tonge, and who bring to the markets of the west and south livestock, products of local industries, salt, and a small assortment of European goods.[11]

Commerce was the first sector to see its barriers erode. It had never been the exclusive domain of any one ethnic group, although the technical problems associated with trade over long distances favored an "ethnic" or religious solution.[12] Conquest made travel safer and the arrival of the railhead in Bamako and then Koulikoro in 1904 made travel easier. Access to trade goods was facilitated by the general expansion of production and an increase in the demand for ecologically specialized products as well as imported manufactured goods. Even small amounts of capital could now be converted into an assortment of goods, albeit relatively small, that could be transported easily over long distances.

The end of slavery accelerated the erosion of ethnic monopolies over resources. Many freed men and women moved into occupations whose skills they had learned as slaves. Some moved into weaving and dyeing, thus catering to the huge expansion of the market for locally produced cloth.[13] Others moved into commerce and transportation. And still others established themselves as farmers, herders, and fishermen. Some became individual producers; others service providers. The end of slavery also profoundly transformed the most commonly used forms of capital investment. This point is central to Félix Dubois's 1911 observation:

> In Western Sudanese society, the slave or captive corresponded . . . to an institution of our modern society—the savings bank. Agricultural and commercial profits were quickly invested in slaves. . . . At the present time, the suppression of domestic slavery is a problem that has been resolved in all its forms. . . . New economies are constituted. And available funds no longer go into purchases of slaves; the owner is very judiciously advised to place them . . . in livestock.[14]

Livestock was one of the principle exports to neighboring colonies of Senegal, Côte d'Ivoire, and the Gold Coast during the early twentieth century. As capital was steadily invested in livestock, ownership of cattle, sheep, and goats was diversified among all ethnic groups. Investment in livestock emerged as one of the primary forms of capital investment during this period.[15] I discuss disputes over livestock and the creation of "new property" in Chapter 7. Many of the disputes between former masters and former slaves in Gumbu took the form of disputes over property. Because property was a product of labor and social relations, disputes over property were also disputes over social relationships and obligations.

COURTS AND THE END OF SLAVERY IN GUMBU

The district of Gumbu along the desert-edge in the French Soudan provides an excellent laboratory for examining the social history of the end of slavery. Located along the desert-edge, Gumbu sat astride the northern limit of rainfed agriculture. In the course of the nineteenth century, the economy of Gumbu expanded around slave-based agricultural production of grain and cotton. Much of the grain and cotton was destined to supply the ecologically specialized trade with the Maures. The core of Gumbu district consisted of the town of Gumbu and some 20 or so outlying villages. The system of slavery that developed in Gumbu differed somewhat from the forms established in the region of Banamba, located more fully in the savanna region, but also catering to the desert-side trade. Around Banamba and the seven other Maraka towns of Beledugu (*Marakaduguw wolonwula*), slaves tended to live together in outlying agricultural villages, which resembled plantations. According to Meillassoux, the slaves of Gumbu had distinctive "relations of production" depending upon their social status. Newly acquired slaves had virtually no rights and worked for their masters in exchange for their subsistence. Once the slave was "seasoned" and did not show signs of flight, he or she entered a new status that influenced the work regime because these slaves now had "rights" to a certain portion of the day for themselves. These slaves worked for their masters 6 to 14 hours per day, 6 days per week. The rest of the time, they worked on their own plots. The final category of slaves was the *woroso* or "slaves born into the house" of the master. These were second or subsequent generation slaves who could, if their master approved, work entirely on their own fields in exchange for an annual rent customarily fixed at 150 *muule* [a local measure equal to around 2.4 kilograms] of grain. Meillassoux calls this "rent slavery."[16] This relationship of an annual transfer of millet or sorghum (the French lump both millet and sorghum together under the generic term *mil*) featured significantly as the former masters of Gumbu sought to prevent their former slaves from leaving in the period after 1908. *Worosow* probably lived in small hamlets dispersed throughout this ecologically sparse and fragile region. Because masters usually provided their slaves with domestic partners, most lived in some form of domestic unit. Masters and slaves also developed mutually entangling webs of dependency, reinforced by loans of livestock and goods and by ritual practices. The end of slavery put to the test the depth and elasticity of these webs of dependency.

The meaning and experiences of the end of slavery in Africa are the subject of considerable debate. Some have argued that the end of slavery was a smooth transition, leaving most former slaves and former masters within the same social world conducting their business more or less as before. Others have argued that the end of slavery set in motion a powerful set of changes that left very little the same as before. Igor Kopytoff has advanced the most compelling argument about the relative smoothness of the transition. He argued that most of the slaves in Africa probably remained with or near their former masters. Kopytoff, however, was not content to postulate that most slaves did not leave their former masters. He insisted that only those slaves least integrated into the social lives of their masters' household left. The vast majority, Kopytoff argued, remained because they were bound to their former masters through affective and cultural ties of dependency and because departure plunged former slaves into a form of social death due to their kinlessness. Moreover, those slaves who remained were further integrated into their masters' social worlds. According to the Kopytoff model of "African" slavery, we can assume that such integration was relatively free of conflict. Had there been conflict, then these former slaves would have, like their less integrated compatriots, simply left their master's households.[17]

Kopytoff's provocative argument was based not only on negative evidence—the absence of evidence of social conflict—but on no evidence. Evidence on social and cultural integration is hard to come by, especially if it is so smooth and seamless that the process does not generate conflicts. The court records from Gumbu district provide a relatively untouched body of source material to examine the social history of the aftermath of the end of slavery. By their very nature, court records exacerbate the perception of conflicts in social relations rather than their smooth functioning. Contextualizing the evidence in the court records against the wider patterns of change and examining trends in the types of disputes brought to court provide historians with a means of examining the social history of the end of slavery.[18]

SLAVES LEAVE GUMBU

Beginning first in the region of Banamba in the spring of 1905 and spreading outward in time and space, slaves from the sahelian districts of Sokolo and Gumbu began to leave their masters by early spring 1908. After initial confusion, hesitation, and efforts to prevent the slaves from leaving, French policy on the slaves' exodus—and on slavery itself—became clear. In December 1905, Governor-general Ernest Roume formally decreed an end to practices leading to the alienation of a person's liberty, effectively prohibiting new enslavement. The December 1905 decree built on the principle that French colonial law (and colonial policy) did not recognize the legal status of the slave as decreed by the 10 November 1903 legal system.

Slaves were quick to understand the implications of these twin decrees: slaves were the ones who pushed the limits of the colonial state's willingness to support the rights of slaves over those of their masters. In the spring of 1908, when the slaves of Gumbu first started to leave their masters, the French district officials were prepared to issue *laisser-passer* (official permission to move from one district to another) and to collect whatever taxes may be owed by those individuals seeking to leave the district.[19] The exodus of slaves from Gumbu had a seasonal quality, reflecting the agrarian nature of most slaves' work, but also indicating the strategic nature of the slaves' plans. Between 1908 and December 1910, 6,279 slaves requested formal permission from the Gumbu district officer to leave the district. Not included in this number were the slaves who simply declared themselves free and either moved to other parts of the district, set up new, independent villages, or simply severed relations with their former masters.[20] Most slaves left during the period from the end of the harvest to the beginning of the new planting season, from roughly December through early June. Slaves probably wanted to reap whatever benefits they could from their harvests or to leave early enough to start farming somewhere else. In contrast, leaving during the agricultural season put slaves at the greatest risk for survival.

As the volume of the slaves' departures for 1909 began to exceed that of 1908, the French worried about the impact of the slaves' exodus on the agricultural productivity of the district. Assistant commandant Thoron de Laur tried to dissuade the slaves from leaving, but he could not prevent them from doing so. Nonetheless, he appealed to what he assumed was their own economic rationality in his efforts to stem the flow of slaves from Gumbu.

> With each slave, I hold the following discussion. "The rainy season has started. You are absolutely free to work for yourself, to pawn yourself, or to hire yourself out. In one word, make whatever decision you want. . . . The season of agriculture is here and we seek to avoid all disruption during this period. Work now, the harvest will come, the best season for traveling will come, and your resources for making such a voyage will be much better."[21]

We have no way of knowing how effective de Laur's speech was in persuading slaves not to leave the district. However, the volume of official slave departures from Gumbu fell dramatically by June 1909 and never regained the volume it had achieved during 1908 and the first half of 1909. Some slaves did leave their masters in Gumbu after the 1909 harvest and probably some continued to leave well into the next decade. By end of 1910, however, there are no more records on the numbers of slaves requesting permission to leave the district. Either the French administrator no longer bothered to keep records of those who requested permission to leave the district, or those who left simply picked up and moved without informing anyone.

The end of slavery offered slave men and women three broad choices and an almost infinite variation within them. Slaves could leave their masters and either return to their original homelands (if they remembered or imagined where they were) or set up new homes elsewhere; they could simply declare themselves free without having to leave; or they could renegotiate relations with their former masters. In my earlier work,[22] I examined primarily the first option, because I had evidence on requests for *laisser-passer* and I had archival evidence from several districts the freed slaves indicated their intentions to move to. I also used interviews with former slaves, former masters, and their descendants to reconstruct the history of those freedmen and women who remained together with their former masters. Most of my informants described the establishment of what several called a "type of kinship," which allowed former slaves to become enmeshed within the households of their former masters. While many now "ate from the same bowl," former slave status was not forgotten and subtle forms of dependency and deference remained central to this new relationship.[23] This is exactly what Kopytoff would have anticipated: the relatively smooth and conflict-free integration of former slaves into their masters' household.

Memories of such smooth integration may well have been encouraged by the context in which my interviews were conducted. As Paul Escot found in his critical examination of the oral history contained in the marvelous Federal Works Project Administration slave narrative project, freed men and women of the American South recalled the most paternal aspects of the master-slave relationship. Recorded in the Deep South during the seemingly unending difficulties of the Depression and being interviewed mostly by white researchers, freed slaves tended not to discuss the harsher side of slavery.[24] Most researchers for the WPA were also not very interested in the era of Reconstruction and thus did not solicit information on the contested nature of that period.[25] The same kinds of distortions in the oral record probably occurred in my interviews and in the interviews most of us collected on slavery and the end of slavery. I collected most of my interviews on slavery and the end of slavery in the late 1970s and early 1980s during the immediate aftermath of the devastating sahelian drought and in the midst of the collapsing national economies of French West Africa. My presence as a foreign researcher arriving with formal government approval to conduct research and the very questions I posed must have contributed to the ways my informants, consciously or unconsciously, discussed the past. We could speculate that when my informants responded that a "form of kinship" emerged between former masters and former slaves, they were not only describing the past as they remembered it, but they were also foreclosing further questions about social conflict. Evidence from the court registers of the Gumbu *tribunal de province* provides precious data on the social history of the end of slavery as it was lived during this period.

SOCIAL CONFLICTS IN GUMBU DURING
THE END OF SLAVERY

The statistical evidence on *laisser-passer* and on population movements does not capture the contested nature of the slaves' decisions to leave their masters. Figure 4.1 shows the requests for *laisser-passer* from Gumbu and should be used as background against which to see the changing incidence in debt, property, and marriage disputes also from Gumbu. Leaving was never easy, because it often meant leaving behind friends and families. But exactly how difficult leaving was can be gleaned from an examination of the court records. Already at the beginning of 1908, the district officer of Gumbu described increased activity at the provincial tribunal. "The numbers of disputes brought before the tribunal de province have increased significantly over the course of the quarter due to the departures of slaves (*serviteurs*) wishing to return to their homelands. These disputes have been brought by the former masters. Almost all of the disputes that are presented have to do with questions of debt, division of property, divorces, and the like."[26] As the planting season of 1908 approached, even more cases were brought by former masters to the provincial tribunal, which was forced to convene three or four times per week in order to meet the case load and to "minimize as far as possible the delay of departure for the former slaves wanting to return to their

Figure 4.1 Slaves Departures from Gumbu, 1908–1910, n = 6,279

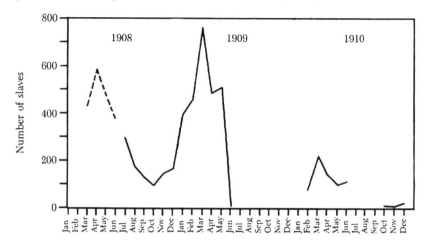

Slaves departures between January 1908–December 1910. The data from 1908 were presented as an annual sum in the records. The dotted line for 1908 is esti-mated monthly departures based on patterns evident in 1909 and 1910 departures. The 1908 departures were 76 percent of those of 1909. Original chart appeared in Roberts, "The End of Slavery in the French Soudan." Source: ANM 1 E 38–39

homelands."[27] Former masters quickly saw the new colonial courts as a way to entangle their former slaves in litigation in order to delay their former slaves' departures. Former masters also saw these courts as a means to force their former slaves to honor the contractual bases behind the master-slave relationship as it had emerged in Gumbu. Not surprisingly, many of the dis-putes dealt with debts of grain, division of property, and loans of livestock. The 3rd Quarter 1908 report on the provincial tribunal indicated that the num-bers of plaintiffs coming before the tribunal increased dramatically. "One must attribute this significant increase to the exodus of the slaves (*serviteurs*) which continues in a very steady pace. Before the departure of their former slaves, their masters seek through all means to keep them in place either by claiming debts or by leveling against them all sorts of accusations."[28]

By 1909, the numbers of cases brought before the provincial tribunal had diminished by two-thirds, despite the fact that the volume of slave departures was higher in 1909 than in 1908. The district officer explained this diminu-tion of disputes to his perception that both the former masters and their for-mer slaves "have come to understand our ideas [about justice] and no longer decry each other as enemies as they did at the outset of the exodus of the slaves."[29] Instead of attributing the decline in disputes to the growing knowl-edge of French ideas of justice or to some greater sense of mutual respect, we could just as easily argue that after the first year of transition the freedmen understood their former masters' strategies to entangle them in legal disputes and preempted the disputes by settling before their departures or by departing without announcing their intentions. The colonial state did not have the institutional capacity to pursue defendants in civil disputes who simply skipped town before their court appearances.

Most of the 597 disputes recorded in the Gumbu court registers fall into one of the following six categories: divorce and bridewealth; child custody; debt; damages or compensation; property; and inheritance. I have also included a residual category of "other," which contained only four disputes I could not otherwise categorize (household fission and several cases of rape).[30] Figure 4.2 indicates the breakdown of the cases by category of dispute. Cases involving ruptured marriages, debts, and property disputes constitute fully 81 percent of all the cases in Gumbu between 1905 and 1912. These cases reflect very different patterns of court use and social conflicts. Disputes over contracts/property and debts mushroom at the start of the planting season in 1908, at exactly the time when the slaves of Gumbu were making their first sustained efforts to leave. Of the total disputes over property, 29 percent occurred in between March and July 1908. Similarly, 31 percent of all the dis-

Figure 4.2 Distribution of Disputes, Gumbu, 1905–1912, n = 597

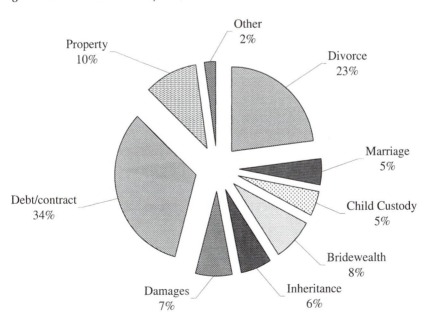

Source: ANM 2 M 122

putes over debts occurred in April and July 1908, and 23 percent of all the debt cases were heard in June and July 1908 alone. In contrast, the incidence of divorce disputes reflected a different pattern (peaks occurred annually in April in the midst of the planting) and between November and January during the harvest time with increasing incidence of divorce cases appearing in the spring of 1911, roughly three years after the first wave of slave departures and during a time when those freed men and women who were going to leave had already left. Whereas many cases of debt and disputes over contracts and property may reflect masters' strategies to encumber their former slaves with legal obligations, the cases about divorce reflect some of the social consequences of the end of slavery in the region. Divorce cases illustrate just how deeply the end of slavery ramified into slave and free households alike.

FORMER MASTERS USE THE COURTS TO PREVENT THEIR FORMER SLAVES FROM LEAVING

Former masters seem to have quickly understood that while the colonial state was no longer prepared to keep their slaves on the fields and working for them, they could use the newly established colonial courts to impose the logic of the debt and property rights on their former slaves. In the Gumbu district, the master-slave relationship that was particularly susceptible to these new strategies by former masters was what Meillassoux calls "rent slavery" formed mostly between masters and slaves "born into the house of the master" or *woroso*. We have no evidence of the relative proportion of slaves in Gumbu who fell into this category. In the absence of a strong state to coerce surplus production from slaves, masters spun webs of dependency around all their slaves. These webs of dependency were designed to keep slaves from running away and to tie them more fully to their masters.[31] These webs of dependency often took the form of masters providing wives for their male slaves, permitting slaves to guard livestock in exchange for a share of the offspring, and in sharing the harvest. Each year following the harvest, the slave presented his master with a set amount of grain.

Disputes over Debts

Debt cases constitute 34 percent of all the cases heard in the Gumbu provincial court during the period being investigated here. Most of the cases dealing with debt between early 1908 and harvest time of 1908 were claims focusing on transfers of grain and guinée cloth—transfers that lay at the heart of what Meillassoux calls the "rent" that slaves owed their masters. Cases dealing with grain and guinée cloth certainly persisted beyond end of 1908, but increasingly after 1908 debt cases reflected commercial disputes and no longer primarily those between former masters and former slaves. Gumbu was well within the guinée currency zone, where guinée cloth served as a multipurpose money.[32] Debt cases involving millet almost certainly continued to reflect the ways former masters and slaves adapted to the end of slavery.

Most common among the debt cases in Gumbu in 1908 were disputes over the transfers of "rent" that defined the master-slave relationship. Such was likely the cause of the claim Demba Diko made against Samba Sigiri on 16 April 1908 for the recovery of 600 kilograms of millet. Samba Sigiri did not deny the claim, but requested a delay from the court in order to wait for the current harvest. The court granted Sigiri's request to delay the transfer, while upholding the plaintiff's claim. Dia Coulibaly denied in court on 7 May 1908 that he owed Dougouni Kone 540 kilograms of millet. However, witnesses supported Kone's claim and the court ruled in his favor. Witnesses also supported Mohamet Cira's claim to 200 kilograms of millet from Mari Diabou "Ngolokoro" [*sic*], who denied owing that quantity. The court ruled in the plaintiff's favor.[33] It could be that former masters now understood how powerfully persuasive it was to have witnesses to the debts they claimed. In three cases heard on 18 June 1908, in two cases heard on 21 June 1908, and in four cases heard on 22 June 1908, the defendants all denied the claims, but the plaintiffs had witnesses who supported their claims. The court ruled in favor of the plaintiffs in all six cases. In the absence of written contracts, witnesses provided the court with its principle evidence.[34]

Defendants often tried to deny the claims made by plaintiffs, as Dia Coulibaly and Mari Diabou "Ngolokoro" did above, and sometimes they

Figure 4.3 Incidence of Debt Disputes, Gumbu, 1905–1912, n = 197

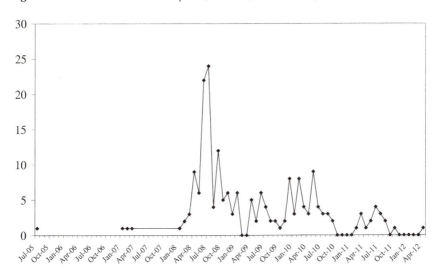

Source: ANM 2 M 122

sought to argue extenuating circumstances. On 14 May 1908, Sidiki Dembele did not deny Bamady Ely's claim to 620 kilograms of millet, but he claimed that this millet was stolen. The court was not swayed; it ruled against Dembele and required that he repay his debt to Bamady Ely. Sometimes the excuses were barely logical, as in the 18 May 1908 case in which Dembele Sambou claimed that he no longer had the 450 kilograms of millet Mabako Gakou sought to recover, because he admitted to having eaten it. The court was not swayed in this case either and ruled against the defendant.[35]

The cases involving debts in guinée cloth in 1908 can probably be read as the cases involving the substitution of cash for grain or other property debts, because guinée cloth was a commodity currency and a unit of value. On 19 March 1908, Mohamet Konate took Noumou Daha to court to recover one and a half guinées. The court ruled in Mohamet Konate's favor. Diagueli Diko sought to recover two guinées from Coumien Ture on 9 July 1908 and brought a witness to support his claim. The tribunal ruled in his favor. The size of the debts in guinée could be substantial. Garba So sought to recover 11 guinées from Amadou Bary on 5 April 1909. Amadou Bary did not deny the debt, but told the tribunal that he only had five guinées at the moment and requested a delay of 20 days to repay the rest. When a defendant failed to deliver the promised goods by the date set by the tribunal, plaintiffs were sometimes obliged to haul the defendant back to court, as happened on 17 May 1909 when Niamakolo Dantioko failed to meet the payment deadline fixed by the tribunal. Sometimes the debts plaintiffs sought to recover mixed commodities, which probably stemmed from different parts of the webs of obligations. This was the case on 2 July 1908, when Mohamet Taliki sought to recover 15 guinées and 20 sheep from Amady Kata. Amady Kata responded that he would repay the guinées, but that he only had one sheep. Witnesses supported Mohmet Taliki's claim and the court ruled against the defendant.[36]

Particularly in the cases of disputes over transfers of commodities and property, the nature of the court registers and the verdicts rendered by the magistrates tended to exacerbate the "contractual" nature of the master-slave relationships. The judgments recorded at the provincial court in Gumbu tell us very little about whether or not former masters tried to negotiate with their former slaves to find a mutually acceptable middle ground to resolve their disputes. The judgments awarded winners and punished losers of the disputes in no uncertain terms. In reaching their decisions, the magistrates probably reduced much more complex negotiations to simple formula of unambiguous rights and obligations.

Disputes over Property

Disputes over property begin to appear sporadically before the provincial court starting in July 1905. They became much more pronounced in the spring of 1908. On 23 March 1908, three of the four cases heard clearly stemmed from the rupture of relations between former slaves and their former masters. In each of the three cases, the defendant was identified as the "former servant," but the pattern of these disputes appears again and again in the records without the defendant being labeled as "servant."[37] In some cases, former masters wanted their share of the harvest, which several former slaves had already transferred into livestock, presumably because they were a more mobile form of wealth. "Baba So claims that his former servant, Ahmary Diallo, had bought one donkey and eight sheep with millet belonging to Baba So. Witnesses confirm." The court ruled in favor of Baba So and ordered Ahmary Diallo to return the livestock to him. In another case heard that day, a former master, Amady Abdoulay Mocar, brought suit against his former slave, Hamady Souka, for a share of the goods the latter bought "largely with the product of his harvest." Here, too, the former slave probably transferred millet into more liquid forms of wealth, although the court record does not indicate what kind. The tribunal ruled in Amady Abdoulay Mocar's favor and forced the former slave to share the goods "in two equal parts."[38]

The threat of the freedmen's departures probably also set in motion efforts to recover the former master's goods left in trust with the former slaves. A crucial part of the master-slave relationship in contexts without strong states to support the masters' rights were webs of debt and obligations. Masters may well have left livestock in the care of their slaves. Slaves may have tended the livestock over many years and expected a share of the offspring. The end of slavery forced some of these relationships, built over many years, into the courts. On 6 April 1908, Samba Kadra brought Amady Toure to court to recover one heifer. "Amady Toure claims that he returned the heifer to Samba Kadra, but that it came back to him." The court ruled in Samba Kadra's favor and ordered Amady Toure to return the heifer to him. On 23 April 1908 Modiba Dembele took Tiema Coulibaly to court to recover property "he entrusted to Tiema Coulibaly, but which he sold." The defendant acknowledged his actions and the court ruled that Tiema Coulibaly must return the goods to the plaintiff.[39]

The end of slavery led to the reshuffling of property relations of all kinds. In Sidibeme cases, the conflict was actually over land. "Kaoura Kone claims that Ahmady Sidibe took away his land. Ahmady Sidibe claims that it belongs to him and that he had been prevented from plowing it."[40] This case is not detailed enough for us to peer beyond the stated dispute to see the sets of Sidibecial relations behind it. Was Ahmady Sidibe the former master, who was now claiming the land his former slaves had worked? Clearly the court ruled in favor of Ahamdy Sidibe's rights to the land, which indicates his rights as a free member of the community, and required Kaoura Kone to return the land following the harvest. This case is interesting first in that Ahmady Sidibe did not claim a share of the harvest and second in that armed with stronger property rights, he seemed relatively powerless vis-à-vis Kaoura Kone's refusal to move from the land.

Figure 4.4 Incidence of Property Disputes, Gumbu, 1905–1912, n = 62

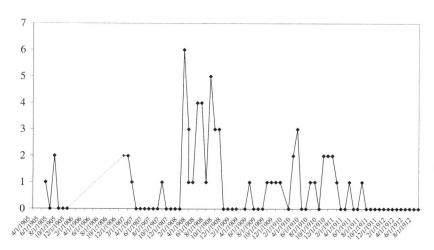

Source: ANM 2 M 122

Given the fact that loans of property and livestock were parts of the webs of debt and obligations between masters and slaves, many of these loans were probably quite old and the circumstances of the original loan could no longer be reconstructed. This was the case when Mohamet Mint took M'Bare Diamana to court to recover a cow that he claimed he had lent the defendant. M'Bare Diamana brought witnesses along to prove to the court that Mohamet Mint had actually "given him that cow."[41] Providing the courts with admissible evidence to prove ownership was not always easy. Thus, a significant number of the property cases were dismissed, probably for lack of evidence.[42] The following section on divorce provides a different perspective into the social consequences of the end of slavery. I will read the divorce cases in this section less in terms of the contractual nature of marriage—which indeed marriage had—but as indicators of social change.

THE END OF SLAVERY AND HOUSEHOLD TENSIONS: DIVORCE

Cases of divorce appear in the court records of the tribunal de province of Gumbu from the moment that the court began to meet in 1905. "Almost all the disputes that were presented to the tribunal de province during the course of the first quarter dealt with questions of divorce," reported the district officer from Gumbu in 1906.[43] By 1908 as the slaves' exodus was becoming a flood, the Gumbu administrator noted that requests for divorce were "particularly abundant." The officer linked the high incidence of requests for divorce in Gumbu to the weak bonds of affection between African women, their husbands, their husband's kin, and from their own children.

> It is regrettable to acknowledge just how little a native woman is attached to her husband and her new family. Many among these women following the exodus of the slaves do not dread to abandon their children to their husbands who wish to remain in their district so that they can return to their homelands.[44]

Although the cases the district officer was referring to were obviously cases of slave wives, the officer should have known that in patrilineal, patrilocal descent systems in which bridewealth has been paid, women, whether free or slave, have no legal claims on their children. Cases of divorce differ from those of contract/property and marriage disputes in that the majority of the plaintiffs were women. Marriage disputes, in contrast, were brought exclusively by husbands or their male kin in order to force their wives to return to the conjugal home. I explore the differences between divorce and marriage disputes more fully in Chapter 5.

In Gumbu and throughout the French Soudan, women were bringing suits for divorce against their husbands because of the ways in which the new colonial legal system provided women with new opportunities to take control over at least a part of their lives. The new tribunals were also significant in that they often supported women's requests to terminate marriages in which

Figure 4.5 Gumbu, Divorces, 1905–1912, n = 138

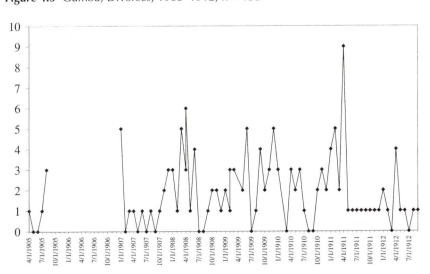

Source: ANM 2 M 122

husbands mistreated their wives or even when women simply wanted to leave their husbands. Fully 36 percent of all the cases heard by the tribunal de provincial in Gumbu stemmed from marital disputes (divorce, marriage disputes, and bridewealth disputes). Divorce alone constituted 23 percent of all the disputes heard at the Gumbu provincial tribunal.

Divorce cases reflect a very different trend than those observed in the case of property/contract and debt disputes. Whereas most of the property/contract and debt disputes coincided with the first significant wave of slave departures from Gumbu in the spring of 1908, divorce disputes have three distinctive characteristics. First, divorce disputes had a marked seasonality. Divorces peaked twice annually: a larger spike occurred in April and a smaller one in November–December. April marked the period when the heavy work of field preparation and planting was getting underway in the sahel region. November through January marked the high point in the harvest, when demand on labor was also great. Second, the incidence of divorce increased each year up to April 1911, after which the number of divorce disputes declined and then leveled off. And third, the two most prominent causes for divorce were women accusing their husbands of mistreatment (44%) and of abandonment (16%).

While some cases of slave marriages are clearly indicated in the court records, most of the cases for divorce in Gumbu probably occurred in non-slave households. Some slave husbands may have wanted to "regularize" their marriage by the payment of bridewealth, because most slave marriages were not formalized. Hence, divorce among slave households would not likely have made their way to court because the rupture of the marriage had no bearing on the recovery of bridewealth and the disposition of children. Children of slave women customarily belonged to the master of the woman, which has led Meillassoux and others to point to the lack of paternity as one of the defining features of male slave status.[45] Nonetheless, there are a handful of divorce cases that are indicative of former slave status, such as the case that Kumba Diallo brought against her husband, Ousmane Sigiri on 24 April 1911. Kumba Diallo told the court that "she no longer wants to live with her husband and that she wants to accompany her brother who is leaving for Bouguni." Bouguni was the destination of choice of the slaves who left Gumbu between 1908 and 1910.[46] Another indication that the marriage between Ousmane Sigiri and Kumba Diallo was a slave marriage or a marriage between former slaves was the size of the bridewealth that Ousmane Sigiri wanted returned. It was a mere 120 *muules* of millet, which was a symbolic transfer.[47] Among free men and women, bridewealth transfers usually represented significant value, whether transferred in goods, labor service, or cash. Between 1905 and 1912, the value of bridewealth payments averaged around Fr 150 in the districts of Bamako and Segu. Values of bridewealth transfers in Gumbu were slightly less and varied with the status of the bride. Among the Bambara inhabitants of Gumbu, the average bridewealth in 1909 was 120,000 cowries or Fr 120.[48]

As I develop more fully in Chapter 6, marriage transferred rights to a woman's wife's labor, reproductive power, and rights of sexual access from her natal group to her husband and his kinship group. Bridewealth was a central mechanism of this transfer. Divorce usually initiated the return flow of bridewealth from the wife's kin to her husband's. The obligation to return bridewealth upon the dissolution of marriage was certainly a barrier to divorce, because the bridewealth a household head received was usually used to transfer brides into his household for his sons and other male dependants. The Gumbu administrator, who was charged with overseeing the operation of the provincial courts, noted in 1909 that a wife who wanted to leave her husband usually found that "her parents have already dissipated the bridewealth received at the time of her marriage and are thus not willing to return it. Instead, they force their daughter to return to the conjugal home, but not before administering a serious beating."[49] The same administrator who penned this note was the one who kept the court registers that indicated that divorce occurred. The significance of divorce set against the need to repay bridewealth is all the more striking and reflects the degree of conflict between men and women in the immediate aftermath of the end of slavery.[50]

As indicated above, most slaves left their masters between the end of harvest and the beginning of the new planting season, roughly from January through June. Those former slaves who wanted to establish themselves as independent peasant households had to be ready to plant when the first rains arrived, usually around April. Data from the official *laisser-passer* indicate that most slaves left Gumbu between February and April, with peaks each year in March. February and March departures were probably ideal for former slaves wishing to start a new farm. February and March departures also meant that formers masters were scrambling for labor in order to put their own crops in. Thoron de Laur, the assistant district officer in Gumbu reflected in May 1909 on the changes to Gumbu's economy and society that he was observing.

> [The departure of slaves was] a just punishment for the race which considered their relatives [i.e., other Africans] as their slaves and who have pushed them to leave. But there are some significant difficulties created by their departure. Destructions of the family, abandonment of children, raping of children, litigenous questions [are] all connected events. The movement [of slaves] appears to be diminishing and the exodus proceeds without incident. Nevertheless, it does cause profound changes in the customs of the land. . . .[51]

De Laur's assumption that the slaves' exodus was diminishing was merely the end of the annual cycle of departures, because the slaves continued to leave in significant, though decreasing numbers into 1910. De Laur was right to see "destructions of the family, abandonment of children . . . and litigious questions" as being linked processes. As indicated in the charts on divorces (Figures 4.5 and 4.6), the incidence of divorce coincides remarkably with the seasonal peaks of slaves' departures and with the onset of heavy agricultural labor. Reflecting patterns of adjustments to the departures of slaves from nearby Banamba and Bamako, former slave-owning household heads turned increasingly to their own wives and children to make up the agricultural labor shortfall. The women of Gumbu probably felt like the woman quoted in a 1907 report from Bamako when she stated that "my husband gives me nothing; my husband forces me to work. My husband does nothing himself, and I, I work continuously."[52] It should not be surprising that 30 percent of the divorce disputes heard in Gumbu cited "mistreatment" as the cause for the suits. Mistreatment is the category I used to sort the complaints by women against their husbands for either failure to provide sufficient food and clothing or for actually beating them.

On 23 April 1908, Oumara So sought divorce from her husband, Lansana Konare, because of "bad treatment, brutality." Three of the six divorce cases heard in April 1909 cited mistreatment as the cause for the divorce. Douba DDansira, for example, sought a divorce from her husband, Diba Taliki, because, she told the court, "he mistreats her and does not give her enough to eat."[53] Nielle Sidibe was in court seeking a divorce form her husband, Bakary Kone, because she was beaten not only by her husband, but also by his mother. We do not have any surviving court records for April 1910, but in April 1911, five of the nine divorce disputes identified mistreatment as the cause of their action, including Aissata Gakou, who accused her husband, Sousoukone Taraore, of not feeding her, and Marama Sambou, who wanted a divorce because her husband "does not give her anything."[54] The court records in these cases are too brief to ascertain whether the mistreatment or abuse wives complained about was a long-standing problem or one that was caused by the restructuring of household labor following the end of slavery. The household head's need to organize (or coerce) household labor for the planting season, the incidence of divorce cases peaking annually in April, and the high proportion of mistreatment as the cause for divorce during the month of April are not just unrelated coincidences. They form a pattern of household social change.

HOUSEHOLD INSTABILITY AND THE AGRICULTURAL CYCLE IN THE AFTERMATH OF SLAVERY

Marital disputes in Gumbu reflected the pressures of the agricultural cycle. The departure of the slaves meant that masters had to rely on themselves and their households for most of their agricultural labor needs. In Gumbu, preparation of the fields and the crucial, first weeding (April, May, June) and harvest (November, December, January) were the labor bottlenecks. Not surprisingly, these were also the months with the highest proportion of

Figure 4.6 Gumbu, Divorces by Month, 1905–1912, n = 138

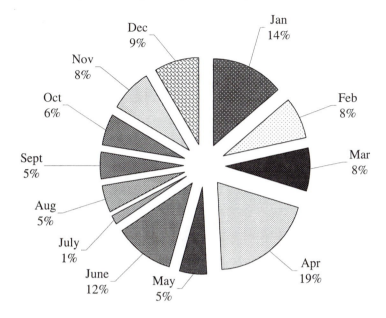

Source: ANM 2 M 122

divorce disputes. Because divorces were usually introduced by wives, their actions during these months indicates that they were reacting to increased pressures on their household and their lives.

In contrast to divorce cases, marriage disputes were exclusively brought by husbands seeking the courts to force their wives to return to the conjugal home. The data on divorce and marriage disputes clearly indicate the importance of the agricultural cycle. During the periods of heaviest agricultural labor 77 percent of the divorce disputes occurred. During the three months of the planting and weeding season 36 percent of the divorce disputes occurred and 41 percent occurred during the three months of the harvest. Data on marriage disputes show a slightly different pattern, still embedded in the agricultural cycle, but demonstrating a strategic intentionality by husbands. What is striking in the distribution of marriage disputes is that men sought to have the courts force their wives to return exactly one month prior to the beginning of the heavy labor period, thus 30 percent of marriage disputes occurred in March (17%) and in October (13%). Given the pressures on women to increase their labor in the households, it is not surprising that we should see mistreatment and abandonment prominently in the causes women cited for divorce.

Figure 4.7 Gumbu, Marriage Disputes by Month, 1905–1912, n = 30

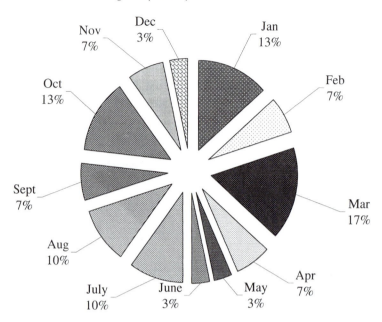

Source: ANM 2 M 122

Women seeking divorce in the courts of the French Soudan had to explain their reasons for seeking the dissolution of their marriages. Among the most common reasons for seeking divorce were abandonment, mistreatment, failure to complete payments of bridewealth, illness of one of the spouse, and incompatibility. Table 4.1 provides data on the distribution of the causes cited in divorce cases in Gumbu. Abandonment cases refer to situations where the husband has absconded and provided neither support nor news of his whereabouts. Mistreatment refers to cases where wives complained of their husbands beating them or failing to provide adequate food or clothing. Incompatibility refers to cases where both spouses agreed mutually to a divorce or when one spouse complains that she or he no longer wants to remain in the marriage. The court records are not detailed enough to interrogate the meanings of incompatibility more fully. To cite incompatibility usually meant an amicable separation, but the incidence of amicable separations could also stem from changes in status and expectations of security within households and thus be tied to the end of slavery. Illness refers to a chronic disease that prevents one spouse from fulfilling the marriage contract either sexually or physically (such cases include impotence, sterility, blindness, and leprosy). Bridewealth as a cause for divorce was cited by wives when their husbands had not fulfilled their promises to transfer wealth, thus rendering the marriage contract incomplete. This had implications both for the respectability of the spouses in the marriage and for custody of the children.[55] The Other category refers to any other stated cause for divorce. This includes the handful of cases in which husbands sued for divorce, in which they usually cited their wives as being disobedient or disrespectful. This category also refers to what is occasionally referred to in the court records as "numerous complaints" that are not specified.

I am particularly interested in abandonment and mistreatment causes. As I have argued previously, given the acute labor demands facing household heads, they would most likely have turned to their households to make up for the labor needed after their slaves had left. I would have anticipated that mistreatment cases would appear as household heads used or forced their wives to work in the fields. We have already seen indications of this in the seasonal distribution of marriage disputes. In contrast, I would have anticipated that we might see abandonment cases lag several years as the remained spouses (usually the wives) sought to have their marriages dissolved so that they might remarry. When we graph out the abandonment and mistreatment causes for divorce cases, we get a clearer sense of the importance of each over time.

Mistreatment in Gumbu coincided with the slaves' exodus in 1908 and 1909. It declined sharply in 1910, spiked in 1911, and declined again in 1912. We have a few random cases of abandonment before 1908, but the trend was for those cases to increase after the slaves' exodus ended in 1909. Abandonment cases continued to increase until the end of our records.

Not all abandonment cases stemmed from slave households nor can all absconding husbands be linked directly to the end of slavery, although contemporary French observers of the slaves' exodus pointed first to the "destructions of the family" as a consequence of the end of slavery. The end of slavery initiated a huge population movement that Klein estimates to con-

Table 4.1 Causes of Divorce Disputes, Gumbu, 1905–1912

Date	Divorces	Divorces as % of all cases	Abandonment (% of divorces)	Mistreatments (% of divorces)	Incompatibility (% of divorces)	Bridewealth (% of divorces)	Illness (% of divorces)	Other/numerous complaints (% of divorces)
1905	5	29%	40%	40%	0	0	0	20%
1906*								
1907	15	37%	33%	20%	13%	7%	7%	20%
1908	23	14%	0	48%	26%	0	4%	22%
1909	34	30%	9%	65%	24%	0	3%	21%
1910	22	19%	14%	9%	18%	0	5%	55%
1911	28	35%	14%	25%	11%	4%	4%	43%
1912*	11	48%	45%	18%	0	0	0	36%
Total	138	23%	16%	30%	17%	1%	3%	32%

*1906 data missing; 1912 data from January through September.

*1906 data missing; 1912 data from January through September. Source: ANM 2 M

Figure 4.8 Abandonment and Mistreatment as Causes of Divorce Disputes, Gumbu, 1905–1912

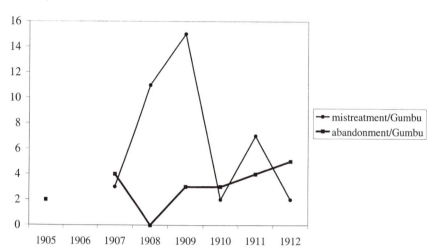

Source: ANM 2 M 122

sist of upward of one million from throughout French West Africa.[56] This was a huge population on the move during a relatively short period of time. Picking up and leaving often meant leaving family behind. But former slaves were not the only group to be on the move during this period. Faced with the prospect of increased labor on the household farm, sons of former masters probably followed some of the same routes as former slaves that led to the new opportunities in mining, construction, and temporary agricultural work in Senegal, Guinea, and the Côte d'Ivoire. In their study of the Soninke of the Nioro district to the west of Gumbu, Pollet and Winter argue that the liberation of the slaves weakened the hierarchical principles of both the family and society.[57] Sons could leave because there were new opportunities outside the household economy and because with the departure of the slaves, sons had little to anticipate in terms of inheritable property and much to fear from increased labor obligations.

In the court records describing abandonment cases women do not usually explain why husbands left their families. They merely describe the facts and underscore the gravity of the plaintiffs' condition. Sadio Konare brought one of the very first requests for divorce due to abandonment before the Gumbu court on 2 April 1908. "Sadio Konare requests divorce from her husband Ahmadou Diaba, who has abandoned her for more than five months without leaving money and giving no sign of his existence."[58] Amadou Diaba's flight from Gumbu preceded the massive slave exodus of early 1908, but it could be

related. It was not uncommon for individuals or small groups to leave whenever they felt ready. Amadou Diaba left before the harvest was in and thus
before he could accumulate some wealth for traveling. However, the crops
were still in the ground and he could have either sought temporary work
along the way or simply scavenged food until he arrived at his destination.
The court records don't tell us why Diaba left his wife and family, only that he
did. And in leaving, he left Sadio Konare without resources to survive. Sadio
Konare requested a divorce so that she could remarry. The court approved her
request for a divorce.

Sana Toure requested a divorce after her husband abandoned her for six
months "without leaving anything for her to eat and without sending any
news." Both Fatouma Diefaka and Tene Soumare waited three years before
they requested divorce from their husband who had abandoned them. Abandonment cases do not seem to reflect any clear seasonal pattern, although
most occurred during the harvest season, when being without subsistence was
a grim reminder of what was to come again, and just before planting season,
when both male and female labor was needed to prepare the fields and to
plant. The courts were sympathetic to abandoned wives and granted them
divorces, usually without any requirement to repay the bridewealth.[59]

SUMMARY

The end of slavery in Gumbu provides a context in which to examine the
linked sets of transformations and the disputes set in motion by the end of
slavery and the establishment of the new courts in 1905. The exact experience
of the end of slavery and the linked changes varied over time and by district,
but the period 1905 to 1912 was one in which men and women, Africans and
colonial officials, former masters and former slaves, household head and their
dependants negotiated new relationships and established new understandings
of their rights and obligations. Glimpses of these struggles are evident in the
court records used in the following chapters addressing disputes over marriages (Chapter 5), bridewealth (Chapter 6), child custody (Chapter 6), property (Chapter 7), and inheritance (Chapter 8).

5

WOMEN SEEKING DIVORCE; MEN SEEKING CONTROL

The new native courts, established by Governor-general Roume on 10 November 1903, were up and running in several districts of the French Soudan by April and May 1905. Most Soudanese were probably skeptical of the courts, preferring to wait and see what transpired in them. But a trickle of litigants brought disputes before the new tribunaux de province. Sara Diallo, mother of four children, brought the very first case before the Bamako court on 4 April 1905. The plaintiff asked the court to grant her a divorce from her husband, Moriba Sangare, "who has left her nothing for her survival and given no notice to his family" since his departure from the region more than one year ago.[1] The court approved her request. The Bamako court heard five cases throughout the entire month of April 1905, of which three, including Sara Diallo's, were about divorce. The second divorce case was heard 10 days later. Both husband and wife appeared together and sought an amicable separation: "Samba Sako and Makasouba declare that they do not want to live together because they are of different race and of different religion."[2] The court granted their divorce. In the third divorce case heard in April 1905, Mariam Fofana sought from the provincial tribunal a formal separation from the family of her widowed husband. Her husband had died two years ago and her husband's male kin, under the custom of levirate, had the rights to retain the widow as a wife, but had not done so, leaving the widow in a marital limbo.[3] The court declared the plaintiff free to remarry, thus effectively divorcing her from her deceased husband's kin.[4]

This chapter examines how women in particular traversed the new landscapes of power in the French Soudan established by the native courts and by the end of slavery. This chapter begins in 1905, when the courts in Bamako and Segu were first established and traces who these initial litigants were and what their disputes were. Women seeking divorce were among the first clients of the new native courts. Based on the aggregate data of court use, it is clear that marriage was one of the most troubled domains of African social life. In Bamako, marital disputes (marriage, divorce, and bridewealth) constituted 56 percent of all the disputes heard at the provincial tribunal between 1905 and 1912. Marriage and divorce alone constituted 45 percent. In Segu, marital disputes were somewhat less significant, but nonetheless comprised 39 percent of the total disputes between 1905 and 1912. Marriage and divorce in Segu constituted 25 percent of all disputes. Women brought 74 percent of all the divorce disputes before the Bamako provincial tribunal and 80 percent in Segu.

Women's actions in seeking divorce from the new native courts stimulated a discussion among colonial officials about why they were in court. Colonial officials began to elaborate a discourse about African women and the African family. Between 1905 and 1910, this discourse contributed to the changes in the landscapes of power by encouraging African magistrates to grant women divorces. By 1909 and 1910, some colonial officials began to worry about the consequences of granting divorce in favor of women. They worried about independent women and family instability. By 1910 an alternative discourse began to appear that sought deep roots to family stability in the French Soudan and expressed itself in the unquestioned authority of the male household head. We can trace the impact of this alternative discourse on the outcomes of marital disputes in the native courts. After 1910, increasing numbers of judgments in divorce cases moved against women, and men began to use the courts to force their runaway wives to return to their conjugal homes. This chapter traces the interplay between court use, judgments, and competing discourses about the African family.

EARLY LITIGATION BY WOMEN

Women were clearly among the chief protagonists in the shaping of the early jurisprudence of the newly established provincial tribunals in regard to matters of divorce. During its first year of operation, 34 percent of the cases heard by the Bamako tribunal involved either the rupture of marriages or efforts to repair marriages. Of these cases, women brought 72 percent of the cases. All the suits brought by women were for the dissolution of marriage; men were the principal litigants in cases to repair marriages.[5] One third of the suits for divorce brought forward by wives were based on alleged mistreatment. The burden of proof fell on the plaintiffs. Aissata Tal brought three witnesses with her when she sought to divorce her husband, Amadu Koita. All three witnesses supported the plaintiff's claim that her husband beat her. In this case, Asisata Tal had already complained three times about her husband's abuse. The court finally granted her a divorce.[6] Niane Koyaute easily received a divorce from her husband when she complained in court that he had kept her in chains "under the pretext that she had brought bad luck to the family."[7] Not so successful was Ma Sidibe, who sued her husband for divorce because he "mistreats" her. The court rejected the suit claiming that the plaintiff lacked proof of her allegations.[8] Ma Sidibe may not have gotten satisfaction from her effort to divorce her husband, but by publicly airing her allegations of mistreatment, she may have shamed her husband into treating her better.[9] On the other hand, her husband may have punished her for her actions, although because the litigants do not appear again in the court record we have no way of pursuing this line of inquiry.

While women might not have consistently been the plaintiffs in the disputes brought before the Segu court, women were clearly the agents in marriage and divorce cases. Even though men were the usual plaintiffs in marriage cases, they were in court in response to their wives having left them. The first two cases brought before the Segu in April 1905 both dealt with husbands or fiancés seeking to recover their bridewealth payments from their fathers-in-law since their wives or brides refused to live with them. Niafily Camara sued his father-in-law, Sibery Doumbia, because Doumbia's daughter had left him and Camara wanted to recover the 50,000 cowries transferred as bridewealth.[10] Five days later, Boliba Taraore brought a case against his prospective father-in-law because his daughter did not want to live with Taraore as his wife. Taraore wanted to recover the 43,000 cowries he had given Diosei Coulibaly as bridewealth for his daughter.[11] In both cases, the court ultimately ruled in favor of the women's choice and ordered a divorce and the restitution of the bridewealth. Daro Camara was the first woman in Segu to use the new courts to seek the end of her marriage. Camara approached the court to divorce her husband, Kamisoko, who had "gravely injured her mother." The record of the case does not elaborate the nature of these injuries, but the court recognized the seriousness of the charge and ordered Daro Camara divorced. Moreover, the court ordered that the plaintiff did not have to repay the bridewealth, an uncommon outcome in divorce cases.[12]

The incidence of divorce cases in Segu from the opening of the new courts in April 1905 to the end of the year is smaller than in Bamako. Divorce accounted for only 15 percent of the total litigation in Segu in 1905, although when combined with other disputes over marriage (but not including bridewealth, which had a clearer contractual character as I shall discuss in Chapter 7), the total number of disputes rises to 28 percent. In divorce disputes, women were the plaintiffs in 92 percent of the cases, including one case where the wife sued for divorce and the husband agreed to a consensual settlement at court. In all but one of the cases brought by wives for divorce, the court ruled in favor of the plaintiff. The most prominent cause for women seeking divorce in Segu in 1905, as recorded by the register, was because of alleged mistreatment. Two cases were brought forward for the cause of abandonment, in which the husbands had disappeared for several years, including one case in which the husband had not been heard from for six years. In only one case did a husband bring suit against his wife, who had left him to return to her family. In court, the defendant claimed that she was sick and went home to recover. She promised to return when she was able. The court ruled against the husband and ordered his wife to return as soon as she was well enough.[13] In one suit, a woman who claimed Muslim legal status sued for divorce on the grounds that her husband now had more than four wives. In addition, she claimed compensation for child rearing expenses for her two daughters. The court ruled in her favor, approved the divorce, and ordered her husband to provide ten *muules* and 1,000 cowries in child care expenses to his former wife.[14]

The dispute category of "marriage" is not the mirror image of divorce, although the plaintiffs were almost all men. In only one case in 1905 did a woman bring suit to force a fiancé to recognize her rights to marry her daughter.[15] Husbands and fiancés constituted 75 percent of the plaintiffs in marriage suits in Segu in 1905.[16] Husbands wanted the court to force their wives to return to their conjugal homes; fiancés wanted their brides to consummate the marriage. These men were in court because their wives or fiancées had either left them or refused to agree to the marriage in the first place. As in the divorce cases, these cases were ultimately caused by women's actions, because wives left their husbands and fiancées refused to marry their fiancés. Even in these cases, the verdicts largely supported women's choices. In three of the four cases where husbands sought to force the return of their wives, the court ruled in favor of divorce. In the remaining one, where the defendant claimed that she was mistreated, but did not provide proof, the court ordered her return. In the other three cases, the court listened to women's defenses of their actions and ultimately sided with them, although it ordered the wives to repay the bridewealth to their former husbands.[17] In the two cases in which aggrieved fiancés sought to oblige their brides' kin to force them to fulfill their pledges of marriage—in both cases the fiancés sued their fiancées' guardians or fathers—the court once ruled in favor of the plaintiff against the wishes of the fiancée ("the fiancée is obliged to marry the man chosen by her father" ruled the court) and once in favor of the defendant.[18] In the second case, the fiancée did not want to consummate the marriage because her fiancé had a "contagious disease." The court agreed that such a condition voided the marriage contract and ordered the fiancée's kin to repay the bridewealth.[19]

Taken together, women's actions in bringing divorce proceedings against their husbands, leaving their husbands, or refusing to marry their fiancés constituted 91 percent of the cases dealing with divorce and marriage. Women were clearly the "actors" in the litigation heard by the new courts in Segu and Bamako. Even more surprising was that fully 75 percent of the Segu divorce cases in 1905 were ruled in favor of women, regardless of whether they were the plaintiffs or the defendants. Two questions immediately emerge from the evidence of women and the newly established native courts in the French

Soudan: first, why were women so prominent in the cases surrounding marriage and divorce? And second, why did the new courts act in favor of women's demands in so many of the cases? The remainder of this chapter will examine these questions in some detail, but an appeals case heard in Bouguni in November 1905 and a 1906 report on the Sikasso native court provide some of the evidence needed in interpreting why the court seemed sympathetic to women seeking divorce.

The provincial courts opened for business in Bouguni only in September 1905 and heard in total seven disputes and two appeals over the next four months. Six of the cases dealt with marriage and bridewealth. The final case involved the custody of a child whose father had died. The case that is most germane to this discussion was first heard on 1 November 1905, when Mamadi Dembele brought suit against his wife, Souzouroudie Fane, to force her return to their "conjugal life." Dembele had given his permission for his wife to visit her parents. Fane, however, refused to return to her husband telling the court that "she no longer loves him." The tribunal ruled in favor of the plaintiff and ordered Souzouroudie Fane to return to her husband's home. Fane appealed the case, which was heard at the district tribunal the next day. The *tribunal de cercle* was presided over by the French administrator, who was assisted by two notables from the district. At the district tribunal, Souzouroudie Fane repeated the arguments that she had used the previous day without apparent success. She indicated to the court her resolve when she stated that she "again refuses" to live with her husband. In its judgment, the district court reversed the provincial court's ruling, which had ordered the defendant to return to her husband's home, and instead granted Souzouroudie Fane's request for the dissolution of her marriage on the condition that she repay her husband 400 francs equal to the original cost of her bridewealth plus the cost of her "upkeep" since their marriage. The court also permitted Fane to keep her child.[20] The French administrator's reversal of the lower court's ruling sent a clear signal to the African magistrates of the newly created native courts about what the French administration had in mind.

These newly appointed African magistrates were obviously trying to learn their jobs. The French district administrator who was charged with supervising the new court officials and the operation of the courts was either in the court when it was in session or hovering nearby. Although they were supposed to apply "custom," the new magistrates may have wanted to do a "good" job or at least to keep their jobs, so they paid very careful attention to what their supervisor had in mind. The fact that the French district officer reversed their decision to force the return of an unhappy wife to her husband sent a clear signal that they should be attentive to what their supervisors had in mind. During the early days of the new courts, some French administrators were decidedly interventionist, particularly in their willingness to listen to and to act favorably upon women's grievances regarding marriage.

A remarkable report was filed from Sikasso at the beginning of 1906 described the "education" of African magistrates who sat on the provincial tribunal. Despite their claims of respecting native customs, this report also indicates the willingness of the French to intervene in the nature of Soudanese marriages and the treatment of women.

> The general spirit of the law is to guarantee to the natives under our control the maintenance of their customs based upon a *droit privé* (family law) appropriate to their mentality and to their social development with the exception of that which is contrary to our core principles of humanity and civilization. . . . Our task of education is much more delicate in the area of civil disputes, which also see undeniable amelioration. Thus, in the cases of marriage and divorce, we have brought the judges to the point where they take into consideration the personal wishes of the women, whom one rarely consulted during the previous state of things. . . . The results we have obtained in such little time are much appreciated, and the manner in which we understand justice will contribute significantly to our ability to win over the populations [of the colony].[21]

The establishment of a colonial legal system replete with native courts in 1905 was part of a set of wider transformation in the landscapes of power and authority in the French Soudan. Colonial administrators liked to claim credit for the "progress" in the administration of native justice. But they often only saw part of a much more radical transformation. I am not sure how much of this more radical transformation the French actually understood. In the next section, I will examine more fully the initial ways in which the French district officers, who were charged with supervising and reporting on the performance of the provincial courts, reacted to their observations that women seeking divorce were among the statistically most prominent cases brought before the new courts during the first several years of their operation.

INITIAL RESPONSES BY THE COLONIAL ADMINISTRATION

Almost immediately after their establishment, the African magistrates newly appointed to these courts and French officials charged with supervising them were confronted by African women seeking divorce. The Bamako administrator wrote in the third quarter of 1906, just one year after the new courts were established, that "the incidence of divorce cases is slightly less than last quarter, but are nonetheless very frequent. It is almost always the woman who brings the request for divorce before the provincial tribunal."[22] The Gumbu administrator in 1906 echoed his Bamako counterpart when he wrote that "nearly all of the grievances brought before the provincial tribunal during the course of this quarter concerned divorce."[23] From Segu, the administrator noted in his first quarter's report for 1907 that "it is to be noted that almost all of the requests for divorce come from women, who often give no reason for their desire to leave the conjugal home."[24] Women seeking divorce continued to preoccupy the native courts as late as World War I. The Mopti administrator wrote in 1911 that "the principal category of civil process [in the district] are the divorces; many women come forward to demand the rupture of their marriages."[25]

Faced with the incidence of women seeking divorce through these new courts, administrators were forced to explain why women were seeking divorce. Some reports identified "poor treatment women receive" and physical abuse, while others described cases where wives were abandoned by their husbands.[26] French administrators began to construct a model of African families as being inherently unstable due to the lack of women's volition in marriage and of African women as beasts of burden, commodities, and exploited workers. Drawing upon recent changes in French family law and a general republican sentiment that the ideal marriage was the "free association of individuals," many colonial officials were inclined to listen to women's grievances and to act favorably to their requests for divorce.[27]

Within the first year or two of activity, administrators began to discern some patterns of African use of the new legal system. In Bouguni district, the district administrator wrote that "natives present themselves before the tribunals for grievances of little importance: tensions within households, incompletely paid bridewealth, and so forth. Others come to complain of acts committed before our occupation, and especially during the time of Samory." By the end of the year, the administrator noted a further narrowing of the range of cases brought before the tribunals. "All the affairs presented deal with household quarrels: husbands abandoned by their wives; wives abandoned by their husbands; or bridewealth incompletely paid."[28] More striking was how quickly African litigants used the legal system for their own ends. Already by 1906 Africans were bypassing the village tribunal in favor of bringing their cases directly before the French administrator—presumably at the district tribunal (but possibly at the provincial tribunal if the African assessors were not yet in place). "The natives prefer to come to the district headquarters and each day the administrator must listen to numerous litigants who talk at length about their domestic quarrels."[29]

This strategic use of the new courts took place throughout the French Soudan. From the Jenne district, the administrator wrote that in 1907 the number of cases brought before the village tribunals were surprisingly small. Instead of seeking the assistance of the village chief in reconciling their differences, "the parties prefer to submit their grievances before the *tribunal de province,* thinking that at the district headquarters, they will find a more impartial jurisdiction. Instead, they find that they are sent back to the village tribunals, which are competent to hear their cases." Nonetheless, he noted that the provincial tribunal "heard a great number of cases, many more civil cases than criminal ones."[30] In his assessment of the previous two years of the new court system, the native affairs officer in Segu wrote in 1907 that the judgments of the village tribunal, rendered by the chief, were not binding and thus its legal activities "hardly important." In contrast, he wrote, was the provincial tribunal, de province, which had a "different importance." It is the "veritable native court" because it sees before it "all of native life in its multiple variations."[31]

That African litigants wanted to avoid the "reconciliation" of the village chief's tribunal and sought instead a more "impartial" judgment hint at two important aspects of their strategies in these early years of the new legal system: first, African litigants sought to avoid the efforts of the village chief, who was, after all, one of the elderly males of the community; and second, they sought not just "impartial" judgments, but decisive ones. An indication of this second point is presented in the 1909 remark by the Bamako district administrator. He noted 17 affairs were brought by "parties soliciting from the tribunal an arbitrary sentence as well as a condemning one."[32] By creating an arena in which decisions awarded were "decisive," the new courts developed a "speculative air" especially for those with the least to lose and the most to gain.[33]

The administrators in the French Soudan noted exactly this kind of "speculative air" in cases brought by those with the least to lose and the most to gain. Moreover, this search for "decisive" judgments, suggesting that the litigants did not wish to be reconciled, is even more pronounced in the case of women seeking divorce. Already in 1908, the Bamako administrator saw this as a trend. "Most of the cases submitted to the provincial tribunal in civil and commercial matters are concerned with divorce or the repayment of bridewealth. It is to be remarked that in this regard, it is almost always the women who demand the dissolution of the marriage."[34]

Administrators were also concerned that the incidence of divorce both reflected and contributed to "familial anarchy."[35] Already in 1906, the Bamako administrator had written in response to his assessment that so many of the civil disputes brought before the native courts dealt with marriage and divorce. "It is to be remarked," he wrote, "that because the bonds of family are relatively fragile, marriage is easily dissolved."[36] The Gumbu administrator qualified this general assessment when he attributed the incidence of divorce to the "weak bonds attaching the native woman to her new family."[37] Linking women seeking divorce to the organization of the African family and to marriage practices, French district administrators developed components of a discourse about African women and the African family. One of the earliest reports emerging out of the need to explain the high incidence of women seeking divorce was penned by the Bamako administrator following his observations of the second month of the new courts' operation. "The young girl is married, or more precisely exchanged for a bridewealth payment, by those who exercise paternal power over her: her father, grandfather, uncle or brother." The Bamako administrator underscored the commodity nature of daughters when he noted that if a household head died leaving a son and a daughter, the son "literally" inherits his sister and the rights to acquire the bridewealth. The administrator's interpretation of inheritance was not quite right in this case, but it led logically to his conclusion. "The social condition of the married woman is very close to that of slavery. She is given the most difficult work and frequently beaten." The administrator contrasted the social condition of the woman married by her male guardians to that of the widow not inherited by her husband's kin. "The widow is declared free and she can remarry following her own wishes. More independent than the female married as a young girl, she is able to earn her own goods, she is much better treated, and generally does not abandon the home of her [new] husband."[38]

Other administrators began to articulate a causal link between the commodity nature of marriage, the bride's lack of choice in partners, and requests for divorce. The Gumbu administrator developed this argument in his assessment of the operation of the provincial tribunal in his district.

> The cases heard before the *tribunal de province* concern above all with divorces, which reflect the social development of the native. In effect, the authority of the head of the family permits him to marriage his daughters as he wishes. This results in his efforts to squeeze as much as possible from the transactions. The girl is never consulted on the choice of her future husband and she is almost always given to the suitor who furnishes the largest bridewealth.

Faced with the significant outlay of capital to secure his new wife, the husband usually gave his new wife the hardest work and mistreated her. Soon, the Gumbu administrator concluded, the husband "tires of his wife's complaints (*doléances*) and in pursuit of peace in the household, divorce is requested."[39] The high incidence of divorce, wrote the Koutiala administrator in 1909, was due to the "conception that the woman is a captive, an instrument of work and of exchange, who can be sold, given away, and repossessed according to the [husband's] whims and means without ever consulting her."[40] Many of the French administrators overseeing the operation of the new courts were sympathetic to the plight of African women and to their efforts to end unhappy marriages.

As much as the French seemed to want to respect custom, they were guided by what they understood as natural human rights, which were sharply influenced by the French Revolution (which provided women with avenues to seek divorce), the maturing Napoléonic Code in France during the course of the nineteenth century (which closed many of these avenues), and the movement to empower women's rights during the Third Republic (which again allowed women to sue for divorce). For most of the nineteenth century,

French women had few rights to initiate divorce. This changed when the anti-clericism of the Third Republic coincided with the emerging women's rights movement and resulted in the Naquet Law of 1884. For the first time since the heady days of the Revolution, French women could initiate divorce proceedings against their husbands on the grounds of abandonment, adultery, grievous injury, or criminal conviction.[41] The timing between changes in the metropolitan legal system and the drafting of the 1903 colonial legal system is not accidental. Crucial here, however, was French willingness to "listen" to women in the new courts and to "respect" their wishes. Such willingness to listen to women's grievances and to act favorably on them is clearly evidenced in Charles Correnson's 1907 report on the functioning of the native courts in Segu.

> Cases for divorce are brought exclusively, or nearly so, by women and the reasons offered are relatively few. In first order one finds divorces requested following a prolonged absence of the husband, who has departed to pursue commerce in distant lands, and has left his wife without resources and without news. The tribunal does not demand a very long absence before imposing a divorce, never more than three years. Incompatibility of personalities is often invoked and sometimes simply the refusal on the part of the wife to stay with her husband is sufficient to justify divorce with certain reservations made regarding the bridewealth.

Correnson concluded this section of his report by noting that "women have benefited from these changes. [The condition of] women [is] incontestably moving toward social improvement."[42] Correnson's remarks and the practices of the new native courts suggest a significantly different pattern from the one Chanock and Ranger have described for British Central Africa, where the "invention" of tradition and custom bolstered the power of elderly men.[43]

In 1910, the Koutiala administrator pressed his attack on African marriage by calling them "disguised sales." By describing marriages as "disguised sales" the administrator was invoking the powerful antislave trade provisions of the 12 December 1905 decree.

> Under the pretext of marriage, in effect, the exchanges of young girls or women are practiced. In reality, these exchanges are nothing less than disguised purchases and sales. It is thus that one see young girls, still small children and far too young to be married, taken from their mothers and given by their fathers or some other male relative in exchange for a women he wants to marry.
>
> In her new milieu, this child is, in reality, considered to be a captive, subject to the capricious demands of her new environment. She is [often] exchanged a second time, either for another woman or for a horse, cattle, or some cowries. In the latter case, under the pretext of bridewealth exchange,

this is nothing less than a brutal sale. All the profound troubles that constantly plague the family and result in multiple unhappy consequences can be traced to this [practice].

The Koutiala administrator argued that those practices masquerading as marriage should be considered "acts of trade" in people, which was prohibited by the December 1905 decree abolishing the trade in slaves and the deprivation of another person's liberty.[44]

In a marginal note scribbled on that report, someone from the governor-general's office in Dakar responded forcefully to the challenge raised by the Koutiala administrator. "Do not meddle in native custom except with the utmost circumspection. The act of agreement among two families to exchange two women is the guarantee of reciprocity. Marriage, in both Muslim practice and native custom has all the characteristics of a sale. Do not, however, treat this as an infraction of the slave trade ordinance." The note suggested that the "only amelioration" that should be brought to the practices of marriage is to request that young women "give their consent."[45] For marriageable women to give their consent was, however, a radical attack on the authority of the household head and threatened the presumed stability of traditional African society. By 1910 the practice of favoring women's requests for divorce or respecting their decisions not to return to their husbands began to crack. By 1911, the opportunities married women had created for themselves to dissolve unhappy marriages by bringing suits for divorce against their husbands were under considerable pressure. Fewer cases brought by women for divorce were successful and thus fewer were heard. Equally important, husbands were finding it much easier to use the courts to force their wives to return to their conjugal homes.

HUSBANDS IN COURT TO CONTROL THEIR WIVES

On 5 February 1907, Demba Diara brought suit against his wife, Dale Tangana, asking the Bamako provincial court to require that his wife return to the conjugal home. This was the very first case heard at Bamako in which a husband as plaintiff sought the power of the court to force his wife to return to him. Instead of forcing the plaintiff's wife to return, the court ruled in favor of the defendant and granted her a divorce, although it did require that she return the bridewealth to her husband.[46] In only one marriage case heard that year was the husband-plaintiff successful in having the court order his wife to return to his home.[47] By 1911, the practices of the Bamako court in marriage disputes had changed in two discernible ways. First, the number of marriage cases increased both numerically and proportionately to the overall number of cases. In 1907, marriage cases constituted 10 percent of all the cases heard at the Bamako court. The proportion fell to 7.5 percent in 1908, fell further to

5.7 percent in 1909, and fell again to 3 percent in 1910. By 1911, marriage disputes constituted 19 percent of the cases heard and by 1912, the proportion jumped to 32 percent. The second significant change occurred in the nature of the judgments reached by the Bamako court in marriage disputes. As a proportion of the overall number of marriage disputes, the court ordered the return of runaway wives in 9 percent of the 11 cases in 1907, 50 percent of the 10 cases in 1908, 50 percent of the 4 cases in 1909, and none of the 2 cases in 1910. The numbers of marriage disputes was relatively small to the overall numbers of disputes until 1911. By 1911, the number of marriage disputes increased to 35 and the court ordered wives to return to their husbands in 54 percent of the cases, and by 1912, the court heard 107 marriage disputes and ordered the return of wives in 63 percent of the cases. Even more revealing than the judgments to return runaway wives was the changes in judgments favorable to husbands. In 1907, the court ruled in favor of husbands in only one out of the four return cases heard. In 1908, husbands were successful in two out of the four return cases heard. The 1909 and 1910 return cases are statistically too small (2 in 1909 of which both were successful; 1 in 1910, which did not succeed). In 1911, when the court ruled on 25 return cases, husbands were successful in 80 percent of the disputes; by 1912, the number of return cases reached 67, the court ruled in favor of the husband-plaintiff in 87 percent of the disputes. The period from 1911 through 1912 thus represents something of a sea change in the political landscape of dispute resolution in the Bamako provincial court. Changes were also underway in the court's disposition of divorce cases, the area where women had been most successful in achieving their goals of ending marriages that either did not work or did not please them.

Even though women constituted 73 percent of the plaintiffs in all divorce cases heard in Bamako between 1905 and 1912, there were subtle changes in the court's disposition of these cases. The proportion of divorce cases and judgments rendered moved in a more or less inverse direction from those of marriage disputes. In 1905, divorce cases constituted 31 percent of all the disputes heard at the Bamako tribunal and 90 percent of the cases resulted in divorce. In 1907, divorce cases constituted 29 percent of the total number of cases and resulted in 72 percent divorce rulings. In 1908, divorce cases composed 36 percent of the total litigation, but the divorce ratio had dropped to 67 percent. In 1909, the proportion of divorce cases had declined somewhat to 29 percent of the total caseload, but resulted in 90 percent divorce rate. Moreover, women constituted 80 percent of the plaintiffs that year. In 1910, however, an anomaly stands out in the records, and hints at changes in the court's orientation to divorce. Women constituted only 23 percent of the plaintiffs in divorce cases. Proportionally more men were bringing divorce cases against their wives, often for what the records referred to in the records as "misconduct."[48] Significantly, the divorce rate in 1910 rose to 95 percent and divorce cases constituted 39 percent of the total caseload. However, the number of cases heard in 1910 was the smallest on record, with a total of only 57 cases. By 1911, the divorce caseload for the Bamako court had more than tripled again and the proportion of women bringing divorce cases resumed its "normal" course. Women constituted 69 percent of the plaintiffs. However, two important changes can be documented. First, the proportion of divorce cases to the total caseload that year began to decline to 26 percent and second, the court ruled favorably in divorce cases only 54 percent of the time. This pattern persisted into 1912. That year, women again constituted 69 percent of the plaintiffs, but the proportion of divorce cases fell to only 16 percent of the total caseload. The courts only granted 59 percent of the divorces requested.

Perhaps the most telling feature of the changes in the court's disposition toward women seeking divorce are the statistics linking the gender of the plaintiff to the judgment rendered by the court. During its first year of operation, the Bamako provincial court heard 10 divorce cases in which women were plaintiffs in 8 of them. The court granted women divorce in all eight of those cases (100% divorce rate). In 1907, the court heard 34 divorce cases in which women were the plaintiffs in 26 cases (77%). Women were granted divorce in 18 of those cases (69% divorce rate). By 1908, the divorce caseload had increased to 48, of which women were the plaintiffs in 33 cases. Women's success in securing divorce fell to 55 percent, although in an additional 9 percent of the cases divorce was provisionally granted subject to various delays to determine whether a husband would return or whether a

Figure 5.1 Marriage and Divorce Disputes, Bamako, 1905–1912. Divorces n = 224, Marriages n = 173

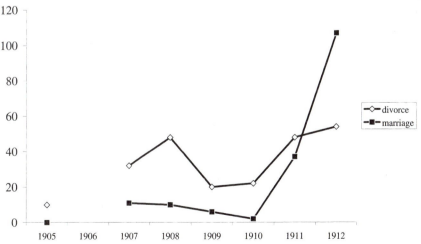

Source: ANM 2 M 104/105

husband's impotence would prove temporary. In 1909, the numbers of divorce cases (21 cases) fell to less than half of the number heard the previous year. Women constituted 81 percent of the plaintiffs in divorce cases and were successful in 88 percent of the cases. The year 1910 stands as a watershed in the divorce disputes heard before the Bamako tribunal. Women were the plaintiffs in only 5 out of 21 cases that were heard (24%). Women were granted divorce in four of those cases (80%). More significantly, husbands now brought the majority of divorce cases before the Bamako court, fully 15 of the 21 cases heard (71%). Men were successful in all of their cases that year. In 1911, the caseload for divorce disputes more than doubled, returning to the caseload heard in 1908. Women again predominated among the plaintiffs, constituting 72 percent of the plaintiffs. However, the judgments rendered in divorce cases brought forward by women now moved against women's efforts to end marriages that either did not work or they did not like. Of the cases brought by women, 59 percent were dismissed or rejected. The disposition of the magistrates against women seeking divorce persisted in 1912, although it was slightly more muted. Women were the plaintiffs in 77 percent of the divorce cases, but they were successful in only 51 percent of those cases. In contrast to the court's changing disposition of listening to and acting favorably on women's suits for divorce, suits for divorce brought by husbands nearly always resulted in a judgment of divorce. Of the 62 divorce cases brought by husbands between 1905 and 1912, the court ruled in favor of husbands in all but one case in 1908.

The trends in marriage and divorce cases heard at the Bamako tribunal can be seen in Table 5.1.

The data on marriage cases are equally revealing of the sea change underway in the native courts in 1911 and 1912. Marriage cases were rare until 1911 and of the total number of marriage cases heard in the Bamako tribunal, women brought only 10 percent of these cases. Women were successful in only 47 percent of the cases. In contrast, men brought 81 percent of the marriage cases. Male plaintiffs in marriage cases were granted their requests in 82 percent of the cases. I used the category unclear in Table 5.1 to refer to cases that were not brought by wives or husbands or their immediate kin. Some of these cases refer to rights to marry a ward.

These data on marriage and divorce disputes in the Bamako court point to two significant changes in the nature of the cases brought before the court and in the judgments rendered. The first is that by 1910, men had become increasingly willing to bring their runaway wives to court, either to force their return or to divorce them. And second, the court increasingly ruled in favor of husbands over wives in marital disputes. What accounted for the closing of the opportunities women had discovered in using the newly created native courts to end marriages they no longer wanted?

The patterns of change evident in the Bamako data are not as obvious in the Segu data on marriages and divorces. In regard to divorce cases heard by the

Table 5.1 Judgments in Divorce and Marriage Disputes by Plaintiff's Gender, Bamako, 1905–1912

Year	Dispute	Gender	Favorable	Unfavorable	Unclear
1905	Divorce n=10	Female	8	0	0
		Male	1	0	0
		Unclear	1	0	0
	Marriage n=0				
1907	Divorce n=34	Female	18	8	0
		Male	8	0	0
	Marriage n=11	Female	1	1	
		Male	6	3	0
1908	Divorce n=48	Female	18	15	0
		Male	9	1	0
		Unclear	3	0	2
	Marriage n=10	Female	1	0	0
		Male	8	1	0
1909	Divorce n=21	Female	15	2	0
		Male	4	0	0
	Marriage n=4	Female	0	0	0
		Male	3	1	0
1910	Divorce n=21	Female	4	1	0
		Male	15	0	0
		Unclear	1	0	0
	Marriage n=2	Female	0	1	0
		Male	0	1	0
1911	Divorce n=47	Female	14	20	0
		Male	12	0	0
		Unclear	1	0	0
	Marriage n=39	Female	1	1	0
		Male	24	8	0
		Unclear	1	1	3
1912	Divorce n=56	Female	22	21	0
		Male	12	0	0
		Unclear	1	0	0
	Marriage n=102	Female	5	6	0
		Male	70	11	0
		Unclear	2	5	3

Divorces n = 237, Marriages n = 168. Source: ANM 2 M 104/105

Segu court, female plaintiffs constituted 68 percent of the total between 1905 and 1912. This is consistent with the gender composition of plaintiffs in Bamako, but changes in the court's disposition to women's suits did not show a parallel change against women's grievances. Of the 45 divorce cases brought by women, the court ruled favorably in 39 (87%), dismissed 3 (7%), and ordered a delay in granting divorce to assess whether the medical conditions at the core of 3 disputes (75) would resolve themselves within a period ranging from 6 months to 1 year. In striking difference from the Bamako court, the Segu court continued to grant women divorce in the period after 1910, although the number of divorce cases brought forward between 1910 and 1912 only constituted 11 percent of the total number of divorce cases heard. It is not clear from the evidence whether wives were more content with their husbands in Segu than in Bamako, but Seguvian wives tended not to bring divorce disputes before the Segu court in the same numbers as their counterparts in Bamako did. Running parallel with the disposition of the Bamako court was the Segu court's rulings in divorce cases brought by husbands. Husbands brought 11 cases (17% of the total number of divorce cases) and secured divorce in all of them.

Disputes involving marriage follow the pattern of declining numbers of divorce cases from 1907 onward. The numbers of both divorce and marriage disputes peaked in 1907 and then declined steadily to 1912. Compared with Bamako, the gender composition of plaintiffs in Segu marriage cases was considerably different. Whereas husbands brought forward 72 percent of the marriage disputes in Bamako, husbands together with fiancés were the plaintiffs in only 57 percent of the Segu marriage cases. In Segu, 32 percent of the marriage disputes were brought forward by kin, usually the bride's or wife's kin, and most of these cases were challenges to the authority to arrange marriages and thus ultimately to collect the bridewealth. In the marriage dispute heard on 3 August 1905 in Segu, the bride's widowed mother, Sabou Taraore, argued in court that she had not given permission for her daughter to marry and thus wanted the marriage annulled. The defendant was her daughter's husband, Lasana Kouma, who argued that he had married Taraore's daughter with the permission of her deceased father, but had no proof to offer the court. The court ruled in favor of the plaintiff and declared the marriage annulled. We cannot tell from the record, but it is likely that following the court's decision, the defendant made overtures to Sabou Taraore to resume marriage payments, because he had declared in court that he had started to do so with his wife's deceased father.[49]

The number of marriage disputes heard by the Segu court was relatively small. What was striking was that of the 35 total marriage disputes heard, 21 (60%) were ruled against the plaintiffs. When husbands or fiancés were the plaintiffs, as they were in 20 cases, the court ruled favorably in 12 (60%). The court ruled favorably in 75 percent of the four marriage cases heard in 1910 and 1911 and brought by husbands or fiancés. Unfortunately, the numbers of disputes regarding marriage and divorce in Segu do not lend themselves to an unambiguous determination of either changes in litigants' strategies or in the disposition of the court's judgments.

Despite the ambiguous patterns regarding marriage disputes and divorce cases from the Segu court, the evidence nonetheless leads to the conclusion that the opportunities women had created for themselves by using the newly created native courts to end marriages they did not want began to close. The opportunities closed as judges decided more cases against female plaintiffs or decided cases in which they no longer considered women's wishes as forcefully as they had before. The opportunities also closed as women began to understand the changing dispositions of the judges and no longer brought their disputes to these courts. I have not found a smoking gun in the archival record that allows me to pinpoint the exact moment of change; however, the announcement of Governor-general William Ponty's *politique des races* as his government's new native policy in September 1909 set in motion a reaction—partially political, partially cultural—that sought to establish family stability as the core of political stability in Soudanese societies.[50] Reaction may be too strong a term here. As we shall see in the next section, two long-time colonial administrator-scholars, Maurice Delafosse and Charles Monteil, put a particular spin on Ponty's native policy that probably contributed to the wider context in which the declension I have identified in the courts can be understood. Clearly, women seeking divorce or wanting more choice in marriage partners could not coexist with those promoting family and political stability.

THE INVENTION OF FAMILY STABILITY: DELAFOSSE, MONTEIL, AND THE COURTS

François-Joseph Clozel was named lieutenant-governor of the French Soudan in 1908. Clozel had had a successful career in the Côte d'Ivoire, where he had been lieutenant-governor since 1903, and Governor-general William Ponty wanted the Soudan in capable hands. Clozel, in his turn, wanted to apply an Ivorian template to the work of his administration. Part of what Clozel had learned during his tenure in the Côte d'Ivoire was just how essential it was to have a systematic assessment of the colony's social, economic, and political assets. To that end, Clozel appointed three rising stars of the colonial administration to different parts of this assessment: Maurice Delafosse, Jacques Méniaud, and Jules Brevié.[51] Clozel was especially keen to have Delafosse collaborate on his project because he had already worked with Delafosse during his Ivorian tenure. He thus appointed Delafosse administrator of Bamako and charged him with producing a compendium of African customs.

To assist Delafosse in his assignment, Clozel in 1909 ordered his district administrators to complete lengthy surveys on the customs in their districts.[52] These surveys constituted the raw material Delafosse used to construct his magisterial three-volume work, *Haut-Sénégal-Niger,* published originally in 1912. Volume III of *Haut-Sénégal-Niger* was Delafosse's intellectual effort to distill out of the detail and variety of African customs a framework to help administrators in their oversight over the new colonial legal system and in their role as magistrate in the district level appeals court. Delafosse came to

Bamako at the beginning of 1909 with a budding reputation as a scholar-administrator. Delafosse had spent the majority of his colonial career in the Côte d'Ivoire and had already published a long list of practical and ethnohistorical studies. Delafosse was reluctant to leave the Côte d'Ivoire, but did so because of the pressures from and loyalty he felt for Clozel. However, in contrast to his long experience in the Côte d'Ivoire and thus with his familiarity with the subjects he wrote about, he stayed in his Bamako posting for barely six months before leaving for France. He never resumed his post in Bamako and he returned to Africa only when Clozel was appointed governor-general in 1915 to serve as director of the natives' affairs bureau.[53]

Haut-Sénégal-Niger was much more than a mere compendium of native customs distilled from the range and variety of African practices. Instead, *Haut-Sénégal-Niger* was a major contribution to the emerging field of French ethnography and the practical tasks of training French colonial administrators at the École Coloniale. Once back in Paris in 1909, Delafosse's mandate from Clozel was transformed by three other contemporary pressures. The first was the movement to define a vision for French ethnography, which resulted in the founding of the Institut d'Ethnographique in 1910. The second was the establishment of new courses in West African languages and customs at the École Coloniale late in 1909. And the third was the reaction to William Ponty's republicanism, and in particular, the conservative spin Delafosse put on Ponty's *politique des races*.

Delafosse's return to Paris coincided with increased efforts by a handful of ethnographers associated with Van Gennep to establish a "scientifically based ethnography." A crucial step in that direction had been Van Gennep's establishment of the new journal, *Revue des études ethnographiques et sociologiques* in 1907. Even before his return from Africa, Delafosse published a detailed ethnography of the Senufo in the first and second volumes of that journal.[54] In Paris, Delafosse worked closely with Van Gennep toward the establishment of the Institut d'Ethnographique, founded late in 1910. Its charter defined ethnography not merely as the "study of customs, practices, beliefs, traditions, and industries of man" but as the study of the evolution or development of "civilizations." At the first conference of the new Institute in 1911, Delafosse gave the welcome address in which he stated that "ethnography is the science of civilization" which is to be examined in all its diversity from the most ancient to the most modern civilization and from the most organized to the most primitive.[55] The imprint of Van Gennep's evolutionism can be seen in Delafosse's *Haut-Sénégal-Niger,* drafted during this period.

The second influence was Delafosse's assignment to teach at the École Coloniale. The École Coloniale was founded in 1899 as a means of providing prospective colonial administrators with the foundational training in subjects that would serve their needs and those of the colonial ministry.[56] Delafosse clearly benefited from his admirers' patronage in Paris because the Minister of Colonies decided late in 1909 to authorize the creation of two new areas of study and to appoint Delafosse to teach them. The first was a course in West African languages (Malinke, Fulfulde, and Hausa); the second was instruction in the customs of the region. Delafosse was simultaneously appointed to the École des Langues Orientales, where he was charged with instructing courses in the "Soudanese dialect." Delafosse's course on "native customs of French West Africa" served as a draft of his important volume three of *Haut-Sénégal-Niger,* which he was composing at the same time.[57] The net result of the twin influences of the ethnographic movement and his appointment at the École Colonial was to give his *Haut-Sénégal-Niger* a practical orientation, both as a handbook for district administrators as well as a conceptual guide to those interested in the ethnography of civilizations.

The third influence on Delafosse was William Ponty, and particularly his 1909 *politique des races,* which became the framework for Dakar's native policy. Ponty's policy was aimed at undercutting the "feudal aristocracy" of French West Africa, whose tyrannical rule had led to the massive devastation of the land and its people. Under what Alice Conklin terms a "republican vision of colonial policy," Ponty saw the role of the French to liberate Africans from the tyranny of their rulers, most of whom were, according to Ponty's formulation, forced upon the Soudanese by wars and conquest. These chiefs, kings, and marabouts (Ponty also railed against radical Islamic leaders) were essentially outsiders, strangers to the societies they ruled. Many of these rulers had been put into place—or reasserted in their roles—during the period of military conquest often as rewards for assisting the French. Ponty wanted native policy to respect the customs and logic of native societies, but to do so through direct contact with the population and not through the intermediary of kings and provincial chiefs. Ponty was not opposed to village chiefs, but to those intermediaries who interceded between the French and the Soudanese and who imposed their own exactions on top of those the French required. Ponty wanted French colonial policy to liberate the Soudanese from these forms of feudal obligations and to win the loyalty of the Soudanese through efforts to promote the development of their societies through the genius of their own customs.[58]

Maurice Delafosse was not opposed to the principles of ethnic solidarity and gradual evolution. Instead, he opposed the egalitarianism and antiauthoritarianism in Ponty's republicanism and sought to shift colonial policy toward an appreciation of the organic nature of patriarchy and power in the Soudan. Instead of crushing the native aristocracy, Delafosse wanted colonial policy to recognize, consult, and guide existing native leaders gradually in the direction of ameliorating social, economic, and political conditions. Far from endearing the French to the Soudanese, Delafosse accused Ponty's policies of generating revolts and social disorder. Although Delafosse was to develop his critique of Ponty more fully once he was back in Dakar in 1915,

his defense of patriarchy, power, and social order can already be seen in his
Haut-Sénégal-Niger.[59]

For Delafosse, the unity of his Soudanese civilizations was that "the guiding
principles of customary law are the same; the organization of property, the
organization of the family, the conception of justice, and the state of social and
political development are everywhere very analogous at the base and hardly
vary in form."[60] The deep reef of commonality in Delafosse's "Soudanse civilization" can be found in the organization of the family: "[b]ased uniquely on
patrilineal lines in which each family constitutes a State, which is universal in
West Africa." It is often the case, Delafosse added, that many "household
chiefs live in a condition of nearly absolute political independence." In most
regions, "each village is composed usually of one extended family" which
meant that the household chief was actually the chief of the quarter or chief of
the village and "no intermediary existed between him and the canton chief."[61]
By extension, "the canton chief is naturally the patriarch of the extended family, whose ancestor founded the canton." Moreover, the powers of the canton
chief are "analogous to those of the village chief, that is to say, the head of the
assembly of village chiefs of the canton. . . . We have here a sort of federal
state, in which the canton chief is the hereditary chief executive."[62] The under-
lining character of this polity was its family nature; it was, as Delafosse later
defined it, a "family State [*état famille*]."[63]

Because family is the core of the Soudanese civilization, customs necessarily reflect this organization. "The customs of the natives of the Soudan appear
to differ least in regard to the organization or property than in regard to other
branches of civil law, for example, inheritance, marriage, etc."[64] The most
important piece of property was the "family property," which was owned col-
lectively by all members of the family and which "is administered by the
chief of the family" for the benefit of all the members of the family.[65]
Delafosse recognized a greater variability in family law, but he nonetheless
proceeded to define its basic characteristics. These basic features included
polygyny—"polygamy is universally recognized through West Africa, even
if it is not always practiced. . . . The number of spouses is only limited by
the resources of the husband. A large number of spouses is a sign of wealth,
but only the rich may so aspire and it is often the case that poor men are
monogamous"[66]—and the modes of obtaining a wife and divorce. The range
of custom, according to Delafosse, was actually quite narrow. He identified
five modes of obtaining a wife, for example. Marriage custom, Delafosse
argued, had physiological, economic, domestic (i.e., women's interests), and
natural foundations and served to channel man's sexual needs. "Custom
wants in so far as possible to stop this potential disturbance to the family and
to society."[67] Whereas Delafosse was concerned with the logic of marriage
customs as a way to guide administrators in their disposition of legal disputes,

his contemporary scholar-administrator, Charles Monteil, advanced a major argument about household stability and the household head's authority.

Charles Monteil, one of the leading scholar-administrators of France's West African empire, published *Les Bambara du Ségou et du Kaarta* in 1924.[68] Monteil based his reconstruction of Bambara history and ethnography on information he collected while serving as a district administrator in Jenne between 1900 and 1903.[69] Monteil had already drafted pieces of his book as administrative reports and in publications.[70] Monteil's influence on Delafosse was probably considerable. Both were in Paris together from 1909 to 1911, when Delafosse was drafting *Haut-Sénégal-Niger;* both published in Van Gennep's new journal; both served together at the École Coloniale. Indeed, Delafosse nominated Monteil to serve with him on the 1910 examining committee for students who had just completed Delafosse's course on the customs of French West Africa. Monteil and Delafosse maintained a lively correspondence throughout this period.[71]

Although the core concepts had appeared in earlier publications, the appearance of *Les Bambara* marked the first detailed ethno-history of the Bambara. Monteil's book, in the words of Maurice Delafosse, "managed to disentangle the chaos [of Bambara history and ethnography] and substituted a scientific basis upon which it is possible to establish the definitive."[72] Monteil's ethnography of the household builds directly on Delafosse's ideas of patriarchy, power, and family stability. Monteil was particularly interested in the etymology of certain key words, such as the family and the household head. But he read his ethnology through the history of the Bambara kingdom, much as Delafosse had read the state through the family. The rise of the powerful Bambara rulers of Segu was linked sociologically to the foundation of the household head's authority. The power of the Bambara *faama* was analogous to the *faya* or power of the *fa* (household head) simply amplified on the scale of a kingdom.

> In the Bambara language, there are no terms equivalent to our word family, understood in a juridical sense. The collectivity placed under the authority of a *fa*[73] is called by different names depending upon how one conceives of the collectivity itself or even the location which that collectivity occupies.
>
> Note first of all the collectivity that occurs when one forms an association, that is the *ton* . . . . and all the people placed under the authority of the *fa* are considered the *ton den[w]* = literally, children of the *ton* . . . .
>
> If one considers the family as the association of the people issued from the same relatives, one can employ the term *ba-denya,* derived from *ba-den[w];* the word *ba* meaning the mother and more broadly as the genitor mother or father, then the term *ba-den[w]* indicates those who have issued from them and commonly means children, brothers, relatives and thus *ba-denya* connotes fraternity and lineage.[74]

The key category upholding the authority of the household was his *faya*. There is a circularity of sorts here—the authority of the household head resides in his status as household head—but that does not alter its importance to Monteil's sociology. "The whole of the prerogatives of all kinds, which uphold the *fa* above the others, constitute a form of eminent dignity of which the essence is its omnipotence, *faya,* which is derived from the status of *fa* (*seigneur, maître*)."[75]

Later in that section, Monteil elaborated on the qualities of the *faya*. "The powers of the *fa* over his community are, in principle, absolute. He can, if he chooses, loan, pledge, sell and even put to death [any member of his community]; he may also dispose of everything that they possess, people and things. In contrast, he has in relationship to them responsibilities, especially to sustain the members [of the community]."[76] Central to the authority of the household head were also reciprocal responsibilities, made possible by the collective nature of household property.

> The material possessions are indivisible, the *fa* is obliged to use them for the well-being of all the members. It is thus that, when it is due, he provides the bridewealth which permits one of his members to found a family; he ransoms the members who have fallen into slavery; he renders care to those who are ill, even if this requires extraordinary expenditures; he is responsible for all civil or legal or other debts of any of the members of his community, especially when the community is responsible as a whole. . . . [77]

According to Monteil's ethnographic sociology of the Bambara household, the power of the household head was absolute and unchallenged. He stood at the head of a complex, multigenerational unit, but it was his capacities to organize and manage that provided the deep stability to African family and political structures.

SUMMARY

Delafosse and Monteil provided the conceptual blueprint for a model of Soudanese society that linked family stability to political power and social order. In addition, Delafosse was on the ground serving as the Bamako district administrator in 1909, when the numbers of marriage and divorce disputes brought before the provincial court began to decline. However, the numbers of marriage and divorce disputes continued to decline into 1910, when Delafosse had already left the district. The increasing numbers of judgments against women can be dated from the time of Delafosse's appointment. I would like to argue that the declension of opportunities for women seeking divorce can be unambiguously dated to Delafosse's tenure, but I cannot. Moreover, I have not found a "smoking gun" in the archival record. The closest we come to such a statement was the marginal note scribbled on the 1910 Koutiala report on divorce, which stated "Do not meddle in native custom except with the utmost circumspection. The act of agreement among two families to exchange two women is the guarantee of reciprocity. Marriage, in both Muslim practice and native custom has all the characteristics of a sale. Do not, however, treat this as an infraction of the slave trade ordinance."[78] The timing of this note fits the declension hypothesis. The sentiment expressed in that note may have circulated more fully throughout the colonial administration and may thus have contributed to the direction Delafosse took in his *Haut-Sénégal-Niger*. Certainly, the ideas of patriarchy, family stability, and social order so clearly represented in Delafosse's project were circulating throughout the colonial world in late 1909 and 1910 in part because Delafosse was teaching these ideas in his courses at the École Coloniale.

The evidence from the native courts discussed in this chapter suggests that the landscape that African women and men had to traverse to accomplish their goals continued to shift during the first and second decade of the twentieth century. In traversing this landscape and in making strategic use of the new courts that dotted this landscape, African women and men and colonial officials were clearly acting on their assessment of "rules and resources."[79]

Married women's abilities to traverse this new landscape and to succeed at least briefly in ending marriages that they did not want depended in part on their capacity to make autonomous decisions. Women were clearly vulnerable in the world after 1905, but women could mitigate their vulnerabilities by choosing lovers or by drawing on their own wealth to end their marriages. The following chapter explores the nature of the bridewealth contract and the ways in which women could use their own resources to overcome the barriers toward divorce that were intrinsic to the marriage transfers. Chapter 7 pursues this line of inquiry by examining how the end of slavery created conditions for the emergence of "new" forms of investment and property relations and how women participated in these new areas. Women's own wealth provided them with some capacity to shape their own lives within the broader cultural and economic conditions in which they lived.

6

BRIDEWEALTH AS CONTRACT

Whether the provincial tribunals ruled in favor of divorce or ordered a runaway wife to return to her husband's home, the judgments all underscored the contractual nature of marriage. The central component in marriage, particularly among the Bambara and Malinke, whose practices have permeated widely in the area I am examining in this chapter, are the strategic investments made between those kinship groups entering into the marriage contract. These strategic investments—"the circulation of goods and personnel in social streams"—revolve around building and maintaining webs of kinship and in organizing and controlling labor.[1] Marriage certainly builds kinship between groups. It also creates conditions for the generation of recognized descendants: children. Marriage also transfers to her husband and his kinship group rights to his wife's labor, her reproductive power, and rights of sexual access. In a recent ethnography, Toulmin describes Bambara marriage as "a particularly long term investment. While the woman's labour and services provide some immediate returns for the heavy wedding costs, many of the benefits will accrue over the following 30 years or more." Toulmin further notes that because the consequences of marriage are likely to be with the family for decades, care in making marriage choices are not left to the potential spouses. Spouses often come from groups already bound by existing marriage ties. "In this way, the household head hopes to ensure that marriages endure and are free of conflict."[2]

Our understanding of the nature of multiplex relationships that constituted marriage are encumbered by the normative biases inherent in ethnographies and legal studies. Marriage is a complex enterprise and the challenges to it are many. The household head may hope that the marriage he has entered his daughter into will endure and be free of conflict, but the realities are often quite different. The view of marriage from the courts clearly exacerbates the conflictual nature of the relationships in and surrounding marriage. But the use of court cases provides precious detail on actual marriages and allows us to identify trouble spots in these relationships. Bridewealth was clearly one of the trouble spots in the social history of households. Bridewealth was both the object of disputes—who owed what to whom?—and the consequence of failed marriage arrangements—what happened to bridewealth when marriages failed?

We might want to consider marriage as a kind of moral economy in which there is a range of relationships determined in part by limits on exploitation. As long as husbands and wives relate to each other within the limits of these acceptable conditions of exploitation, then the marriage will persist. What we see in the courts are cases where the limits on exploitation have been exceeded. In the courts, husbands and wives appealed to these limits in seeking dissolution of their marriages. The dissolution of the marriage was by no means the end of the relationships entered into by husband and wives and their respective kin. Despite the fact that the household head sought to spin social webs around his dependents and in-laws, these webs were often ruptured by the actions of husbands and wives and even earlier by the fiancés themselves. This chapter seeks to explore the "contractual" part of marriage that took the form of bridewealth and to explore what happened to these transfers of wealth in the face of changes to the wider landscapes of power in the French Soudan.

BRIDEWEALTH, CONTRACTS, AND NEGOTIATIONS

In response to Clozel's 1909 questionnaire on customs, the Gumbu administrator provided precious detail on the Bambara marriage customs prevailing at the time.

> When a man has chosen a woman or more precisely, when a young man is not yet married, the household head chooses a woman for his son or younger brother. He begins by charging one of his friends or a *griot* to visit the parents of the young girl chosen to request a marriage. He is called *furusentigui*. The household head gives the *furusentigui* 40 meters of cotton bands and ten kola nuts to present to the father or ward of the young girl. If the father or guardian accepts the request, he keeps the cotton and the kola. If not, he does not accept the cotton or the kola.
>
> It is to be noted that just as the future groom is not consulted on the choice of his wife, neither is the future bride. Often, they do not meet until the day of their marriage. If the family of the groom is rich, they send presents from time to time to the future bride. Throughout the period of engagement, the young girl is obliged to hide from the presence of her future husband. . . . [T]he size of the bridewealth varied directly with the status of the parties involved. Nevertheless, among the Bambara, the bridewealth for a young girl is 120,000 cowries or 120 francs.[3]

In nearby Bandiagara, custom was slightly different. Instead of 40 meters of cotton bands, the *furusentigui* approached the parents of the future wife ("who is still very young") with a calabash containing between 120 and 1,000 cowries. If the father or the guardian of the girl accepted the engagement, then the groom began to work in his future father-in-law's fields, usually every other year often together with his age grade association (Bambara: *ton*) until the marriage took place. The bride's father determined when she was old enough to marry.[4] "Custom," the Gumbu administrator remarked in his discussion of marriage, "is quite expansive and does not impose on marriage the same severe and ineluctable rules as our civil code." Nor, he continued, "was it a simple matter to determine precisely the distinctions between different sanctions. Because custom is not written, the native interprets it in his own best interests."[5] The following discussion of marriage, bridewealth, and the court cases surrounding bridewealth must be understood within the context of the linked transformations set in motion by the end of slavery.

While marriage was surrounded by significant ritual involving coming of age for the bride, the ceremony was merely the culmination of a complex set of transfers known as bridewealth.[6] Precolonial Bambara and Malinke marriage involved exchange marriage, although by the beginning of the twentieth century, bridewealth had come to represent the exchanges of other "equivalences."[7] Bridewealth often involved the transfer over a number of years of goods (grain, livestock, and cash) and services (weaving and occasional farm work) flowing from the husband's kin and his age mates to those of his bride. In return, the husband and his kin group received the rights to the bride's labor power (at least for that portion of the day customarily devoted to household chores and other activities which contributed to the well-being of the household, such as farming and weeding, spinning, etc.), her reproductive power, and her domestic services. Within the framework of the tightly structured gender division of labor, women also had access to income from work within their own "economic spheres," which they controlled independent of their husband's income and the needs of the household economy. Although women had customary rights to enjoy the product of their own labor during their "leisure" times, men could still lay claim on their wives' wealth if there was an identifiable need to support the general good of the household.[8]

Bridewealth constituted not only a significant investment, but it also represented a considerable flow of goods between households, permitting further marriages.[9] Given the customary obligations of household heads to provide a wife for each of their sons and younger brothers, it was unlikely for household heads to accumulate bridewealth payments. Thus, the more or less continuous circulation of bridewealth served as a major barrier against divorce, which usually required that the bride's family return the bridewealth it had received. Toulmin describes contemporary practice that probably reflected earlier times.

> A woman who is unhappy with her husband can return to her parents and try to persuade them that she should not be forced to go back to him. This is

usually not successful, as the girl's father knows that the stability of the unions into which he and his brothers have entered would be upset by his taking the side of his daughter in this case. In addition . . . the husband may try to get back part of the money he has given to the girl's family. This will be difficult for the bride's father to return, since the money will have been paid over a number of years and spent as it was received.[10]

Toumlin's description echoed the Gumbu administrator's remarks from 1909, when he stated that a wife who wanted to leave her husband usually found that "her parents have already dissipated the bridewealth received at the time of her marriage and are thus not willing to return it. Instead, they force their daughter to return to the conjugal home, but not before administering a serious beating."[11] Toumlin thus concludes that official divorce among the Bambara is very low and "people, when asked, will say that it hardly ever occurs."[12] Toumlin's ethnography reflects a normative bias contained in most discussions of custom. Divorce was clearly recognized by custom, especially if the wife committed adultery, if she aborted a pregnancy, if she was sterile, if she abandoned her children, or if she heaped abuse on her husband's kin. Divorce was also possible if the husband was impotent, if he abandoned his family, or if he was abusive. Although there were barriers against divorce, as we have seen in Chapter 5, women and men used the newly created courts to end marriages or to force their partners to return. In most cases following the breakdown of marriage, the bridewealth was to be returned. Only if the husband repudiated his wife (as is the accepted Muslim practice), if the husband abandoned his wife, or if the wife died was bridewealth not consistently returned.[13] Even in these situations, the court record shows considerable inconsistency.

The life cycle of a marriage usually had four phases: (1) a preliminary set of negotiations, sometimes conducted through the assistance of an intermediary, but often without the consent of the future groom and bride; (2) a set of advanced negotiations, in which a substantial amount of the bridewealth transfers took place; (3) the actual marriage; and (4) divorce, rupture of the marriage, or the death of one spouse or the other. Each of these phases was marked by anticipated outcomes. In negotiating marriage, the groom's kin and the bride's kin, as well as the groom and the bride thus entered into contracts. Contracts are mutually acceptable promises to do or to forbear; failure to honor contracts usually has consequences.[14]

The earliest survey of the customary practices of contracts in the Middle Niger valley comes from Trentinian's 1897 questionnaire. Although his responses to the questionnaire were generally flat, the Segu district officer was nearly effusive on the subject of contracts. "The common contract among the Marka is the 'fatia' or a verse from the Koran; among the Bambara, a handshake." Agreements exist in which "a price is agreed in advance, payable in such and such conditions at such a date." "Bonds (or pawnship) are widely used."[15] The Segu officer's response to the 1897 questionnaire did not directly address issues of bridewealth, although the notion of a "bond" and a "handshake" to cement the agreement between two parties lay also at the heart of bridewealth transfers. We can consider bridewealth as a form of contract in which the parties agree to a set of transfers, which could be identified, tracked separately, or bundled together. Similarly, bridewealth could be understood as a "bond" holding the marriage together.

The persistence of marriage was the bond against the wife's return to her kin and the reciprocal return of bridewealth. The difficulty of returning bridewealth was thus in principle a "bond" against marriage instability. Because marriage often involved transfers over a number of years, promises to fulfill the agreed upon transfers constituted a contract. But promises were often unfulfilled and parties to agreement were often in court to recover bridewealth.

In the absence of oral data on turn of the century contracts, a quick glance at Bamana terminology may reveal some aspects of contracts that apply to bridewealth transfers. According to Gérard Dumestre, *fátiya* (the term identified in the 1897 report on legal customs) is a "collective incantation to bless or to curse." It is usually pronounced by the imam. Père Charles Baillaud identifies the Bamana term *láyidu* as promise, verbal agreement, or contract. According to Dumestre, the phrase *kà láyidu tà* is "to make a promise;" *kà láyidu wuli* is "to break a promise." The Bamana proverb, *láyidu mán gèlen fó à tíimeko,* evokes the sense the difficulties of adhering to promises: "to enter into an agreement is easier than to respect it."[16]

Fátiya and *láyidu,* collective incantations and verbal promises, suggest that agreements are webs of relations. This concept fits the nature of expectations and sets of obligations entered into upon marriage and represented by the bridewealth. We can thus assume that marriage agreements—contracts— were secured by their embeddedness within dense networks of relationships. Disputes over bridewealth transfers often occurred where those networks were either not dense or had weakened.

Cases regarding the recovery or disposition of bridewealth can be used to provide evidence for the contractual nature of the phases of marriage identified above. This method entails some potential distortion, because the process of dispute resolution involving bridewealth exacerbated the jural nature of the agreements entered in marriages.[17] On the other hand, this approach has the advantage of identifying particular practices—or the rupture of particular practices or expectations—at specific historical moments rather than the presentation of custom as timeless tradition. Figures 6.1 and 6.2 indicate the trouble spots within the marriage and bridewealth process for the provincial tribunals of Bamako and Segu. The trouble spots in bridewealth disputes differ considerably between Bamako and Segu especially in the areas of broken

Figure 6.1 Types of Bridewealth Disputes, Bamako, 1905–1912, n = 108

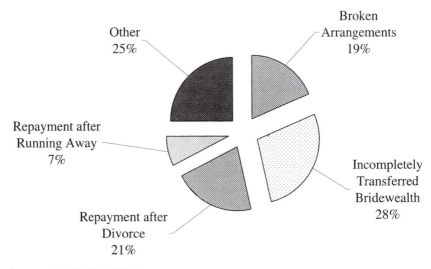

Source: ANM 2M 104/105

Figure 6.2 Types of Bridewealth Disputes, Segu, 1905–1912, n = 48

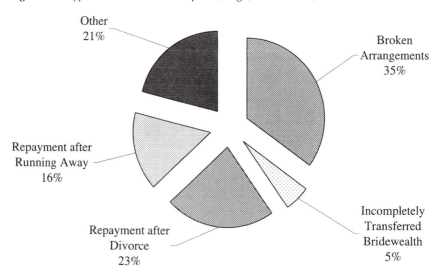

Source: ANM 2 M 143

arrangements and in incompletely transferred bridewealth. The incidence of broken arrangements prior to the formal marriage was much more pronounced in Segu and the incidence of incompletely paid bridewealth was higher in Bamako.

In the sections below, I will explore these findings as I examine the broader issues of bridewealth disputes. The method used here moves back and forth between the aggregate data that identify patterns and the individual cases that provide texture to the dispute and the relationship in question.

Preliminary Negotiations

According to the early twentieth-century reports on marriage customs, two sets of negotiations constituted the preliminary phase. The first was the agreement of the household head to enter into negotiations on behalf of his son or younger brother. The second set involved the work of the intermediary in testing the interest of the bride's guardian to the future marriage. On 14 November 1911, M'Pie Diara brought the head of his household to court to force him to provide bridewealth for a wife. Soriba Diara, the head of the household, argued that he had no obligations to M'Pie Diara, because M'Pie Diara had left the family four years earlier and thus had extinguished his claims on the household for bridewealth. The court agreed with the defendant and dismissed the case.[18] The court ruling seemed to uphold the idea that the obligation to provide bridewealth to all male members of the household rested upon the reciprocity of members to the household. As long as sons and younger brothers worked for the household head, then the household head was responsible for bridewealth. When younger male dependents did not "work" for the household head, then the household head was not responsible for helping them secure a wife. Less than a year later, the Bamako tribunal reversed its position on the household head's responsibility. Amadu Koyaute brought his elder brother, Ousmane Keita, to court to force him to pay his bridewealth, just as M'Pie Diara had done in 1911. Ousmane Keita argued in court that because Amadu Koyaute did not fulfill his obligations to the family—"Amadu Koyaute did not do the family work"—he was not entitled to the household's assistance for his bridewealth. Amadu Koyaute did not dispute this assessment of his contribution to the family well-being, but he argued that whatever his behavior, this did not extinguish his rights as a member of the family and thus his rights to bridewealth. The court ruled in Amadu Koyaute's favor and ordered Ousmane Keita to pay his bridewealth.[19]

These two cases provide only an entry point into the issues of household reciprocity. In both cases, the heads of households, Soriba Diara and Ousmane Keita, argued consistently on their obligations only to the members of their communities who served the well-being of the community. Both plaintiffs sought to force household heads to honor the "custom" that household heads provide bridewealth to their sons and younger brothers regardless of the underlying assumptions of reciprocity. The court's rulings were inconsistent. In one ruling it upheld the principle of reciprocity over the strict application of "custom"; in the other it ruled in favor of "custom" without regard to practice. While we can not pursue this line of argument further, because neither case was appealed, these two cases reveal the likely sets of negotiations within the household of the groom that proceeded the willingness of the household head to begin negotiations with the household of a potential bride.

Once the household head agreed to embark on the search for a wife for one his dependants, he often turned to a *furusentigui*, or an intermediary, to help open negotiations with kin of a prospective bride. The *furusentigui* was usually a friend of the groom's family or a trusted *jeliw* (Bambara: griot).[20] Occasionally, the *furusentigui* was entrusted with delivering the bridewealth itself; sometimes the *furusentigui* was tempted by the capital entrusted to him and kept it. This was clearly the case when Fako Dihko sought to recover the money he gave Sienou Koita to give to his future father-in-law as bridewealth. Fako Dihko alleged that Sienou Koita kept the bridewealth, because he failed to deliver it to the father of his son's prospective bride. Sienou Koita apparently did not dispute this charge and the court ordered him to reimburse the bridewealth.[21] A similar situation arose when Kini Coulibaly gave his kinsman, Samba Coulibaly, Fr 120 to give to the father of the bride, Bakata, as part payment of bridewealth. The plaintiff accused the defendant of keeping the money for himself. The court ruled that the defendant must repay the "debt."[22]

These two cases are not difficult to interpret, because the court consistently ruled in favor of the aggrieved household head. Custom was not at issue in these cases. Instead, the failure of the *furusentigui* to fulfill his obligations to serve as a conduit for bridewealth transfers was seen by the court as a breach of trust (hence, contract) and thus the court ruled against the intermediaries in both cases. Both sets of cases—disputes over custom and disputes over trust—involve breaches of expected behavior attendant upon the promises to perform acts agreed upon in the "contract."

Advanced Negotiations

As soon as preliminary negotiations were successfully completed and as parties to the marriage intensified their relationships and transfers, potential breaches multiplied as well. While the range of breach of contract was potentially unlimited, the court record indicates three of the most common areas of dispute: double-dipping on the part of the bride's guardian; reluctance on the part of either the groom or the bride to consummate the union; and household disputes over control of the bridewealth. A fourth area of dispute, incompletely paid bridewealth, will be addressed in the following section on marriage, although the roots of the dispute lie in this phase of advanced negotiations.

As the exchange of "equivalences" became more common than the exchange of sisters in the course of the twentieth century, bridewealth became a source of potential accumulation. Some unscrupulous guardians did not hesitate to accept multiple offers of marriage, occasionally pursuing them simultaneously or serially. The exasperated administrator from Koutiala wrote to Lieutenant-governor Clozel in 1911 that

> most of the judgments in misdemeanor cases punish the same offense. Almost always, they occur when a father or a brother or sometimes a male member of a family, who, having married his daughter or relative for the first time and having acquired the bridewealth, refuses to let the bride go to her husband, either by threats or by force. He then promises her in marriage for the second time in order to acquire a second bridewealth. This infraction, so common, as I have indicated in previous reports, always has the same character.[23]

Such double-dipping was not limited to Koutiala. On 12 May 1908, Soumoumery Ture took Oualama Kasse to the Bamako tribunal to recover bridewealth that he had given for marriage to his daughter, Seradie Kasse. The problem, as Soumoumery Ture told the court, was that even though he was the first to provide the bridewealth, Seradie Kasse was being married by her father to Bi Dembele, who had also paid bridewealth. The court ordered the defendant to reimburse Soumoumery Ture his bridewealth.[24] Niani Kone of Segu found himself in court because he had accepted bridewealth from Nene Tangara for his daughter, but had also accepted bridewealth from another party to whom he married his daughter. The court ruled that Niani Kone had to return to bridewealth he had received from the plaintiff, but also ordered the defendant to pay a Fr 20 fine.[25]

Occasionally unscrupulous male guardians not only collected multiple bridewealth, but tried to dispute the value of them when confronted in court with their actions. This occurred when Mata Sako promised his daughter to Demba Ouattara, accepted Demba Ouattara's bridewealth installment, and then married his daughter to another man, from whom he also collected bridewealth. Demba Ouattara sued Mata Sako in court for the return of his bridewealth. Mata Sako claimed to have received only Fr 45 from Demba Ouattara. Demba Ouattara, however, brought to court two witnesses who proved that Demba Ouattara had actually paid a Fr 100 installment. The court ordered Mata Sako to repay the full amount.[26]

While male guardians were the chief defendants in double-dipping disputes, women were not above engaging in matrimonial fraud. In second or subsequent marriages, women often received bridewealth themselves rather than their male guardians. Makan Kamara from Segu was duped into giving Mama Coulibaly "many presents" as part of a pledge for marriage only to discover that Mama Coulibaly was already married. Coulibaly, it turned out, was actually a bigamist, being married to two other men. The court ordered the defendant to return the presents she had received from the plaintiff and to serve two months in prison. Because the *tribunal de province* had jurisdiction over both civil disputes and over misdemeanor cases, it was competent to order civil and criminal judgments.[27] This case indicates that women could also claim bridewealth as well as "presents" as part of marriage strategies, a topic that I shall develop below. But before we address the issue of women's claims on bridewealth, we will need to examine the agency of brides and grooms in the breakdown of marriage arrangements.

Ethnography, whether the Gumbu administrator's 1909 version or Toulmin's postcolonial one, consistently reports that marriage is contracted by male guardians on behalf of their wards. District administrators were more or less agreed, as discussed in Chapter 5, that one of the primary causes of the high incidence of divorce in the French Soudan was that brides had no choice in marital decisions, at least in first marriages. A number of cases heard at the provincial courts in Segu and Bamako suggest that the authority of household heads to contract marriage was often challenged and that some brides and grooms broke marriage arrangements made for them without their consent. Such was the case when Alabassane Diara promised his niece in marriage to Nianguima Sidibe. Diara received an installment consisting of 45,000 cowries and 179 kola nuts as preliminary tokens of bridewealth. However, Diara's niece refused to marry Nianguima Sidibe and actually ran away rather than marry the man her uncle chose. The Segu court ordered Diara to repay both the bridewealth installment and the presents he had received.[28]

Brides sometimes refused to marry if, after the start of bridewealth transfers, they discovered that their fiancés were ill or incapacitated. This was the case when Faramata So discovered that her fiancé had leprosy and when Mamakan Taraore's sister discovered that her fiancé has become "crazy."[29] The options available to grooms to avoid marriages arranged by their household heads were probably larger than those available to brides. While women could flee, as Alabassane Konare's niece did, their survival certainly depended upon finding a male protector. The court record contains numerous references to matrimonial disputes in which no bridewealth had been transferred, indicating some sort of common-law arrangement.[30] This was probably the situation when Bala Diallo complained in the Bamako court that his daughter had "gone to live with Difa Diara. He is demanding payment of bridewealth according to custom." Bala Diallo's daughter had clearly left her father and moved in with her lover, Difa Diara, thus bypassing altogether the negotiations and network building so common to the ethnographic literature. The court ruled in Bala Diallo's favor and ordered the defendant to pay Fr 200 bridewealth within six months.[31]

Given the increasing commercial and labor opportunities in the early twentieth century, young men could more easily find means of establishing their own independent households. In the span of three months, four cases of runaway grooms were heard in the Bamako provincial court. Two of the cases were brought by the grooms' father or guardian seeking to end the marriage contract and to recover the bridewealth that they had advanced. Bogori Doumbia had entered into negotiations with Lamine Soumare regarding the marriage between his son and Lamine Soumare's daughter. Both parties had agreed and initial bridewealth was transferred. However, Bogori Doumbia's son left the district and had not been heard from for over three years. Bogori Doumbia was in court to annul the marriage contract and to recover the bridewealth already transferred. The court agreed and ordered the defendant to return the bridewealth. A similar suit was brought by Sory Fofana to annul the marriage agreement between his son and Dialimoussa Diallo's daughter and to recover bridewealth already transferred, because his son has not returned during the past five years.[32] It was also clearly in the interests of the bride's father to end marriage agreements if the groom had gone missing. Another case was brought by the father of the bride against her fiancé, charging that the fiancé had disappeared and thus asking the court to annul the marriage agreement. The father of the bride was prepared to return the bridewealth, but wanted a clear verdict that the contract was annulled. The court agreed with the plaintiff.[33] It may only be a coincidence (although historians are always intrigued by coincidences), but the cases of the runaway grooms all trace the initial departure to the years from 1906 to 1908. This was exactly the moment when the end of slavery was making its most significant initial impact on the economies of the Middle Niger region and when household heads were redoubling their efforts to use their household labor in new ways.

I have used these examples of brides and grooms contributing directly to the breakdown of marriage arrangements to demonstrate that despite the ethnographic assumption that male household heads or guardians decided marriages, brides and grooms had some say in whether marriages actually took place. Brides and grooms probably played an even greater role in the breakdown of marriage arrangements than the court cases suggest. Most of the court cases regarding the breakdown of marriage arrangements do not specify the cause; they are primarily efforts by the groom or the groom's guardian to recover bridewealth. The incidence of the breakdown of marriage arrangements before the consummation of marriage was significant. Of the bridewealth disputes, in Segu 35 percent and in Bamako 19 percent were due to the breakdown of marriage arrangements before marriage took place. Most of these records resemble the one heard in Segu on 31 May 1907. "Sala claims the return of a bridewealth advance. The marriage negotiations have been broken."[34] This fairly typical record does not provide sufficient evidence to determine what or who caused the breakdown in negotiations, only that the negotiations broke down. The judgment ordered the repayment of the bridewealth advanced, but did not specify who was to repay the bridewealth. We do know that Bamba Ballo was the named defendant, but we do not know whether Bamba Ballo was the father, uncle, brother, or guardian of the unnamed bride.

Knowing who had agreed to repay the bridewealth in cases of broken marriage arrangements is important because it points to agency. For example, Boa Kamara wanted to recover the bridewealth advanced to Lassana Sidibe, who had promised his daughter, Tene Sidibe, in marriage. However, Lassana Sidibe had since died and his daughter did not want to marry Boa Kamara. In court Tene Sidibe claimed that she had no resources with which to repay the bridewealth, since her father had apparently used the bridewealth for other purposes, but she did pledge to repay the bridewealth as soon as she married someone "she would like." The court ruled exactly as Tene Sidibe wished. "Tene Sidibe will return to Boa Kamara the bridewealth received by her deceased father as soon as she received one from a husband she chooses for herself."[35] This is a wonderfully revealing case, precisely because it indicates the nature of the dispute and because it indicates women's agency in marriage negotiations. The case certainly hints at the willingness of the new courts, particularly during their very early years, to listen to and respect women's wishes. It also hints at a significant factor in bridewealth disputes: under certain conditions wives actually "controlled" their own bridewealth payments. I shall develop this issue below.

Disputes over who had rights to bridewealth in the bride's household form the third site where disputes were most common. Such disputes constituted 12 percent of the cases in Segu and 22 percent in Bamako. These disputes indicate that there were considerable challenges from within the household to the "custom" that the household head both received the bridewealth from marriages of female wards and that he was responsible for the bridewealth of his male wards. The most pronounced bridewealth dispute axis within the household occurred between the household head and his younger brothers. In polygynous households, it was quite common for brothers to have a common father but different mothers. Disputes over the bridewealth of daughters and sisters occasionally ruptured the idealized harmony of the extended household. Although the members of the household were supposed to be members of a corporate community managed by the household head for the benefit of all, the attraction of a significant amount of capital flowing from bridewealth probably led to conflicts over rights to it. On 15 November 1907, Bandiougou Keita brought Fake Soumare to court to recover the bridewealth the latter had received. The plaintiff accused Fake Soumare of falsely representing himself as the head of the household and thus accepting the bridewealth of Fr 140 for the marriage of one his nieces, who was probably the daughter of the household head. The court ruled that Fake Soumare must return the bridewealth to the plaintiff.[36] The following case indicates that household members sometimes sued each other for the recovery of bridewealth one member accepted under false pretenses. Karounga Coulibaly, the head of the household, took his younger brother, Fanouma Coulibaly, to court to recover the bridewealth the latter had received from the marriage of his sister. The court ruled not only that the bridewealth must go to the household head, but that the marriage itself was annulled because it was conducted without the approval of the bride's guardian.[37]

Fathers were not the only ones to receive bridewealth. Uncles, brothers, and occasionally other male guardians were identified in the court records. It could be that these individuals were in fact household heads and receiving or repaying bridewealth because of their positions. A case heard in Bamako in 1911 suggests that even women could serve as plaintiffs in suits to recover bridewealth. Diara Fofana, the mother of the bride, brought Baba Diara to court to force him to transfer to her the bridewealth owed for her daughter. Baba Diara did not dispute his obligation to Diara Fofana, he merely requested a delay in the payment. The court agreed to the defendant's request for a delay, but ordered him to pay the bridewealth of Fr 150 to Diara Fofana within three months.[38] Given the high incidence of divorce in the court records, it is possible to imagine that Diara Fofana was the head of her own household, however unlikely that may be. She could have been divorced or separated from a man who had never paid bridewealth and therefore had no legal claims on his child. In the situation of a "natural child," as it was referred to in the records, the father or male guardian of the mother was usually considered the child's guardian. Nonetheless, the records clearly indicate that Diara Fofana brought her son-in-law to court to recover the bridewealth for the marriage of her daughter. This act indicates that household norms during the first two decades of the twentieth century were potentially quite fluid. More research needs to be conducted on household organization during this period of rapid change.

BRIDEWEALTH AND MARRIAGE:
THE INSTALLMENT PROBLEM

Bridewealth was a considerable investment. Table 6.1 provides a view of the range of bridewealth figures between 1905 and 1912 as drawn from the court records.

From the data cited in Table 6.1, it is clear that bridewealth represented not only a long-term investment in Toulmin's terms, but a considerable fortune. The data range in the chart is not large enough to demonstrate an unequivocal increase in bridewealth. The data suggest that bridewealth payments were higher in Bamako than in Segu, often by as much as 100 percent. Because of the considerable capital involved, bridewealth was often transferred over

Table 6.1 Value of Bridewealth

Year	Segu	Bamako
1905	9,000K, 40F range 9-40F	200F, 200F, 5 cattle, 200F range 200F-500F, average 275F
1907	40,000K, 340,000K, 70,5000K, 14,000K, 60,000K range 14-340F, average 105F	84F 140F, 150F, 200F, 300F, 500F range 84F-500F, average 229F
1908	25,000K, 45,000K, 148,740K, 115F, 22,600F range 23-149F, average 71.5F	260F
1909	40F (plus 3 gros gold), 53,600K, 106,000K range 54-106F, average 82F	230F, 25F (plus one cow), 3 cows range 125-300F, average 152F
1910	65F, 85F, 225F range, 65-225F, average 125F	150F, 225F average 188F
1911	No data	200F, 217.50F, 150F, 279F, 225F, 150F, 165F, 69.50F, 100F range 70-279F, average 173F
1912	No data	420F, 150F, 235F, 81F, 65F, 175F, 155F, 30F, 130F, 220F, 270F range 30-420F, average 176 (w/o installment, 198F)

Notes: Sources ANM 2 M 104, ANM 2 M 105, ANM 2 M 143; Gumbu 1909 report cited above; Chapter 7 estimates on cattle prices; for cowries equivalences, see Jan Hogendorn and Marion Johnson, *The Shell Money of the Slave Trade* (Cambridge: Cambridge University Press, 1986), pp. 141–142. Gros gold = 15,000K; cow = 100F; cowries, 1,000 = 1F; figures of 65F, 81F are installments, not figures for total BW. The 1912 figure of 30F is total bridewealth paid for a former slave.

time. Payments over time eased the burden on the groom's household, but gave rise to conflicts over the actual value transferred and over noncompletion of payments. When faced with disputes over the value of bridewealth transferred, the court often tried on its own to discover the value by soliciting testimony from witnesses. When none was available, the court was not above fixing the value of bridewealth at what it considered normal. In a case heard in 1911 where no proof was available, the Bamako court fixed bridewealth at Fr 250.[39] The notion of marriage as a long-term investment has a very concrete character in the sense that it also took a long time to complete the bridewealth transfers.

Faced with the significant investment in bridewealth and the practice of completing those transfers over time, household heads allowed their daughters or female wards to cohabit with their husbands even before the transfers were completed. Marriages probably took their ceremonial course, but the bridewealth transfers continued after the bride entered her husband's home. Herein lay one of the major trouble spots in bridewealth disputes in the Bamako district: once having his wife live with him, a husband's or the household head's ardor to complete the bridewealth transfers may have waned. Incompletely transferred bridewealth constituted 28 percent of the bridewealth disputes in Bamako. In contrast, incomplete transfers constituted only 5 percent of the bridewealth disputes in Segu. I shall examine the implications of this difference in the section on trends that follow, but it is safe to conclude that household heads in Bamako faced a greater risk of noncompletion of bridewealth transfers than their counterparts in Segu. This may help to account for the higher bridewealth costs in Bamako than in Segu, where the risks of nonpayment were smaller.

Typical of these cases was that brought by Siradie Doumbia against Togouta Sangare for failing to complete the final bridewealth transfer. We can only imagine the conversations between father-in-law and son-in-law that led to the situation where Siradie Doumbia arrived in court with "witnesses [who] confirm the exact amount" of unpaid bridewealth. In this case, the court ruled that Togouta Sangare must transfer the missing Fr. 69.50 in bridewealth.[40] Suits brought to the provincial tribunal for noncompletion of bridewealth sometimes hinged upon the initial vagueness of the marriage contract regarding the time frame for transfers. This is the argument that the defendant Fatoumata Diallo used in explaining why he had not yet completed the transfers for his marriage to Biratigui Kone's sister. Since his father's death, Biratigui Kone had become head of the household and thus eager to receive the remaining bridewealth. "Fatoumata Diallo claims that the deceased father of Biratigui Kone had accorded him a long delay. No proof presented." Although the defendant admitted that he still owed bridewealth to his wife's kin, neither the plaintiff nor the defendant had witnesses to prove their cases. In its judgment, the court not only ordered that Fatoumata Diallo pay the bridewealth, but in absence of an agreement about the size of the bridewealth committed actually fixed the bridewealth at Fr 150 and one cow (or roughly Fr 250).[41]

The installment nature of bridewealth transfers is revealed by the following case. This case was brought to court because the husband did not honor his commitments to complete bridewealth transfers after his wife began living with him. In this case, Aicha Kouyate, the wife, left her husband because he did not complete payments. As the case was presented, Aicha Kouyate was suing for divorce, although she was obviously willing to return to her husband's home. Aicha Kouyate was probably using the court to force her husband to complete payments. "Aicha Kouyate wants a divorce because her husband has not completely paid the bridewealth. He wants her to return home. He agrees to pay bridewealth monthly." The court ruled that Aicha Kouyate will return to the conjugal home and that Moussa Taraore will pay Fr 12.50 per month until the bridewealth was completed. In this verdict, the installment nature of bridewealth was given greater temporal regularity, but the judgment stemmed from the accepted practice of allowing bridewealth payments over time.[42] The fact that the plaintiff in this case was a woman raises important issues about whose responsibility it actually was to collect and to repay bridewealth in case of marriage rupture, which I shall examine below.

THE RUPTURED MARRIAGE AND THE RECOVERY OF BRIDEWEALTH

The ethnographic logic of bridewealth is that it serves as a bond for the persistence of the marriage and as compensation for the transfers of rights to a daughter's labor and reproductive power to her husband and his kin. Should the marriage fail, then the wife returns to her kin and her kin return the bridewealth to her husband's kin. I have discussed the difficulties the wife's kin often faced in repaying bridewealth in the event of a divorce. Indeed, Toulmin's argument about the persistence of marriage is that the obligation to repay bridewealth served as an effective barrier against divorce.[43] Nonetheless, marriages failed and divorce happened. Indeed, 23 percent of the bridewealth disputes heard by the Segu court and 21 percent of the cases heard in the Bamako court were suits to recover bridewealth after divorce. Given the barriers against divorce due to the requirement to repay bridewealth, what can the court records tell us about who was responsible for bridewealth payments following marriage breakdown?

Of the many possible causes of divorce, I will examine three contexts in order to examine the assignment of responsibility for the repayment of bridewealth: upon the death of a spouse, when the wife was abandoned by her husband, and when either the wife or the husband requested divorce. Custom, as the Gumbu administrator acknowledged, was an expansive domain where rules were inexact and where individual interests shaped its expressions. The elasticity of "custom" permitted its accommodation to changing circumstances, as in response to the increasing value of bridewealth transfers. While the cases used here reflect practices only during a brief seven-year period, they provide precious detail on actual practices, which seem to conform broadly to "custom" but reveal significant differences in patterns of agency.

Death, except by one's own hand, cuts a broad swathe through all populations. It provides a good entry point into the discussion of bridewealth recovery because it does not appear to muddy the perspective with the troubling issues of agency. Bridewealth was the transfer of value between kinship groups surrounding marriage and residence patterns. According to the ethnographies, the death of a wife obligated the wife's kin to replace the deceased woman. The same would prevail in principle if the wife proved to be infertile, which was akin to a form of social death.[44] This was the case in Bouguni, where several cases involved the replacement of deceased or infertile wives with another sister.[45] Where bridewealth had come to replace the exchange of sisters or daughters, then the death of a wife set in motion the return of bridewealth. The court records are too brief to extract from them the sense of grief that would have followed the death of Ayoua Diara, who died in childbirth. Nevertheless, her husband, Djeli Dembele, was in court to demand the return of bridewealth transferred to her family. The court ruled that Ayoua Diara's father must return the bridewealth.[46] The principle of the return of bridewealth following the death of the wife was maintained in the appeal to the case brought by Makan Kasse against Ticoura Coulibaly. Makan Kasse claimed that he should recover bridewealth since his wife had died while back at her father's house.[47] Usually more complex and thus more interesting are cases involving the death of the husband. I deal with levirate in greater detail in Chapter 8, but I will preview the problem here because bridewealth lay at the core of widow inheritance disputes as well.

Marriage, as we have discussed, involved fairly significant transfers of value from the groom's kin to the bride's kin. Bambara and Malinke practiced a form of levirate, in which the wife became part of the "wealth" inherited by her husband's kin following his death. A widow would likely find herself becoming a new wife of her husband's brother, his father, or even his son by another wife, although never her own son.[48] A fairly simple levirate case was heard in Bouguni on 17 March 1910, when Moro Coulibaly went to court to force the return to his home of his deceased brother's wife, Masseui Dembele, who had returned to live with her brother. Moro, no doubt, also wanted to claim Masseui Dembele's four children. The court ordered Masseui Dembele to return to Moro Coulibaly.[49]

Widows did not always go willingly into the homes of their deceased husband's kin. Had they done so, there would not have been any levirate cases at all. The following case indicates clearly the widow's efforts not to live with her deceased husband's brother. "Zan Doumbia inherited Fene Kone, the wife of his deceased brother. She lived with Zan until last year, when she left with her three children. Zan Doumbia requests that she and the three children return. Marriage [he argued] had been conducted by the exchange of wives, following Bambara custom." Exchange of wives also meant that there was no obvious bridewealth to return. The court ordered that the widow and her three children return to Zan Doumbia's home. However, the court provided Fene Kone, the unhappy widow, with an option. She could return her children to the plaintiff and be separated from him (and them). Fene Kone was not pleased with this judgment and filed an appeal with the district tribunal. At the appeal hearing, Fene Kone claimed that her marriage to Zan Doumbia's brother was not formalized, because there was no transfer of bridewealth. Under questioning (which the reader of the case does not see), Fene Kone "acknowledges that her family received a sister from Doumbia's family in exchange for her. This was legitimate Bambara custom." The district administrator was responsible for a court that was charged with applying custom. Hence, the court upheld the lower court's decision and ordered "Zan Doumbia to take the children, [even if] Fene Kone refuses to return to him."[50]

Levirate was not, however, recognized by Islamic law, even if local practices sometimes condoned it. Muslim widows could use Islamic prohibitions against levirate to secure their separation from their husbands' kin. Nano Cisse and Nale Bari, widows of the deceased Koni Kamite, refused to live with Koni Kamite's brother and heir. Moreover, they refused to release their children to Kano Ba, the paternal uncle, because he was an animist. The two widows claimed that allowing their children to live with animists was against their faith. The tribunal may have been sympathetic to the widow's argument except for the fact, as it was discovered in the court, that Koni Diara, their deceased husband, had also been an animist. The tribunal argued that "custom was not violated" because their husband had been animist and that "following custom, children are placed under the guardianship of the eldest of the family." The court did not, however, force the widows to live with Kano Kamite.[51]

Coincident with the hardening of the courts to the wishes of women seeking divorce as I have discussed in Chapter 5, the rulings regarding levirate claims moved against women in the Bamako provincial tribunal in 1912. Of the levirate cases, 75 percent (8 cases) heard before 1912 were ruled partially or completely in favor of women. By partially, I mean that widows were not obligated to return to their deceased husband's kin. In 1912, the Bamako court was hearing twice as many levirate cases (15 cases) than it had in the previous seven years, and 73 percent were being ruled in favor of male plaintiffs (11 cases) claiming their rights to widows.

Even as the courts were hardening their attitudes to widows who did not want to live with their husband's kin, the courts were often willing to recognize divorce as an option to unhappy widows. In Bamako, three of the four cases ruled in favor of widows in 1912 all hinged upon the willingness to return bridewealth. In one case, the father of the widow agreed to return the bridewealth; in two other cases, the widows themselves were willing to return the bridewealth in order to secure their divorce. For example, the widow Initio Ouattara refused to live with Manion Diara, the heir to her deceased husband. Manion Diara agreed to accept the divorce as long as Initio Ouattara reimbursed the bridewealth. Initio Ouattara offered a cow, a goat, and Fr 27.50 as the value of her bridewealth. Manion Diara accepted the offer and the court gave the widow two months to complete the transfer.[52] Initio Ouattara's offer to return the value of the bridewealth her family had received for her marriage is illustrative of the capacity women had to use their own wealth to overcome the bridewealth-return barrier to divorce. As the economy of the region began to expand in the early years of the century, women increasingly had access to income and property. As we shall see the next section (Women's Agency in Bridewealth Recovery), wives and widows turned increasingly to their own property to end marriages they no longer wanted. But not all ruptures of marriages required that women draw on their own resources to extricate themselves. The following section examines the disposition of women seeking divorce in abandonment cases and how the courts ruled in terms of bridewealth recovery.

Abandonment

Abandonment occurred when either the husband or the wife left the conjugal home and provided neither news of their whereabouts nor, in the case of husbands, subsistence for their wives and children at home. Abandonment was almost always an unambiguous cause for divorce, because it ruptured the fundamental "moral economy" of the marriage contract between spouses. Husbands and wives were usually willing to remain together as long as they felt that their partners were upholding their share of the gender-specific tasks necessary for the survival of the household. Because men had more geographical mobility than women, not surprisingly, women constituted two-thirds of the plaintiffs in abandonment cases. Most were like Dicoumba Keita, who went to court to seek a divorce because "her husband is absent for two and a half years and refuses to send money necessary for the family" or Ma Silla, who sought a divorce because her husband had disappeared three years ago.[53] The court ruled in favor of the plaintiffs' requests and granted them divorces. Abandoned wives usually represented themselves in court. Occasionally, male guardians represented abandoned wives.

Because the abandonment of a wife fractured the moral economy of the marriage, the courts were initially willing to grant wives their requests for divorce without conditions. Beginning in 1908 in Bamako and in 1909 in Segu, however, the courts began to tighten the rules for divorce on the bases of alleged abandonment. Kourabe Coulibaly came to court to have her marriage to Fode Sidibe annulled because the latter had gone to the Côte d'Ivoire four years ago and had not been heard from since. Whereas in previous cases of abandonment of this nature, the court ruled quickly in favor of the plaintiff; in Kourabe Coulibaly's case, it granted a delay of six months to the plaintiff's request, pending, we can assume, efforts to contact Fode Sidibe.[54] Abandoned wives often were back in court when the waiting period had ended. Fatimata Diara was back in court after the year delay imposed by the court to claim her divorce from her missing husband. Fatimata Sako, accompanied by her father, Sina Sako, was back following the six months delay ordered by the court in their case against her husband, who had left without word three years ago. "They asked for a divorce six months ago and the court imposed a delay before pronouncing the divorce. They now want the divorce." In Fatimata Diara's case, the court granted her a final divorce without stipulating the need to repay the bridewealth. In the Fatimata Sako case, the court granted the divorce, but ruled that should the husband return within one year, the bridewealth of Fr 140 must be returned. If the husband failed to return within one year, the husband forfeited the bridewealth, "which will be acquired by the wife."[55] Wives in their second or subsequent marriages often received the bridewealth given by their husbands, which helps account partially for the numbers of female plaintiffs in bridewealth cases.

The Segu court's disposition in abandonment cases was slightly different from its Bamako counterpart. The Segu court applied a rough formula of a moral economy of the household when confronting the recovery of bridewealth. Mama Fane returned to the Segu court on 11 September 1907 following a mandated three month waiting period to demand once again a divorce from her husband, Oumarou Kamite, who had been missing for the past three years. She stated that no word from the husband had been received. The court ruled in favor of Mama Fane's request for a divorce without reimbursement of bridewealth and left the custody of the children with their mother until the return of their father. In ruling that Mama Fane did not have to repay the bridewealth, the court was arguing that bridewealth had served as a substitute for the subsistence that the husband should have provided.[56] By 1909, the Segu courts were still applying the moral economy formula, although it now insisted that the abandoned wives return the bridewealth less the cost of subsistence for the years in which the husband was absent.[57]

The Bamako court's jurisprudence regarding the recovery of bridewealth was slightly different from that of Segu. Up to 1911, it ordered the return of bridewealth only when husbands brought suits against their wives for abandonment. Indeed, up to 1911, 79 percent of the abandonment cases resulted in a simple divorce verdict. Divorce was linked to the recovery of bridewealth in only 6 of the 28 abandonment cases that resulted in divorce rulings (only 1 case up to 1911 resulted in a postponement). The court's disposition toward women in abandonment cases changed in 1911, which coincided also with the increase in numbers of abandonment cases brought by husbands against their wives. This increased incidence of men using the courts to recover bridewealth from runaway wives in 1911 and 1912 can be clearly seen in Table 6.3 tracing the incidence of bridewealth disputes in Bamako.

Abandonment cases brought by husbands differed from return cases discussed more fully in Chapter 5. In these return cases (referred to as marriage cases in Chapter 5), husbands used the courts to force the return of their runaway wives. In abandonment cases, husbands did not want their wives to return, but wanted a clean separation. Such was the case that Digui Diallo brought against his wife, who had abandoned the conjugal home and committed adultery. Digui Diallo told the court that his wife refused to return home and he wanted a divorce. The court granted his request.[58] Whereas wives' abandonment suits against their husbands were distributed throughout the court record, husbands' suits against their wives for abandonment were concentrated in 1911 and 1912. The cases brought by husbands in these two years

Figure 6.3 Bridewealth Disputes, Bamako, 1905–1912, n = 101

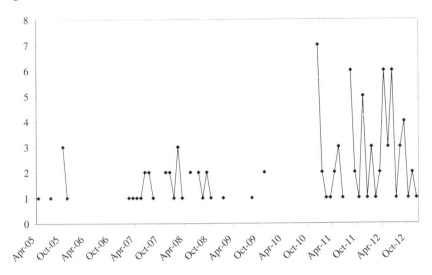

Source: ANM 2 M 104/105

constituted fully half of all the suits brought by husbands for abandonment. The pattern of increasing male use of the courts in domestic disputes after 1910 is congruent with evidence discussed in Chapter 5. Equally interesting is the disposition of the verdicts linking divorces to the recovery of bridewealth. More than half the cases that linked divorce to the recovery of bridewealth occurred in 1911.

In general, if cause was found with the husband's claim, then the courts ordered the wife to repay the bridewealth. Consistent with its recognition of the moral economy of the household, if the court found fault with the husband who had abandoned his family, and if no news had arrived following the delay introduced in the period after 1908, the court ruled, as in the case brought by Aissata Sy against her husband Amadou Tangana, "divorce is pronounced against the husband and Aissata is not responsible for the reimbursement of bridewealth."[59]

From the standpoint of the social history of households, the court record provides some fascinating clues regarding both claims on bridewealth and the responsibility for returning bridewealth. The following section examines the issue of the wife's responsibility for repayment of bridewealth following the breakdown of marriage.

WOMEN'S AGENCY IN BRIDEWEALTH RECOVERY

Early colonial and postcolonial ethnographies portray marriage as a set of relationships between male household heads in which the bride and groom had little choice. Most also identify the transfer of bridewealth as a significant barrier to the rupture of marriages, because the father or guardian had little opportunity to accumulate the wealth received. He was under considerable pressure to put that wealth back in social streams thus providing wives for his younger brothers and sons. Rather than return the bridewealth of an unhappily married daughter, according to the 1909 Gumbu report on custom, the household head beat her for disobedience and sent her back to her husband. This was custom as represented by the elderly male informants most administrators and ethnographers consulted. The actual practice of the courts where divorce and bridewealth cases were heard, however, indicates that practice was considerably different. The most significant wedge in the apparent architecture of patriarchy and female powerlessness was women's willingness and abilities to repay the bridewealth themselves.

The court records for civil cases heard at the provincial courts are sparse at best and the verdicts are usually noted in the passive voice or with an indeterminate subject. For those of us interested in agency, such language is unfortunate. Most of the judgments in successful divorce cases were noted simply that "divorce is pronounced." Such judgments (49% in Bamako and 41% in Segu) made no mention of bridewealth. Can we assume that because bridewealth was not mentioned in the judgment that none was required following the pronouncement of divorce? Unfortunately, no, negative evidence of this nature is not sufficient to determine causality and consequence. On the other hand, the court rendered a second type of judgment that indicated the repayment of bridewealth by adding a subordinate clause, but most court clerks unfortunately rendered these judgments in the passive voice as well and thus foreclosed a determination of responsibility: "divorce is pronounced and bridewealth is to be returned." The court clerk failed to indicate whose responsibility it was to repay the bridewealth. Such judgments appeared in 31 percent of the cases in Bamako divorce cases and 18 percent in those from the Segu court. The difference between these two judgments suggests that recovery of bridewealth was not part of the types of judgments in the first type of ruling, but was in the second because it was mentioned. Again, we can not assume this to be the case because the factual weakness of negative evidence.

In 41 percent of the cases in Segu and in only 20 percent of the cases in Bamako, the court record clearly indicates responsibility for the repayment of bridewealth. The logic behind the ethnographic studies of marriage would suggest that household heads, as the patriarchs spinning the webs of social relationships between kinship groups and as those who benefited from the original bridewealth transfers, were ultimately those responsible for the repayment of bridewealth. However, male household heads or other relatives were named defendants responsible for the repayment of bridewealth in only 1 percent of the judgments in Bamako and 2 percent in Segu. In contrast, wives were the named defendants in 15 percent of the total judgments in Bamako and 30 percent in Segu. An additional 4 percent of the judgments in Bamako and 9 percent in Segu ruled that either no bridewealth be returned or only a fraction of the original value be returned. In some cases, the judgments were recorded in the passive voice; in others, wives were held either responsible or freed from their responsibility to return the bridewealth. In the judgments where responsibility to repay bridewealth was indicated, wives were responsible in 79 percent of the cases in Bamako and 74 percent of those in Segu. This evidence clearly suggests that the financial responsibility for ending marriages during the period under study fell disproportionately on women. In Segu, the judgments ordering women to repay bridewealth are distributed throughout the record from 1905 to 1912. All the judgments in divorce cases in 1910, 1911, and 1912 identified wives as the parties responsible for the return of bridewealth or ruled that no or only partial bridewealth be returned. In Bamako, a tiny number of rulings against wives appear in 1905, 1908, and 1909; none against wives appear in 1907 and 1910. However, the numbers of judgments against wives for repayment of bridewealth increased significantly in 1911 and 1912. Increased judgments against wives in 1911 and 1912 in the Bamako court is consistent as well with the trends in judgments against women in that court more generally.

Faced with a judgment ordering them to repay the bridewealth that their fathers, brothers, uncles, or other male guardians probably accepted at the time of their marriage, divorced wives could approach their male guardians for help. Few women would find help there. Instead, wives could draw on their own personal wealth or forge new relationships with men who would transfer bridewealth to the woman's former husband. Most of the court records indicate summarily the wife's responsibility to repay the bridewealth. Because of the emergence of new forms of property and a booming regional economy in which women's work had increasing value, women could accumulate considerable wealth. Women with access to their own wealth may well have used it to free themselves from unhappy marriages.

Divorced women could also negotiate a new marriage. Second or subsequent marriages often provided women with more choice of partners, and the wife's new lover might provide bridewealth thus facilitating both the judgment for the recovery of bridewealth and the legitimation of the second marriage. Such was the situation when Fako Kouma sued his former wife to recover bridewealth. The court ordered Soutoura Diabite to repay the Fr 200 bridewealth. As stated in the court, Soutoura Diabite's new husband, Paul Diop, "is working to repay the [first] husband. He will pay Fr 50 this month and then Fr 15 installments until completed."[60]

A slightly different variant of the same set of strategies employed by women to escape from unhappy marriages was that used by Tene Sidibe. Tene Sidibe had been engaged to marry Boa Kamara by her father, who had already accepted the bridewealth. Tene Sidibe, however, refused to marry him and when brought to court by her aggrieved fiancé, she pledged that as soon as she found a husband she would have him transfer the bridewealth to Boa Kamara.[61] Drawing on her own financial resources or by seeking a husband more of her own choosing, a woman could escape marriages arranged for her. I develop this argument more fully in Chapter 7. The court record thus provides evidence that forces us to fundamentally reappraise the model of a supremely powerful male patriarch overseeing a complex, multigenerational yet harmonious household. The rupture of marriage by divorce, abandonment, or death not only led to disputes over bridewealth, but also over the custody of children.

BRIDEWEALTH AND THE CUSTODY OF CHILDREN

Delafosse attributed the ubiquity of polygyny (he actually uses the vaguer term polygamy) in the Soudan to the African's primary occupation as an agriculturalist. The African, therefore, "needs many arms, and so it follows that children are for him a source of wealth."[62] Precisely because children were a source of wealth, marital instability translated directly into conflicts over custody of children. The Bamako administrator noted in 1909 that "parents, particularly those belonging to the Bambara race, fiercely dispute after divorce or the death of one of the spouses the questions of guardianship and custody."[63] One of the central functions of bridewealth was the transfer of rights of unborn children from the mother's kin to that of the father. Relationships between men and women that resulted in children but which were not regularized by bridewealth were exactly those that produced the heated disputes the Bamako administrator identified.

Delafosse's quote about children being a source of wealth had at least two dimensions, although he only seemed to recognize one. He saw children as sources of extra labor on the fields and in the homes. Children were clearly a source of joy, a means of reproducing the community, and a source of labor to assist both the male household head and the women of the household in their domestic duties. What he did not recognize was that girls were a source of wealth precisely in terms of their potential to secure goods, cash, and services in the form of bridewealth payments.

In reflecting on the relatively high incidence of civil cases regarding custody of children, the administrator of Sikasso in 1911 argued that the

> disputes surrounding the reclaiming of children have as their source the custom that permits the wife to freely abandon the conjugal dwelling and to take her young children with her. The husband, most of the time, leaves the girls with their mothers until they have reached a certain advanced age and only then does he reclaim them. The mother opposes their departure and in

many cases the girls, used as they are, to living in the household of their mother, also refuse to leave. This situation gives rise to problems without end.[64]

Only rarely, however, did the wishes of the mothers and children influence the decisions taken by the African magistrates of the provincial courts.

On 12 July 1907, Faraba Taraore of Bamako district sued for the recovery of his children. Taraore's wife had apparently left him, taken her children, and moved back to her father. There is a hint in the record that Taraore's wife had left because he had been away from the household ("en raison de ses absences"). His wife had subsequently died, although it is not clear how long she had been dead before Taraore introduced his case. Her children were raised by their maternal grandfather, the deceased mother's father. But now Taraore wanted his children back. The court agreed and ordered that Taraore's children be returned to him.[65] Despite the fact that Taraore had not taken any responsibility in providing for his wife and his children, the court ruled in his favor because he had obviously paid bridewealth and the children thus belonged to him.

In situations where bridewealth or other modes of formally recognizing a marriage were not adequately completed, then the custody of children often remained with mother's kin group. Extramarital affairs were a common feature of marriages where women had little choice in marriage arrangements. Aggrieved husbands could sue the adulterer for damages, as discussed in Chapter 3. Sometimes, however, adulterers sought custody of the children they had fathered. This was the case that Dielimori Coulibaly brought against Lamine Konare. Coulibaly was in court to secure the custody of his daughter, "born of his relations with the woman named Dicouia Diakite." Konare did not dispute Coulibaly's paternity, but argued that he had raised the child to the present and as the "representative of the family of the husband of Diecouia Diakite, the child should belong to him." The court ruled in the Konare's favor.[66] In the case of an adulterous relationship, the child belonged to the husband's kin regardless who the father actually was.

Adultery was only one variant of such informal relationships. The Sikasso administrator described a common form of temporary union in his district, but his particular interest was on the disposition of the children born of these unions. He reported in 1911 on what he saw as a common trend with inverted domestic roles. "It often happens that a woman claims the child that she has had with a man following temporary unions (*relations passagères*). This child belongs to the mother following the custom, but often she frees herself from the care of raising her child by leaving him with her lover and does not reclaim the child until he is of an age to render her service."[67] The Sikasso case appears to be a mirror image of the Tanaore case from Bamako, where the father, who had paid bridewealth, sought to recover his children when they could render service to him. The central differences between the two cases were the transfers of bridewealth and the gender of the caregiver.

Because of marital instability, the frequency of informal domestic relationships, and the value of children, child custody disputes were "without end." The handful of cases presented here, however, point to the broader custom surrounding child custody and often the timing of child custody cases in the life cycle of the child. First, even if cases where paternity might be uncertain or certainly not the husband's, custody was attributed to the husband of a formal marriage in which bridewealth had been transferred. Second, control over children became a dispute only when the child was ready to "provide some services," whether in the form of labor or as a repository of exchange value in the form of a girl's sexual, domestic, and reproductive services. Third, child custody disputes were also related to the social consequences of the end of slavery. Child custody disputes in Bouguni, home to many of the freedmen and women who left their masters in the years after 1905, constituted 28 percent of the total number of cases filed with the provincial court. Marriages were also unstable, composing 32 percent of the disputes heard in Bouguni. What is also intriguing is that 73 percent of all the child custody cases heard in Bouguni took place in 1910. I do not have enough data on the context in Bouguni to explain why child custody cases clustered around 1910. Bouguni was, however, the destination of many freed slaves who returned from Gumbu in 1908 and 1909. The appearance of child custody cases in 1910 could, therefore, reflect the difficulties freed men and women had in sustain-

Figure 6.4 Child Custody Disputes, Bouguni, 1905–1912, n = 49

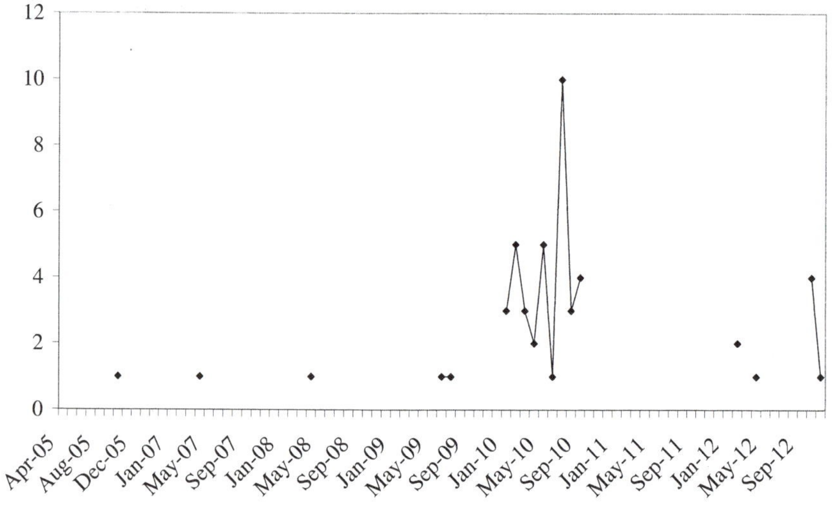

Source: ANM 2 M 110

ing marriages during these turbulent years immediately following the end of slavery.[68]

The disposition of the courts in child custody cases hinged upon evidence of the regularization of marriage through the completion of bridewealth. If bridewealth was transferred, even if only partially, then the courts generally ruled in favor of the male claimant. Breastfeeding infants remained with their mothers until they were four or five.[69] Freedwomen actually benefited from the fact that few slave marriages involved formal bridewealth transfers: female slaves usually gained custody of their children following the rupture of the informal marriage. The Koutiala administrator noted that many child custody cases have their origins in "the former state of slavery, where a couple is married without other formalities. From this union issue one or more children. Upon emancipation, each person has freedom of action. The women often refused to deliver the children and kept them. This gave rise to numerous disputes."[70] Kelebana Diara and Kouma Fane had two children while they were slaves. They were not formally married. When slavery ended, Kouma Fane took the children and left her slave husband. In 1911, Diara was in court to seek custody of children. The court ruled in favor of Kouma Fane and ordered that the children remain with their mother.[71] The lack of formal marriage while slaves also hindered Kalfa Toure's claims for the custody of the three daughters he had with Fatima Fofana. The court awarded custody to the mother.[72] Sometimes slave women left without their children only to try to recover them later. This was the case on 14 October 1912, when Guine Kamite brought a case against Lahi Koita, her slave "husband." Kamite argued in court that while she was a slave, her master had forced her to live with Lahi Koita, another slave. They had children. In his defense, Koita claimed that they were regularly married, but he had no proof to offer. Nor could he recall whether any bridewealth had actually been paid. In absence of proof, the court ruled in favor of Guine Kamite and ordered that she be given custody of the children.[73]

Occasionally, slave parents went to court to recover children retained by their former masters. In a case heard before the Jenne native court, a freed man accused his former master of taking his children under the guise of being their grandfather. The former slave did not convince the court, which ruled against him. He then appealed the case and the administrator ruled in his favor.[74] Leaving children behind as freed men and women fled appears to have been common, especially in Gumbu during the height of the slave exodus. The Gumbu administrator regretted "how little attached the native woman is to her husband and his family. Following the exodus of the slaves, many among them do not fear abandoning their children to their husbands who wish to remain in the region as they seek to return to the homelands."[75] The administrator's comments reflected his views on the sanctity of marriage, but the reality of marriage in the French Soudan was that if bridewealth transfers had been made, then the mother had little claim on her children. The administrator may have been describing marriages between female slaves and their masters, otherwise freed women would have had a better claim on the custody of their children. Clearly, the end of slavery provided opportunities for freed women to define their own futures, although sometimes this meant painful choices of leaving children behind.

Marriage practices, marital instability, and child custody issues often grated against French administrators' sense of justice and equity. The Koutiala administrator railed against the custom of exchange marriages, which he admitted were disappearing, but which nonetheless contradicted French concepts of humanity. Bridewealth as well as exchange marriages, he suggested, were evidence of "faits de traite," the persistence of the slave trade, which had been declared illegal in December 1905.[76] Governor-general Ponty reprimanded the Koutiala administrator for suggesting that the provincial tribunal be more activist in shaping African marriages in order to bring them closer to French "practices of humanity."

Despite Ponty's concern that changing custom would unleash potentially serious social disruption, such tinkering over child custody issues did occasionally take place. The following case from Sokolo district in 1911 reveals a willingness on the part of the French administrator to intervene and overturn a provincial tribunal ruling on custom that he felt was contradictory to French concepts of civilization. The administrator's actions in this case is instructive because the case came under his jurisdiction as head of the district tribunal, which heard appeals from the lower court.

Among the cases dealing with matrimonial questions, the district tribunal has decided to act, in order to safeguard the principles of civilization, and to overturn the judgment rendered by the *tribunal de province* in conforming to custom. Here is the summary of the case: the husband, a native from Bouguni, Sooule Sangare, requested from the court of the first instance a ruling conferring to him the custody of two of his deceased brother (Bakary Assa Sangare)'s children and, in consequence, requiring that their mother, Tene Taraore, deliver the children to him. In strictly applying custom, the tribunal acceded to this request, despite Tene Taraore's supplications. The latter decided to appeal the ruling and, following an in depth examination of the issues, the district tribunal annulled the decision of the magistrates of the lower court based upon the following reasons.

The district tribunal acknowledged that both parties were of animist status and that custom would apply as long as it was not contrary to the principles of civilization. Acknowledging also that according to one interpretation of custom, the children of a deceased animist are to be confided to the brothers of the deceased, as Soaule Sangare argued, but, in considering the other part, that the woman, Tene Taraore, was after the declaration of those of the community, an honorable mother and, despite a second marriage, has done her best to raise her two children with any contribution from Sooule Sangare since the death of her husband, Bakary Asdsa Sangare, more than one year now.

And because Sooule Sangare has the intention, if he receives the custody of Sadio and Ya Sangare, to take them back to Bouguni, this would lead to a definitive separation of the mother from her children, ages thirteen and seven, who still need their mother's care.

In addition, the elder child, Sadio, declared strongly that he wished to stay with his mother; the second, the younger Ya, is considered too young to have an opinion.

Because of these reasons, [the court ruled] that it would be inhumane to separate Sadio and Ya Sangare from their mother, Tene Taraore, and thus declares that the provincial tribunal had made application [in its original ruling] to a custom contrary to our principles of civilization and thus overturn the judgment rendered by that court on 4 May 1911. [The district tribunal] confers the custody of Sadio and Ya Sangare to Tene Taraore, but adds that Sooule Sangare has the right to supervise their upbringing and the right to visit as often as he judges useful.[77]

In applying his own cultural sensibilities to the rights of children and mothers, the Sokolo administrator was directly contravening the principles of respecting indigenous customs of the 1903 legal systems. A similar subjectivity was evidenced in a report from Bamako in 1912. Here, too, the French administrator was using the courts in an instrumental fashion to engineer a fundamental change in Bambara society by demanding that the magistrates begin to take into consideration "individual" rights and the rights of children.

Discrete counsels to disputants are given daily through the intermediary of the tribunal in order to modify the custom on this point and to induce an evolution of Bambara society in the direction of a more just conception of individual liberty and the rights of children. The results will certainly not be immediate, but the native judges are convinced that the utility of their advice in the present state of the organization of the family will bear fruit in the following generation.[78]

The Sokolo and Bamako administrators' expectations that parents would increasingly appreciate their children as individuals and not merely as units of labor or exchange confronted the tendency within the courts to rule cases in favor of husbands and household heads. These rulings supported the principle of bridewealth as the foundation of marriage transfers. The French administration revisited the issue of marriage and bridewealth under the Popular Front government and actually introduced legislation to limit bridewealth and require female consent in marriage.[79]

Despite the property bias of bridewealth transfers, husbands and household heads did not reign supreme. The period after 1905 witnessed profound changes in the meaning and nature of property. Women participated in these changes and women's abilities to end marriage that they did not like rested in part on their abilities to control sufficient property to return the bridewealth that had been received for their marriage. The next chapter examines some of the new forms of property and the new meanings of property that emerged particularly after 1905 and that can be seen from an examination of the court records.

7

CONFLICTS OVER PROPERTY

The establishment of the new native courts in the Soudan coincided with the linked sets of transformations set in motion by the consolidation of French conquest in the 1890s and with the end of slavery beginning around 1905. These linked sets of transformations ushered in a period in which men and women, masters and slaves, elders and youth redefined their relationships to each other and to wealth. As Africans struggled with one another in the process of defining individual and collective wealth and the nature of obligations both within and outside the household, the French tried to make sense of African customs as part of their efforts to regularize and control the practices of power.

This chapter examines the ways in which the end of slavery, as discussed in Chapter 4, contributed to new forms of investments and to new forms of property relationships established through these new investments. Women were active participants in this new economy. Pursuing the lead taken in Chapter 6, this chapter examines women's property and the ways in which women sought to protect their property within the context of marriage. Women's property was central also to their strategies to leave marriages that they did not want. Women needed access to wealth in order to return the bridewealth that their guardians had received. This chapter also examines conflicts over "old property," particularly the notion of communal or household property. These conflicts demand that we reappraise the nature of the relationships between individual members of households and the household head. Distinctions between household and individual property are particularly important in many of the court cases dealing with property disputes.

HOUSEHOLD AUTHORITY AND THE DOUBLE CONCEPTION OF PROPERTY

Maurice Delafosse was the architect of the notion of a distinctive Soudanese civilization, which drew on a set of core ideas about property and legal relationships borrowed from contemporary European thinking about

Roman law and French ethnographic ideas of the bounded nature of African communities. For his synthesis of customary law, Delafosse drew on the 1897 and 1908–1909 surveys of African custom that first Lieutenant-governor Trentinian and then Lieutenant-governor Clozel ordered. The intellectual orientation of these questions was drawn from contemporary continental historical and ethnographical thinking about early societies and kingdoms and about the stages of development, which had only recently found a new home in the emerging field of colonial sociology.[1] Delafosse used the results of these surveys in his course on African customs at the École Coloniale and in his book, *Haut-Sénégal-Niger*. Delafosse's project played an important role in French colonial ideologies and debates about African societies and especially the stability in property relations, because this was supposed to be a guide for administrators in the application of customs.

In the final volume of his magisterial historical and cultural overview of the new colony of Haut-Sénégal-Niger, Maurice Delafosse reflected on the idea of "civilization" and its applicability to French West Africa:

> If, by "civilization," one understands the state of social, moral, and material culture to which important nations of Europe and America have arrived, it is certain that one can not consider the natives of the Sudan as part of what one commonly calls "the civilized world". . . . If one speaks of "civilizations" and not "the Civilization"—ours—one is obliged to admit that to have a culture and a social state different from ours, the natives of the Sudan do not have less [claim on the concept of] civilizations, which are worth the effort to study and describe.[2]

By broadening the concept of civilization, Delafosse engaged in a process of constructing difference. Delafosse's Soudanese civilizations were filtered through a cognitive model of French society, but were defined by their opposition to it.[3] They were also shaped by prevailing French colonial and ethnographic ideas about "race," categories of religion, and by a materialist conception of livelihood.[4] He identified three Soudanese civilizations: pastoralists (who were linked to the white races), Muslims (who were only marginally influenced by Islamic law), and the vast majority of settled agriculturalists (who remained animists).

Although not formally trained as an ethnographer, Delafosse was a product of the École de Langues Orientales and well versed in the French orientalist-Maghrebian school. At 20, Delafosse volunteered for a stint in Cardinal Lavigerie's Institut des Frères Armés and served briefly in the Algerian campaign against Arab slave traders.[5] He was thus conversant with contemporary European ethnographic efforts at categorization of human societies, of which his "civilization" was a variant. Such ethnographic categorization was an important part of the imperial experience of "ordering" the colonial landscape into spaces and behavior recognizable to Europeans.[6]

By 1912, when *Haut-Sénégal-Niger* was published, Delafosse was one of the undisputed scholar-administrators of French West Africa. Indeed, Lieutenant-governor Clozel commissioned Delafosse to synthesize the vast and untidy evidence collected in 1909–1910 regarding African customary law and history in the Soudan.[7] Volume III of *Haut-Sénégal-Niger* was Delafosse's intellectual effort to distill out of the detail and variety of African customs a framework to help administrators in their oversight over the new colonial legal system and in their role as magistrates in the district level appeals courts.

For Delafosse, the unity of his Soudanese civilizations was that "the guiding principles of customary law are the same; the organization of property, the organization of the family, the conception of justice, and the state of social and political development are everywhere very analogous at the base and hardly vary in form."[8] Because of the way Delafosse dismissed the influence of Islam ("it is very rare that native Muslims have adapted at least in its integrity Koranic law"[9]) and because of his search for deep commonalities, it is not surprising that he found only *one* primary "native civilization" of the Soudan: the settled community of farmers.

Among these farming communities, the deep reef of commonality was found in the organization of property, called *le régime foncier.* "The customs of the natives of the Soudan appear to differ least in regard to the organization or property than in regard to other branches of civil law, for example, inheritance, marriage, etc."[10] According to Delafosse's historical sociology, the organization of property varied with the nature of the soil and with the means by which it was utilized. Besides the gathering mode, which Delafosse relegated to colonies deep in the forest zone, the organization of property in the Soudan was characterized by the division between the farmer and the pastoralist. Delafosse tempered his ecological determinism with a historical sensibility (volume II of this project was devoted to the rise and fall of Soudanese kingdoms and provided the first precolonial history of the colony). Delafosse was keenly aware how historical processes, especially conquest, had transformed the organization of property rights. Armed conquest established rights superior to those of the first inhabitants, but he remained convinced that the legal and social foundations of the rural order remained stable.

> Despite the nature of political control over territory ("anarchy is relatively unknown in the Soudan"), the organization of property everywhere followed similar principles. The immense majority of the Soudanese constitute, par excellence, a rural and agricultural population. . . . The soil is rapidly depleted and it is necessary for the inhabitants to possess huge expanses in order to relocate their fields. That is why customs have

reserved for the native state or the collective group ownership over all the territory, cultivated or not: if the vast expanses of land are vacant, none is without its master.[11]

Delafosse's historical sociology established a seamless linkage between the *régime foncier* and the *régime politique*. "The soil and all that which is produced naturally is the property of the collectivity represented by its chief, or by the king in polities of the monarchical form." In turn, the chief or the king, whether hereditary or elected, divided the land among the village chiefs, who in turn divided the land among chiefs of families according to the needs of the group.[12]

Delafosse's Soudanese civilization, which rested upon community ownership of land and that tied communities to overarching, but often-distant polities, echoed popular and scholarly perceptions of medieval French customary law.[13] In these terms, land was a collective good and must be used to support the common good. Delafosse may have been influenced by the French legal concept of use rights referred to as *seisin* (or *saisine*). *Seisin* meant possession of land protected by tradition and separate from "ownership." In a medieval French environment of multiple layers of "rights," *seisin* gave priority to the user.[14] Use rights stood in opposition to "private" ownership of land. Delafosse here juxtaposed "traditional" Soudanese to modern French concepts of property. "From the native point of view, it is thus illegal on the part of the French authorities to consider the land the domain of the French state and to offer to private companies or individuals, under the form of concessions, specific parcels of land." The French state cannot cede land in the colonies "without violating the traditional rights of the natives."[15]

Delafosse confounded, however, his simple notion of collective ownership of the land based on common enjoyment of the fruits of the land, by introducing what he called "a double conception of the idea of property." Delafosse's double conception of property separated the land (and its "spontaneous products") from "the product of the labor of man."[16] Although ownership of particular fields was vested in the collectivities, families enjoyed usufruct. "In practice," Delafosse admitted, "long usufruct of a field in the same family becomes almost a veritable property: this usufruct can be inherited; it can be ceded in total or in part by the head of the family to another native; it can be ceded, with certain reservations, for example that the product of fruit trees or the first harvest must remain with the original *usufructier*. But usufruct can not be transferred to a stranger without agreement of the village chief or the chief of the [polity]." Property was not transferred, only rights to use it.[17] Thus, the authority of the village chief or the household head rested upon his abilities to allocate land and to command labor to work it. Yet, individuals as individuals had rights to part of the product of their labor.[18]

It is here, in the tension between the collectivity—in the form of the household head with his ability to allocate land and to command labor from household members—and the individual's rights to the product of his or her labor that Delafosse's "double conception of property" obscures more than it reveals. Delafosse was on the right track, however. There was a profound tension between the collective and the individual, but these tensions rested upon a more complex set of tensions than Delafosse admitted. In his efforts to generate a single Soudanese civilization with deep commonalities, Delafosse could not (or would not) account for significant varieties in the uses to which property was put and to the influences of economic and political change. Instead of a static notion of a "double conception of property," it may be more useful to view the late nineteenth and early twentieth centuries in the Soudan as constituting an economic system in which there were at least two dynamic and changing superimposed systems of production in which the uses of property differed.

I have elsewhere used the notion of superimposed systems of production to interpret changes in the gender property relations within Maraka households. I argued that at the base of the household economy was a system of production designed to maintain the household at a constant level. Under this system, the household head acted as manager of a complex firm, balancing household stocks with subsistence and making strategic investments in kinship and marriage in order to provide for the reproduction of the unit over time. Members of the household, which was often a multigenerational unit, owed their labor to the household head in return for promises of subsistence. The household cultivated sufficient acreage and varieties of crops in anticipation of a "normally" poor harvest, oftentimes reaping significant surplus to ensure survival over periods of drought, for trade, and to provide for marriage costs.[19] Household collectivity rested upon practices of reciprocity. This is more or less consistent with Delafosse's conceptualization of the "Soudanese civilization."

Superimposed on this system of "subsistence" was a system of production designed for commerce and accumulation. This system was marked by efforts to expand production and to accumulate wealth. Slaves, polygyny, and efforts to articulate property rights were associated with it. This system of expanded production often led to conflicts over control over the product of labor and over property rights. These two systems of production (and probably several other variants) could coexist, each waxing or waning in relationship to climate and to the webs of economic relationships stretching through regional economies and into the wider West African subcontinental economy.

Delafosse's "double conception of property," which pitted collective against individual property, provides an entry into the property disputes examined in this chapter. These disputes, however, have to be read against the grain of Delafosse's project. Those men and women who were engaged in challenging others over rights in property were also struggling over the nature of social relationships. This chapter examines conflicts over property that were presented to the *tribunaux de province* between 1905 and 1912. Marriage and bridewealth, of course, should be understood as a set of property transfers and the analytical separation between property and promises on one hand and marriages on the other is arbitrary, because marriages involved transfers of property in social streams between individuals and households linked by promises and bound by property transfers. For the Bamako district, domestic disputes involving marriages and their dissolutions constituted 56 percent of the 928 cases brought before the Bamako provincial tribunal. Disputes over property, loans and contracts constituted 27 percent of the cases. Cases involving disputes over inheritance (see Chapter 8), while clearly linked to households and marriages, were essentially over competing claims to property and divergent paths to accumulation. These cases constituted another 5 percent of the total Bamako cases and together with the other property and contract cases equaled 32 percent of the total litigation. In Segu, cases involving property, loans, and contracts constituted 35 percent of the total litigation. Segu also had a considerably higher proportion of inheritance disputes than Bamako, nearly three times a high and constituting 14 percent of total cases heard.

While smaller in number than marital disputes, cases involving property reflect changes in the constitution of the landscape of social relations following the end of slavery and the consolidation of French colonial rule. Martin Chanock reminds us that disputes over property were not merely about "rights in things, but about relations between people. . . . It is clear that to the people involved [in colonial court cases], at least, that commodity relations were social relations."[20] Moreover, these cases need to be read against French colonial surveys of African custom collected during this period. As I have argued in Chapter 5, these surveys and Delafosse's reading of them in *Haut-Sénégal-Niger* can be seen as an effort to invent a stable African society under the guise of enduring patterns of authority, in which the male household head sat supremely unchallenged at the head of a complex, multigenerational community. Suits by women, younger brothers, and sons provide a very different perspective on the range of relationships established across gender and generations.[21]

THE END OF SLAVERY AND THE EXPANSION OF COMMERCE: NEW PROPERTY AND NEW PROPERTY RELATIONS

Colonial conquest stimulated the regional economy, but not necessarily in ways the French had anticipated. Although French colonial expansion stimulated economic demands for labor and goods, much of the expansion of production in the Soudan from 1890 followed the deep patterns of ecological specialization that had characterized the precolonial continental economy of West Africa. Nonetheless, French conquest created the conditions in which Africans struggled over the nature of productive relationships made possible by the erosion of ethnic boundaries over economic resources and the end of slave labor. The reorganization of access to economic resources was probably the most revolutionary shift during the period under investigation and which the French probably did not fully understand. This reorganization of access to resources is also the most difficult for historians to trace.[22]

As I discussed in Chapter 4, the erosion of the ethnic boundaries around access to resources was linked to changes in the regional political economy. The end of slavery was a vital part of the erosion of ethnic monopolies over resources and accelerated the process. Many freed men and women moved into occupations whose skills they had learned as slaves. Some moved into weaving and dyeing, thus catering to the huge expansion of the market, locally produced cloth.[23] Others moved into commerce and transportation. And still others established themselves as farmers, herders, and fishermen. Some became individual producers; others as service providers. The end of slavery also profoundly transformed the most commonly used forms of capital investment. This point is central to Félix Dubois's 1911 observation quoted in Chapter 4 that with the end of slavery, capital was no longer invested in slaves. Instead, "new economies are constituted. And available funds no longer go into purchases of slaves; the owner is very judiciously advised to place them . . . in livestock."[24]

Livestock was one of the principle exports to neighboring colonies of Senegal, Côte d'Ivoire, and the Gold Coast during the early twentieth century. Herds of cattle, which had been badly depleted by a bovine epizootic in 1891, had by 1905 been reconstituted to a large extent.[25] As capital was steadily invested in livestock, ownership of cattle, sheep, and goats was diversified among all ethnic groups. Investment in livestock emerged as one of the primary forms of capital investment during this period.[26] The monopoly long held by the FulBe and the Maures over livestock ownership was broken, although some FulBe and Maures found themselves providing services as herders for others who owned livestock. Dubois and French administrators on the ground described four important facets to this new economy: first, Africans were now participating in all types of productive activities regardless of ethnic boundaries; second, livestock became an increasingly important part of commerce and a store of wealth; third, owners of livestock often contracted out the care of their animals to those prepared to perform that service; and fourth, men were on the move all over and in the process challenged assumptions about social boundaries and trust.

The expansion of commerce, the opening up of ethnic boundaries over productive resources, and the end of slavery thus contributed to the changing meanings of property, strategies for accumulation, and led to efforts to redefine relationships between mean and women, fathers and sons, and among brothers. The large, multigenerational household became a site for struggles over security and accumulation and between individual interests and collective identity.

Following Martin Chanock, historians of this period of transition must be mindful of the differences between "old" and "new" forms of property. By old property, Chanock has in mind food, cattle, land, people (as in brides, slaves, and pawns) and the kinds of prestige goods that Claude Meillassoux privileged in his structural interpretation of male elders' control over their younger male dependents.[27] New forms of property constituted both new kinds of things, such as imported clothing, bicycles, watches, dishes, money, as well as older forms of property transformed by new contexts. Most evocative of the changing sets of relationships embedded in the new forms of property are the multiplex social relationships stemming from cattle ownership, especially because after 1905 cattle increasingly became the most important source of capital investment. As livestock emerged in 1905 as the primary form of accumulation, and as livestock ownership spread throughout Soudanese society, livestock ownership, its use, and its care became a trouble spot of the new property relations.[28]

DISPUTES OVER LIVESTOCK

Disputes involving livestock appear in the court registers as cases involving the recovery of debts, disputes over property, efforts to recover damages, torts over sales and contracts, and disputes over wages or compensation for services. It is unfortunate that the registers for 1906 have been lost for both Segu and Bamako districts.[29] Given the available data, cases involving livestock were very rare in the 1905 records, but appear with increasing frequency in 1907 and 1908. There was a single livestock case for Bamako in 1905, when Brahima Daode, the owner of a cow sought to recover its value from Nama Darako, the herdsman employed to care for it.[30] In Segu, however, disputes over livestock appear in the fall of 1905 records dealing primarily with claims seeking recovery of damages by cattle to standing crops and in cases involving property rights. For the period 1905 to 1912 taken as a whole, livestock figured centrally in the recovery of debt in 15 percent of the Segu debt cases and 11 percent of those in Bamako. For the same period, damage claims involving livestock constituted 22 percent of damage cases in Segu and 66 percent in Bamako. Livestock also figured prominently in disputes over property: 50 percent of all property disputes in Segu involved livestock and 65 percent of those in Bamako. In cases involving disputes over

Table 7.1 Selected Livestock Prices, 1889–1912

Dates	Types of Livestock		Region	Source
1889	Horses	400-1500F	Middle Niger	Jaime, *Koulikoro*, p. 106
	Oxen	100F		
	Donkeys	70F		
	Sheep	8-10F		
1890			4,500 head of cattle in Bamako district 40-45,000 head of cattle in Macina	Notices historiques, géographiques, Bamako, ANM 1 D 33-1 D 1
1905	Pack oxen	60-70F	Bamako	Enquête sur les productions animales, Bamako, 1905, ANM 1 Q 257
	Ordinary cattle	35-40F		
	Cows of Beledugu	90F		
	Horses	800-1500F		
1905	Ordinary cattle	15-50F	Bandiagara, 60,000 head of cattle in the district	Enquête sur les productions animales, Bandiagara, 1905, ANM 1 Q 257
	Pack oxen	25-100F		
	Cow	30-150F		
1905	Ordinary cattle (zebu)	65F	Segu, 35,000 cattle divided between zebu and mère breeds	Enquête sur les productions animales, Segu, 1905, ANM 1 Q 257
	Ordinary cattle (mère)	50F		
	Milk cow (zebu)	100F		
	Milk cow (mère)	80F		
	Pack oxen (zebu)	90F		
	Pack oxen (mère)	70F		
1909	Ordinary cattle	40-50F	Jenne	Monographie du cercle de Jenne, 1909, ANM 1 D 33-3
1912	Ordinary cattle	35-40F	Interior Delta	Meniaud, *Haut-Sénégal-Niger*, II, 50, 138
	Cows 3 times value of cattle			
	Horses	175-200F		
1912	Ordinary cattle	35-45F	Sokolo, Gumbu, Nioro	Meniaud, *Haut-Sénégal-Niger*, II, 50
	Cows 3 times value of cattle			
1912	Ordinary cattle	40-50F	Bamako, Sikasso, Kita (horses in Banamba)	Meniaud, *Haut-Sénégal-Niger*, II, 50, 138
	Cows 3 times value of cattle			
	Horses	350-1000F		

commercial transfers or sales, livestock appeared in 67 percent of sales cases for Segu but only 17 percent of such cases in Bamako. Contract disputes during this period involved a significant incidence of disputes over livestock: 60 percent of contract disputes in Segu and 41 percent in Bamako.

The incidence of livestock disputes within cases involving property, contracts, and damages are indicative of the struggles surrounding the investment of wealth in new forms that took place after the end of slavery. In Segu, 80 percent of the property cases involving livestock took place in 1907 and 1908, coinciding with the period of accelerated transition following the end of slavery. In Bamako, property disputes appear throughout the records distributed fairly consistently between 1907 and 1912, indicating that livestock remained a consistent, if low-level trouble spot in relationships both within and outside of the household. In contrast, damage claims in Bamako concentrated in the period 1911–1912. In a commercial environment where returns on investment were limited to agricultural labor and profits on successful commercial ventures, livestock provided significant returns as well as significant risks. As a store of value, livestock increased investment through reproduction. Livestock also provided a source of milk and green manure.[31]

Livestock and Property Disputes

In Segu, a father welcomed his daughter into the world by giving her a cow, which he retained as part of his herd. Nineteen years later and now married, Hinna Camara was in court pressing her brother and her uncle to release her share of the herd. Her father had died 15 years earlier ("at the time of Fama Bodian"), when Hinna Camara was too young to manage her share of the inheritance on her own. Three named witnesses testified on behalf of the grown daughter that her cow had been productive and her share of the herd now increased to 18 head of cattle. The court ordered the defendant to give his sister her cattle. Her brother appealed the case, which now involved not only Hinna Camara's livestock by her own cow, but also her share of her father's estate, which was managed by the deceased's brother, her uncle, Gado Bale. The appeals court ordered her brother and uncle to give Hinna Camara 30 head of cattle, of which half were to be breeding stock.[32]

After 15 years, her herd had increased considerably in value. An adult cow had roughly three times the value of an ox (about Fr 80–100 in Segu); at two years, a heifer has 5–6 times the value (Fr 40–50 in Gao) of a newly born calf.[33] The plaintiff's herd had a value of at least Fr 1650, a considerable fortune at the time. Very few Soudanese could accumulate such large herds. More common was the ownership of 10 or fewer cattle.[34] However, given the investment potential of livestock, ownership of fractions of an animal provided a means of entry into the livestock market.

Although the following case derives from an inheritance dispute, it speaks to the issue of the value of even fractions of an animal. On 2 November 1907, Djeneba Togora brought Babile Fane to the Segu tribunal to recover his one-quarter share of a horse his father owned. Togora claimed that Fane had sold the horse, but did not give him the market value of his share. The court ordered Fane to pay the plaintiff 40,000 cowries.[35] Transactions regarding fractions of an animal were also the cause of the case heard in Segu on 23 January 1908. The plaintiff argued that he sold one-half share of his mare to the defendant in exchange for the rights to receive two foals. The plaintiff admitted that he had already received one colt, but it had died two months later. He did not consider that this colt constituted even partial payment of his one-half share, and wanted the court to recognize his claims on two additional colts. The court dismissed his claim, although it did encourage the defendant to honor the remaining promise to deliver the first filly.[36]

Because livestock could be a substantial investment, it was probably not uncommon for kin or friends to purchase shares of livestock together. In 1908, Bakary Kouyate and Soulemane Diabite bought a cow together for Fr 100, each owning half shares. Bakary Kouyate was called up for military service that year and when he returned three years later, he sought out his old friend and his investment. Diabite told him that their original cow had since died. Kouyate wanted his half share of the value of the cow's meat and half the value of the surviving calf. Diabite countered that since he had taken care of the cow for three years, he deserved to be compensated for that labor. Kouyate responded that Diabite's "compensation" was the value of the cow's milk over the past three years. The dispute between two old friends over the terms of their investment found its way to court in Bamako. These arguments were rehearsed in the court, where Diabite continued to claim "compensation" for his caretaking role and Kouyate equally refused. Diabite provided the court with "proof" that the value of the meat and the calf was Fr 172. The court accepted that figure and ruled that Souleymane Diabite was to pay Bakary Kouyate the half-share of the value of the meat and the calf, which was Fr 86. Despite the loss of his original investment, Bakary Kouyate saw his investment increase by 72 percent over three years.[37] Investment in livestock was good, if risky, business.

As part of the webs of relations between kin, friends, and between masters and slaves, livestock were loaned from one household to another. On 20 December 1905, the Segu court heard the plaintiff seek the recovery of his cow lent to the defendant, who claimed that it had died. The defendant brought no proof to his claim and the court ordered him to reimburse the owner with the value of the cow.[38] Cases involving competing claims on cattle held by members of the same household were probably the messiest kinds of livestock disputes. These disputes illuminate specific forms of individual property within the orbit of the household's collective wealth and how these forms of property were tracked by their owners. On 4 October 1911, Neti Soumare sued her own son for the recovery of that seven cattle she claimed were in his herd. Under examination by the judges, they agreed that Neti Soumare's share was actually four cattle, not seven. Her son agreed to return these to his mother.[39] Neti Soumare was not pleased with this ruling and was back in court five weeks later to reclaim the remaining three cattle from her original dispute. This time she was better prepared. She came to court with two witnesses who supported her claim. The court ruled in favor of Soumare's suit and ordered her son to return the three remaining cattle.[40]

Claiming their property in livestock was also part of the difficulties former slaves had in extracting themselves from their masters' household. As we have seen in the case of Gumbu (Chapter 4), loans of goods and livestock between masters and slaves formed dense webs of entanglements that the courts often had to adjudicate. On 23 July 1909, Zele Coulibaly took her former master,

Djounie Kouma, to court to recover what she claimed were her seven cattle, which she had accumulated through her own industry while in captivity. In this case, the plaintiff offered no proof to convince the court of her claims and her case was dismissed. Bani Diara, the former "servant" of Moussa Diara, brought his former master to court on 22 July 1911 with a claim of ownership over five cattle in his master's hands. Three witnesses for the defendant claimed that the cattle actually belonged to him. Two witnesses supported the plaintiff's claim. Faced with the contradictory evidence, the court nonetheless moved to dismiss the case rather than seek to reconcile these competing claims. Noumouke Doumbia, the former slave of Buka Keita, was more successful in his claim to recover 17 cattle that he left in his former master's herd when he fled his master's compound to declare his independence. Doumbia was fortunate to have several supporting witnesses, who were also willing to swear an oath on behalf of his claim. The court ordered the defendant to return 17 cattle to the plaintiff.[41]

Precisely because livestock had become such an important store of wealth and a significant capital investment in the years after the end of slavery, and because they were mobile, livestock were often lost or stolen. Lost or stolen livestock frequently were sold in local markets and wound up in the hands of an innocent buyer brought to court by the original owner. *Caveat emptor* certainly prevailed in the courts of the French Soudan. Boke Sow appeared to be the innocent buyer of a horse, which Samba Barro claimed was stolen. The court ordered Boke Sow to return the property to the plaintiff.[42] Witnesses were often needed to provide the plaintiff with a sufficient cause to seek the recovery of his stolen livestock. This was the situation when Amadou Sako sought the recovery of his cow from Sani Ouele. Witnesses confirmed Sako's claim and the court ordered the hapless Ouele to return the animal.[43] When the reseller of stolen livestock could be identified, then the buyer was urged to seek recovery of his losses from that person. This was the case when Demba Diallo found his stolen cow in the possession of Isa Ndiaye, who claimed that he had bought the animal from Dade Konate. Unless claims of original ownership could be substantiated, then the rights of the purchaser were usually protected.[44] For example, Naturu of Sokolo claimed that several of Seribu Gadiagou's livestock had been stolen from him, but witnesses supported the defendant's claim that he had bought those cattle. Naturu's claim was probably weakened because he could neither prove ownership rights nor that those cattle were stolen from him.[45]

The court often had to wade through what appeared to be opportunistic claims over livestock. Moriba Fofana brought Nanioume Keita to court to claim that with the assistance of Moussa Ture, he had stolen six cattle from him. The defendant, Nanioume Keita, proved to the court that the cattle were actually hers and the court dismissed the case.[46] The court's decision in this case is important for our larger story because it indicates that the court recognized women's rights to own livestock.

Livestock and Damage Cases

Farmers in the sahel and savanna regions of the Middle Niger had long welcomed the dry-season arrival of the large herds of the desert-edge nomads. These herds grazed on the stubble of the cereal crops and in exchange deposited green manure into fields before the planting season. With the arrival of the rains, the nomads led their herds back to pastures of the drier sahel.[47] This was the model of the symbiotic exchange between the desert and the sown, when most of the larger livestock was owned by ethnically bounded groups working their specialized economic niches. Many farmers in the sahel and savanna owned a few goats and sheep to serve the domestic needs of the households. With the increasing investment in livestock and the diffusion of cattle ownership among farmers came a series of unintended consequences, which included increasing conflicts between farmers and herders and contract disputes between the owners of livestock and hired shepherds.

A significant number of the damage cases in Segu stemmed from farmers seeking to recover crops lost to foraging herds. Most of these suits named the herdsmen as defendants and often claimed huge losses. On 23 April 1907, Babile Cooulibaly sued Aliou Diode for damages to his standing crops, which he estimated to be equal to 100 baskets of millet. The plaintiff offered no proof and was not willing to swear an oath to corroborate his claim. The court awarded the plaintiff a mere four baskets of millet.[48] Two months later, the court heard another case for the recovery of damages from a farmer who claimed to have lost 100 *muules* (equal to 250 kilograms) of millet to the herd poorly guarded by Badia Balo. Neither party was prepared to swear an oath on the size of the damages and the court decided on a claim of 40 *muules*.[49] Faced with claims for damages that were often fictitious, the Segu tribunal introduced in August 1907 a "fact-finding committee" that actually went to the plaintiff's fields to ascertain independently the scale of damages. This "committee" reported to the tribunal several times in 1907.[50] By 1908, farmers bringing damage claims against herdsmen increasingly came to court with witnesses to support their claims. An analogous "commission of inquiry" was operating in Bamako crop damage cases in 1912.[51]

As livestock ownership diffused throughout Soudanese society and across the previous ethnic boundaries, farmers often hired herdsmen to watch over their investment. Hired herdsmen had certain occupational risks in regard to their exposure to suits seeking to recover losses. The court record is inconsistent on whether the owners or the herdsmen were responsible when their herds ravaged farmers' fields. For example, when Birama Diara's fields were damaged by herds belonging to Mamadi Diabite and Tonemaka Konate, the court ordered that shares of the damage were the responsibilities of the owners in proportion to their ownership of the herd.[52] When Dumbia Kone sought to recover damages to his fields, he brought the herdsmen Sidi Sow and Baka Barro to court and they were held responsible.[53] The herdsman, N'To Dembele, who was guarding a herd of cattle belonging to "diverse proprietors," was brought to court by four farmers from Segu because he let his herd ravage their fields. After the commission of inquiry examined the evidence, the court ruled that the defendant "must pay Fr. 103 divided among the various plaintiffs."[54] Herdsmen were also responsible for welfare of the livestock under their watch. On 7 February 1908, for example, the owner of several cattle sued his herdsman for the loss of one of his cows, which the plaintiff argued had died due to his herdsman's negligence. The herdsman was forced to pay Fr 65 in compensation.[55] In another case heard by the Bamako tribunal in 1908, the owner sued his herdsman for the value of a cow that ran off from the herd and which the herdsman did not pursue. The shepherd was forced to pay the owner Fr 107.[56] For herdsmen earning perhaps Fr 10 per month, a judgment of this size was ruinous.

Judgments in damage suits for losses to livestock or to crops were sometimes quite high. More common in damage claims for losses to crops, however, were judgments payable in kind, including 8 baskets of millet and 5 baskets of fonio or 40 baskets of cotton and 4 baskets of millet.[57] These damage claims were more or less equivalent to the actual value of the losses incurred. In so doing, the native judges were not applying in a strict sense the French concept of *damages-intérêts,* which empowers judges to award punitive damages on top of actual losses.

Farmers were clearly acting in their rights to bring damage suits against herdsmen for failing to control their herds. However, when a farmer sought to protect his fields, he risked incurring damage claims as well. On 1 July 1908, Bouba Diallo found a herd of cattle grazing on his fields and in the course of protecting his crops, he killed one of the cows. In determining the nature of damages, the Segu tribunal turned to their "experts" whose testimony helped the court reach its decision. The court ordered the farmer to repay the value of the cow less the value of the damages to his crops.[58] The Bamako tribunal often struggled to reconcile the competing damage claims of farmers and livestock owners. Doussa Koro Taraore found several of Diatouru Samake's cattle grazing in his millet fields. In protecting his crops, Taraore killed two cows. The court reached a damage award through its efforts to "conciliate" the two claims, but awarded Samake Fr 180 for the loss of his two cows.[59]

A case heard in Bamako on 12 November 1912 indicated that farmers could insulate themselves from damage claims against destruction of livestock if they had established a history of complaints about crop loss due to marauding livestock. Such was the case when Moussa Sidibe sought compensation from Faguinba Koita for poisoning seven of his sheep. In his defense, Koita argued that Sidibe's sheep had continuously ravaged his fields and that he had finally consulted the village chief. The chief had suggested that Koita put poison on his fields, which Sidibe's sheep subsequently ate and seven died. The court dismissed Sidibe's case and argued that Sidibe was responsible for his own loss because his herd was "badly guarded."[60]

Increased investment in livestock after 1905 meant that there were more animals permanently residing in farming areas than before 1905. More animals living in close proximity to farmers increased the likelihood of accidental damages to standing crops. Such indeed was the situation that led to the high incidence of damage claims due to livestock. Increased investment in livestock throughout the population also led to the development of a service industry: owners of livestock needed herdsmen to care for their herds. The model of ethnically distinct herders watching over herds that they themselves did not own had precolonial roots. The Segu state, for example, used captive FulBe (Bamana: *forobafula*) to guard the vast herds owned by the *faama*. Maraka and Bambara farmers who owned livestock often engaged FulBe herders to care for their animals in exchange for the milk and a share of the newborn animals.[61]

The employment relationship between the proprietor and the herdsman formed another side of the "trouble" increased livestock ownership induced in the region. The disputes between owners of livestock and their herdsmen that came before the Bamako and Segu courts usually involved failure to honor provisions of the service contract. Although written contracts were admissible in court and encouraged by the colonial state, I have no evidence that written contracts were entered as evidence in the native courts.[62] These grievances suggest that there were two major types of herding contracts. The first had clear precolonial roots and involved the caring of animals in exchange for a portion of the daily milk supply and a share of the offspring. This was an especially attractive arrangement for herders without their own herds, because it provided a means to acquire livestock. It also suited owners of livestock who might be short on cash, because the wages for herding were paid in kind. This arrangement also limited the owner's direct involvement in decision making, because owners frequently did not inquire about their investments for years. On 16 June 1911, Satigui Keita took Coumba Keita to court to recover his investment made over seven years ago when he left one cow with the defendant. The cow had since had four heifers, but the defendant refused to return the animals. The court ruled that defendant had to return the cattle less one cow, which was to be the defendant's compensation.[63] In addition to the milk, the herdsman received one-fourth share of the offspring. Other cases heard in both Bamako and Segu indicate that one-half or one-third shares were common. On 1 July 1907, the herdsman, Babou Demba, took the owner of a horse to court to recover his compensation. As presented to the court, the owner left his horse with the plaintiff with the understanding that each third colt was to be his. The owner sold the horse after the second colt was born and bought another horse, which also had two colts before it too was sold. The owner always seemed ready to sell his horse before the third colt was born, thus depriving the herdsman of his compensation. The court agreed with the plaintiff and ordered that he receive the first colt from the second horse, which was equal to the third born colt.[64] In Bamako, a herdsman successfully defended his claim for one-half the value of a horse as compensation for taking care of it, although the more common practice was probably the one-third share as reported in another case: "the owner agrees to provide 1/3 share to the person who cares for the animals."[65]

Because of the verbal nature of these contracts between owners of livestock and hired herdsmen, disputes sometimes arose over the kinds of claims presented in court. This was clearly the case when Diogondime Diara claimed to be the owner of two cows also claimed by his former employer, Mory Konate. The witness brought to court declared that the cows had been purchased by Mory Konate and that Diogondiame Diara was charged with caring for them. The court dismissed Diogondime Diara's claim without clarifying the nature of the contract.[66]

The Segu court also heard another form of in-kind compensation as revealed when Mahmadou Barro took Bouboukar Tal to court to recover his compensation for serving as herdsman. The court established that Barro and Tal agreed that Barro would receive a heifer after nine months in service. Barro apparently broke his "contract" after four months and Tal refused to provide the promised heifer. Barro subsequently sued Tal to recover his lost wages. The court dismissed the case, because it had discovered that the two parties had indeed entered into a contract for nine months and that only four were served.[67]

The second form of contract between the owner of livestock and the herdsman was monthly wages. The range of salary as evidenced in the judgments rendered in both Bamako and Segu was considerable. For example, on 26 May 1908, a herdsman sued his employer for two months wages and a return for the Fr 5 rent the employer demanded for the shepherd's use of a dwelling. The owner of the livestock was ordered to pay Fr 17.50 in wages and return the Fr 5 in rent.[68] As Koura Seck departed on a voyage, he left a cow and two heifers with his brother, who asked Souleyman Diallo to watch over the animals. Upon his return, one month later, Koura Seck wanted his animals returned, but the herdsman first wanted to be paid for his services. The court ruled that Diallo was to return the animals, but he would receive payment from Seck for his services.[69] Occasionally, owners and shepherds disagreed over the length of service. On 14 May 1907, Kefa Coulibaly sued the owner of a horse he was guarding in court to recover his wages for seven months. The owner, Tiekoura Ouattara, claimed that Coulibaly only worked for him for four months. Asked to swear an oath supporting his claim, Coulibaly demurred.[70] The court ordered the defendant to pay Fr 20, or four months worth of wages. Rates of pay were also disputed. The shepherd, Diade Ould Moctar, took his employer, Koitee Dembele, to court to recover his wages in the form of millet. The plaintiff argued that he was promised 300 *muules* of millet, but the defendant disputed this amount. The court settled on 120 *muules*, considerably less than what the shepherd had sought.[71] The Segu court heard a case brought by Sidi Balo against the owner of the herds he had been guarding for the past nine years. He claimed that he has never been compensated, although he likely used the milk from the herds. In any case, the court order the defendant, Karamoko Keita to pay the plaintiff 100 calabashes of millet and 14,000 cowries within one month.[72]

Although the contracts between owners and employees had precolonial roots, they increasingly came to be monetized. And because the risk-return factor was so significant for both parties, owners and herdsmen each sought to maximize their shares of the arrangements. Herdsmen took considerable risk in the performance of their duties because they were often held responsible for the damages done by the herds under their supervision. On the other hand, herdsmen who managed to negotiate contracts involving shares of the offspring were in positions to acquire the core of their own herds and were thus on the route to independent accumulation. Herdsmen who found themselves in wage relationships, whether paid in cash or in food, were vulnerable to negligence suits and could find themselves slipping into the ranks of the very poor.[73] The herdsman, Almani, barely escaped this future in a case brought before the Bamako court on 26 June 1908. Bougani Konate brought his kinsman Brama Konate to court to recover the value of a cow the former had entrusted to the latter. Brama Konate admitted that the cow was lost, but put the blame on his herdsman, Almani, and argued that the herdsman should be liable for this loss. Almani was also in court that day. The details surrounding the loss of the cow were not recorded in the register, but we do hear that Almani claimed that he was not responsible, and in any case, he argued that his "salary was too low to pay." The court ruled that Brama Konate was responsible and ordered him to pay the plaintiff Fr 85.[74]

The period of transition following the end of slavery witnessed significant changes in investment and in contracts between herdsmen and owners. This period also witnessed women's struggles to maintain control over their property within marriages and to redefine their wealth in relationship to their husbands' and their paternal kin.

WOMEN'S WEALTH: OLD PROPERTY RIGHTS AND NEW MEANINGS

Women had distinctive rights to property that remained separate through their life course. Women often brought property into a marriage and even in marriage, women had the right to acquire and maintain separate property. Women usually had clearly delimited financial obligations within marriage and to the household, her husband, her children, and to her spouse's lineage.

In the eighteenth century, Willem Bosman observed this practice of separate gender property relations when he remarked during his travels in the Gold Coast that "married people have no community of goods, but each hath his or her own particular property."[75] I have elsewhere argued that such separate gender-spheres of property led to the "materialization" of marriage because marriage brought together complementary male and female tasks that led to household subsistence.[76] Such complementarity of gendered tasks was probably experienced by men and women as natural as long as the demand for the products of gender-specific tasks remained anchored in subsistence. Men and women derived mutual benefits from marriage, not only through the exchange of gender-specific tasks and services, but also often through affection. Affection was not, however, always strong enough to weather the stresses of marriage and thus various forms of reciprocity led to the mutuality of marriage benefits. For example, in response to a question about the pre-colonial household, Sane Tambara explained that while indigo-dyeing was women's work, women often dyed their husband's cloths even though they were not "obliged" to in order to ensure the smooth running of the household economy. In return, husbands often sent their slaves to tend their wives' plots of indigo.[77] Another one of my informants, Cemoko Ture, noted that it was common for the newly wed wife to give to her husband her entire output of dyed cloth during the first year of marriage. This gift served the nucleus of her husband's commercial capital.[78] In subsequent years, however, husband's often traded their wives' goods for their wives' accounts and returned to them their profits or other goods they wanted. Once market demand increased the value of men's or women's tasks or gender-specific property rights, then frictions over control of the final marketable product or disposition over actual property emerged.[79] With the expansion of economic activity and the reshuffling of ethnic boundaries over economic resources in the period around 1905, it should not be surprising that we find considerable evidence of women's property in disputes brought to the *tribunaux de province*. Extracting women's property from the conjugal household was part of the messiness of the overlapping household and individual property system.

In a study of eighteenth-century criminal prosecutions in the English county of Surrey, John Beattie argued that the victims of crimes committed by men and by women were telltale signs of the universes in which men and women traversed. Men committed crimes at home, in their places of work, and in public arenas such as pubs and markets. Women's victims, on the other hand, were almost exclusively spouses, relatives, and visitors to their homes or gardens.[80] A similar pattern can be discerned from the study of civil disputes involving women's property: the vast majority of these cases stem from inheritance and familial disputes involving loans between wives and husbands. The handful of exceptions reveal the strategies women pursued in seeking to enhance the value of their property.

On 16 April 1907, Aminate Diara sought to divorce her husband before the Bamako tribunal and to recover money she had lent him. The court granted the plaintiff her divorce and ordered her husband to repay the Fr 20 his wife had lent him within eight days.[81] The tribunal probably did not find in favor of the wife's claim for divorce solely on the basis of her husband's failure to repay the money she had lent him. The court's ruling in two other cases indicate that failure to repay loans from their wives was insufficient cause for divorce. Mohamed Diara went to court to force his wife's return to his home. She left, as she told the court, for a variety of reasons including her husband's failure to repay a loan made by her to him of Fr 55. Diara agreed to repay the loan as a condition of the court's ruling ordering his wife's return.[82] Women seeking to recover debts from loans made to their husbands were not always successful. Kanna Sidibe sued the brother of her deceased husband to recover the money she had lent her husband in order to help him assemble the bridewealth needed for his marriage to Nene Konate, his second wife. As I shall discuss in Chapter 8, levirate was practiced in many parts of the Soudan. Widows often found themselves absorbed into the households of their brothers-in-law. Widows could extract themselves from levirate by repaying the bridewealth.[83] Kanna Sidibe's thus sued her brother-in-law to recover the bridewealth he demanded in order to release her from his household.[84]

In a similar case, the Bamako tribunal ruled in favor of a widow's claim on her husband's estate for the recovery of a loan made to him. Aoua Diabite claimed in her suit against her husband's heirs that her husband, Magate Kone, owed her Fr 400 for loans she had made to him. In the course of testimony, Diabite revealed that she lived on property her husband had acquired that was equal to the value of the loan she had given to him. The court thus ruled that the plaintiff was to keep her husband's houses and property, which the court valued at the sum equal to the original loan.[85]

It is clear from these cases that women kept track of their property, even if they lent it to their husbands. Although women were active merchants in local markets, women did not usually trade over long distances. When their husbands planned long distance commercial ventures, wives sometimes consigned goods or cash to their husbands to trade on their behalf. Usually these arrangements worked out well. But this was not the case between Mariam Cisse and her husband, N'Ky Togora. Before his voyage to Guinea, Cisse gave her husband Fr 77.50 in cash and two sacks of dried tamarind to trade on her account. Upon his return, Togora explained that he had lost her goods en route. She was not satisfied and brought her husband to court to recover her goods. The court ruled in her favor and ordered her husband to restitute the value of her goods within two months.[86]

Women brought their own property to the household of their husbands when they first married and augmented it during the course of the marriage through their own industry. Vivian Paques argues that among some Bambara, the bride's guardian returned some of the bridewealth he received to the bride as her own property to bring into the marriage.[87] All members of the household had rights to a certain amount of time (either per day or per week), which they could use as they wished. Many young males and married women devoted their leisure time to their own fields (*jonforaw*, Bamana: fields of the slave, or *forawso,* Bamana: fields of the night) or their own artisanal activities. The product of these activities was considered individual property. Even if women could acquire and maintain property separate from their husbands, recovering it once marriages failed or her husband died was not always easy. This is what Nio Coulibaly discovered when she brought her brother-in-law, Ba Ture, to court in Segu to recover her property following the death of her husband of 14 years. Nini Coulibaly explained to the court that she had repaid her bridewealth to her brother-in-law, thus formally separating herself from marriage ties that persisted even following the death of her husband. Her brother-in-law let her remain in the house she had occupied with her deceased husband and she continued to work on the household's fields. Nini Coulibaly claimed that she had worked hard while she was married. She also used her leisure time to making baskets from palm fronds and had used this income to acquire four cows, three oxen, and 104,000 cowries. Ba Ture, she claimed, had taken her property and refused to let her have them. The transcript does not provide the defendant's responses regarding his claims on the contested property, but he must have made a fairly convincing case because the court awarded him one cow, one steer, and 4,000 cowries of the contested amount. He was not, however, satisfied with this offer and appealed the judgment.[88]

As the *Coulibaly v. Ture* case indicates, tracking individual property within the context of the household's collective fund of wealth was sometimes difficult. An individual's livestock would be guarded together with the communal herd under the authority of the household head. Other forms of individual property might commingle with communal goods. Retrieving such property when relationships within the household ruptured became one of the trouble spots of property relationships. This was certainly the case when Fatimata Ouele demanded the return of a heifer and a gold ring she claimed that she had lent her former husband. The court dismissed her claim when her former husband denied those claims and when a witness supported the defendant's denial.[89] The record of this case is too thin to evaluate the plaintiff's claims further; however, another case heard on 11 December 1908 indicates that notwithstanding the customary rights to maintain individual property, a husband could equally claim individual property that had probably blended into the household's collective wealth. The transcript in this case is also not full enough to be certain of this interpretation, but the two cases suggest that women's abilities to track their individual property within the sphere of household goods was becoming uncertain. Djeli Kani Diakite sought divorce from her husband, Diani Dembele, for "using her money without her permission." Her husband claimed that "it was his right to use the money." The court dismissed the wife's suit for divorce probably because her claim that her husband used her money without her permission did not constitute sufficient grounds for divorce. The court ruled only in the plaintiff's request for divorce and did not respond to the plaintiff's complaint about the erosion of her property rights.[90] In a third case involving a wife's suit for divorce because of her husband's disrespect of her property, the court ruled in favor of the plaintiff. On 7 September 1909, Nanko Fofana brought her husband to court because she wanted a divorce. Fofana accused her husband of "squandering her goods." The court granted her a divorce.[91] The court did not grant a divorce to Aoua Sako, when she sued her husband, Diatrou Taraore, in order to recover her property that her husband had taken to support his commerce. The plaintiff also claimed that her husband had not completed his bridewealth payments (on incompletely paid bridewealth, see Chapter 6). Her husband argued in court that on the contrary, his wife had given him her money in order for him to pursue his commerce. The court ruled against the plaintiff by denying her request for a divorce, but the court did order her husband to complete the bridewealth payments and to repay the money he took from his wife.[92] Although the court did not rule consistently in such cases, all four cases involved a wife's complaints that her husband had eroded the boundaries separating women's property from that of the household.

In one of the most detailed records we have of the difficulty women experienced in extracting themselves and their property from marriages, Tabara Keita brought a case against her former husband. Dene Balo, her former husband, challenged each item Keita raised and then countered with a flurry of claims of his own. The court examined each issue in turn before reaching a judgment. The transcript is worth including in its totality not only for what it tells us about property rights within marriages, but also for what it reveals about how the native court went about its business of adjudicating conflicting claims.

> Tabara Keita, divorced wife of Dene Balo claims personal property that Dene has retained after their divorce: 17 cattle, loans of 150, 120, 300, 80, 20, 75, and 795 F. Dene asserted his rights in the property of 17 cattle. All of the sums of money listed have been returned. Dene counter-claims as follows: reimbursement of bridewealth of 48,000 cowries and one piece of white cloth, 140,000 cowries given after marriage, gifts of 600F in gold and 300F in cash, four cows, and 90F in food provided to Tabara's mother. Tabara did not acknowledge any debt that she owed Dene. Various witnesses were heard either directly or through rogatory commissions sent to Bandiagara and Bamako. Each claim was examined separately in order to judge whether it was founded or not.

The court's verdict is worth reproducing as well.

> The herd was examined and assessed to be 20 head, which will be divided. A horse, valued at 120F is known to belong to Tabara. The debts of 80F, 20F, and 75F are not proven. Those of 150F and 300F concerning Tabara are dismissed. Dene has the right to be reimbursed for the bridewealth of 48,000 cowries and one piece of white cloth. Concerning the 300F in cash claimed, Tabara recognizes 90F; the rest was value which was acquired during the length of the marriage. This will be equally divided. The remainder of Dene's claims are dismissed.

The judgment satisfied neither party and they both submitted the case to appeal, where the provincial tribunal's judgment was upheld.[93] The case is useful for historians because it provides an indication of the degree of precision with which men and women tracked their property within marriages. The case also reveals that when confronted with such divergent claims, the court engaged in a process of discovery that was quite complex. Requesting that witnesses be deposed from as far away as Bamako and Bandiagara in an age before reliable telegraph was a serious enterprise and one that the court also took seriously. Certainly not all cases required such detailed discovery; nor were all property disputes so obviously irreconcilable.

Some of the cases involving women's property also reveal the social worlds in which they lived. Women in early twentieth-century Soudan were not limited geographically or socially to the borders of their homes or gardens. Women dominated the lively regional markets of the colony, usually selling small quantities of local agricultural or artisanal goods. As they engaged in the buying and selling of goods, women entered into contracts with non-kin and occasionally found themselves with businessmen who did not live up to the promises they made. This was clearly the case when Koko Tamoura gave Fr 100 to Bala Sidibe, who promised to buy her a cow. The defendant neither delivered on his promise to buy her a cow, nor did he repay the money he had received. Koko Dembele thus brought him to court to recover her debt and the court ruled in her favor.[94] Boli Sy produced cloth and approached Moussa Dembele to sell this cloth on her behalf. Dembele failed to deliver the proceeds to Sy and Daillo found himself in court where the plaintiff sought to recover the value of her cloth.[95] A female entrepreneur, Sebe Soumare, asked Sykary Kouma to help sell her gold and livestock. The commercial deal was successful, but Kouma did not repay Sambare because there was disagreement about the terms of the transactions. She was in court to claim her share of the profits, which she estimated to be worth Fr 200. Kouma acknowledged Sambare's share of the gold profits, but he disputed the profits from the livestock transactions. Neither party had witnesses and neither was prepared to swear an oath. Given the contradictory evidence, the court ruled partially in favor of the plaintiff. The court ordered Kouma to return the value of the gold, but only one-half of the herd of livestock.[96]

Women often needed men to serve as commercial agents or brokers for them (Bamana: *tefew*). Most commissioned sales were based on trust, but sometimes trust turned fragile and women were forced to turn to the courts to recover their goods.[97] In 1907, Naba Ture gave her amber[98] to Naibu Ndiaye to sell for her. He did not deliver on his promise and thus found himself in court, where he was ordered to pay the plaintiff 20,000 cowries.[99] For a variety of purposes, including commercial investments and obligations to repay bridewealth (see Chapter 6), women occasionally had to borrow money. Loans were granted on trust, but when trust alone was insufficient the loan was secured by an object or a person pawned to the creditor. Because interest per se did not accrue from holding inanimate objects, creditors often passed the goods on to third parties in exchange for other goods or objects.[100] Recovering the pawned object was thus not always a simple transfer of the borrowed sum for the goods pawned. This was the case when Oumurou Kamara took Ahmadi Oulare to the Segu tribunal to recover the six gros of gold she had left with the defendant as security for a loan. The defendant argued that he has since given the gold to a third party, who then sold it. Despite this defense, the court held the defendant responsible and ordered him to repay the value of the gold to the plaintiff.[101]

The scale of women's transactions as revealed in the court evidence suggests that some women were major entrepreneurs. One woman commissioned the building of a commercial canoe to facilitate long distance trade. While it was unlikely that she would venture out as the primary merchant, this woman probably saw investment in a freight canoe, which could be rented, as a way to participate in the booming commercial environment involving the movement of bulky commodities such as cereals.[102] Women also participated in the burgeoning economy involving new property, especially livestock. Women were often in court as plaintiffs seeking to recover their livestock and as defendants in the range of damage claims associated with livestock ownership.

Inheritance was another opportunity for claimants to dispute their rights to property. Inheritance cases were usually messy, because they pitted kin against kin, including very close relatives. I shall take up inheritance cases in Chapter 8. But before turning to inheritance, we need to examine the handful of disputes over land that appear in the court records of this period. As an icon of "old property," litigants should not have been in court debating their rights to land and other natural economic resources. However, some forms of "old property" were taking on new meanings and Africans were in court to debate those meanings.

POWER AND PROPERTY: ECONOMIC RESOURCES

This chapter began with a presentation of Delafosse's conceptualization of the deep reef of stability in what he described as the Soudanese civilization.

Delafosse had quite consciously built the stability of African agrarian society on the capacity of the household head to manage the multigenerational unit under his authority. As head of the family, he represented the family to the wider community and was responsible for meeting all financial obligations. "Each member of the family is obliged to devote to the community a part of his labor, whether in the form of one or several days per week, or in the case when a member lives far away, a portion of his earnings or salary."[103] The household head managed, according to Delafosse's argument, the economic resources necessary to the well-being and survival of his members. These economic resources were both the labor of his community and access to the means of livelihood. As we have seen, Delafosse drew a distinction between immobile and mobile property and complicated the discussion by linking two concepts of property rights to these two categories of property. In this section, I will use the handful of examples of disputes over "old" property as a way of examining the nature of the relationship between property and authority and between household head and community members. Many of these cases are not household-specific cases but disputes over old property by neighbors. I am particularly interested in disputes over land, houses, and economic resources, such as the rights to fish. The cases need to be examined in relationship to changes taking place within the wider context of changes in property and property relations set in motion by the end of slavery, the expansion in commercial activity, and the ease of physical movement.

According to Delafosse's model of African societies, cases involving land, houses, and economic resources should not be appearing in the records. The fact that they do indicates a dissonance in Delafosse's model of African societies and the reality on the ground. For the Bamako district, "old" property cases consisted only 12 percent of the total property cases heard by the provincial tribunal; for the Segu district, these types of disputes constituted 25 percent of the cases involving property.

On 15 May 1905, shortly after the provincial tribunal first opened for business, the Bambara inhabitants of Segoubougou, ten kilometers south of Segu, the seat of the new tribunal, brought suit against the Somono of Segoubougou for control over fields farmed by the Somono in that village. The exposé of the dispute in the records provides only the briefest sketch of the grievance: the Somono of Segoubougou started to farm the disputed fields, which had been left fallow for several years. The Bambara, as the original inhabitants of the village, now reclaimed these fields. The court ruled in favor of the Somono, applying the principle (paradoxically reminiscent of the French *seisin*) that rights of possession take precedence over other rights. "Considering that the land is not the property of individuals, that the land was not occupied for two years, it can be considered available for use (*disponible*); considering that the Bambara had ceased to cultivate the land for many years, the tribunal dismissed the suit of the plaintiffs."[104] The plaintiffs appealed the judgment.

Two days later, the district tribunal, presided over by the French district officer assisted by two native assessors, sat in attendance of the appeal requested by the Bambara of Segoubougou. The exposé of the appeal reads as follows:

> Sougoba Diara appealed the judgment of 15 May which declared that the Bambara of Segoubougou no longer had rights to the fields cultivated over the past two years by the Somono, who had taken the land from them. The Somono, represented by Mama Sako, reported that they had requested permission from the Bambara before they occupied the land and that it was their intention to use the land exclusively. The *tribunal de province* decided against the Bambara [based on] a decision by the commandant of the cercle that all land not cultivated for two years is considered free.

The judgment rendered by the district tribunal overturned the earlier judgment and ruled in favor of the plaintiffs. "The Somono of Segoubougou must return to the Bambara the land which the later claim the Somono have taken."[105] I am not certain how to interpret this ruling, especially because the presiding magistrate was none other than the *commandant de cercle,* who had apparently issued the order transforming unused fields into freely available land. Because the provincial tribunal had just been implemented and was likely under the watchful eye of the French district officer, it could be that the African members of that tribunal on 15 May acquiesced to the commandant's desires in rendering their verdict in favor of the Somono. It could be that two days later the native assessors at the district tribunal had argued persuasively against eroding collective property rights and that the commandant was prepared to change his mind. There seems, however, to be another side to the context of this case. Around the same time as this case was being heard, the Somono of Segu were involved in some undisclosed form of political action against the French, which took the form of an Islamic grievance. The reversal of the ruling in favor of the Somono (and overturning the commandant's order regarding vacant land) may be part of a broader punishment against the Somono.[106] We do not have enough information to interpret this case further, but the fact that the Bambara of Segoubougou felt themselves obliged to bring this suit to the new courts hints at significant erosion of the "principle" of collective property rights and the powers of the village chief.

Segoubougou, where I have conducted interviews during earlier research in 1976–1977 and 1981, was an ancient Bambara village located along the Niger River.[107] The Somono, primarily fishermen but also entrepreneurs of tobacco and onions produced for the market, were newcomers to the village. They were thus dependent for their land rights upon the Bambara village chief. That the Somono saw unused land as an economic resource, which they were willing to utilize, also suggests significant changes in the regional economy. The economy of the Middle Niger valley had been undergoing dramatic changes following the French conquest in 1890, which unleashed pent-up regional demand for goods and services. The growing grain market in Bamako, the demand for cloth, dried fish, and other products of the Middle Niger valley in the wider West African sub-continental market spurred the expansion of production and led to tensions between the two systems of production, which I argued better explained the social conflicts and tensions inherent in Delafosse's "double conception of property." It was also linked, as I shall argue below, to challenges to authority, whether at the level of village chiefs or household heads.

Disputes over fields, the principle economic resource for farming communities, are uncommon in the court records. The Segu tribunal heard only seven cases (less than 2%) dealing directly with land disputes among the 402 cases it heard altogether. The disputes over land are obviously not important numerically; they are important, however, as indicators of increasing valuation and competition for access to productive resources. On 19 November 1909, two villagers from neighboring villages brought to the Segu tribunal their dispute over the same field. With neither party bringing forward "historic" claims to the land, the court ruled that the field was to be divided equally between the two villages, but only after the current harvest was completed.[108] Disputes over land also erupted between neighbors of the same village. This was the case when Inchi Diallo "seized" four meters of his neighbor Inchi Korate's field. The court dispatched "experts" to the field to examine the claims and they reported back to the court. The court ruled in favor of the plaintiff and ordered Inchi Diallo "to restore the land inappropriately taken."[109] In Delafosse's conception of the deep stability of Soudanese African farming communities, land per se would not have any value, merely its use rights. What Delafosse had failed to incorporate into his argument was how changes in the wider political economy were transforming the value of economic resources, such as land, as more people came to produce commodities for an expanding market.

Four of the eight disputes over fields in Segu occurred in the summer of 1907. Kori Samake brought Ibrahima Diawara to court on 11 June 1907 to force Diawara to return to him his field, which Samake claimed to have worked "uninterruptedly" for the past 20 years. Samake "proved" to the satisfaction of the court that these were the facts and the court ordered that "satisfaction be given to the plaintiff."[110] A similar case was heard 10 days later when Bodian Kone brought Lamine Fofana to court to recover his field that Fofana had started to farm. Bodian claimed that he had worked the field for the past 11 years and the court found in his favor.[111]

The following case provides further evidence of the principle that working the land provided the farmer with enduring property rights. Mohamed Doade took Boakary Togora to court to contest the latter's claim on the land he was cultivating. Apparently, Mohamed Doade gave Boakary Togora permission to cultivate his land. Over the past five years, Boakary Togora had erected dwellings and cultivated maize. Boakary Togora was willing to return the fields to Doade, but not the dwellings or the standing crops. The court ordered a visit to the fields in question, and upon presentation of the findings, the court ruled that the land "that had been constructed" belonged to Boakary Togora, which included the dwellings and the cultivated fields. Mohamed Doade, the original owner, has rights to the land that had not been "constructed." The language used in the judgment is significant: "the constructed land is recognized as Boakary's property. The sowed field without its crops will be returned to Mohamed."[112]

The most intriguing case of this set was an appeal from the village tribunal of Markadougouba to the Segu provincial tribunal. The provincial court heard an appeal of the Markadougou chief's ruling on a local land dispute, which probably involved household fission. The provincial court overturned the chief's decision and returned the land in question to the household head.[113] This case indicates that the village chief's authority was being challenged not only by women seeking divorce (as discussed in Chapter 5), but by young men of the village as well.

These four cases indicate that access to some land, probably land in close proximity to villages or markets, was coming under increasing pressure in response to individual's efforts to increase their output of farm produce. As access to land was becoming more valuable, it was also emerging as a site of potential conflict. The cases cited above indicate that the sphere of conflict was between neighbors or between "owners" of different types of fields adjacent to each other. Delafosse had placed the village chief in a position as representative of the village inhabitants and thus responsible for the allocation of rights to use village land. The chief was to serve the common good of the community. As rights to land were beginning to have economic value, conflicts between chiefs and residents also emerged as a potential flashpoint. This was clearly the case when Sibiri Diara of Kala village brought suit against his village chief, Teneman Sankara, for reallocating his family's land to another resident. The chief responded that he had merely reallocated the land because the plaintiff had left the village. The court gave priority to Sibiri Diara's claim on the field and ruled against the chief. "The field will be returned to its true proprietor, Sibiri Diara."[114] This ruling on top of those others discussed here indicates that the Segu tribunal had a more or less clear concept of individual property rights and was prepared to act in favor of individual's claims on land against the idea presented by Delafosse that land had no value.

In his reconstruction of the rural property regime, Delafosse had provided for contractual agreements between owners and users of property. Disputes over "rental" agreements are generally few, but those from Bamako are more frequent than from Segu.[115] On 23 June 1908, the proprietor of a house brought his tenant to court to recover the Fr 30 rent the tenant owed. The tenant argued that he was forced to make improvements to the house and thus should not have to pay the full price. The court agreed and ordered the tenant to pay Fr 12.[116] Tenants had some rights, especially if the proprietors sought to annul their agreements, as the case when Issa Silla wanted to evict Dado Dembele from land Silla owned. Silla claimed that Dembele's activities were "disturbing the peace" of the neighbors. What these activities were were not mentioned, but the court ruled in favor of the proprietor although it charged the proprietor with a bill for Fr 40 to compensate the tenant for the improvements he made to the property.[117]

The nature of proprietorship comes into clearer focus in the course of the judgments in 1909 and 1910. Courts in both Bamako and Segu obviously accepted the concept of enduring individual property rights to land that been extensively worked and that these rights were not diminished by absence. This was clearly the ruling in the *Diara v. Sankare* case cited above, but also clearly reiterated in the *Coulibaly v. Coulibaly* case heard in Bamako on 17 August 1909. According to testimony presented in court, Mori Coulibaly tilled his plot and then left the district. Negueda Coulibaly took possession of fields and planted his crops while Mori Coulibaly was away. Despite the value added by his labor, the court ruled that Negueda Coulibaly must return the fields and the crops to the plaintiff.[118] Rights of individual ownership were also upheld in the case brought by Mamadou Diko to regain possession of his house, which had been occupied by Mamadou Sumare during Diko's absence.[119] As Bamako city continued to develop, housing remained scarce and disputes over urban houses and lots increased.[120]

As in the case of the Somono and Bambara of Segubougou, the emerging market for agricultural commodities raised the stakes of access to economic resources. The inhabitants of two riverine villages, Mereninkoro and Guendo, along the Niger brought a case against each other for the exclusive rights to fish streams between their two villages. Exclusive rights to economic resources, such as fishing grounds, had been a central part of the political economy of the precolonial Segu state. This was constituted when the Segu state provided exclusive rights to fish and provided new recruits to the Somono in exchange for the provision of ferry and communication services to the state.[121] With French conquest and with the breakdown of ethnic boundaries over occupations and economic resources, conflicts such as those between Mereninkoro and Guendo over access to exclusive rights to fish indicated that the boundaries between groups was dissipating, but also that the Somono of these different villages were still invoking the precolonial model of exclusive access to bounded economic resources. In its ruling, the Segu tribunal did not dispute the exclusive nature of access to fishing rights, but merely divided the contested area equally between the two villages.[122] This resolved the particular grievance without creating a new dispensation in regard to economic resources.

Four years later, the Bamako tribunal dismissed a case brought by Bafin Coulibaly against the inhabitants of Bougoula village for exclusive rights to fish. Coulibaly claimed that he had exclusive rights to fish the Korodum creek. Soumano Coulibaly, representing the village, argued that the rights to fish were a common good and open to all members of the village. The tribunal sided with Soumano Coulibaly. We do not have enough detail in this case to assess whether Bafin Coulibaly's claim had any precolonial roots, but even if it did, the tribunal's decision indicates that the precolonial concept of exclusive access to economic resources were being steadily challenged by many people fishing. Taken together, these two cases suggest that precolonial rights to exclusive use of economic resources was being eroded by the pressures of the new colonial economy and the actions of men and women into new areas of economic activity and forms of accumulation.

SUMMARY

This chapter has taken up the Martin Chanock's challenge to interrogate the meanings of "new" property and the construction of new property relationships in colonial Africa. The end of slavery in the period after 1905 was a central component to these efforts to redefine social and productive relationships within households and between individuals not bound by kinship. Ownership of cattle, especially those owned by women, illuminated some of the dynamics of household property relations that were far more complex than those identified by Delafosse in his classic ethnography of the region.

Ownership of cattle was, in the terms used in this book, a trouble spot in household social relations. It became a source of trouble precisely because it was such a potentially powerful genitor of wealth. In the agrarian world of the Middle Niger valley in the early twentieth century, the avenues to wealth were rarely through hard work and thrift. Hard work and thrift could generate subsistence, but little else. Wealth could be achieved through ownership of productive investments, such as cattle and slaves, through theft (which had been the primary means of generating wealth during the era of the slave trade and warrior societies), and through inheritance. I take up the issue of contested inheritance in the next chapter.

8

DISPUTING INHERITANCE

There is no code that unifies the rules of Bambara life. Everything is in the customs: that mysterious thread, at once fragile, links generations one to the other. It sustains the individual unbeknownst to him; if one falls outside of custom, he is completely abandoned and alone. Bequeathed by the ancestors, conserved superstitiously, it imposes itself by fear of punishment against those who wish to transgress it. At first glance, custom seems an amalgam of the most heterogeneous things. To Europeans, custom seems at once respectable and ridiculous, good and bad, useful and senseless, sometimes atrocious but at other times excellent. Upon careful analysis, custom reveals itself to be founded on common sentiments found throughout humanity and fully compatible with the indigenous milieu. Custom is based upon natural morality, which doubles as positive law.[1]

Thus wrote Charles Monteil, one of the French administration's leading scholar-officials, in the major ethnographic and historical study of Bambara published during the colonial period.[2] As I discussed in Chapters 5 and 7, Monteil's research on the Bambara Empire under French colonial rule complemented Delafosse's project and became a central part of France's efforts to promote stability and authority in its newly acquired territory. Monteil's arguments on custom as that "mysterious thread" that binds generations and individuals together formed a cornerstone to the efforts by part of the French colonial administration to shore up the authority of the family and the male household head within it. This "mysterious thread" of custom was a central part of the intellectual template behind Ponty's *politique de races.*

Monteil further elaborated the qualities of the *faya,* the authority of the male household head. "The powers of the *fa* over his community are, in principle, absolute. He can, if he choses, loan, pledge, sell and even put to death [any member of his community]; he may also dispose of everything that they possess, people and things. In contrast, he has in relationship to them responsibilities, especially to sustain the members [of the community]."[3] Central to the authority of the household head were also reciprocal responsibilities, made possible by the collective nature of household property. Thus, the household head was responsible for the well-being of members of his community and they were in turn obliged to respect the household head and work for the benefit of the community as a collectivity. The power of the household head was absolute and unchallenged. He stood at the head of a complex, multigenerational unit, but it was his capacities to organize and manage that provided the deep stability to African family structures.

In Chapter 3, I briefly introduced the Konate case heard in Kita in 1910, in which the elderly chief of Komakana village brought suit against his own son from the latter's refusal to work for his father. After "discovering" what the "custom" regarding filial responsibility was, the tribunal ruled in favor of the elder Konate. "Respecting custom. . . . the Tribunal has decided that Famoussa must furnish four days of labor per week for his old father."[4]

How can we explain the discrepancies between the Konate case in 1910 and the apparent authority of the *fa* in Monteil's ethnographic sociology? Was the Konate v Konate case in 1910 an anomaly? Did Monteil get his sociology of the household wrong? Certainly the African magistrates serving the Kita tribunal drew on custom to support the elder Konate's claim to the labor of his son and Monteil drew on the intelligence of his two primary informants regarding the customary authority of the household head. But, the fact that the elder Konate actually went to court to force his son to adhere to "custom" tends to support Sara Berry's notion that

> colonial regimes imposed themselves on societies already engaged in strug-
> gles over power and the terms of which it was exercised. By announcing
> their intention to uphold "traditional" norms and structures of authority,
> colonial officials were, in effect, declaring their intention to build colonial
> rule on a foundation of conflict and change. The result was a "blizzard of
> claims and counterclaims" to rights over land and people, which served as
> "a mechanism for generation factional struggle" rather than eliminating it.[5]

Monteil's informants in the early years of colonial occupation may well have used their patron as a vehicle for "inventing" the authority of the household head.

Monteil's "mysterious thread" of custom linking generations and individu-als—and its counterpart, the anomie of lying outside of it—would suggest that the newly established native courts, which began operations in the spring of 1905, would not hear any cases regarding inheritance. Orderly forms of inheritance would seem to be central in the continuities of domestic units over time. But men and women did bring cases of disputed inheritance before the native courts throughout the French Soudan. The presence of these cases and the patterns of resolving them suggest a number of important issues:

1. disputes over inheritance reveal far more dissent than agreement over the "mysterious threads" of inheritance and household organization. These dis-putes support Sara Berry's notion that colonial rule was built on fluid and highly contested patterns of access to productive resources and wealth. Mon-

teil's characterization of the orderliness of inheritance may in fact have been part of a discursive tradition in colonial rule aimed at promoting certain patterns of accumulation and authority over others and certain individuals over others.

2. disputes over inheritance, which made their way to the newly established native courts, suggest that individuals may have been acting as individuals in taking their grievances before third parties. In disputing inheritance, these individuals were challenging both the presumed orderliness of custom, the presumed authority of tradition, and the presumed ubiquity of the idealized multigenerational African family. When Muslims disputed inheritance in the native courts, they were challenging the authority of local qadis and entrusting judgments to colonial courts composed also of nonbelievers.

In bringing cases of disputed inheritance before the tribunals, litigants raised issues of the authority of Muslim law and custom and forced the colonial state to intervene ever more fully into the most intimate issues of domestic life. Precisely because these records are about the most intimate matters of domestic life, they also provide a starting point for our efforts to reconstruct what David William Cohen calls the "interior architecture" of African societies.[6] This chapter will focus on the patterns of inheritance disputes in the Segu court.

In the post-abolition social world of the early twentieth-century French Soudan, what separated the well-off from the poor was not very great: a few head of cattle, some gold and amber, some stores of trade goods, and of course, many children. To accumulate was not easy, given the vicissitudes of the harvest and the claims of kinsmen. Hard work and good fortune often paid off, but also generated covetous kinsmen. It is safe to say that few kinsmen were interested in the estates of their poor relatives. However, the estates of those who had managed to accumulate gave rise to intense interest among those with claims on the inheritance and led to disputes over the definition of property and households. The inheritance of wealth was a means of rapidly transiting from poverty to relative comfort and for solidifying the status of those who had already managed to accumulate. Inheritance was one factor in the persistence of social inequality in the French Soudan.[7]

This chapter examines disputes over inheritance as a way of demonstrating that the end of slavery and the expansion of new forms of property gave rise to opportunities for kinsmen to articulate ideas about kinship and identity that strengthened their claims on the estates of those who had died. Inheritance disputes challenged the orderly custom that Monteil and Delafosse sought to establish, revealing a messier universe of individuals often acting in their own interests rather than for the benefit of the collective household unit. In this chapter, I am particularly interested in cases that demonstrated points of tension within the Bambara custom of collateral inheritance (within the generation). In several cases discussed below, I examine how brothers clashed with brothers and with their sisters over the disposition of their elder brother's or their father's estates (which represented transmission of wealth between generations). Another group of cases illuminate how the death of "outsiders," including former slaves and itinerate merchants, challenged the assumptions of orderliness in custom and kinship. I also devote a section to exploring what the death of a husband meant for his wives who had managed to accumulate wealth and how the death of wealthy women also put different groups of kinsmen into conflict. I end this chapter with a discussion of the ways in which Islam and Muslim legal status changed strategies of kinsmen and redefined the locus of interested parties upon the death of well-off Muslim women in particular.

Inheritance disputes brought before the Segu provincial tribunal comprised 14 percent of 436 cases heard between 1905 and 1912. Figure 8.1 indicates the distribution of inheritance cases in Segu. The sharp increase in inheritance cases heard in 1905 indicates that litigants were interested in testing the disposition of the new courts in regard to their interests in inheritance disputes. The new courts were part of a new landscape of power and litigants who were not confident of the outcomes of their disputes in other venues may have decided to try their cases in the new courts. The second spike in inheritance cases occurred in 1908. That year probably represented the first signs of post-emancipation household tensions following three years of slaves' departures or renegotiations. All these disputes about inheritance

Figure 8.1 Inheritance Disputes, Segu, 1905–1912, n = 64

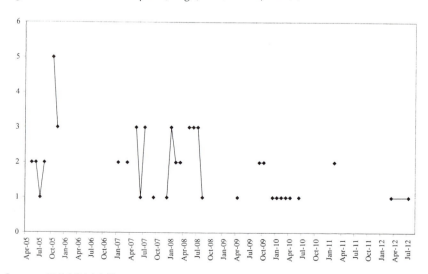

Source: ANM 2 M 143

contribute to our understanding of the social history of African households in this region.

INHERITING DISPUTES AND DISPUTES OVER INHERITANCE

On 20 October 1905 two brothers, Boa and Amara Kone of Togo village, brought suit against their uncle, Benoko Kone, for failure to "divide" their father's estate fairly. Boa and Amara Kone claimed "customary" legal status and thus sought adjudication according to Bambara customs. Benoko, in his turn, accused his two nephews of "withholding" certain goods from the estate. Benoko, however, did not provide proof of his accusations. The tribunal ruled in favor of the plaintiffs: "Benoko must return to his nephews their father's estate with the exception of that which he can justify legally as his."[8] Boa and Amara Kone were pleased with the court's decision; Benoko, however, chose to appeal the verdict.[9]

This case provides a starting point for assessing Monteil's "mysterious threads." Beyond the gloss on the deep and enduring traditions in the Monteil passage cited above, there is little in Monteil's account to help interpret this case. We need to turn to Maurice Delafosse, whose *Haut-Sénégal-Niger* was probably the most influential study of the new colony during the entire colonial period. Published in 1912, *Haut-Sénégal-Niger* provided an interpretation for what Delafosse perceived as the deep commonalities among all Soudanese societies and therefore a blueprint to colonial administration. The deepest commonality of all (like Monteil's "mysterious thread") was the linkage between the family and property.[10] Delafosse recognized two distinct property spheres, one which undergirded the multigenerational "family" and the other which stemmed from personal efforts and individual accumulation.[11] The much larger sphere of property, that which linked the family to the soil and to the political world of chiefdoms and kingdoms, rested on household control over fixed property. The other sphere of property was that which was accumulated individually through personal efforts during times of the day or week in which the individual was free from collective chores to pursue her or her own ends.

Each time that one must deal with a disputed inheritance among the natives in the Soudan, one must know at the outset whether it deals with the transmission of private or personal property, independent of the collective goods of the family, or whether it deals with collective property. In the first case, the deceased may have disposed of all or part of the property through verbal testaments made before witnesses. But since these possessions are usually objects of little value, they are usually left to the natural (sic) and unique heir, determined by his kinship to the deceased. In the second case, the heir is always unique and his inheritance consists of the control and administration of the collective goods of the family, including the authority and the prerogatives of becoming the head of the family. The collective good of the family is inalienable, and because of that, can never be subject to testamentary considerations.[12]

The head of the family's estate thus consisted of two parts: the status, power, and fiduciary responsibilities of the head of the family and his private possessions. The Bambara practice collateral succession, which means that the younger brother of the head of the family inherits. Such collateral succession generates discrete points of tension in the household between generations and between members of different units of reproduction. Jack Goody has helped interpret the persistence and organization of complex, multigenerational households by dividing the household into functionally separate units: units of production, units of reproduction, and units of consumption.[13] Goody's schematic orientation is especially useful for dealing with the large LoDogaaba household of Northern Ghana, which can contain upwards of 100 members, but it also helps make sense of the morphology of the smaller, but still complex Bambara households (Bamana: *gwa,* hearth). As late as the 1980s, the mean household size of the Bambara living in the Kala district of Segu consisted of 23.8 people. It is possible that the turn of the century, when the Segu courts heard these inheritance cases, the mean household size was even larger. The large Bambara household provided strong advantages to its members, because if offered better subsistence security and access through collective control over resources to scarce goods needed for bridewealth payments. In contrast, division of the household exposed it to considerable subsistence and reproduction risks.[14]

In her study of Bambara households in the Kala region of Segu, Toulmin examined not only household persistence but also household division. Although household size depended upon ecological, economic, and political variables, Toulmin noted that as households get larger, they can be expected to divide. While some households contain men related over four generations, household fission often occurred when the head dies and sons of the same father but different mothers split apart. The sons of the same mother usually remained together. Another point of tension in household is related to the two overlapping systems of authority, one based on generations and the other on age. Under collateral succession, it is likely that the household head's younger brothers may well be younger than the household head's sons, thus confounding the foundations of authority of age versus the authority of generations. At this point, the elderly son of the household head may resent the authority of his younger uncle and lead his followers to found a new *gwa.*[15]

Delafosse and Toulmin provide some ethnographic context to examine the case brought by Boa and Amara Kone against their uncle Benoko for his refusal to share their father's estate with him and his brother. It could be that

Boa and Amara sought to leave the household and thus claimed their share of their father's possessions. Benoko's counter claim that his nephews had withheld part of the inheritance and that he wanted it returned rested on his assertion of his rights to claim both of the position household head and possessions of the household. The court records do not provide sufficient detail of the objects being contested, which would have facilitated our analysis of the case. Nonetheless, Delafosse's proposition of the separate nature of the household head's possessions helps us interpret the tribunal's decision: "Benoko must return to his nephews their father's inheritance with the exception of that which he can justify legally as his." What Benoko, who was likely in line for collateral succession, could legally claim was his brother's possessions that were linked directly to the collectivity of the household. What his nephews could legally claim was the "small property of little value" possessed individually by their father. Because the household head managed a complex unit of production, reproduction, subsistence, and accumulation, he could, in principle, amass a significant wealth, of which the boundaries between collective and individual rights could be blurred. Of course, the household head was supposed to invest the household's wealth in the broad patterns of household reproduction, namely the matrimonial exchanges so necessary for marriage, which would logically lead to the rapid redistribution of any accumulated wealth.

On the other hand, the division of the Kone household would seem to be a natural pattern of the development cycle of the Bambara domestic group. If this were the case, however, we could hypothesize that there would be no need for Bao Kone and his brother to sue their uncle for their share of the inheritance in the provincial tribunal. The fact they Boa and Amara Kone were actually in court on 20 October 1905 suggests that someone in the Kone family was not playing according to those "mysterious threads" of custom that linked generations and individuals together.[16] The evidence is much too thin for us to analyze the proximate causes of this case, except by reference to the ethnographic material already cited. But this approach cannot explain why this case occurred in 1905.

Chapters 4 and 7 addressed the changes occurring in and after 1905 that were set in motion by the end of slavery. As I argued, the period from 1903 to 1905 witnessed the beginning of a considerable reshuffling of economic, social, and cultural practices. This reshuffling—the linked sets of transformation—may have contributed to household tensions as household heads sought to extract greater effort from their dependents at exactly the same time when new economic opportunities (a booming economy and the erosion of ethnic boundaries over economic resources) may have encouraged junior men to establish their own households. This is what Pollet and Winter have described as the erosion of patriarchal authority.[17]

The Kone case suggests that changes in the wider social and political landscape of the French Soudan may have contributed to the articulation of structural tensions in Bambara household between paternal uncles and nephews. Not all cases of inheritance challenged by nephews were successful. On 1 October 1905, Ba Moa Taraore sued his uncle, Bagoba Taraore, for a share of the wealth accumulated by his deceased father. Citing Bambara custom, Bagoba Taraore argued that upon the death of his brother, he in fact became head of the household and thus custodian of all the household's wealth. No elaboration of what constituted the household's wealth was indicated in the court records, so it was not clear whether Ba Moa Taraore was claiming a share of the "smaller" individual wealth of his father or the "larger" possessions of the household. In any case, the court dismissed the plaintiff's claim and ruled that Bagoba "in becoming the household head has rightful title to the estate of his deceased brother."[18]

Writing in 1932, Alfred Aubert, commandant of Bouguni, noted that "judgments relating to inheritance are rare, in part because the interested parties are reluctant to discuss the possessions of the deceased, and in part because they may not have confidence in the rules that we impose regarding their inheritance."[19] Indeed, disputes regarding inheritance in Bouguni constituted only 2 percent of the cases heard between 1905 and 1912. But this was not the case in Segu. What social factors contributed to the interests individuals had in bringing cases of disputed inheritance before the new courts in Segu?

There was clearly something about the patterns of social change after 1905 that contributed to Natie Konare's willingness to pursue her claims on her deceased father's wealth 30 years after his death. The court records are too sparse to provide any insight in Konare's decision, but she was in court on 15 January 1907 claiming her share of her deceased father's estate. The defendant, Fadouga Dembele, did not challenge her claims, but merely noted to the court that after such a long wait, it was due only to his efforts that there was anything of value still to inherit. The court ruled that Dembele and Konare are to divide her father's wealth into two equal parts.[20]

A similar case of delayed claims on inheritance was heard on 12 August 1908, when Issa Sako brought her brother to court seeking her share of her father's estate. Her brother, Celouki Sako, argued that the division of the inheritance had actually taken place 15 years ago under the rule of Bodian, the French-appointed puppet king of Segu, and under the authority of the late Sekou Kone, qadi of Segu. Kone's son affirmed in court that his father had actually ruled in this case, but he did not know whether his father's judgment had been executed. Issa Sako had two witnesses who swore that the qadi's ruling was never executed and who estimated that the size of Issa Sako's share of the inheritance was 30 cattle. The court ruled in Issa Sako's favor.[21]

The Issa Sako case indicates that in addition to the structural tensions in Bambara households between uncles and nephews and nieces, another trouble spot appeared to be between brothers and sisters. Dienebou Ballo was in court on 18 June 1908 claiming that her brother was withholding her share of her father's estate, which included one cow and one calf. Her brother, Hama Kadia Ballo, in turn argued that his sister was not fit to possess anything, because she has left her husband and was living as a vagabond. Dienebou Ballo replied that she had indeed left her husband but that she was actually living with her mother. The court ruled that Hama Kadia Ballo was to give his sister that which was hers.[22] In claiming that his sister had left her husband and was a vagabond, Hama Kadia Ballo was probably trying to sway the court by disparaging his sister's status as a respectable woman, who should not be trusted with valuable possessions.

Nor did the "mysterious threads" of custom stop two brothers, Baiamory Coulibaly and Alkao Coulibaly, from fighting over the inheritance of their father. Each brother further accused the other of "wasting" the inheritance. The court must have been exasperated by these claims and by the animosity expressed by the litigants because it ordered the inheritance to be divided equally among all the deceased father's children and his wives.[23] The court probably understood that this household could no longer be put back together again.

The collapse of the Coulibaly household suggests that households have their own histories. Chayanov and Goody have drawn our attention to the discrete life cycles of domestic groups.[24] But such life cycles are not enduring processes, constantly reproducing themselves in the same manner. They are instead deeply influenced by the larger landscape in which they are embedded. Inheritance disputes can thus be read as moments of change in a household's development and as opportunities to redefine kinship relations. In the cases discussed below, I am particularly interested in assessing the articulation of kinship claims during this period of social change. I have selected two different types of cases to illustrate this point: the first set deals with fictitious claims to inheritance and the second with inheritance where no kin could be found.

Igor Kopytoff and Suzanne Miers have argued that one of the characteristics of African slavery was its capacity to absorb outsiders, such as slaves, into kinship systems. Kopytoff later argued that when given the opportunity to free themselves, most slaves chose instead to integrate themselves more fully into their masters' households and kin-based systems of dependence.[25] If former slaves integrated themselves more fully into their masters' households, then masters would also extend "kinship" to their former slaves. Na Keita was in court to claim on behalf of his niece the estate of Sira Keita. This was a somewhat complicated case in that several brothers and their children were claiming the estate of Sira Keita, who had been head of a fairly large, but fractious household. Na Keita claimed that his niece was the daughter of the deceased's brother, and thus a paternal niece. Amary Keita, who currently possessed the estate, claimed that Na Keita's niece was actually his brother's "domestic." Amary Keita added to the authority of his claim by bringing witnesses. The court ruled in favor of Amary Keita and dismissed the suit.[26] Former slaves, no matter how well integrated into their masters' households, were still not considered kin when there were things of value to be inherited. This was also the case when Zane Kante tried to claim a share of the Fagnouma Diallo's estate, who died without male heirs. Diallo's wife, Fatimata Cisse, argued that Zane Kante was not a male kin, but was in fact "in service" in her husband's household. The court rejected Kante's claim.[27]

Webs of kinship were also put to the test when former masters tried to claim kinship with their former slaves in their effort to claim their estates. Bamoussa Kone tried exactly this strategy when he claimed to be the brother of Sadiki Sumare, also called Sadiki Kone. Sadiki Sumare had obviously prospered, because he was a district guard and had two wives. Bamoussa Kone's suit was challenged by Sumare's two wives, who claimed that Sumare was actually Bamoussa Kone's "servant" and not his brother. Witnesses supported the defendants and the court rejected Kone's claim.[28]

Under slavery, masters had rights to their slaves' possessions. Slaves had rights of usufruct only and could not bequeath their goods to their children.[29] Former masters probably assumed that they still had these rights. Thus, when Koke Diara's wife, who had been a "servant" in Cedougou Diabite's household, died, the Diabite family assumed that it should inherit her possessions. Koke Diara's wife had no children and no other known kin. But, given the new dispensation of the 1903 legal system that the status of the litigants could not be considered in court, Cedougou Diabite's claim over the inheritance of his former slave was dismissed because he could not prove kinship ties. In the absence of any claims of kinship, the court awarded the deceased's estate to her husband.[30]

Koke Diara's wife's condition—to be without kin—was clearly an anomaly within a world defined by kinship. Koke Diara's wife was not, however, unique in the aftermath of the end of slavery. Many former slaves left their masters and set themselves up in independent households. Birama Konare, like Sadiki Sumare, probably set up a new household, married, and began a new life. Like Sumare, Konare also became a district guard. Upon his death in 1908, he had no paternal kin. His wife, Aissata Konare, was in court to claim her husband's estate. The court agreed.[31]

The court also heard cases of individuals who died in transit. Some were merchants and others merely travelers who were upon the roads because the regional economy provided increased security of movement and more reasons to travel away from one's home. But travelers did die and if they had possessions, the court was called upon to decide how to dispose of these goods. Sabou Diallo, a merchant, died while staying with Alam Traore. Traore did not know Diallo and thus could not identify any known heirs, but Diallo had left one donkey and one ox in Traore's care. Traore was in court to have the court decide what to do with Diallo's livestock. The court gave Traore temporary rights to the livestock as it conducted an inquiry into

Diallo's potential heirs.[32] We would expect merchants to be away from home, but not necessarily a single woman. But this was exactly the case when Tene Keita, "unknown and in transit," when she died in the village of Zambougou. Keita was carrying the sum of 171 francs. The chief of the village brought the Keita estate to the Segu native court, which declared the inheritance to be "vacant." A vacant estate reverted to the state.[33] We have no way of knowing what Tene Keita was doing in Zambougou or where she was ultimately headed. But the fact that she was on the move alone and with considerable cash points to the problems of deciding what happens to their wealth when women or their husbands died.

WHEN WOMEN OR THEIR HUSBANDS DIE: INHERITANCE AND WOMEN'S WEALTH

Women had rights to own property. Because women were enmeshed in several overlapping systems of affiliation, they were surrounded by dense webs of obligations and rights. Death put these webs and the disposition of women's wealth into sharper focus. It is not surprising that women, their kinsmen, their husbands, and their husbands' kinsmen should be in court to seek shares of women's wealth. Disputes over the disposition of women's wealth or inheritance disputes in which women were the plaintiffs account for 57 percent of all the inheritance disputes heard in the Segu native court. Statistically, this is a telling indicator that women's wealth and women's rights to possess wealth were significant factors in the social conflicts within households.

On May 3, 1905, just two weeks after the new courts opened for business in Segu, the provincial tribunal heard a disputed inheritance. Fa Sankare of Bandiagara brought a dispute against Ba Kamite regarding his rights to the estate of his deceased sister, Fatimata Sankare. "Fa claims the inheritance of his sister, Fatimata, retained without rights by Ba Kamite. The value of the claim was not fixed. Ba affirmed by oath that it [the inheritance] consisted only of four baskets of grain and a number of clothes." Records of the judgment noted that "Ba will remit to Fa Sankare the estate of Fatimata Sankare."[34]

Death of a woman was not the only reason why women or their heirs were in court. The death of a woman's husband often signaled the beginning of the widow's struggles to extract herself from the webs of her husband's household. On 24 June 1905, Ali Taraore of Segu brought a case against Fatimata Kone of Seribougou. Ali Taraore accused Fatimata Kone, who was the widow of his father, Saidou, of having left the household with a part of the possessions he believed belonged to him upon his father's death. Taraore also accused Kone of using this wealth to benefit her daughter. Taraore did not provide evidence to support his claims. In contrast, Fatimata Kone affirmed by oath not to have taken any of the possessions of her deceased husband. She swore that what she had taken was her own property. In going to court, Ali Taraore was attempting to claim as his through inheritance of his father's estate that which actually "belonged" to Fatimata Kone. The tribunal dismissed the charges.[35]

The Segu native court heard a fascinating inheritance case on 27 March 1907 that showed how women used the courts to protect their wealth and how they used their wealth to enhance their control over their lives. Ba Diawara brought his deceased elder brother's wife, Nia Fane, to court to claim what he considered his rightful share of his brother's estate. Nia Fane told the court that she was married for 14 years to Ba Diawara's brother and upon her husband's death, she returned the bridewealth. She did not indicate why she returned the bridewealth, but as I discussed in Chapter 6, women could avoid levirate if they returned the bridewealth to her husband's kin. Ba Diawara was obviously not satisfied with the return of the bridewealth. He claimed that as part of the extended household of his elder brother, he had "worked very hard" and wanted a share of the wealth that Nia Fane now possessed, which included four cows, three oxen, and 104,000 cowries. In effect, Ba Diawara claimed that Nia Fane had commingled her individual property with the collective property of the household. It is not clear from the court record how Nia Fane responded to this claim, but the court's ruling hints that they agreed only partially with the plaintiff's claim. The court ruled that Nia Fane was to give to Ba Diawara one cow, one ox, and 4,000 cowries. Had the court believed Ba Diawara's claim that Nia Fane had actually taken the bulk of her husband's wealth as her own, it would probably have ruled more strongly in the plaintiff's favor and ordered a greater restitution of the contested possessions. That the court ruled only partially in Ba Diawara's favor indicates that the court believed that most of Nia Fane's wealth was actually her own.[36]

Taken together these three cases underscore that the two property system—collective and individual property—also favored women. "The woman," according to Delafosse, "has the same rights as the man in that which concerns the possession, use, and disposition of individual property and that which concerns the use and disposition of collective property. From the point of view of the acquisition of property rights, however, it often occurs that the rights of the woman are different from those of the man. Certain groups prohibit women from the capacity to inherit. . . . "[37] Delafosse's second sentence may refer to the contingency of women's capacity to acquire property rights within their husbands' patrilineages, because wives usually marry in. The first sentence, however, underscores that fact that women have the right to acquire individual property on the same basis as do men.

In Chapter 6, I described women's capacities to acquire property stemming from their labor as gender specific spheres of property. Work throughout the Soudan was gendered and marriage can be understood as a process of uniting male and female labor. Women worked for the collective well-being of the household and they had rights to *suraforaw* (Bamana: fields of the night, also referred to a *jonforaw*, fields of the slaves) or free time to devote to their own pursuits. Women could thus acquire property, which was separate from her husband's and the household's. Women tended to dispose of their property to their children, especially their daughters.[38] This pattern of disposition of women's property is born out in the case Ali Taraore brought against Fatimata Kone, the wife of his deceased father. "Ali accused Fatimata, widow of his father, Saidou, of having a part of his possessions, which she used for the benefit of her daughter." Ali was most likely the son of the household head by a different mother, which forms a natural cleavage in polygynous households. Like Nia Fane in the third case cited above, Fatimata Kone's property was probably commingled with that of the larger Taraore household. Such circulation of a wife's wealth within the household of her husband was probably very common. It made no sense to maintain their respective livestock separately, because one herder managed the combined herd. Commingling women's and household property produced both efficiencies and denser webs of affiliation. Extracting oneself from these denser webs became one of the extra hurdles women faced upon the death of their husbands.

Bafing Kamite was in court representing his sister's interest in recovering her wealth from the household of her deceased husband. During the course of the marriage, Kamite's sister "advanced" a cow to her husband, which in turn had produced five calves. Upon her husband's death, Kamite's sister extracted herself from the Diara household, which was headed by her husband's brother Ceko Diara, probably by returning the bridewealth to avoid levirate. Now she wanted Ceko Diara to return the loan she had made to her deceased husband. Ceko refused to acknowledge her claim. Without indicating who actually swore, the court records indicate that "proof was made by oath." The court ruled in favor of Kamite's sister and demanded that Ceko Diara return her property.[39]

This case also supports the proposition that wives often lent their property to their husbands to help him establish or augment their own wealth. Such commingling of husbands' and wives' property was probably quite common as it served to establish the complementarity and reciprocity of marriage.[40] Because of the commingling of property in the household, the wife had an interest in tracking her property should the marriage fail or her husband die. Under Bambara inheritance, her husband's wealth would be controlled by his brothers and his sons following the distinctions between collective and individual property. Thus, if Bafing Kaminte's sister had not kept track of the original "loan," she would not have been in a position to reclaim her property upon her husband's death. Thus, her husband's death was a moment of crisis in which she had to articulate and prove her claim to her property. If she had not done so, her husband's brother would have retained her property as his or as his household's.

Tracking of a wife's possessions in marriage was complicated when the wife died while still married. Occasionally a husband recognized his deceased wife's separate property and gave his wife's possessions to another of his wives in order to hold in trust for her children. This was the case brought by Modyba Haidara. In this case, the husband and father of Modyba had carefully tracked his wife's wealth, but had allowed it to commingle with that of another wife, who was caring for the child. Modyba Haidara's father apparently died before he reached maturity, because he did not appear in court. In 1908 Modyba Haidara was ready to claim his inheritance from his mother's estate, but his father's other wife and custodian of his inheritance claimed "nothing that would have belonged to Modyba remained." Modyba Haidara brought witnesses who "without being able to make precise identifications" estimated the value of his inheritance to be eight cows and two oxen. The court was persuaded and ordered the livestock to be returned to the plaintiff.[41]

The disposition of a deceased woman's wealth upon her death was indeed a common trouble spot in inheritance cases. Many of these cases in Segu were expressed in terms of Muslim inheritance, which provided for a wider set of interested parties. The major transformation issuing from Muslim inheritance practices was to redefine the locus of inheritance toward smaller domestic units, albeit competing ones, rather than the larger multigenerational Bambara household under the authority of the household head.[42] This had the consequence of interesting husbands in their wives' estates as well as guaranteeing certain portions to her sons and daughters, and to her uterine kinsmen (her father, mother, and siblings) following specific rules of inclusion and exclusions of various potential heirs.[43] Given the possibilities of being excluded from the inheritance, potential heirs were quick to make a case for their standing when a wealthy woman died. This was the case on 2 October 1905, when Amadou Mariko, husband of the deceased Dienma Coulibaly, asked the native court to proceed with the division of his wife's estate. Also attending the court were Dienma Coulibaly's mother, the deceased's uterine sister, her consanguine brother, and two consanguine sisters. The court divided the estate into tenths, with three-tenths going to the husband, one tenth each to her mother, brother, and uterine sister, and two tenths each to her two consanguine sisters.[44] Of course, such divisions of estates only made sense if there was something there to inherit. The court records did not indicate the value of Dienma Coulibaly's estate.

Something of the scale of women's wealth is indicated in the disposition of Fatimata Kouma's estate. When she died, she left seven cattle, a gold necklace, and four large amber beads. Her half-brother, Sori Bari, claimed to be the only rightful heir. He argued that his half sister had been divorced from her husband and that the other claimant, Maire Kouma, was not actually Fatimata's uncle. Fatimata Kouma's husband and uncle were in court to challenge Bari's claims.

Mohamed Diara proved that he was still married to the deceased when she died and Maire Kouma proved that he was actually her paternal uncle. The court ruled that Fatimata Kouma's estate should be divided into four parts: her husband and uncle each received three cattle and her half-brother received one cattle, the necklace, and the amber. This division of the estate did not conform to prevailing Malikite practice, but was considered equitable by the parties.[45]

Sina Barro's estate consisted of 26 cattle when the court considered the inheritance on 9 May 1908. The court ruled more in line with Malikite practices in awarding three parts to her widowed husband, two parts to her nephew, and one to her sister. Siradori Demba left a considerable fortune in terms of eleven cattle, five goats, and a gold necklace, which engendered a considerable debate over shares of the inheritance between the interested relatives. The court ruled that Siradori Demba's estate be divided into thirteen parts, of which two were to go to the deceased woman's mother, three parts to her husband, and the rest to her two daughters.[46] The Siradori Demba case demonstrates how Muslim inheritance in particular provided transfer of wealth to female relatives. These disputes over Muslim inheritance raise an important question about why did Muslim litigants chose to bring their cases before the colonial courts, which were overseen by both Muslim and animist judges, and not to the local qadi.

MUSLIM INHERITANCE DISPUTES IN THE SEGU PROVINCIAL TRIBUNAL

Following their first month of the new court's operation, the Segu administrator wrote at the end of April 1905 that "we can not yet judge the results of the reform in the organization of justice. During the first days of its operation, the district court did not meet and the provincial court met only to adjudicate a very small number of cases. I should remark, however, that the predominant Bambara element among the judges appears to have discomforted above all the Muslims and made them hesitant to bring forward their disputes."[47] What was merely his initial observations about Muslims' reluctance to use these new courts had by the end of the year become a discernible pattern. Muslims were clearly avoiding these new courts. The 1903 decree mandated that at least one of the judges of the provincial court be of the same personal status as the disputants. For Muslims, this meant at least one judge at the provincial court or one assessor at the district court was the qadi or other Muslim notable. This, indeed, was the case in Segu. "At both the provincial and district courts, the disputants will find at least one judge of the same personal status. Despite this, it is necessary to note that in the first efforts of the new courts, Muslims have demonstrated a certain reluctance about bringing their disputes before these mixed courts. The numbers of civil disputes has diminished and one can suppose that the reasons are that the litigants are choosing other ways to resolve their disputes."[48]

This is a telling remark and reminds us that the colonial courts were not the only venue for dispute resolution. Indeed, the establishment of the colonial legal system merely introduced a new element into the landscape of the plural legal system operating in the Soudan. Such a plural legal environment essentially empowered litigants to chose which venue would provide the best chance of success for the outcome they wanted. It should therefore not be surprising that women gravitated to the new colonial courts. These courts offered women new opportunities to resolve their disputes, especially ones regarding marriage, because qadi courts only recognized a handful of causes for divorce and usually required the husband's approval, and certainly not in village courts, where the elders were likely the kin of a married woman's husband. Muslims, as the Segu administrator noted, and especially males, probably took their cases before local qadi's courts. Local qadi courts persisted in the plural legal environment of the Soudan even if they no longer had "official" recognition. In addition, litigants could pursue a multiple strategy of trying out their disputes in a number of different venues until they got the outcome they wished. For the colonial provincial courts for which I have examined the records, there is no indication that the litigants tried or did not try other venues before bringing their cases to the new native courts. But the presence of Muslim inheritance cases in the provincial tribunal suggest that African litigants were certainly making calculated choices about the sequence of courts to use to resolve their grievances.

Muslims preferred, however, to avoid bringing their disputes before courts in which non-Muslims served as magistrates. Muslim *originaires*—the inhabitants of the Four Communes of Senegal who were granted metropolitan legal rights—protested the implementation of the 1903 decree that put their disputes before a French magistrate, who, while obliged to consult with a Muslim assessor, nonetheless ruled in ways that fundamentally changed gender and spousal relations in Muslim households. Rebecca Shereikis found the same pattern in Kayes. The Muslims of Kayes also protested the 1912 judicial reorganization, which eliminated the Muslim tribunal and directed Muslims to the native courts, where Muslim family law was merely one of the variety of other native customs. The nature of the Muslims' grievances is probably indicative of earlier sentiments as well. Shereikis quotes a 1913 Kayes petition:

> As a consequence [of the Decree of 1912], we Wolof Muslims, who came from Senegal to bring commercial and industrial knowledge to this new country, we who are for the most part literate, [who] exercise a profession or a trade and who for a long time have been used to a modern civilization, we find ourselves currently being treated . . . like the most backward

natives of the Soudan. In effect these subdivisional tribunals are composed of natives of Bambara and fetishist races, and because they apply fetishist customs . . . we find ourselves returned to the laws and customs of a previous generation.[49]

This and other petitions concerning the suppression of the Muslim tribunals in French West Africa reveal the cultural universe in which many Muslims lived. They clearly considered themselves part of the modern world and saw themselves participating in the advance of commerce and industry. They were thus defining themselves in opposition to animists, whom they lumped together as "uncivilized." These Muslims were also concerned that animist judges on the native courts would not and could not apply Muslim family law to their disputes involving their families.

A similar sentiment can be seen already in 1905 in Segu. While this document was not written by Seguvian Muslims, it captures the same concerns expressed by the Muslims in Kayes in 1913. In explaining why the Muslims of Segu were avoiding bringing their disputes to the new native courts, the administrator attributed this refusal to "the arrogance and the spirit of independence of a caste that would like to be superior—and believes that to be the case—and who want their cases judged by their peers."[50]

Among the Segu court records, I have found only a handful of registers that mention the religious status of the litigants. These data may be anomalous, reflecting specific local events that influenced short term decisions to use the native courts. Despite the fact that the Segu administrator wrote as late as July 1905 that Muslims "have demonstrated a certain reluctance about bringing

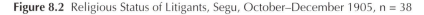

Figure 8.2 Religious Status of Litigants, Segu, October–December 1905, n = 38

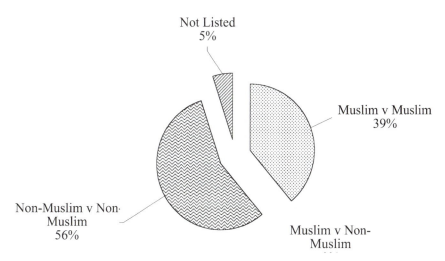

Figure 8.3 Types of Cases, Muslim Litigants, Segu, October–December 1905, n = 15

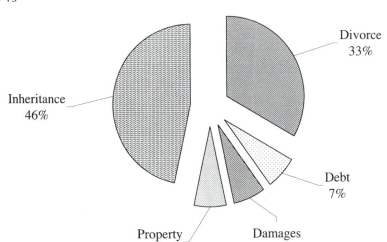

their disputes before these mixed courts," data from the Segu provincial court from October to December 1905 indicates that Muslim litigants made up a sizeable minority of the cases (38%). Those claiming customary status brought 54 percent of the cases. In a region where Muslims composed a significant part of the population, the data suggest that Muslims were underutilizing these courts relative to their population. This makes those Muslims who actually went to the provincial courts even more significant.

Figures 8.3 and 8.4 illustrate the nature of the disputes that Muslim and non-Muslim litigants brought before the Segu provincial court. These charts are revealing of the kinds of grievances Muslims and non-Muslims brought before these new courts. Inheritance cases clearly predominated among the kinds of disputes Muslims brought before the native courts, followed by divorce cases. A third of the cases were requests for divorces and nearly all of these were brought by women. This is consistent with the evidence on divorce from Bamako discussed in Chapter 5. Somewhat surprising, given the dominance of Muslims in the commercial sector of the regional economy, is the relatively insignificant number of disputes involving property, debt, and damages. Given the small sample of these cases, a momentary surge in inheritance cases could easily skew the data.

In contrast, the Segu litigants claiming customary status brought a fuller range of cases before the new courts. Inheritance disputes constituted only 15 percent of the cases for non-Muslims compared to 46 percent for Muslims. Similarly, non-Muslims brought relatively fewer divorce cases (25%) compared to Muslims (33%), but the difference is not significant. When taken together, divorce, marriage, bridewealth, and child custody cases composed 55 percent of all the disputes brought by non-Muslims. This suggests that marriage was a cause of most of the disputes that non-Muslims brought.

There are two explanations for the appearance of Muslim inheritance cases in the colonial courts. The first is the increased physical movement of people that coincided with other social and economic changes. These included the coincidental erosion of social boundaries around occupations, which encouraged former slaves and others to enter crafts or skilled activities that had been hitherto restricted to those who were endogenous to the group.[51] People were moving physically and socially, thus undermining that presumed symmetry between group, location, and custom. This change was captured in a 1907 report from Segu. Reflecting on the end of slavery and changes in what he called the mores of the people of the region, Administrator Charles Correnson wrote that

> it is important to note the progressive emancipation of the individual in relationship to the domestic group. From being a mere cog in the machinery of the household head, the individual begins to develop a distinct personality that is related to the emerging distinctions between communal property and personal property. The latter emerges to the detriment of the former and

Figure 8.4 Types of Cases, Litigants Claiming Customary Status, Segu, October–December 1905, n = 20

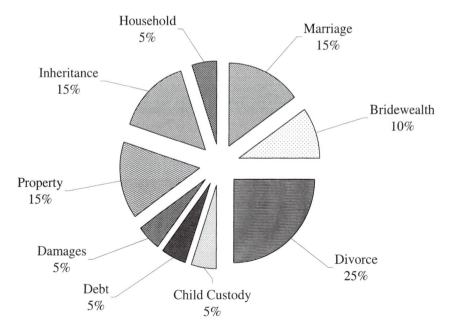

Household 5%

Marriage 15%

Inheritance 15%

Bridewealth 10%

Property 15%

Damages 5%

Divorce 25%

Debt 5%

Child Custody 5%

has the effect of encouraging the commercial activity, which had been shackled by the immobilization of goods and the lack of individualization in the communal domain.[52]

The second explanation has to do with the litigants' strategies to succeed in their disputes. The new courts offered a relatively new arena for litigants who may have wanted to avoid the other arenas of dispute resolution. Even though these courts were staffed by animist and Muslim magistrates, the custom of the litigants was to prevail. Used as they were to the idea of a "code," they could fairly easily turn to the French translation of Sidi Khalil's Maliki law, the Seignette edition of which was published in 1898. Administrators could easily locate the appropriate section on marriage, divorce, inheritance, guardianship, and so on.[53]

Such presumed naturalness in the application of shari'a law, however, obscured a much more dynamic process of legal adaptation and change. It also obscured the meaning of Muslim identity in an era of rapid conversion to Islam. Despite its written traditions, shari'a law never remained static, especially in contact with "customary law." As J. N. D. Anderson notes "Islamic law has never wholly ousted the indigenous law, but either co-exists with it as a separate and distinct system, each being applied in suitable circumstances, or else had fused with it into an amalgam that may be terms 'Islamic law' or 'native law and custom' according to local taste or local practice."[54] Perignon, district officer in Segu in 1900, observed the same kind of amalgam of legal spheres identified by Anderson, when it wrote that "it is necessary to take into consideration that here justice is a mixture (*mélange*) of Koranic principles and local ones."[55]

Delafosse, notoriously anti-Muslim throughout his 1912 study, also noted in passing the same conflation of legal spheres. "There where Islam has profoundly penetrated, the moeurs, rule of inheritance, and even the order of succession have often been notably modified. Thus, among the Muslims of the Soudan, the woman may inherit a part at least of the possessions of her husband, and the children of the deceased each receive an equal portion of the paternal inheritance. These two patterns are absolutely contradictory to the spirit of the primitive natives customs."[56] Delafosse's insistence of the absolute nature of custom was part of his program of demonstrating the deep reefs of continuity in Soudanese society. If some Muslims were wary of the mixed composition of the new tribunals, other litigants probably saw in this composition new opportunities to press cases based on a more "flexible" reading of either shari'a or customary law. I think that this helps explain the significant presence of inheritance cases in cases brought by Muslim litigants.

Where the ideal of Muslim shares of inheritance seems to prevail unambiguously is in the following case. On 23 October 1905, Douba Sissoko of Foni brought suit against her "guardian" Ba Manie Konare of Foni. Both claimed Muslim legal status. "Douba Sissoko requested to receive her portion of father's estate, which Ba Manie, her guardian, was holding for her. Among other possessions, Douba claimed 35 francs. She was able to prove that he was to give her her inheritance." The court ruled in Douba's favor.[57] This case suggests that the power of guardianship, as indicated in the case of the death of Sibery Diallo, where Sibery's brother, Souleyman Diallo, sought control over the inheritance, which he pledged to hold for the use of his minor niece (Sibery's daughter Serimba) until she reached the age of majority, was ambiguous enough to become the site for contestation over control over property held in pledge and likely also over the disposition of the body of minor herself.[58]

The case brought by Douba Sissoko against her guardian touches on one of the most important conclusions we can draw from the close reading of the records of Segu provincial tribunal: women were the initiators in a significant number of cases and even when they were the defendants (as in the case of Fatimata Kone), women often received protections from the court. Women used the new courts to seek dissolution of marriages they did not like, to protect their property, and to regain their property held by others against their will. Women using the new native courts was one of the major transformations in the early colonial period.

The evidence on inheritance disputes presented in this chapter challenge the assumption of the orderliness of custom and the regularity of households and household social relations at least as presented in the classic ethnographies of Charles Monteil and Maurice Delafosse. Monteil and Delafosse were instrumental in the development of the idea of a Soudanese civilization of settled farmers functioning in age-old ways. Instead, the evidence drawn from the inheritance disputes discussed here suggest that the period from 1905 to 1912 was one in which there was considerable debate and challenges to "custom." These inheritance disputes thus provide a lens onto the subtle patterns of social change, which were linked to struggles over property, social relationships, and strategies for accumulation. My concentration on cases dealing with women's wealth and women's estates reveals something of the tensions between individual and collective rights to property within households and the strategies women's used to track their individual property even as it commingled with other household members' property. These disputes also remind us that inheritance disputes were part of wider changes taking place in this period of accelerated social change linked to colonial conquest, the establishment of colonial institutions, and the end of slavery.

9

CONCLUSION: THE IMPORTANCE OF "DISPUTES WITHOUT SIGNIFICANCE"

I began this project by asking two questions: why did Africans bring their most intimate domestic disputes to the newly created native courts in the period after 1905? And what do these disputes tell us about everyday life and social change? To answer these questions, I used all 2,062 civil disputes heard at the *tribunaux de province* of four districts between 1905 and 1912. I concluded that changes in social relations occurring at a time of accelerated change associated with colonial conquest and the end of slavery interacted with institutional changes—namely the creation of the new native courts—to produce discernible patterns of litigation. Moreover, these patterns of litigation point to "trouble spots" in African society, thus providing a lens into the most ordinary aspects of daily life. The lens of trouble spots, however, highlights relationships in conflict; people in harmonious relationship do not have disputes to bring to the courts. In focusing on trouble spots, am I normalizing conflict when conflicted social relationships may not have been the norm?

African Studies may be one of the few academic fields where the notions of harmony persist in shaping our understandings of past times and patterns of social change. Even within this field, few would adhere to the assumption that until the colonial era (or the arrival of European demand for slaves) Africans lived in harmonious social relationships with each other and with the environment.[1] Most students of the African past recognize that individuals sought security and advantages for themselves and their social groups, even if those gains came at the expense of other individuals and groups. Ubiquitous, low level competition for control over resources—labor, land, forests, waterways, and so on—was punctuated by periods of heightened conflict associated with environmental, political, cultural, and economic changes.

The period from 1905 to 1912 coincided with profound changes in social organization set in motion by colonial conquest and the end of slavery. I have described these changes as linked sets of transformations, which in turn altered the landscapes of power in the region. I use the concept of landscapes of power to capture the sense of intentional action as people sought to renegotiate their relationships within households, with those in positions of authority, and with those who offered goods and services. I also use this term to suggest that in acting intentionally, women and men had to understand and traverse a landscape shaped by changing power relations, new institutions, and the changing character of those institutions and the ideas that undergirded them. This was a period when social relationships were under considerable pressure and the court cases I use may well reflect the character of this moment. Indeed, men and women may have sought out the new colonial courts precisely because they were better suited to resolving their disputes than preexisting lineage, village, and qadi's courts. I discuss litigants' choice of courts as venue-shopping, not to suggest that disputants floated about from court to court in search of the best judgment (much as consumers prowl the mall looking for the best price), which they may have done, but to underscore their strategic evaluation of different legal outcomes available at different courts. The data derived from these entry-level civil disputes provides precious detail about social relations and social relations in various phases of deterioration.

The creation of the native courts in the French Soudan generated a new phase of the longer history of the development of plural legal systems in this region, which had been characterized by centuries of cultural and political change. I was particularly struck by the evidence that African disputants who used the new native courts after 1905 were interested in "definitive" judgments, rather than reconciliation. Many people with intimate domestic problems probably sought reconciliation through the agency of lineage and village elders. I do not have evidence of such reconciliation; instead, what the court records provide is evidence of individuals, especially those who were in asymmetrical power relations, who wanted more thorough changes in their relationships, those who felt especially vulnerable in regard to specific property or property rights, and those who sought new means of gaining or controlling property and people. Africans exposed the intimate parts of their lives in courts because doing so was the price of admission into the colonial legal system. As in metropolitan France, the courts were public in order to ensure transparency and accountability.[2]

The incidence of litigation in the provincial courts of Bamako, Bouguni, Gumbu, and Segu between 1905 and 1912 indicate that marital relations, control over property, and debt were the most pronounced trouble spots. By analyzing the incidence of trouble spots in the different districts, I was able to pinpoint with greater accuracy which districts experienced what kinds of trouble more than the average. I used these leads to pursue a more detailed analysis of patterns of litigation and the substance of the disputes. A central part of the methodology I used in this book is to move back and forth between trends in litigation and individual cases. I first identified trends in litigation and then sought to interpret the nature of the dispute through an analysis of individual cases. Two kinds of trends emerged from this research. The first was the dramatic spikes in litigation surrounding specific events. The second was more general trends, indicating changing patterns of litigation, court use, and legal outcomes.

In chapter 4, I examined the evidence surrounding the spike in debt cases in Gumbu in 1908. As I argued, the spike in debt cases coincided with the first wave of the slaves' exodus from Gumbu that began in the spring 1908. A careful review of the cases indicated that most of these debt cases were actually brought by former masters against their former slaves. Although the new native courts were not permitted to consider social status in their assessment of the dispute, evidence from the cases revealed that these debt cases stemmed from the particular sharecropping contract between slaves and masters in Gumbu and that former masters were in court to prevent their slaves from leaving the area without first sharing the harvest. Most of these cases were about shares of the grain harvest; others involved loans of livestock. What is striking about this trend in debt cases was that when the slaves resumed their exodus from Gumbu in spring 1909, the volume of departures was significantly higher than in 1908 but the incidence of debt cases was only a fraction of what it had been the year before.

Figure 9.1 Incidence of Debt Disputes, Gumbu, 1905–1912, n = 197

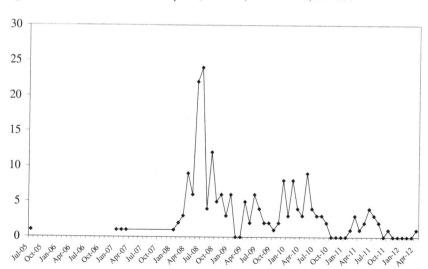

Source: ANM 2 M 122

This example of debt disputes in Gumbu indicates what court records can and what they cannot tell us. By examining the records in 1908, we know that debt cases revolved around contractual issues of sharecropping and return of livestock, which had formed dense webs of relationships between masters and slaves in an environment without strong states to support the masters' extraction of surplus from their slaves. The court records do not tell us why there was such a dramatic decline in debt cases in 1909, even in the face of larger numbers of slave departures.

The Gumbu debt series reminds us that the court records of the provincial tribunal used in this study do not tell the whole story. They rarely reveal the history between the litigants, most of whom had been in long-term relationships with one another, nor the story of what happened after the court ruled in the case. More importantly, because each case focuses only on the proximate wrongs in that dispute, we do not see the wider context. I knew in advance that Gumbu was the site of a major slave exodus in 1908–1909, so I knew what kinds of clues to look for in the individual cases. Had I not known about the slave exodus in advance, the spike in 1908 would have altered me to inquire further about the wider context of 1908. Either way, trends in litigation point to interesting intersections of agency and structure.

In thinking about what happened after the court ruled in each case, we need to ask how judgments were enforced. We can assume that with the authority of the colonial state behind the judgments of its native courts, the loser would be intimidated into delivering on the judgment. However, the colonial state did not have the resources and probably lacked the interest to track down and prosecute those who refused to obey the court or simply left the region without fulfilling the court's rulings in its civil cases.[3] Thus, the former slaves who left in 1909 may have learned from the experiences of the year before what the courts could and could not do and just departed without informing anyone. The court records do not tell us whether a plaintiff may have filed some sort of summons, which the defendant may have ignored. With the exception of women seeking divorce from husbands who had abandoned them, we only read about cases in which both parties came to court together. Absent the coercive capacity of the court to require attendance of defendants, the cases we read probably formed a limited set of disputes where the litigants were willing to play by the rules of the new courts and thus willingly accept its judgments. It also suggests that most defendants were probably close by and had enough interest at stake to come to court to seek the best outcome they could get.

The second type of trend evident from court records was the gradual movement of litigants and judgments in particular directions or, more interestingly, reversals of patterns. My favorite examples of these types of trends are the Bamako marriage and divorce cases. I used this figure in Chapter 5, but it is worth revisiting again here (see Figure 9.2). In contrast to the Gumbu debt

Figure 9.2 Marriage and Divorce Disputes, Bamako, 1905–1912. Divorces
n = 224, Marriages n = 173

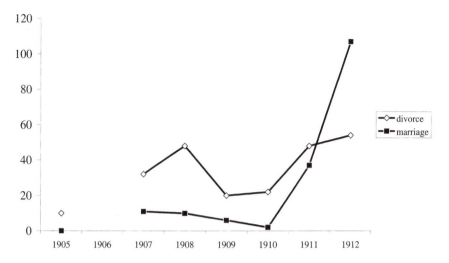

Source: ANM 2 M 104/105

trend, I had no background to interpret the trends in marriage and divorce in
Bamako. I knew that divorce cases were important because I had read the
monthly reports from Bamako in which the district administrators had described
the earliest clients of the new courts as women seeking divorce. But I did not
know until I plotted the incidence of divorce and marriage that divorce had fallen
off after an initial surge in cases between 1905 and 1908 and then rose again only
to begin to level off in 1911–1912. In contrast, marriage cases accelerated dramatically from 1910–1912. These trends demanded further analysis. In contrast
to the Gumbu debt cases, where I knew some of the context in advance, in the
Bamako case, I needed to learn more about the wider environment. Rather than
finding the solution in changes in the wider political and economic context as in
Gumbu, I found clues in the changing nature of European discourses about
African women and families. A careful reading of the archives indicated that
European administrators had an initial predisposition in favor of African women,
who were represented as being akin to slaves in the sense that they were "bought"
with bridewealth and were thus in marriages in which they had no choice. These
representations and the roles of European administrators in the courts during
these early years influenced the African magistrates, who ruled mostly in favor of
women seeking divorce. By 1910, however, an alternative representation of
African families became ascendant. The principal author of this alternative discourse was Maurice Delafosse, who in 1910 began teaching African customs at
the École Coloniale and who in 1912 published his seminal *Haut-Sénégal-Niger.*

Delafosse's course on customs and his *Haut-Sénégal-Niger* made a powerful case
for stability of African families that rested on the unquestioned authority of the
male household head. These changing discourses about African women and the
family provided an entry point into a study of the judgments rendered in divorce
and marriage cases. A comparison of the judgments in divorce and marriage cases
provided substantive proof that the emerging discourse on African family stability was having an effect on the courts. For the first time since the courts opened in
1905, judgments in divorce cases in 1911 began to move against women seeking
divorce. Whereas prior to 1910, women were overwhelmingly granted the
divorces they sought, after 1911 half or more of the divorce suits brought by
women were dismissed. Further supporting this trend of courts finding in favor of
husbands and family stability, the judgments in marriage cases in which men
sought the power of the courts to return their runaway wives consistently favored
husbands in 1911 and 1912.

   These trends in marriage and divorce suggest two important conclusions.
The first is that the courts provided only a brief window of opportunity for
women seeking divorce from unhappy marriages. While the data for 1911 and
1912 indicate that women continued to seek dissolution of unhappy marriages
in the native courts, they were no longer assured of a positive outcome.
Women were still granted divorces by the native courts, but the courts raised
the bar considerably by demanding more proof of accusations of mistreatment and abandonment and by requiring a cooling-off period before granting
divorce. More research needs to be conducted on the period after 1912 to see
what trends emerged in divorce and marriage cases. It could be that the closing of the window favorable to women evident in the data from 1911–1912
persisted. Such a conclusion would support Toulmin's assertion that divorce
rarely occurred in postcolonial Mali, Barbara Cooper's conclusion that
African women in the interwar period and afterwards shunned the native
courts because they knew that the courts favored their husbands, and Sean
Hawkin's conclusion that the colonial courts in Northern Ghana ruled consistently in favor of marital stability and husbands' rights to their wives over
women's choices, thus eroding women's freedoms.[4] Such an argument about
the opening and closing of opportunities for women supports Jean Allman
and Victoria Tashjian's argument about the need to identify both long-term
and short-term historical trends that empowered and disempowered women's
control over resources.[5]

   The second conclusion is that courts have always been susceptible to the
political and ideological pressures.[6] Civil law courts were at once insulated
and more directly tied to these pressures. Judges are considered civil servants
and thus somewhat immune from the ideological litmus tests applied to the
appointment of judges in some common law traditions. On the other hand,
judges were empowered to rule according to the code, which is made by leg-
islative action. In colonial French West Africa, judges on the native courts

were not civil servants, but appointees subject to selection by senior colonial officials, making them doubly vulnerable to the agenda of the colonial state. Moreover, in the colonies, laws were made by decree with some, often token, consultation with civil society. But the colonial state was not a monolithic entity; instead, as I described in Chapter 3, magistrates and administrators often fought over the nature of the courts and the degree of judicial accommodation to political policy. The courts could thus be harnessed to the social agendas of the dominant forces within the colonial state.[7] Governor-general Ponty's *politique des races* found a ready partner in Delafosse's Soudanese civilization. In contrast, the Popular Front, which never articulated a coherent colonial policy, nonetheless favored social reform in the colonies and renewed the debate about women's choice in marriage in the Mandel Decree of 1939, which itself fell victim to Vichy's profamily orientation.[8]

My conclusion stated at the beginning of this chapter is that changes in social relations interacted with institutional changes to produce discernible patterns of litigation. By institutional change, I mean the establishment of the native courts in 1905. From an analytical perspective, it would have been much neater to assume institutional stability and thus attribute the discernible patterns of litigation to social change. However, the courts were not stable institutions. They were subject to political and ideological pressures. And they were also subject to institutional change. Thus, analysis of discernible patterns of litigation needs to factor in both social and institutional change.

The French never quite got the native courts right in part because they were operating on the assumptions of stable ethnic groups linked to clear territorial units. Instead, African men and women were on the move during the early years of the twentieth century, into new areas and into new occupations and new social relations. The assumption that the provincial chief sat supreme over his territory composed of a homogenous ethnic group was out of touch with realities on the ground. In 1912, the government general of French West Africa issued the first of a series of periodic efforts to tinker with the architecture of the native courts. In this decree, the provincial tribunals were suppressed in favor of newly created "subdivisional tribunals," which eliminated the role of the provincial chief as president of the tribunal. The subdivisional tribunal model also mandated a different spatial distribution of native courts, although it is not clear how well they were actually implemented. Nor is it clear to me what procedural changes were implemented. The new decree mandated greater scrutiny over court personnel, including the secretaries who kept the court records.[9] World War I, however, interrupted the progress of institutional change, by withdrawing several layers of French administrators from local affairs. Much more research is needed to assess the impact of institutional change on the patterns of litigation and thus on the ability of court records to yield evidence of the social change I have been looking for.

I began this study deeply concerned about historians' decreasing ability to mine African oral histories for evidence of daily life at the beginning of the colonial period. I remain convinced that we need to find new sources capable of providing evidence of African encounters with the changes set in motion though colonial conquest and colonial rule. I gravitated to the study of court records because I wanted to explore whether these records might provide evidence of daily life, which I am convinced that they do, evidence of African agency, which they do as well, and evidence of African voices.

The African disputes we read in the court records of the provincial tribunals are expressed by African litigants—we have their names, residences, and the dates on which they spoke—and they do recount wrongs, strained or broken relationships, and requests to the court to act on those claims. These are records of Africans expressing their grievances, but the voices we hear have been altered by the processes that transformed the dispute as understood by the litigants into categories that the court recognized. The 1903 decree establishing the native courts mandated that court registers be kept in French. Thus, the African dispute underwent several layers of transformation through translation before it appeared as written text in the registers. The act of translating Banama, Mandinka, or Fula into French was only the tip of much more substantive transformations. I have found helpful the Felstiner-Abel-Sarat model of tracing a perceived injury through the phases of naming, blaming, and claiming before it appears in court. In the process, the grievance is renarrated and rearticulated to conform to prevailing legal categories so that the courts can act on it. Susan Hirsch has complicated this process further by insisting that we recognize how gender and gendered norms of speech profoundly shape the narration of trouble.[10] I have concluded that the transcript we read is but a shadow of a much more complex understanding of wrongs and of the complex set of interactions that actually went on in the court. What we have is a summary of the dispute that was produced by an intermediary, whose understanding of the dispute was shaped by translations of interactions that took place in the court and by various economies of recording. These translations and summaries served to channel talk of trouble into simplified categories of dispute. These are African voices, but the voices we read are not the same as those that spoke in the court.

Research into the everyday life during an era of accelerated social change demands that we pay careful attention to the sources that we have and to the evidence that we do not have. Historians need to be aware of what their sources can and cannot provide. As we learn more about how Africans used courts during the colonial period and more about the changes in narrating trouble as it is translated into texts, historians will develop more sophisticated tools to use the rich evidence that is clearly available in colonial court records.

NOTES

PREFACE

1. *Richmond Newspapers, Inc. v. Virginia,* 44 U.S. 555 (1980); *Globe Newspapers v. Superior Court,* 457 U.S. 596 (1982); *NBC Subsidiary Inc. v. Superior Court,* 20 Cal. 4th 1178 (1999). See www.thefirstamdendment.org/courtaccess.html.

2. Maryland Rules of Procedure, Title 6: The Courts, Judges, and Attorneys; Chapter 1000, Access to Court Records, March 4, 2004. See www.courts.state.md.us/access/.

CHAPTER 1: INTRODUCTION: "DISPUTES WITHOUT SIGNIFICANCE"—AFRICAN SOCIAL HISTORY AND COLONIAL COURTS AT A TIME OF SOCIAL TRANSFORMATION

1. Arthur Girault, *Principes de colonisation et de législation coloniale: deuxième partie: les colonies françaises depuis 1815,* 4th ed., 3 vols. (Paris: Sirey, 1921–1923) I, p. 486. The original and much shorter first edition of this book appeared in 1895 and framed the issue as follows: "Not French citizens, the natives in our colonies do not enjoy political rights. Our private law is not applicable to them. They conserve their social organization, their customs, and their laws," *Principes de colonisation et de législation coloniale* (Paris: Larose, 1895), p. 303.

2. Lt-gov. Colonel de Trentinian, Note circular, Bamako, 3 February 1896, ANM 2 M 4.

3. Martin Klein, *Slavery and Colonial Rule in French West Africa* (Cambridge: Cambridge University Press, 1998), pp. 170–173. Klein estimates that around one million slaves left their masters throughout French West Africa.

4. Lt-gov. Clozel, Rapport politique, Haut-Sénégal-Niger, 1911, ANS-AOF 2 G 11–9.

5. John Henry Merryman, *The Civil Law Tradition: An Introduction to the Legal Systems of Western Europe and Latin America* (Stanford: Stanford University Press, 1969), pp. 24–39. For the French West African case, Dominique Sarr has studied the appeals brought to the highest court, *cour d'homologation,* which did identify problems in legislation and practice. See especially Dominique Sarr, "Le chamber spéciale d'homologation de la cour d'appel de l'Afrique Occidentale Française et les coutumes pénales de 1903–1920," *Annales Africaines* 1 (1974).

6. Girault, *Principes,* I, 464–473. See also Jeswald W. Salacuse, *An Introduction to Law in French-Speaking Africa* (Charlottesville: Michie, 1969), I, pp. 21–23.

7. See the classic anthropological study about Lozi judges, Max Gluckman, *The Judicial Process among the Barotse of Northern Rhodesia* (Manchester: University of Man-

chester Press, 1955). Martin Chanock, *The Making of South African Legal Culture, 1902–1936: Fear, Favour, and Prejudice* (Cambridge: Cambridge University Press, 2001) is very much concerned with the competing discourses regarding the law and with the judiciaries' role in shaping the complex South African legal system.

8. The Malian Court Record Project at Stanford University is in the process of coding the complete run of all the provincial court records for the French Soudan from 1905–1912 that have survived. Once completed, the coded cases and copies of the court registers will be available to students and scholars. All 1906 court registers were sent to Dakar for the *procureur-général* to examine and approve. Most of these have been lost, with a few exceptions of partial registers available in the Senegalese National Archives. I have not included these records in this data set because they are incomplete. The Bamako provincial tribunal continued to hear and record disputes into March 1913. During this first quarter of 1913, it heard 91 disputes. I have not included these disputes in the data used in this study because the other district data end in December 1912.

9. E. Beurdeley, *La justice indigène en Afrique occidentale française: mission d'études, 1913–1914* (Paris: Publication de la comité de l'Afrique française, 1916). See also Gouvernment général de l'Afrique occidentale française, *Justice indigène: instructions aux administrateurs sur l'application du Décret du 16 Août 1912, portant réorganization de la Justice indigène en Afrique occidentale française* (Dakar: Imprimermie Ternaux, 1913). See also Pierre Meunier, *L'Organisation et fonctionnement de la justice indigène en Afrique occidentale* (Paris: A. Challamel, 1914).

10. Richard Roberts, "The End of Slavery in the French Soudan, 1905–1914," in *The End of Slavery in Africa,* eds. Suzanne Miers and Richard Roberts (Madison: The University of Wisconsin Press, 1988), p. 288.

11. Richard Roberts and Martin Klein, "The Banamba Slave Exodus of 1905 and the End of Slavery in the Western Sudan," *JAH* 21 (3) (1980); Richard Roberts, "The Emergence of a Grain Market in Bamako, 1883–1908," *Canadian Journal of African Studies* 14 (1) (1980); Klein, *Slavery and Colonial Rule,* chapter 10.

12. A provincial tribunal was first established in Banamba in 1907. I compare the evidence from the Banamba tribunal with that of Gumbu in Richard Roberts, "Women, Household Instability, and the End of Slavery in Banamba and Gumbu, French Soudan, 1905–1912," in *Women and Slavery: In Honour of Suzanne Miers,* eds. Gwyn Campbell, Suzanne Miers, and Joseph Miller (London: Frank Cass, forthcoming). I do not include the Banamba evidence in this book.

13. For a sample of this debate see, Igor Kopytoff, "The Cultural Context of African Abolition," in *The End of Slavery in Africa,* eds. Suzanne Miers and Richard Roberts (Madison: University of Wisconsin Press, 1988), pp. 485–503; Roberts, "The End of Slavery in the French Soudan, 1905–1914," pp. 282–307; Klein, *Slavery and Colonial Rule.*

14. Richard Roberts, *Warriors, Slaves, and Merchants: The State and the Economy in the Middle Niger Valley, 1700–1914* (Stanford: Stanford University Press, 1987), pp. 191–207.

15. Richard Roberts, *Two Worlds of Cotton: Colonialism and the Regional Economy in the French Soudan, 1800–1946* (Stanford: Stanford University Press, 1996), pp. 11–36.

16. Karl N. Llewellyn and E. A. Hoebel, *The Cheyenne Way: Conflict and Case Law in Primitive Jurisprudence* (Norman: University of Oklahoma Press, 1941), pp. 20–40. See M. B. Hooker, *Legal Pluralism: An Introduction to Colonial and Neo-Colonial Laws* (Oxford: Clarendon, 1975), pp. 35–39.

17. Laura Nader and Harry F. Todd, eds., *The Disputing Process: Law in Ten Societies* (New York: Columbia University Press, 1978), pp. 14–15. See James C. Scott, *Domination*

and the Arts of Resistance: Hidden Transcripts (New Haven, CT: Yale University Press, 1990), for discussions of off-stage expressions of resentment regarding injustices.

18. See especially Laura Nader, *Harmony Ideology: Justice and Control in a Zapotec Mountain Village* (Stanford: Stanford University Press, 1990); Michael J. Lowy, "A Good Name is Worth More than Money: Strategies of Court Use in Urban Ghana," in *The Disputing Process,* eds. Laura Nader and Harry F. Todd (New York: Columbia University Press, 1978), pp. 202–207. See also Marc Galanter, "Justice in Many Rooms: Courts, Private Ordering, and Indigenous Law," *Journal of Legal Pluralism* 19 (1981).

19. Jane F. Collier, *Law and Social Change in Zinacantan* (Stanford: Stanford University Press, 1973), pp. 252–256; June Starr, *Dispute and Settlement in Rural Turkey: An Ethnography of Law* (Leiden: Brill, 1978), pp. 140–141, 179–185; June Starr and Jane F. Collier, "Introduction: Dialogues in Legal Anthropology," in *History and Power in the Study of the Law: New Directions in Legal Anthropology,* eds. June Starr and Jane Collier (Ithaca, NY: Cornell University Press, 1989), pp. 1–3, 6–9.

20. Collier, *Law and Social Change,* chapters 2–3; Sally Falk Moore, "Individual Interests and Organizational Structures: Dispute Settlements as 'Events of Articulation,' " in *Social Anthropology and the Law,* ed. Ian Hamnett (London: Academic Press, 1977); Lawrence Rosen, "Islamic 'Case Law and the Logic of Consequence,' " in *History and Power in the Study of the Law,* eds. June Starr and Jane Collier (Ithaca, NY: Cornell University Press, 1989), pp. 311–312. See also Richard Abel, "Introduction," in *The Politics of Informal Justice: Volume 2, Comparative Studies,* ed. Richard Abel (New York: Academic Press, 1982), p. 3.

21. Collier, *Law and Social Change,* p. 57.

22. Starr and Collier, "Introduction: Dialogues in Legal Anthropology," in *History and Power in the Study of Law,* ed. Starr and Collier, p. 17. See also June Starr and Jane F. Collier, "Historical Studies of Legal Change," *Current Anthropology* 28 (3) (1987): pp. 367–372.

23. A. L. Epstein, "The Case Method in the Field of Law," in *The Craft of Social Anthropology,* ed. A. L. Epstein (London: Tavistock, 1967), p. 208.

24. Gluckman, *The Judicial Process.*

25. Max Gluckman, "Introduction," in *The Craft of Social Anthropology,* ed. A. L. Epstein (London: Tavistock, 1967), p. xvi.

26. Lloyd Fallers, *Law without Precedent: Legal Ideas in Action in the Courts of Colonial Busoga* (Chicago: University of Chicago Press, 1969), pp. 85–86.

27. In the United States, less than 3 percent of civil filings (that is disputes that led to legal action by calling the police, contacting a lawyer or a government agency) went to trial. There are many stages along the way to court that provide exit options from litigation. See Patricia Ewick and Susan S. Silbey, *The Common Place of Law: Stories from Everyday Life* (Chicago: University of Chicago Press, 1998), p. 19.

28. Sally Falk Moore, *Social Facts and Fabrications: "Customary" Law on Kilimanjaro, 1880–1980* (New York: Cambridge University Press, 1986), pp. 1–12.

29. I have found Richard Abel's discussion in "Western Courts in Non-Western Settings: Patterns of Court Use in Colonial and Neo-Colonial Africa," in *The Imposition of Law,* eds. Sandra Burman and Barbara E. Harrell-Bond (New York: Academic Press, 1979) very suggestive.

30. These statistics refer to cases in which I can identify the plaintiff's gender. I have not included cases in which both parties agreed mutually on divorce. By district, 74 percent of divorce plaintiffs in Bamako were women; 42 percent in Bouguni; 75 percent in Gumbu; and 80 percent in Segu.

31. In French ethnographies describing African and Maghrebian practices, the term *dot* is used to signify bridewealth as a form of matrimonial compensation.

32. Gluckman, *The Judicial Process,* p. 21.

33. District population is taken from ARS K 18–22 as quoted in Klein, *Slavery and Colonial Rule,* p. 254. We do not have very good data on litigation rates for colonial Africa, but for illustrative purposes I have estimated the litigation rate in Bamako in 1908 to be 0.75 (based on number of cases per 1,000 inhabitants) and in 1912 to be 1.9. In contrast to Bamako, litigation rates in Gumbu in 1908 were 3.0 and fell to 0.002 in 1912 following the end of the slaves' exodus. Segu followed the Gumbu pattern of falling litigation rates, from 0.62 in 1908 to 0.2 in 1912. Bouguni, which witnessed significant in-migration during the slaves' exodus saw an increase in litigation rates, from 0.08 in 1908 to 0.2 in 1912. For comparative purposes, Kenya as a whole in 1969 had a litigation rate of 17.9. In Meru district, Kenya, the litigation rate was 3.3 in 1969, indicating significant regional variations. In the United States in 1994, the litigation rate was 74.5 and in France in 1995 it was 40.3. These figures suggest that far from being like the Lozi, the inhabitants of the Middle Niger region of the French Soudan had fairly low rates of litigation as measured by the case load at the provincial tribunal. Kenya data taken from Richard Abel, "Western Courts in Non-Western Settings: Patterns of Court Use in Colonial and Neo-Colonial Africa," in *The Imposition of Law,* eds. Sandra Burman and Barbara E. Harrell-Bond (New York: Academic Press, 1979), p. 183; USA and France data taken from Christian Wollschlager, "Exploring Global Landscapes in Litigation Rates," in *Sociologie des Rechts: Festschrift fur Erhard Blakenburg zum 60. Geburtztag,* eds. Jurgen Brand and Dieter Strempel (Baden-Baden: Nomos, 1998), pp. 587–588.

34. Abel argues that litigation rates in rural areas will decline, whereas those in urban areas may remain constant or even increase because "tribal social structure" persisted in rural areas, which bound individuals together in ways that were "difficult and costly to sever." This was less true in modern, expanding urban centers. Abel, "Western Courts in Non-Western Settings," pp. 182–184.

35. European microhistorians have access to a wider variety of church, village, and state records. See for example Carlo Ginzburg, *The Cheese and the Worms: The Cosmos of a Sixteenth Century Miller,* translated by John Tedeschi and Anne Tedeschi (Baltimore: Johns Hopkins University Press, 1980); Edward Muir and Guido Ruggiero, eds., *Microhistory and the Lost Peoples of Europe,* translated by Eren Branch (Baltimore: Johns Hopkins University Press, 1991). See also Hans Medick, *Weben und Überleben in Laichingen 1650–1900: Lokalgeschichte als allgemeine Geschichte* (Göttingen: Vandenhoeck & Ruprecht, 1996) and István Szijártó, "Four Arguments for Microhistory," *Rethinking History* 6 (2) (2002): pp. 209–215.

36. This focus on women and the law builds on the important leads taken by Margaret Jean Hay and Marcia Wright, *African Women and the Law: Historical Perspectives* (Boston: African Studies Center, 1982); and Martin Chanock, *Law, Custom, and Social Order: The Colonial Experience in Malawi and Zambia* (Cambridge: Cambridge University Press, 1985).

37. Cognitive psychology may provide some leads on guiding our understanding of human processes of perception, knowing, learning, and problem solving. For a study of cognitive problem solving linked to spatial knowledge, see Mary M. Smith, Peter E. Morris, Philip Levy, and Andrew W. Ellis, *Cognition in Action* (London: Hillsdale, 1987), chapter 11. See also Richard A. Carlson, *Experienced Cognition* (Mahwah, NJ: L. Erlbaum Associates, 1997), pp. 195–263.

38. Anthony Giddens, *The Constitution of Society* (Berkeley: University of California Press, 1984), pp. 9, 14.

39. Fernand Braudel, *The Mediterranean and the Mediterranean World in the Age of Philip I*, translated by Sian Reynolds (New York: Harper and Row, 1972), pp. 20–21.

40. See, for example, A. G. Hopkins, *An Economic History of West Africa* (London: Longman, 1973), chapter 4; Robin Law, ed., *From Slave Trade to "Legitimate Commerce": The Commercial Transition in Nineteenth-Century West Africa* (Cambridge: Cambridge University Press, 1995); and Bouboucar Barry, *Senegambia and the Atlantic Slave Trade* (Cambridge: Cambridge University Press, 1998); Terence Ranger, "The Invention of Tradition in Africa," in *The Invention of Tradition,* eds. Eric Hobsbawm and Terence Ranger (Cambridge: Cambridge University Press, 1983).

41. See, for example, Sara Berry, *No Condition is Permanent: The Social Dynamics of Agrarian Change in Sub-Saharan Africa* (Madison: University of Wisconsin, 1993); Jan Hogendorn and Paul Lovejoy, *Slow Death to Slavery: The Course of Abolition in Northern Nigeria, 1897–1936* (Cambridge: Cambridge University Press, 1993); Suzanne Miers and Richard Roberts, eds., *The End of Slavery in Africa* (Madison: The University of Wisconsin Press, 1988).

42. Giddens, *Constitution of Society,* p. 25. Giddens refers to structures as being "structuring properties allowing the 'binding' of time-space in social systems. . . . Those practices which have the greatest time-space extensions within such totalities can be referred to as *institutions,*" p. 17.

43. The debate surrounding the origins of Anglo-American antislavery provides a fascinating discussion of ideology, representation, and agency. See Thomas Bender, ed., *The Antislavery Debate: Capitalism and Abolitionism as a Problem in Historical Explanation* (Madison: University of Wisconsin Press, 1992).

44. Jonathon Glassman, *Feasts and Riot: Revelry, Rebellion, and Popular Consciousness on the Swahili Coast, 1856–1888* (Portsmouth, NH: Heinemann, 1995) captures this sense of unstable and contested institutions and practices. See also Sally Engle Merry, *Colonizing Hawaii: The Cultural Power of the Law* (Princeton: Princeton University Press, 2000).

45. Rapport sur le fonctionnement de la justice indigène, 3rd Quarter 1905, Bougouni, ANM 2 M 59; Rapport sur le fonctionnement de la justice indigène, 4th Quarter 1905, Bougouni, ANM 2 M 59.

46. Rapport sur le fonctionnement des tribunaux indigènes, 3rd Quarter 1906, Bougouni, ANM 2 M 59.

47. Rapport sur le fonctionnement de la justice, 2nd Quarter 1907, Jenne, ANM 2 M 60.

48. Rapport sur le fonctionnement de la justice, 1st Quarter 1909, Bamako, ANM 2M54.

49. Bernard Cohn, "Some Notes on Law and Change in India," *Economic Development and Change* 8 (1) (1959): 72–79; Bernard Cohn, *Colonialism and its Forms of Knowledge: The British in India* (Princeton: Princeton University Press, 1996); Robert Kidder, "Western Law in India: External Law and Local Response," in *Social System and Legal Process,* ed. Harry M. Johnson (San Francisco: Jossey-Bass, 1978), pp. 159–162.

50. Collier, *Law and Social Change,* p. 69. See also Maria Teresa Sierra, "Indian Rights and Customary Law in Mexico: A Study of the Nahuas in the Sierra de Puebla," *Law and Society Review* 29 (2) (1995): 232–236.

51. Rapport de l'Administrateur sur le fonctionnement des tribunaux indigène, 4th Quarter 1908, Bamako, ANM 2 M 54.

52. In a study of contemporary urban American sensibilities about law and society, Ewick and Silbey have described three types of popular conceptualization about the law:

law is majestic, operating according to fixed rules; law is a game, an instrument among others to be used to achieve strategic goals; and law as something external to be resisted, avoided, and deflected. The second category, law as an instrument and the third category, law as a game, applies to this section of the discussion. Ewick and Silbey, *The Common Place of Law,* pp. 28, 47–48, 132–136. These typologies need to be understood as parts of a broader repertoire of actions and cognition in regard to the "state" and that the state was not always hegemonic.

53. Elizabeth Colson, "The Contentiousness of Disputes," in *Understanding Disputes: The Politics of Argument,* ed. Pat Caplan (Providence, RI: Berg, 1995), pp. 71–77. Compare also Elizabeth Colson's masterful "Social Control and Vengeance in Plateau Tonga Society," *Africa* 23 (1) (1953), where village solidarity was still powerful.

54. Lauren Benton, *Law and Colonial Cultures: Legal Regimes in World History, 1400–1900* (New York: Cambridge University Press, 2002), p. 161.

55. Abel, "Western Courts in Non-Western Settings," p. 169. See also Keebet von Benda-Beckman, "Forum Shopping and Shopping for Forums: Dispute Settlement in Minangkabau Village in Western Sumatra," *Journal of Legal Pluralism* 19 (1981); and Sally Engle Merry, "The Articulation of Legal Spheres," in *African Women and the Law: Historical Perspectives,* eds. Margaret Jean Hay and Marcia Wright (Boston: African Studies Center, 1982), pp. 68–76.

56. John Griffiths, "What is Legal Pluralism." *Journal of Legal Pluralism* 24 (1986): pp. 2–9.

57. Starr and Collier have suggested that customary law was a colonial invention that needs to be analytically separate from what they term indigenous law, which was practiced before colonial conquest, *History and Power,* pp. 8–9.

58. Mahmoud Mamdani, *Citizen and Subject: Contemporary Africa and the Legacy of Late Colonialism* (Princeton: Princeton University Press, 1996), pp. 21–23, 108–128.

59. Benton, *Law and Colonial Cultures,* pp. 3–11. See also Sally Engle Merry, "Anthropology, Law, and Transnational Processes," *Annual Reviews in Anthropology* 21 (1992): pp. 357–379. The concept of imposed law, applied by Sandra Burman and Barbara E. Harrell-Bond, *The Imposition of Law* (New York: Academic Press, 1979) was designed to highlight the political context of legal pluralism in the late nineteenth century colonialism and in the twentieth century global legal environment.

60. Benton, *Law and Colonial Cultures,* pp. 128, 137.

61. Sally Engle Merry, "Legal Pluralism," *Law and Society Review* 22 (5) 1988: p. 879. Benton certainly recognized the importance of these dynamics of change by examining cultural intermediaries and the changing law of property as indicators of these processes. Merry applies her principles in her *Colonizing Hawaii.* In *Colonizing Hawaii,* Merry focuses on criminal law in which the state has a stronger interest in the outcomes than in domestic disputes in colonial contexts.

62. For more discussion on the encounter concept, see Roberts, *Two Worlds of Cotton,* pp. 9–13. See Frederick Cooper, "What is the Concept of Globalization Good for? An African Historian's Perspective," *African Affairs* 100 (1) (2001): pp. 189–214; and Frederick Cooper and Randall Packard, eds., *International Development and the Social Sciences: Essays on the History and Politics of Knowledge* (Berkeley: University of California Press, 1997).

63. For a perspective, see Robert July, *An African Voice: The Role of the Humanities in African Independence* (Durham, NC: Duke University Press, 1987). For another perspective, see Jan Vansina, *Living with Africa* (Madison: University of Wisconsin Press, 1994).

64. Roland Oliver's *The Missionary Factor in East Africa* (London: Longmans, Green, 1952); J. D. Fage, *An Introduction to the History of West Africa* (Cambridge: Cambridge University Press, 1955); K. Onwuka Dike, *Trade and Politics in the Niger Delta, 1830–1885: An Introduction to the Economic and Political History of Nigeria* (Oxford: Clarendon Press, 1956); and George Shepperson and Thomas Price's *Independent African; John Chilembwe and the Origins, Setting, and Significance of the Nyasaland Native Rising of 1915* (Edinburgh: Edinburgh University Press, 1958) signaled the departure from imperial history's concern with the heroic character of colonial conquest, the progress of white settlement, the history of administration, and with various versions of the imperial civilizing mission. These new works focused instead on the history of Africans and increasingly on the history of Africans before the arrival of Europeans.

65. For an important assessment of African voices as sources for history and as sources for what shaped the telling of history, see Luise White, Stephen F. Miescher, and David William Cohen, eds., *African Words, African Voices: Critical Practices in Oral History* (Bloomington: University of Indiana Press, 2001).

66. See especially Jan Vansina's autobiography, *Living with Africa* and his two classic statements on oral history methodology, *Oral Tradition: A Study in Historical Methodology*, translated by H. M. Wright (Chicago: Aldine, 1965), which appeared in French in 1961, and *Oral Tradition as History* (Madison: University of Wisconsin Press, 1985).

67. I do not want to suggest that we can gain nothing from oral informants about the history prior to the Second World War. Our informants might be able to provide some first hand accounts of the earlier period, but most importantly, they can set an agenda for what they think is important about their past and define the categories for analysis.

68. Barbara Cooper, *Marriage in Maradi: Gender and Culture in a Hausa Society in Niger, 1900–1989* (Portsmouth, NH: Heinemann, 1997).

69. Liisa Malkki, *Purity and Exile: Violence, Memory, and National Cosmology among Hutu Refugees in Tanzania* (Chicago: University of Chicago Press, 1995); see also Isabel Hofmeyr, *"We Spend Our Years as a Tale that is Told": Oral Historical Narrative in a South African Chiefdom* (Portsmouth, NH: Heinemann, 1993) for another example of the impact of social dislocation on oral history.

70. See especially Stephen Ellis, "Writing Histories of Contemporary Africa," *JAH* 43 (1) (2002): 1–26, who develops a methodology and an assessment of sources for the history of postindependent Africa.

71. Interview with Idrissa Diakite, Hamdullaye, Bamako, 21 December 1996.

72. William Felstiner, Richard Abel, and Austin Sarat, "The Emergence and Transformation of Disputes: Naming, Blaming, Claiming. . . ." *Law and Society Review* 15 (1980–1981): pp. 631–636.

73. John M. Conley and William M. O'Barr, *Rules versus Relationships: The Ethnography of Legal Discourse* (Chicago: University of Chicago Press, 1990); and Sally Engle Merry, *Getting Justice and Getting Even: Legal Consciousness among Working-Class Americans* (Chicago: University of Chicago Press, 1990), pp. 13–16, 112–116.

74. Susan F. Hirsch, *Pronouncing and Persevering: Gender and Discourses of Disputing in an African Islamic Court* (Chicago: University of Chicago Press, 1998), pp. 3–4, 136.

75. John M. Conley and William M. O'Barr, *Just Words: Law, Language, and Power* (Chicago: University of Chicago Press, 1998), p. 89.

76. Conley and O'Barr, *Just Words,* pp. 94–95.

77. The impact of writing on oral cultures has been a major issue in anthropology and history. See especially Jack Goody, *The Logic of Writing and the Organization of Society*

(Cambridge: Cambridge University Press, 1986); Jack Goody's study of the impact of writing on a specific oral tradition, *The Myth of the Bagre* (Oxford: Clarendon Press, 1972); Walter Ong, *Orality and Literacy: Technologizing of the Word* (London: Metheun, 1982); Hofmeyr, *Oral Historical Narrative.*

78. Sean Hawkins, *Writing and Colonialism in Northern Ghana: The Encounter between the LoDagaa and "the World on Paper"* (Toronto: University of Toronto Press, 2002), pp. 10–20, 27–31; see Brinley Messick, *The Calligraphic State: Textual Domination and History in a Muslim Society* (Berkeley: University of California Press, 1993), chapters 11 and 12.

79. James Clifford, *The Predicament of Culture: Twentieth Century Ethnography, Literature, and Art* (Cambridge, MA: Harvard University Press, 1988), p. 290.

80. Hirsch, *Pronouncing and Persevering,* p. 72.

81. Some celebrated legal cases have been televised and copies of the videorecordings may provide historians with good data. Few ordinary cases of the kind used in this study would have been recorded.

82. See especially, David W. Cohen, " 'A Case for the Basoga': Lloyd Fallers and the Construction of an African Legal System," in *Law and Colonialism in Africa,* eds. Kristin Mann and Richard Roberts (Portsmouth, NH: Heinemann, 1991), pp. 239–254; Richard Roberts, "Text and Testimony in the *Tribunal de Première Instance,* Dakar, during the Early Twentieth Century," *JAH* 31 (3) (1999): pp. 447–463.

83. Ernest Roume, *Justice indigène: Instructions au administrateurs sur l'application du Décret de 10 November 1903 portant réorganisation du service de la justice dans les colonies relevant du Gouvernement général de l'AOF* (Gorée: Imprimerie du Gouvernement-général, 1905), p. 41. See Chapter 3 for more details.

84. Mary F. Smith, *Baba of Karo: A Woman of the Muslim Hausa* (New Haven: Yale University Press, 1981). Baba of Karo describes her multiple divorces and marriages and invokes incompatibility as a cause for her unhappiness in her early marriages.

CHAPTER 2: THE FOUNDATIONS OF THE FRENCH COLONIAL LEGAL SYSTEM IN WEST AFRICA, 1673–1903

1. For a general overview of the ideologies of empire and colonialism during the *ancien régime,* see Anthony Pagden, *Lords of All the World: Ideologies of Empire in Spain, Britain, and France, c. 1500–1800* (New Haven: Yale University Press, 1995), especially chapters 3 and 5; Lauren Benton, *Law and Colonial Cultures: Legal Regimes in World History, 1400–1900* (New York: Cambridge University Press, 2002), chapter 1.

2. O. Adewoye, *The Judicial System in Southern Nigeria, 1854–1954: Law and Justice in a Dependency* (Atlantic Highlands: Humanities Press, 1977). Benton, *Law and Colonial Cultures,* chapters 2–3.

3. Emilien Petit, *Droits publics, ou gouvernement des colonies françaises, d'après les loix faites pour des pays* (Paris: Chez Delalain, 1771) vol. II, p. 178, quoted in Arthur Girault, *Principes de colonisation et de legislation coloniale: deuxième partie: les colonies françaises depuis 1815,* 4th edition, 3 vols. (Paris: Sirey, 1921–1923), vol. I, p. 201.

4. Edmon Seligman, *La justice en France pendant la Revolution (1789–1792)* (Paris: Plon-Nourrit, 1901), chapters 1–2. Francois Furet, *Revolutionary France, 1770–1880,* translated by Antonia Nevill (London: Blackwell, 1988), pp. 8–9. See also Natalie Davis,

Fiction in the Archives: Pardon Tales and their Tellers in Sixteenth Century France (Stanford: Stanford University Press, 1987).

5. R. Demogue, "La loi française aux colonies," in *Les colonies françaises,* vol. I of *Pétite encyclopédie coloniale,* ed. Maxime Petit (Paris: Larousse, 1902), p. 32.

6. Dominique Lamiral, *L'Affrique et le peuple affricain considérés sous tous leurs rapports avec notre commerce et nos colonies* (Paris: Dessenne, 1789), quoted in Pierre Pluchon, *Histoire de la colonisation française: Le premier empire colonial, des origines à la Restauration* (Paris: Fayard, 1991), pp. 448–449.

7. See, for example, Jean Meyer, Jean Tarrade, Annie Rey-Goldzeiguer, and Jacques Thobie, *Histoire de la France coloniale: Des origines à 1914* (Paris: Armand Colin, 1990), vol. I, pp. 296–298; Jean-Joel Brégeon, *L'Egypte française au jour le jour, 1798–1801* (Paris: Perrin, 1991), pp. 79–89, 241–249.

8. On the place of regeneration in Napoléon's Egyptian expedition, see especially Jean-Loup Amselle, *Vers une mutliculturalisme française: L'empire de la coutume* (Paris: Aubier, 1996), pp. 56–61.

9. Edward Said, "Orientalism: The Cultural Consequences of the French Preoccupation with Egypt," in *Napoleon in Egypt: Al-Jabarti's Chronicle of the French Occupation, 1798,* translated by Shmuel Moreh and introduced by Robert Tignor (Princeton: M. Weiner, 1993), p. 171. See also Brégeon, *L'Égypte française,* pp. 251–304; Pluchon, *Histoire,* pp. 484–485; Baron Jean Thiry, *Bonaparte en Égypte, Décembre 1797–24 Août 1799* (Paris: Berger-Levrault, 1973), pp. 207–214; Michel Dewachter, ed., *L'Égypte, Bonaparte et Champollion* (Figeac: Association pour le Bicentenaire Champollion, 1990).

10. Amselle, *Multiculturalisme,* pp. 73–84. For more discussion of the cultural administration and the role of scholars in the Egyptian adventure, see Yves Laissus, *L'Égypte, une aventure savante, 1798–1801* (Paris: Fayard, 1998) and Patrice Bret, ed., *L'Expédition d'Égypte: une enterprise des Lumières, 1798–1801* (Paris: Technique & documentation, 1998). See also Jules François Saintoyant, *La colonisation française pendant la période Napoléonienne (1799–1815)* (Paris: La Renaissance du Livre, 1931), pp. 149–150.

11. Furet, *Revolutionary France,* pp. 230–233; Seligman, *Justice,* chapter 2.

12. Furet, *Revolutionary France,* pp. 230–233.

13. Edward McWhinney, "Code Law Systems," in *Encyclopedia of the Social Sciences* (New York: Macmillan, 1968–), vol. 9, p. 214.

14. The Code of 1804 represented a conservative turn away from the fuller rights extended to women during the earlier days of the Revolution, including a women's right to sue for divorce. While divorce was still enshrined in the Code, it was now harder for women than it was following the Constitution of 1791.

15. For background, see Charles-Robert Ageron, *Modern Algeria: A History from 1830 to the Present,* translated by Michael Brett (Trenton, NJ: Africa World Press, 1991); Annie Rey-Goldzeiguer, "La France coloniale de 1830 à 1870," in *Histoire de la France coloniale: Des origines à 1914,* eds. Jean Meyer, Jean Tarrade, Annie Rey-Goldzeiguer, and Jacques Thobie (Paris: Armand Colin, 1991).

16. John Ruedy, *Modern Algeria: The Origins and Development of a Nation* (Bloomington: Indiana University Press, 1992), pp. 52–53; David Prochaska, *Making Algeria French: Colonialism in Bône, 1870–1920* (Cambridge: Cambridge University Press, 1990), pp. 65–91.

17. Raphael Danziger, *Abd al-Qadir and the Algerians: Resistance to the French and Internal Consolidation* (New York: Holmes and Meyer, 1977); see especially, Smaïl Aouli, Randame Redjala, and Philippe Zoummeroff, *Abd el-Kader* (Paris: Fayard, 1994).

18. The Bureaux Arabes were formally instituted in 1848, but their semiofficial proto-
types were in existence earlier. See especially, Jacques Frémeaux, *Les Bureaux arabes
dans l'Algérie de la conqûete* (Paris: Denoël, 1993); Ruedy, *Modern Algeria,* pp.
72–76; Allan Christelow, *Muslim Law Courts and the French Colonial State in Algeria* (Princeton: Princeton University Press, 1985), p. 82, fn. 2.

19. Amselle, *Multiculturalisme,* p. 103.

20. Ruedy, *Modern Algeria,* p. 54. For more detail on this interpretation, see Constantin-
François Volney, *Voyage en Égypte et en Syrie* (Paris: Mouton, 1959), who was the source of
this idea for Napléon.

21. The best study of Muslim courts in Algeria is Christelow, *Muslim Law Courts.*

22. M. Perron, trans., *Précis de jurisprudence musulmane ou principes de législation
musulmane civile et religieuse selon le rite malékite* (Paris: Imprimerie Nationale,
1848–1852); N. Seignette, *Code musulmane, statut réel* (Constantine, Impr. L. Arnolet;
Alger, Jourdan; Paris, Challamel aîné, 1878). For an early twentieth century study of the
place of comparative law in French colonial expansion, see M. E. Jobbé-Duval, "L'histoire
comparée de droit et l'expansion coloniale de la France," *Annales internationales d'Histoire* (1900; reprint, Nendeln, Liechtenstein: Kraus Reprint, 1972), pp. 117–146. The
Seignette edition of the Malikite law was often part of the district officers' libraries in the
French Soudan in the early twentieth century.

23. Girault, *Principes,* 3rd part, pp. 304–323.

24. Jeswald Salacuse, *An Introduction to Law in French-Speaking Africa* (Charlottesville: Michie, 1969), pp. 21–23.

25. The decree of 24 April 1833 further confirmed the principles of the 1830 decree by
declaring that "every free person possesses, in the French colonies, civil rights and political rights under the conditions prescribed by law." See Lamine Guèye, *Étapes et perspectives de l'Union française* (Paris: Editions de l'Union Française, 1955), p. 24.

26. By far the best discussion surrounding the politics of legal jurisdiction of the Muslim tribunals is Bernard Schnapper, "Les tribunaux musulmans et la politique coloniale au
Sénégal (1830–1914)," *Revue historique de droit français et étranger* 39 (1961). Schnapper argues that the debates on the jurisdiction of Muslim tribunals in Senegal date from
1832, fully 25 years before a Muslim tribunal was enacted in 1857. Cruise O'Brien discusses how the anticlericism of the French military and administrators in Senegal contributed to a pro-Muslim orientation, especially toward those Senegalese willing to
collaborate with the French in "Towards an 'Islamic Policy' in French West Africa," *JAH* 8
(2) (1967).

27. Seck Ndiaye, "Les tribunaux musulmans du Sénégal de 1857 à 1914," unpublished mémoire, University of Dakar, 1984.

28. Schnapper, "Les tribunaux musulmans"; Cruise O'Brien, "Towards an 'Islamic
Policy' "; David Robinson, "French 'Islamic' Policy and Practice in Late Nineteenth Century Senegal," *JAH* 29 (3) (1988). For more detail, see David Robinson, *Paths to Accommodation: Muslim Societies and French Colonial Authorities in Senegal and Mauritania,
1880–1920* (Athens: Ohio University Press, 2000). For background, see David Robinson,
The Holy War of UmarTal: The Western Sudan in the Mid-Nineteenth Century (Oxford:
Clarendon Press, 1985); Martin Klein, *Islam and Imperialism in Senegal: Sine-Salou,
1847–1914* (Stanford: Stanford University Press, 1968); and Christopher Harrison, *France
and Islam in West Africa, 1860–1960* (Cambridge: Cambridge University Press, 1988). For
a detailed discussion on Faidherbe's ethnographical orientation in Amselle, *Multiculturalisme,* chapter 4.

29. Alain Quellien, *La politique musulmane dans l'Afrique Occidentale française* (Paris: Emile Larose, 1910), pp. 224–225. See Ghislaine Lydon, "Thus Ruled the Qadi of Ndar (Senegal): Civil Litigation in a Colonial Muslim Tribunal, 1880s–1920s," published paper presented at the Muslim Family Law and Colonialism in Africa Conference, Stanford, May 2001.

30. François Renault, "L'Abolition de l'esclavage au Sénégal: L'attitude de l'administration, 1848–1905," *Revue française d'histoire d'outre mer* 63 (1971); Leland C. Barrows, "Louis Léon César Faidherbe (1818–1889)," in *African Proconsuls: European Governors in Africa*, eds. L. H. Gann and Peter Duignan (New York: Free Press, 1978), pp. 64–71. See also Martin Klein, *Slavery and Colonial Rule in French West Africa* (Cambridge: Cambridge University Press, 1998).

31. Paul Dislère, *Traite de législation coloniale* (Paris: P. Dupont, 1914), pp. 214–215.

32. Frantz Despagnet, "Les protectorats" in *Les Colonies françaises,* vol. 1 of *Petite encylopédie coloniale,* ed. Maxine Petit (Paris: Larousse, 1902), pp. 53–54.

33. See Roberts, *Warriors, Slaves, and Merchants: The State and the Economy in the Middle Niger Valley, 1700–1914* (Stanford: Stanford University Press, 1987), chapter 4.

34. A. S. Kanya-Forstner, *The Conquest of the Western Sudan: A Study in French Military Imperialism* (Cambridge: Cambridge University Press, 1969); B. Marie Perinbam, *Family Identity and the State in the Bamako Kafu, c.1800–c.1900* (Boulder, CO: Westview Press, 1997). See also Sundiata A. Djata, *The Bamana Empire by the Niger: Kingdom, Jihad, and Colonization, 1712–1920* (Princeton: M. Weiner, 1996).

35. Archinard, letter to Gov. Senegal, 9 January 1890, Kayes, ANM B 83.

36. Kanya-Forstner, *Conquest,* pp. 196–198.

37. Jennifer Ward, "The Bambara-French Relationship, 1880–1915," unpublished dissertation, UCLA, 1976.

38. Palabre, Nyamina, 19 April 1890, signed by Archinard, Mamdou Racine, Mademba, Amadou Kuma, Bonnier, Underberg, and Quinquadon, ANS-AOF 15 G 172.

39. Archinard, telegram to Gov Senegal, Bamako, 12 April 1890, ANF-DOM Sénégal et Dependences IV-95.

40. Commandant Superieur Archinard, Rapport militaire, campagne 1889–1890, nd, np, ANS-AOF 1 D 105.

41. Archinard, letter to under secretary of state for colonies, 9 January 1891, Nioro, ANF-DOM Soudan I 1 a. For a preliminary statement on this issue, see Richard Roberts, "The Case of Faama Mademba Sy and the Ambiguities of Legal Jurisdiction in Early Colonial French Soudan," in *Law in Colonial Africa,* eds. Kristin Mann and Richard Roberts (Portsmouth, NH: Heinemann, 1991).

42. For background, see Roberts, *Warriors, Slaves, and Merchants,* pp. 151–161. See also William Cohen, *Rulers of Empire: The French Colonial Service in Africa* (Stanford: Hoover Institution Press, 1971).

43. Archinard, letter to commandant Segu, Kayes, 3 December 1890, ANM 5 D 44.

44. Bulletin politique et militaire, Segu, July 1895, ANM 1 E 71.

45. Sous sec d'état des colonies, Instructions à M. le Colonel Archinard, Commandant sup du Soudan, Paris, 12 September 1892, ANF-DOM Soudan I-4.

46. Archinard, Rapport de campagne, 1892–1893, November 1893, Paris, ANS-AOF 1 D 137.

47. Tony Chafer and Amanda Sachur, *Promoting the Colonial Idea: Propaganda and Visions of Empire in France* (New York: Palgrave, 2002); William Schneider, *An Empire*

for the Masses: The French Popular Image of Africa, 1870–1900 (Westport, CN: Greenwood Press, 1982).

48. The best source for a critical interpretation of the Republican principles of France's civilizing mission in West Africa is Alice Conklin, *A Mission to Civilize: The Republican Idea of Empire in France and West Africa, 1895–1930* (Stanford: Stanford University Press, 1997).

49. By 1898, the French had defeated both Samori and Babemba, the last two remaining rulers of major African polities opposed to the French. The French never fully "pacified" the Tuareg, although they did defeat them militarily following the ignoble defeat of the French at Timbuktu in 1894. The end of the large African military states, however, led to a proliferation of localized raiding and enslavement throughout much of the region. See, for example, Andrew Hubbell, "A View of the Slave Trade from the Margin: Souroudougou in the Late Nineteenth Century Slave Trade of the Niger Bend," *JAH* 42 (1) (2001): pp. 25–47.

50. G. Wesley Johnson, "William Ponty and Republican Paternalism in French West Africa (1866–1915)," in *African Proconsuls: European Governors in Africa,* eds. L. H. Gann and Peter Dignan (New York: Free Press, 1978).

51. William D. Irvine, *The Boulanger Affair Reconsidered: Royalism, Boulangism, and the Origins of the Radical Rights in France* (New York: Oxford University Press, 1989). For more narrative accounts, see James Harding, *The Astonishing Adventure of General Boulanger* (New York: Scribner, 1971) and Jean Garrigues, *Le Général Boulanger* (Paris: O. Orban, 1991).

52. Theodore Zeldin, *France 1848–1945* (Oxford: Clarendon Press, 1973), vol. 1, pp. 483–484.

53. Philip Nord, *The Republican Moment: Struggles for Democracy in Nineteenth-Century France* (Cambridge, MA: Harvard University Press, 1995), chapter 6, esp. pp. 136–137; Jean-Pierre Royer, Renée Martinage, and Pierre Lecocq, *Juges et notables au XIXe siècle* (Paris: Presses Universitaires de France, 1982), pp. 359–370; Jean-Louis Debré, *La justice au XIXe siècle: Les magistrats* (Paris: Librarie Académique Perrin, 1981).

54. Gov. Grodet, letter to Com. Sup., Région Nord-Est (Segu), Kayes, 26 January 1894, ANM B 150.

55. Gov. Grodet, letter to Com. Sup., Région Est (Bamako), Kayes, 11 July 1894, ANM 2 M 59.

56. Gov. Grodet, letter to Com. Sup., Région Nord-Est (Segu), Kayes, 26 January 1894, ANM B 150.

57. See chapter 3 for more discussion on the issue of codification. For an Indian example, see especially Nicholas Dirks, "From Little King to Landlord: Colonial Discourse and Colonial Rule," in *Colonialism and Culture,* ed. Nicolas Dirks (Ann Arbor: University of Michigan Press, 1992).

58. Commandant Quiquandon, Rapport sur le fonctionnement de la justice administrative dans le cercle de Segu, Segu, 1 April 1894, ANM 2 M 92.

59. Robert Kidder, "Western Law in India: External Law and Local Response," in *Social System and Legal Process,* ed. Harry M. Johnson (San Francisco: Jossey-Bass, 1978).

60. Prevailing French ethnography at the turn of the century operated within the essentializing character of "race." Assuming that "race" created a common community of members and interests, they all shared certain distinctive traits. This notion of "race" as

social boundaries is evident in many of the 1894 reports. For more detail, see Jean-Loup Amselle, *Logiques métisses: anthropologie de l'identité en Afrique et ailleurs* (Paris: Payot, 1990) and Jean Bazin, "À Chacun son Bambara," in *Au Coeur de l'ethnie: Ethnies, tribalisme, et État en Afrique,* eds. Jean-Loup Amselle and Elikia M'Bokolo (Paris: Découverte, 1985).

61. Commandant Quiquandon, Rapport sur le fonctionnement de la justice administrative dans le cercle de Segu, Segu, 1 April 1894, ANM 2 M 92.

62. A similar position on corporal punishment was made in the Bamako district report, Captain Porion, Étude sur la justice administrative indigène dans le cercle de Bamako, Bamako, 19 July 1894, ANM 2 M 54. Porion was careful to underline that even though corporal punishment was a precolonial practice and widely accepted by Africans, it was no longer applied in his district.

63. Martin Chanock, *Law, Custom, and Social Order: The Colonial Experience in Malawi and Zambia* (Cambridge: Cambridge University Press, 1985), p. 125 and Chapter 8.

64. Archinard, letter no. 149, np, 23 April 1891, cited in Lt. Sargols, Notice sur la justice indigène et la justice musulmane au Soudan, np, March 1896, ANM 1 D 15.

65. Capt. Porion, Étude sur la justice administrative indigène dans le cercle de Bamako, Bamako, 19 July 1894, ANM 2 M 54. I have not, however, seen this guide.

66. Capt. Porion, Étude sur la justice administrative indigène dans le cercle de Bamako, Bamako, 19 July 1894, ANM 2 M 54. Porion drew a distinction between civil and criminal cases, to which I shall return in Chapter 4. He did indicate that, while he alone rendered judgments in civil cases, he was assisted by two other French officers during criminal trials.

67. Robert Delavignette, *Les vrais chefs de l'empire* (Paris: Gaillmard, 1939).

68. Capt. Froment, letter to gov. Soudan, Kita, 20 March 1894, ANM 2 M 73.

69. Lt-gov. Colonel de Trentinian, Note circular, Bamako, 3 February 1896, ANM 2 M 4.

70. Girault, *Principes,* vol. I, p. 277. Jacques Thobie, "La France coloniale de 1870 à 1914," in *Histoire de la France coloniale: des origines à 1914,* eds. Jean Meyer, Jean Tarrade, Annie Rey-Goldzeiguer, and Jacques Thobie (Paris: Armand Colin, 1991), pp. 685–697, 706.

71. See, for example, Joseph Buttinger, *Vietnam: A Political History* (New York: Praeger 1968), pp. 101–116.

72. Ministre des Colonies, Rapport au Président de la République française, Paris, 16 June 1895, ANF-DOM AOF VII-2. For background, see C. W. Newbury, "The Formation of the Government General of French West Africa," *JAH* 1 (1) (1960).

73. The regulations of the government-general of Indo-China are part of the file dealing with the constitution of the West Africa Federation. Exposé sommaire de la reglementation concernant l'organisation administrative de l'Indo-Chine française, nd, np, ANF-DOM AOF VII-2.

74. Ministre des Colonies, confidential instructions to Gov-gen Chaudié, Paris, 11 October 1895, ANF-DOM AOF I-1.

75. Girault, *Principes,* part 2, vol. 1, pp. 352–371.

76. Girault, *Principes,* part 2, vol. 1, p. 297. See also Newbury, "Formation."

77. The Voulet Affair of 1899, in which a French officer went on a rampage of violence and destruction in the regions of Upper Volta and Ziner, nailed shut the coffin of military autonomy in the Soudan. See the files on the Voulet affair in ANF-DOM AOF I-6, especially Minister of Colonies to gov-gen, Paris, 3 October 1899, and ANF-DOM Soudan

III-3, especially Lt. Voulet, letter to capt., resident of Bandiagara, Tagarou, 24 February 1896. A fuller study of the Voulet affair needs to be written.

78. Dèves and Chaumet, letter to Min of Colonies, n.p., n.d., included in a file sent from Min of Colonies to gov-gen, Paris, 31 January 1900, ANM B 70.

79. Min of Colonies, letter to gov-gen, Paris, 9 November 1898, ANS-AOF 15 G 95.

80. Min of Colonies, Projet de decret, Institue un conseil superieur du gouvernment-général de l'AOF, Paris, 12 September 1895, ANF-DOM AOF VII-2. The conseil supérieur, however, only met once in 1896. It did not meet again until 1902.

81. William Ponty, the délégué to the gov-general (effectively the lt-gov of the Soudan), chastized the commandant of Nioro for inflicting 40 lashes as punishment. Ponty reminded the commandant that corporal punishment was no longer recognized in the colony and that it was reprehensible in the eyes of humanity and civilization. Ponty, letter to commandant Nioro, [Kayes], 26 September 1900, ANS-AOF 15 G 58. The Segu commandant had proposed already in 1895 that in "recently conquered areas" an "Algerian institution" of a tribunal composed of military officers be established to execute swift and severe punishments. I have no record whether this Algerian institution was implemented. Bulletin politique et militaire, Segu, July 1895, ANM 1 E 71.

82. Gov-gen Chaudié, letter to Minister of Colonies with copies to 1ère Direction, 1ère Bureau, and Sec-gen 3ème Bureau, St. Louis, 21 March 1900, ANF-DOM Soudan VIII-2. An even stronger letter in the same vein was sent to Chaudié's lt-govs under his authority: Chaudié, letter to govs of Guinée Française, Côte D'Ivoire, and Dahomey, St. Louis, 19 March 1900, ANF-DOM Soudan VIII-2. These two letters form a central turning point in the struggle between the two models of colonialism prevailing in French West Africa. Chaudié's challenge to the district administrators formed one strand of a wider "crisis" in the administration of justice in French West Africa. The second strand, which also hinged on abuses and irregularities, originated in Dahomey, and was funnelled through Liontel, the president of the conseil d'appel, Grand Bassam, who was appointed to lead a federation-wide inquiry into the application of native justice. A third strand in the crisis occurred as a result of a decision by the Cour de Cassation, 24 November 1900, which rejected a lower appeals court ruling regarding the jurisdiction of a crime committed in Cayor.

83. Commandant Destanve, Projet d'organisation politique, administrative et defensive de l'AOF, n.p., 1898, ANS-AOF 18 G 2.

84. Trentinian, L'organisation d'un gouvernment-général de l'AOF (Soudan, Sénégal, Guinée, Côte d'Ivoire, Dahomey), Paris, 7 October 1899, ANS-AOF 18 G 2.

85. Gov-gen Chaudié, letter to Min of Colonies, St Louis, 6 December 1897, ANF-DOM AOF I-4; Gov-gen Chaudié, Rapport à M. le Ministre des colonies sur les modifications politiques et administratives à introduire dans l'organisation du Soudan, Paris, 26 September 1899, ANF-DOM AOF VII-4; Le Directeur des affaires d'Afrique, Note pour le Ministre, Paris, n.d. [1899], ANF-DOM AOF VII-4. For a narrative background to this period, see Newbury, "Formation."

86. Marie François Joseph Clozel, "Preface," in Roger Villamur, *Les Attributions judiciaires des administrateurs et chefs de poste en service à la Côte d'Ivoire* (Paris: Librairie de la cour d'appel et de l'ordre des avocats, 1902).

87. Chaudié, letter to Minister of Colonies, St Louis, 21 March 1900, ANF-DOM Soudan VIII-2. The same language was used in a letter sent to his lieutenant-governors two days earlier, Chaudié, letter to govs of Guinée Française, Côte d'Ivoire, and Dahomey, St Louis, 19 March 1900, ANF-DOM Soudan VIII-2.

88. For similar concern between arbitrarily harsh punishments ordered at the lower court level in South Africa and the superior court's concern with "a metropolitan standard

of punishment," see Martin Chanock, *The Making of South African Legal Culture, 1902–1936: Fear, Favour, and Prejudice* (Cambridge: Cambridge University Press, 2001), p. 131.

89. Le Chef du cabinet, Ministre des Colonies, Note pour le 1ère Direction, 1ère Bureau, Application dan les territoires de l'ancien Soudan du decret du 30 September 1887, Fonctionnement de la justice indigène, Paris, n.d. [but mid-late April 1900], ANF-DOM Soudan VIII-2.

90. See especially, Tony Asiwaju, "Control through Coercion: A Study of the Indigenat Regime in French West African Administration, 1887–1946," *Bull IFAN, Series B* 41 (1) (1979); Raymond. L. Buell, *The Native Problem in Africa* (New York: Macmillan, 1928), vol. I, pp. 1016–1020; Conklin, *Mission to Civilize,* p. 202. The *indigénat* was abolished in 1946.

91. Acting on the orders of Chaudié, Ponty issued immediate clemency to selected prisoners in 1900. See, for example, Chaudié, telegram to Ponty, Saint Louis, 20 February 1900; Ponty, telegram [to gov-gen], Kayes, 22 February 1900, regarding the clemency of Médoune Gueye, ANF-DOM Soudan VIII-2.

92. The important decrees and letters include Le Chef du cabinet, Ministre des Colonies, Note pour le 1ère Direction, 1ère Bureau, Application dan les territoires de l'ancienne Soudan du decret du 30 September 1887, Fonctionnement de la justice indigène, Paris, n.d. [but mid-late April 1900], ANF-DOM Soudan VIII-2. For the follow-up to this letter, see Instructions données par telegramme du 5 May 1900 en vue de la revision de sentences prononcés par vois d'action disciplinaire contre des indigènes dans l'ancienne colonie du Soudan Français, Principaux actes du Ministre des Colonies, Paris, January 1901, ANF-DOM AOF I-8. Gov-gen Chaudié issued two decrees that initiated the legal reforms. See decrees 12 April 1898 and 19 July 1901 in *Journal Officiel de l'Afrique Occidental Française.*

93. A series of registers of prison sentences issued in the Soudan were assembled beginning in 1900. These registers contain the name of the defendant, the crime committed, the date sentenced, and the date released from prison. The registers are backdated to 1896, but they are lack detail until 1900. Etat nominatif de individus condamnés à la prison, various dates, ANF-DOM Soudan VIII-2.

94. Ponty, letter to cmdt Segu, Kayes, 2 May 1901, ANS-AOF 15 G 60; Ponty, letter to cmdt Segu, Kayes, 5 July 1901, ANS-AOF 15 G 60; Ponty, letter to cmdt Bouguni, Kayes, 8 August 1900, ANS-AOF 15 G 58.

95. Minister of Colonies Gaston Doumergue, letter to Gov-gen, Paris, 23 August 1902, ANM 2 M 459.

96. Ponty, circular to district officers, Kayes, 26 January 1903, ANM 2 M 459.

97. Gov-gen, Rapport sur la situation politique de l'AOF, St Louis, 11 July 1901, ANF-DOM AOF I-8.

98. Liontel, letter to Minister of Colonies, Porto-Novo, 15 January 1901, ANF-DOM AOF VIII-1; Gov Liotard, letter to Minister of Colonies, Porto-Novo, 18 January 1901, ANF-DOM AOF VIII-1. On the Liontel mission to Côte d'Ivoire, see Roger Villamur and Léon Richaud, *Notre colonie de la Côte d'Ivoire* (Paris: A. Cahllamel, 1903), pp. 161–165.

99. Liontel, President du conseil d'appel, chargé de mission, letter to Minister of Colonies, Grand Bassam, 31 January 1901, ANF-DOM AOF VIII-1.

100. Marie François Joseph Clozel, Roger Villamur, and Honoré Cartron, *Les coutumes indigènes de la Côte d'Ivoire. Documents publiés avec une introduction et des notes* (Paris: A. Challamel, 1902).

101. Villamur and Richaud, *Notre colonie,* p. 59.

102. Clozel, "Preface," in Villamur, *Les Attributions judiciaries.*
103. Villamur and Richaud, *Notre colonie,* p. 55–56.
104. Clozel, "Preface," in Villamur, *Les Attributions judiciaires.* See also Georges François, *L'Afrique occidentale française* (Paris: E. Larose, 1907), pp. 76–77.
105. Pierre Meunier, *Organisation et fonctionnement de la justice indigène en Afrique occidentale française* (Paris: A. Challamel, 1914), pp. 44–54.
106. Villamur and Richaud, *Notre colonie,* p. 63.
107. Lt-gov. Colonel Trentinian, Note circulaire, Bamako, 3 February 1896, ANM 2 M 4.
108. Lt-gov. Colonel Trentinian, Note circulaire, Bamako, 3 February 1896, ANM 2 M 4, citing Archinard's circulaire number 149 of 23 April 1891.
109. Gov. Trentinian, circulaire no. 546, Droits des commandants de Région, de cercle et poste en matière de justice, Kayes, 16 December 1896, ANM 2 M 40. The same circular appears in file ANM 2 D 155.
110. Rapport politique, Segu, April 1897, ANM 1 E 71.
111. Rapport politique, Segu, February 1897, ANM 1 E 71.
112. Rapport politique, Segu, July 1897, ANM 1 E 71. Ponty finally clarified the jurisdiction of qadi justice, when he wrote to the Segu commandant that the qadi can only judge disputes among Muslims. Ponty, letter to Cmdt Segu, Kayes, 23 April 1900, ANS-AOF 15 G 58.
113. Perignon, Généralités sur Haut Sénégal et Moyen Niger, Segu, 1900, ANS-AOF 1 G 248.
114. Rapport général sur la situation, Segu, 1st Quarter 1897, ANM 1 E 71. Rapport politique, Segu, July 1897, ANM 1 E 71 echoes this sentiment.
115. Rapport politique, Segu, March 1903, ANM 1 E 71.
116. William Ponty, Délégué permanent du Gouverneur-général, to administrateurs des cercles de la Sénégambie-Niger, Kayes, 5 February 1903, ANM 2 M 459. Ponty framed his instructions in a general sense, although his concern was with the abuses of the *indigénat,* the system of summary administrative law applied already from 1887.
117. Jacques Léotard, "Afrique Occidentale," in *Les colonies françaises au début du XX siècle: Cinq ans de progrès (1900–1905),* eds. Jacques Léotard, R. Teisseire, A. Ramal, and J-B Samat (Marseille, n.p., 1906), pp. 12–15; Johnson, "Ponty," pp. 134–135.
118. Procès verbal, Commission permanente du Conseil du Gouvernement, session 18 May 1903 and 20 May 1903, ANF-SOM AP 1645/3; Procès verbal, Commission permanente du Conseil du Gouvernement, session 6 June 1903, ANS-AOF 5 E 1. See also Conklin, *A Mission to Civilize,* pp. 88–89.
119. Ernest, Roume, *Justice indigène: Instructions au administrateurs sur l'application du Décret de 10 November 1903 portant réorganisation du service de la justice dans les colonies relevant du Gouvernement général de l'AOF* (Gorée: Imprimerie du Gouvernement-général, 1905), p. 5.

CHAPTER 3: CUSTOMS AND LEGAL AUTHORITY IN THE NATIVE COURTS

1. Rapport au Président de la République, suivi de decret portant réorganisation du service de la justice dans les colonies relevant du gouvernement général de l'Afrique occidentale," *Journal officiel de la République française* (24 November 1903); *Annuaire du gov't general de l'AOF,* 1904, p. 54; Procès-verbal, Conseil du gouvernement-général, ses-

sion 6 June 1903, Dakar, ANS-AOF 5 E 1; Ernest Roume, *Justice indigène: Instructions au administrateurs sur l'application du Décret de 10 November 1903 portant réorganisation du service de la justice dans les colonies relevant du Gouvernement général de l'AOF* (Gorée: Imprimerie du Gouvernement-général, 1905), pp. 60–61.

2. The task of the court of homologation was to confirm judgments made by lower courts. It thus provided the final level of surveillance over judgments and was designed to ensure the regularization of judgments and the equality of penalties. The most detailed discussion of the role of the *Chambre Spéciale d'Homologation* appears in Pierre Meunier, *Organisation et fonctionnement de la justice indigène en Afrique occidentale française* (Paris: A. Challamel, 1914), pp. 46–52 and chapter 8. The court of homologation became the site for the clarification of procedures and other jurisdictional issues. See especially Gilbert-Desvillons and Edmond Joucla, *Jurisprudence de la chambre d'homologation: Justice indigène. Jurisprudence de la Chambre d'homologation, publiée sous le patronage de M. William Ponty, gouverneur général . . .* (Gorée: Imprimerie du Gouvernement-général, 1910). Dominique Sarr has been one of the very scholars to work with the records of the *Chambre spécial d'homologation*. See Dominique Sarr, "La Chambre spéciale d'homologation de la Cour d'appel de l'Afrique Occidentale Française et les coutumes pénales, 1903–1920," *Annales Africaines* 1 (1974): 101–115, and "Jurisprudence des tribinaux indigènes du Sénégal: Les causes de rupture du lien matrimonial de 1872 à 1946," *Annales Africaines* 2 (1975): 141–178.

3. I discussed the notion of winners and losers in Chapter 1.

4. Meunier, *Organisation et fonctionnement,* p. 113, quoting Arthur Girault, *Principes de colonisation et de législation coloniale: deuxième partie: les colonies Françaises depuis 1815,* 3 vols. 4th edition (Paris: Sirey, 1921–1923), vol. 2, p. 78.

5. Most of the records available on the proceedings of the *Chambre d'Homologation* deal with criminal cases. The one exception is the 1906 control over the civil and commercial registers of the *tribunaux de province.* Although not all the court registers have survived, ANS-AOF M 119–121 contain selected court registers from the French Soudan for 1906. I had not found the 1906 registers in Bamako, because they were all sent to the procureur-general's office to be examined. I have not located any correspondence regarding whether or not these records were acceptable. Ponty did summarize these concerns in a letter to the lieutenant-gov of the Soudan. Ponty, gov-gen per interim, letter to lt-gov, H-S-N, Instructions et circulaires sur le fonctionnement de la justice, Dakar, 10 October 1907, ANM 2 M 459.

6. Meunier, *Organisation et fonctionnement,* p. 100.

7. Ponty, Rapport d'ensemble sur la situation générale de la colonie, H-S-N en 1904, ANS-AOF 2 G 4–16.

8. Roume, *Justice indigène,* p. 41.

9. Roume, *Justice indigène,* pp. 21–25.

10. Roume, *Justice indigène,* p. 25.

11. Commandant Quiquandon, Rapport au sujet de fonctionnement de la justice administrative, Segu, 1 April 1894, ANM 2 M 92; see also Capt. Porion, Étude sur la justice administrative indigène dans le cercle de Bamako, Bamako, 19 July 1984, ANM 2 M 54; and Capt Froment, letter to gov, Kita, 10 March 1894, ANM 2 M 73.

12. Gov. Trentinian, circular 546, Droits des commandants de région, de cercle et poste en matière de justice, Kayes, 16 December 1896, ANM 2 M 40. The same circular appears in file ANM 2 D 155.

13. Minister of Colonies Gaston Doumergue, circular to Gov-gen, Paris, 23 August 1902, ANM 2 M 459.

14. The text of the 1903 legislation appears in the *Journal officiel de la République française,* 24 November 1903.

15. Rapport sur le fonctionnement de la jusitce indigène, Sikasso, April 1905, ANM 2 M 93.

16. Rapport sur le fonctionnement de al justice indigène, 4th Quarter 1905, Sikasso, ANM 2 M 93.

17. Perignon, Généralités sur le Haut Sénégal et Moyen Niger, Segu, 1900, ANS-AOF 1 G 248.

18. Rapport judiciaire, Sokolo, 3rd Quarter 1910, ANM 2 M 94.

19. Compare with Brinkley Messick's study of Yemen, *The Calligraphic State: Textual Domination and History in a Muslim Society* (Berkeley: University of California Press, 1993).

20. Ponty, Instructions [regarding 1903 legislation], n.d., n.p., [probably 1904], ANM 2 M 2.

21. Rapport sur le fonctionnement des tribunaux indigènes, Koutiala, April 1905, ANM 2 M 75.

22. For example, Rapport sur le fonctionnement de la justice indigène, Sikasso, April 1905, ANM 2 M 93; and Rapport sur le fonctionnement de la justice indigène, 4th Quarter 1909, Sikasso, ANM 2 M 93; for Europeans serving as secretaries, see Rapport sur le fonctionnement de la justice indigène, 2nd Quarter 1908, Jenne, ANM 2 M 60; and Saurin, Rapport concernant la verification du service de M. Faure, administrateur commandant, le cercle de Sokolo, 20 January 1910, ANS-AOF 4 G 11.

23. Rapport sur le fonctionnnement de la justice indigène, 4th Quarter 1905, Sikasso, ANM 2 M 93.

24. Beurdeley, letter to gov-gen, Mission d'études sur le fonctionnement de la justice dans les colonies de l'AOF, 25 June 1914, Dakar, ANS-AOF M 85. See also Ruth Ginio, "Negotiating Legal Authority in French West Africa: The Colonial Administration and African Assessors, 1903–1918," in *Intermediaries, Interpreters, and Clerks: Africans in the Making of Modern Africa,* eds. Benjamin Lawrance, Emily Osborn, and Richard Roberts (Madison: University of Wisconsin Press, forthcoming).

25. Inspecteur Saurin, rapport concernant la verifcation du service de M. Catalogne, resident à Banamba, 23 February 1910, ANS-AOF 4 G 11.

26. Lt-gov Clozel, letter to gov-gen, Bamako, 29 April 1911, ANS-AOF M 83.

27. Rapport sur le fonctionnement de la justice indigène, 1st Quarter 1906, Sikasso, ANM 2 M 93.

28. Hampaté Bâ captures this dependency well in his brilliant novel, *The Fortunes of Wangrin,* translated by Aina Pavolini Taylor (Bloomington: Indiana University Press, 1999). See also Emily Osborn, " 'Circles of Iron': African Colonial Employees and the Interpretation of Colonial Rule in French West Africa," *JAH* 44 (1) (2003): pp. 29–50. See also Benjamin Lawrance, Emily Osborn, and Richard Roberts, eds. *Intermediaries, Interpreters, and Clerks: Africans in the Making of Modern Africa* (Madison: University of Wisconsin Press, forthcoming).

29. Menuier, *Organisation et fonctionnement,* p. 174. Article 53 of the 1903 legislation.

30. Lt-gov. Clozel, Rapport politique, Haut-Sénégal-Niger, 1911, ANS-AOF 2 G 11–9.

31. Procureur-général to gov-gen, 22 December 1908, Dakar, ANS-AOF M 122.

32. Ponty, Rapport d'ensemble sur la situation générale de la colonie du Haut-Sénégal-Niger en 1904, ANS-AOF 2 G 4–16; Ponty, Service judiciaire, Justice, Rapport annuel, Haut-Sénégal-Niger, 1903, ANS-AOF 2 G 3–8/VI.

33. Alice Conklin, *Mission to Civilize: The Republican Idea of Empire in France and West Africa, 1895–1930* (Stanford: Stanford University Press, 1997), pp. 89–90.

34. "Rapport au Président de la République, suivi de decret portant réorganisation du service de la justice dans les colonies relevant du gouvernement général de l'Afrique occidentale," *Journal officiel de la République française* (24 November 1903).

35. Gov-Gen Roume to lieut-govs, Dakar, 4 March 1904, ANS-AOF M 79; the handbook was published in Gorée by the Imprimerie du Gouvernment général, 1905.

36. Roume, *Justice indigène,* pp. 29–30.

37. See Maurice Delafosse, *Haut-Sénégal-Niger* (Paris: E. Larose, originally 1912, reissued Paris: Maisonneuve and Larose, 1972), 3 vols., see vol. 3 in particular. For more detail, see Chapter 5.

38. Procès verbal, Commission permanante du Conseil du gouvernement, session 6 June 1903, Dakar, ANS-AOF 5 E 1. The British also sought to prohibit attorneys in native courts. See O. Adewoye, *The Judicial System of Southern Nigeria: Law and Justice in a Dependency* (Atlantic Highlands: Humanities Press, 1977).

39. Roger Villamur and Léon Richaud, *Notre colonie de la Côte d'Ivoire* (Paris: A Challamel, 1903), pp. 164–165.

40. For example, Marie François Joseph Clozel and Roger Villamur, *Les coutumes indigènes de la Côte d'Ivoire: Documents publiés avec une introduction et des notes* (Paris: A Challamel, 1902).

41. Rapport sur le fonctionnement de la justice indigène, 4th Quarter 1905, Sikasso, ANM 2 M 93.

42. Rapport politique, Segu, February 1897, ANM 1 E 71.

43. Captain Porion, Étude sur la justice administrative indigène dans le cercle de Bamako, Bamako, 19 July 1894, ANM 2 M 54.

44. Charles Correnson, De l'organisation de la justice et des moeurs chez les populations de la région de Segu, Segu, 5 September 1907, ANM 1 D 55–3.

45. Sara Berry, *Chiefs Know Their Boundaries: Essays on Property, Power, and the Past in Asante, 1896–1996* (Portsmouth, NH: Heinemann, 2001), pp. 5–6, 50–55.

46. Rapport sur la justice indigène, 2nd Quarter 1910, Kita, ANM 2 M 73.

47. Rapport sur le fonctionnement de la justice, 3rd Quarter 1908, Sokolo, ANM 2 M 94.

48. Charles Monteil relied on one primary informant, Monteil, *Les Bambara du Ségou et du Kaarta: étude historique, ethnographique et littéraire d'une peuplade du Soudan français* (Paris: originally Maisonneuve 1924, reprinted Paris: Maisonneuve, 1976), p. 7. See also Hervé Jezequel, " 'Collecting Customary Law': Educated Africans, Ethnographic Writing, and Colonial Justice in French West Africa," in *Intermediaries, Interpreters, and Clerks,* eds. Benjamin Lawrance, Emily Osborn, and Richard Roberts (Madison: University of Wisconsin Press, forthcoming).

49. Sec-gen Merlin, Instructions aux administrateurs . . . , Gorée, October 1904, ANM 2 M 459.

50. Meunier, *Organisation et fonctionnement,* pp. 138–139.

51. All colonial powers applied the rights to intervene and to abolish practices concerned "repugnant" to civilization or to good conscience. Such a repugnancy test offered significant power to colonial authorities to interfere in the internal affairs of African societies and households.

52. Lt-gov. Trentinian, Note circulaire, Bamako, 3 February 1896, ANM 2 M 4.

53. Gov. Trentinian, circulair no. 546, Dorits des commandants de Région, de cercle et Poste en matière de justice, Kayes, 16 December 1896, ANM 2 M 40. The same circular appears in file ANM 2 D 155.

54. Lt-gov. Trentinian, Circulaire to commmandants de cercle, 19 December 1896, Kayes, ANS-AOF 1 G 138.

55. Commis des Affaires indigènes Barrat, Coutumiers juridiques, 1897, ANS-AOF 1 G 229.

56. Ponty, serving as interim gov-gen, letter to lt-gov H-S-N, Dakar, 10 October 1907, ANM 2 M 459. Selected 1906 court registers for the tribunaux de province can be found only in Dakar, ANS-AOF M 119–121.

57. See, for example, Christopher Harrison, *France and Islam in West Africa, 1860–1960* (Cambridge: Cambridge University Press, 1988); David Robinson, *Paths of Accommodation: Muslim Societies and French Colonial Authorities in Senegal and Mauritania, 1880–1920* (Athens: Ohio University Press, 2000); David Robinson and Jean-Louis Triaud, eds., *Le temps des marabouts: itinéraires et stratégies islamiques en Afrique occidentale française, 1880–1960* (Paris: Karthala, 1998); James Searing, *"God Alone Is King": The Wolof Kingdoms of Kajoor and Bawol, 1859–1914* (Portsmouth, NH: Heinemann, 2002).

58. Rapport politique, Segu, October 1906, ANM 1 E 72. N. Seignette was an officer in the military interpreters' corps in Algeria and had a degree in law. See N. Seignette, *Code Musulman, rite Malékite—statut reel, par Khalil ibn Ishak al Jundj,* translated by N. Seignette (Constantine, Impr. L. Arnolet; Alger, Jourdan; Paris, Challamel aîné, 1878).

59. Lt-gov Clozel, letter to Gov-gen, Bamako, 29 April 1911, ANS-AOF M 83.

60. De la Brestesche, letter to lt-gov, Segu, 6 December 1906, ANM 2 M 34. On influencing outcomes of court cases, see Brett Shadle, "African Court Elders in Nyanza Province, Kenya, c. 1930–1960," in *Intermediaries, Interpreters, and Clerks: Africans in the Making of Modern Africa,* eds. Benjamin Lawrance, Emily Osborn, and Richard Roberts (Madison: University of Wisconsin Press, forthcoming) and Maurice Nyamanga Amutabi, "Power and Influence of African Court Clerks and Translators in Colonial Kenya: The Case of Khwisero Native (African) Court, 1946–1956," in *Intermediaries, Interpreters, and Clerks: Africans in the Making of Modern Africa,* eds. Benjamin Lawrance, Emily Osborn, and Richard Roberts (Madison: University of Wisconsin Press, forthcoming).

61. Correnson, De l'organisation de la justice et des moeurs, Segu, 5 September 1907, ANM 1 D 55–3.

62. See especially Judith E. Tucker, *In the House of the Law: Gender and Islamic Law in Ottoman Syria and Palestine* (Berkeley: University of California, 1998), chapters 1 and 3 especially. Kathleen M. Moore provides an important framework for thinking about Muslim women and the law in "Legal Studies" in *Encyclopedia of Women and Islamic Cultures: Methodologies, Paradigms, and Sources,* ed. Suad Joseph (Leiden: Brill, 2003), 369–377. For a normative rendering of the Muslim law of divorce, see John L. Esposito, *Women in Muslim Family Law* (Syracuse: Syracuse University Press, 1982), 28–39; Jamal J. Nasir, *The Status of Women under Islamic Law and under Modern Islamic Legislation* (London: Graham and Trotman, 1990), chapter 4; and J.N.D. Anderson, *Islamic Law in the Modern World* (New York: New York University Press, 1959), chapter 3.

63. Gov-gen, letter to lt-gov H-S-N, Dakar, 2 May 1910, ANM 2 M 459.

64. Conklin, *Mission to Civilize,* pp. 108–119.

65. Rapport sur le fonctionnement de la justice, Bouguni, 3rd Quarter 1910, ANM 2 M 59.

66. Rapport sur la justice indigène, 4th Quarter 1908, Sikasso, ANM 2 M 93.

67. Anne Martin-Fugier, *La bourgeoisie: Femme au temps de Paul Bourget* (Paris: Bernard Grassett, 1983), pp. 104–108; Ann-Louise Shapiro, *Breaking the Codes: Female*

Criminality in Fin-de-Siècle Paris (Stanford: Stanford University Press, 1996), pp. 140, 183–186. Adultery was widely used in contemporary literature in France and adultery trials were very popular. See Edward Berenson, *The Trial of Madame Caillaux* (Berkeley: University of California Press, 1992) and Ruth Harris, *Murders and Madness: Medicine, Law, and Society in the fin de siècle* (Oxford: Clarendon, 1989). I thank Lou Roberts for these suggestions.

68. Rapport sur le fonctionnement de la jusitce indigène, 3rd Quarter 1909, Sokolo, ANM 2 M 94; Rapport sur le fonctionnement des tribunaux indigènes, 1st Quarter 1909, Bamako, ANM 2 M 54; Rapport sur le fonctionnement de la justice indigène, 3rd Quarter 1909, Sikasso, ANM 2 M 93.

69. Rapport sur le fonctionnement des tribunaux indigènes, 4th Quarter 1906, Gumbu, ANM 2 M 65.

70. In a similar manner, the Bamako administrator remarked in 1912 that he was concerned with "ameliorating the most severe punishments associated with adultery" and directing those cases to the criminal court. Rapport sur la justice indigène, Bamako, 2nd Quarter 1912, ANM 2 M 54.

71. Sara Berry, *No Condition Is Permanent: The Social Dynamics of Agrarian Change in Sub-Saharan Africa* (Madison: University of Wisconsin Press, 1993), pp. 8–10.

72. Lt-gov, p.i., letter to gov-gen, Kayes, 5 September 1905, ANM 2 M 1. Included in letter was Rapport de l'Administrateur sur le fonctionnement des tribunaux de cercle, Bandiagara, June 1905. I consider this the first because it was the first to be presented to the senior administration as a jurisdictional and procedural problem.

73. Lt-gov, circulaire au sujet de la compétence des tribunaux indigènes, to administrators and commandants de cercle de la colonie, Kayes, 2 June 1906, ANM 2 M 459.

74. Rapport sur les coutumes et institutions juridiques, Cercle de Segu, 1909, ANM 1 D 206.

CHAPTER 4: THE COURTS, THE END OF SLAVERY, AND THE LANDSCAPES OF POWER

1. Rapport du commandant de cercle sur l'affaire de Nyamina, 22 May 1901, ANM 1 E 19. See also Rapport politique, Segu, 1901, ANS-AOF 2 G 1–14; Ponty, Rapport politique, H-S-N, February 1901, ANS-AOF 2 G 1–14.

2. Emily Osborn, "Power, Authority, and Gender in Kankan-Baté, 1650–1920," (unpublished Ph.D. dissertation, Stanford University, 2000).

3. See Denise Bouche, *Villages de liberté en Afrique noire française, 1887–1910* (The Hague: Mouton, 1968), pp. 87–89; Martin Klein, *Slavery and French Colonialism* (Cambridge: Cambridge University Press, 1998), pp. 84–88; also Captain Loyer, commandant of Bamako, letter to commandant supérieur, 5 May 1886, Bamako, ANM 2 D 72.

4. Trentinian, "Instructions à la usage. . . ." *Bulletin du Comité de l'Afrique française,* January 1900, p. 22, quoted in Bouche, *Villages de liberté,* p. 147.

5. Richard Roberts, "The Emergence of a Grain Market in Bamako, 1883–1908," *Canadian Journal of African Studies* 14 (1) (1980).

6. Brevié, Rapport sur l'esclavage, Bamako, 1904, ANS-AOF K 19. See also Richard Roberts and Martin Klein, "The Banamba Slave Exodus of 1905 and the End of Slavery in the Western Sudan," *JAH* 21 (3) (1980).

7. Richard Roberts, *Warriors, Slaves, and Merchants: The State and the Economy in the Middle Niger Valley, 1700–1914* (Stanford: Stanford University Press, 1987), pp. 13–17.

8. Jean-Loup Amselle, *Logiques métisses: anthropologie de l'identité en Afrique et ailleurs* (Paris: Payot, 1990), pp. 71–88.

9. Fredrik Barth, ed., *Ethnic Groups and Boundaries: The Social Organization of Culture Difference* (Boston: Little, Brown and Company, 1969); see also David C. Conrad and Barbara Frank, eds., *Status and Identity in West Africa: Nyamakalaw of Mande* (Bloomington: Indiana University Press, 1995).

10. Rapport commercial et agricole, 1st Quarter 1901, Segu, ANM 1 R 69.

11. Rapport général sur la politique du cercle pendant l'année 1905, Segu, ANM 1 E 177.

12. Abner Cohen, "Cultural Strategies in the Organization of Trading Diasporas," in *The Development of Trade and Markets in West Africa,* ed. Claude Meillassoux (London: Oxford University Press, 1971); Philip Curtin, *Cross-Cultural Trade in World History* (New York: Cambridge University Press, 1984); Paul Lovejoy, *Caravans of Kola: The Hausa Kola Trade, 1700–1900* (Zaria, Nigeria: Ahmadou Bello University Press, 1980).

13. Richard Roberts, "The End of Slavery in the French Soudan, 1905–1914," in *The End of Slavery in Africa,* eds. Suzanne Miers and Richard Roberts (Madison: University of Wisconsin Press, 1988).

14. Félix Dubois, *Notre beau Niger* (Paris: Flammarion, 1911), pp. 135–136.

15. Interviews with Tijani Sylla, 3 August 1981, Baraweli; Batene Kale, 31 July 1981, Segu.

16. See especially Claude Meillassoux, "État et conditions des esclaves à Gumbu (Mali) au XIXe siècle," in *L'esclavage en Afrique précoloniale,* ed. Claude Meillassoux (Paris: Maspero, 1975) and Claude Meillassoux, *The Anthropology of Slavery: The Womb of Iron and Gold,* translated by Alide Dasnois (Chicago: University of Chicago Press, 1991), pp. 280–285. See also Klein and Roberts, "The Banamba Slave Exodus;" Richard Roberts, "Ideology, Slavery, and Social Formation: The Evolution of Slavery in the Middle Niger Valley," in *The Ideology of Slavery in Africa,* ed. Paul Lovejoy (Beverly Hills: Sage, 1981); Ann McDougall, "Banamba and the Salt Trade of the Western Sudan," in *West African Economic and Social History: Studies in Memory of Marion Johnson,* ed. David Henige (Madison: African Studies Center, 1990). Most recently, see Klein, *Slavery and Colonial Rule,* pp. 6–7, 13, 164–165, 170–172, 223.

17. Igor Kopytoff, "The Cultural Context of African Abolition," in *The End of Slavery in Africa,* eds. Suzanne Miers and Richard Roberts (Madison: University of Wisconsin Press, 1988). Kopytoff draws a distinction between what he calls "African" slavery from what he considers nonindigenous forms of slavery, including those practiced by Muslims. Such a distinction essentializes the concept of "African" slavery.

18. The evidence examined in this chapter focuses on what we can learn from court cases regarding changes in social relations between former masters and former slaves and within households as a result of slaves' departures. The evidence I selected for this chapter does not examine the erosion of ethnic boundaries, per se. Aspects of this erosion can be seen in livestock ownership cases examined in Chapter 7.

19. Klein notes that a very telling aspect of the social adjustment to the end of slavery was whether former masters or former slaves paid taxes for the former slaves, *Slavery and Colonial Rule,* p. 206.

20. Rapport politique, Gumbu, June 1909, ANM 1 E 38.

21. Rapport politique, Gumbu, June 1909, ANM 1 E 38.

22. See Roberts, "The End of Slavery in the French Soudan."

23. See Roberts, "The End of Slavery in the French Soudan." Especially interviews with Santa Kulibali, 21 March 1977, Sinsani; Binke Baba Kuma, 21 March 1976, Sinsani;

Binke Sukule, 21 March 1977, Sinani; Sidi Yahaya Kone, 1 February 1977, Sinsani; Fofana Baye, 20 July 1981, Banamba; Mustafa Simpara, Baasi Simpara, Bafu Simpara, Danguien Simpara, Fasumara Simpara, Baramu Simpara, Sadybu Simpara, Mayhamy Simpara, Moktar Simpara, and Sory Konate, 18 July 1981, Banamba.

24. See, for example, Paul Escot, *Slavery Remembered: A Record of Twentieth-Century Slave Narratives* (Chapel Hill: University of North Carolina Press, 1979).

25. See for example, Eric Foner, *Nothing But Freedom: Emancipation and Its Legacy* (Baton Rouge: Louisiana State University Press, 1983); Eric Foner, *Reconstruction: America's Unfinished Revolution* (New York: Harper and Row, 1988); Jonathan Wiener, *The Social Origins of the New South: Alabama, 1860–1885* (Baton Rouge: Louisiana State University Press, 1978); Ira Berlin and Leslie S. Rowland, eds., *Families and Freedom: A Documentary History of African-American Kinship in the Civil War Era* (New York: New Press, 1997); Ira Berlin, Marc Favreau, and Steven F. Miller, eds., *Remembering Slavery: African Americans Talk about Their Personal Experiences of Slavery and Freedom* (New York: New Press, 1998).

26. Rapport sur le fonctionnement des tribunaux indigènes, Gumbu, 1st Quarter 1908, ANM 2 M 65.

27. Rapport sur le fonctionnement des tribunaux indigènes, Gumbu, 2nd Quarter 1908, ANM 2 M 65.

28. Rapport sur la justice trimestriel, Gumbu, 3rd Quarter 1908, ANM 2 M 65.

29. Rapport sur la justice indigène, Gumbu, 3rd Quarter 1909, ANM 2 M 65.

30. Rape should have been defined as a criminal case and brought before the *tribunal de cercle,* which was empowered to hear criminal cases. Some of the other cases, including those involving adultery, also involved criminal acts under French and French colonial law, but these were usually heard by the tribunal de province, because divorce was sought or because damages were sought.

31. Fredrick Cooper discusses how masters used Islam as part of their strategies of hegemony in the absence of a strong state, "Islam and Cultural Hegemony: The Ideology of Slaveowners on the East African Coast," in *Ideology of Slavery in Africa,* ed. Paul Lovejoy (Beverly Hills: Sage, 1981). Klein addresses this issue in terms of honor, *Slavery and Colonial Rule,* chapter 14.

32. See Richard Roberts, "Guinée Cloth: Linked Transformations within France's Empire in the Nineteenth Century," *Cahiers d'Études Africaines* 128 (1992). See also Jane Guyer, ed., *Money Matters: Instability, Values, and Social Payments in the Modern History of West African Communities* (Portsmouth, NH: Heinemann, 1995).

33. Demba Diko v Samba Sigiri, 16 April 1908; Dougouni Kone v Dia Coulibaly, 7 May 1908; Mohamet Cira v Mari Diabou "N'Golokoro," 18 June 1908, Tribunal de Province, Gumbu, ANM 2 M 122.

34. In the absence of witnesses, swearing an oath was an equally powerful form of evidentiary presentation. For a general discussion on oaths in West Africa, see Allan Christelow, "Theft, Homicide, and Oath" in *Law in Colonial Africa,* eds. Kristin Mann and Richard Roberts (Portsmouth, NH: Heinemann, 1991); and Allan Christelow, *Thus Ruled Emir Abbas: Selected Cases from the Records of the Emir of Kano's Judicial Council* (East Lansing: Michigan State University Press, 1994). Even in the absence of witnesses, swearing on the Koran to support claims of debt usually prevailed in court. On 18 June 1908, Galo Kamara denied Kissima Cisse's claim to 420 kilograms of millet, but refused to swear an oath. The court ruled in Kissima Cisse's favor. Swearing an oath on the Koran also served the defendants. In two cases heard on the 13 July 1908, defendants swore an oath that denied the plaintiffs' claims. In one of these cases, Moriba Ture sought to recover from

Fara Diafaka 200 muules of grain, but "Fara Diafaka swears on the Koran that it was only 2,500 cowries that he owed. No witnesses." The tribunal ruled in favor of the defendant and required that he return the 2,500 cowries. Tribunal de Province, Gumbu, ANM 2 M 122.

35. Bamady Ely v Sidiki Dembele, 14 May 1908; Mabako Gakou v Taraore Sambou, 18 May 1908, Tribunal de Province, Gumbu, ANM 2 M 122.

36. Mohamet Konate v Noumou Daha, 19 March 1908; Diagueli Diko v Coumien Ture, 9 July 1908; Garba Keita v Amadou Moctar, 5 April 1909; Menkoro Diara v Niamakolo Couliblary, 17 May 1909; when Mohamet Taliki sought to recover 15 guinées and 20 sheep from Amady Bary, 2 July 1908, Tribunal de Province, Gumbu, ANM 2 M 122.

37. French administration sought to disguise the problem of slavery from metropolitan scrutiny by labeling slaves as "servants" or some other equally vague term. See especially Klein, *Slavery and Colonial Rule,* chapter 8.

38. Baba So v Ahmady Diallo and Amady Abdoulay Mocar v Hamady Souka, Tribunal de Province, Gumbu, 23 March 1908, ANM 2 M 122.

39. Samba Kadra v Amady Toure, 6 April 1908; Modiba Dembele v Tiema Coulibaly, 23 April 1908, Tribunal de Province, Gumbu, ANM 2 M 122.

40. Ahmady Sidibe v Kaoura Kone, Tribunal de Province, Gumbu, 5 September 1908, ANM 2 M 122.

41. Mohmet Mint v M'Bare Diamana, Tribunal de Province, Gumbu, 1 April 1908, ANM 2 M 122.

42. The issue of evidentiary procedure in the tribunal de province is a major issue that I cannot enter into here. However, in the absence of written contracts, the court relied heavily on witnesses and on oaths. Refusing to swear on the Koran in the absence of witnesses was tantamount to pleading guilty.

43. Rapport sur le fonctionnement des tribunaux indigènes, Gumbu, 1st Quarter 1906, ANM 2 M 65. I have court records for only the first two weeks in July 1905. I have not included these records here because they may be anomalous to the wider trends evident with denser court data. Court records for 1906 from all districts seem to be lost.

44. Rapport sur le fonctionnement des tribunaux indigènes, Gumbu, 1st Quarter 1908, ANM 2 M 65.

45. Meillassoux, *The Anthropology of Slavery,* pp. 35, 88–89, 172–173, which is modified by Klein, *Slavery and Colonial Rule,* pp. 10–11. Cases regarding child custody disputes may provide additional information on the issue of male slaves' paternity. More research also needs to be conducted on divorce to see if former slave marriages were more or less stable in the immediate aftermath of the end of slavery.

46. Roberts, "The End of Slavery in the French Soudan," p. 293.

47. Kumba Diallo v Ousmane Sigiri, Tribunal de Province, Gumbu, 24 April 1911, ANM 2 M 122.

48. Coutume Bambara dans le cercle de Gumbu, 1909, ANM 1 D 192.

49. Coutume Bambara dans le cercle de Gumbu, 1909, ANM 1 D 192.

50. To overcome the structural problem of having her kin transfer the bridewealth back to her former husband, the court records indicate that wives were sometimes the ones who actually agreed to return the bridewealth. Since bridewealth was a considerable sum, women who wished to divorce their husbands would either have to draw on their own wealth or seek another marriage in which the new bridewealth would flow directly to the former husband. For more information, see Chapter 6, "Bridewealth as Contract."

51. Thoron de Laur, Rapport sur la tournée de recensement, 5 May 1909, Gumbu, ANM 1 E 38.

52. Rapport politique, Bamako, May 1907, ANM 1 E 19.

53. Douba Dansira v Diba Taliki, 19 April 1909; Oumara So v Lansana Konare, 23 April 1908, Tribunal de Province, Gumbu, ANM 2 M 122.

54. Nielle Sidibe v Bakary Kone, 5 April 1909; Aissate Gakou v Soussoukone Taraore, 3 April 1911; Marama Sambou v Youmari Danitoko, 17 April 1911, Tribunal de Province, Gumbu, ANM 2 M 122.

55. Bridewealth disputes could also occur before marriage occurred or after divorces. I code such cases as bridewealth disputes and not as divorce disputes in which bridewealth is the cited cause.

56. Klein, *Slavery and French Colonial Rule,* p. 197.

57. Eric Pollet and Grace Winter, *La Société Soninke (Dyahunu, Mali)* (Brussels: Editions de l'Institut de sociologie, Universite libre de Bruxelles, 1972), pp. 371, 394.

58. Sadio Kone v Amadou Diaba, Tribunal de Province, Gumbu, 2 April 1908, ANM 2 M 122.

59. Sana Toure v Toumani Diara, 16 December 1909; Fatouma Diefaka v Santina Diallo, 8 April 1909; Tene Soumare v Amadou Diara, 19 January 1910, Tribunal de Province, Gumbu, ANM 2 M 122. Another form of rupture to the reciprocity of the household was when women left their husbands, which constituted 19 percent of the divorce cases heard in Gumbu. At this stage in my research, I am much less certain that I can link wives leaving their husbands to the end of slavery, although I could speculate that some runaway wives fled to escape their husbands' mistreatments and increased labor obligations. In Chapter 6, I analyze the court data on the relationship between abandonment and mistreatment and the return of bridewealth.

CHAPTER 5: WOMEN SEEKING DIVORCE; MEN SEEKING CONTROL

1. Sara Diallo v Moriba Sangare, Tribunal de Province, Bamako, 4 April 1905, ANM 2 M 104.

2. Samba Sako v Makasouba, Tribunal de Province, Bamako, 14 April 1905, ANM 2 M 104.

3. See Chapters 7 and 8 for a fuller discussion of levirate.

4. Mariam Fofana v un-named defendant, Tribunal de Province, Bamako, 28 April 1905, ANM 2 M 104.

5. Men's strategy in repairing marriage was to ask the court to force the return of their wives, who had fled to their kin because of problems in the household.

6. Aissate Tal v Amadu Koita, Tribunal de Province, Bamako, 1 September 1905, ANM 2 M 104.

7. Niane Kouyate v Ko Tangara, Tribunal de Province, Bamako, 15 September 1905, ANM 2 M 104.

8. Ma Sidibe v Siriki Keita, Tribunal de Province, Bamako, 22 December 1905, ANM 2 M 104.

9. Public shaming of lazy or abusive husbands (or abusive warrant chiefs) by wives is fairly widespread in the literature, see especially Judith Van Allen, " 'Aba Riots' or Igbo 'Women's War'? Ideology, Stratification, and the Invisibility of Women," in *Women in Africa: Studies in Social and Economic Change,* eds. Nancy J. Hafkin and Edna G. Bay (Stanford: Stanford University Press, 1976); Majorie Shostak, *Nisa: The Life and Words of a !Kung Woman* (New York: Vintage Books, 1983), chapter 11; see also Dorothy Hodgson

and Sheryl McCurdy, eds., *"Wicked" Women and the Reconfiguration of Gender in Africa* (Portsmouth, NH: Heinemann, 2002).

10. Niafily Camara v Sibery Doumbia, Tribunal de Province, Segu, 19 April 1905, ANM 2 M 143.

11. Boliba Taraore v Diosei Coulibaly, Tribunal de Province, Segu, 24 April 1905, ANM 2 M 143.

12. Daro Kone v Kamisoko, Tribunal de Province, Segu, 8 May 1905, ANM 2 M 143.

13. Diokolo Ture v Gidi Ture, Tribunal de Province, Segu, 25 October 1905, ANM 2 M 143.

14. Indati Kouma v Balla Diara, Tribunal de Province, Segu, 20 November 1905, ANM 2 M 143.

15. Penda Sy v Tene Diallo, Tribunal de Province, Segu, 30 August 1905, ANM 2 M 143.

16. Overall, 32 percent of the marriage cases between 1905 and 1912 in Segu were brought by women or male relatives on their behalf. This contrasts with Bamako, where only 6 percent of the marriage cases between 1905 and 1912 were brought by women or their male relatives.

17. I shall examine in more detail the issues surrounding bridewealth in Chapter 6.

18. Nieba Kouyate v Degi Kouyate, Tribunal de Province, Segu, 20 October 1905, ANM 2 M 143.

19. Tiekoro Keita v Miantou Tangara, Tribunal de Province, Segu, 20 November 1905, ANM 2 M 143.

20. Mamadi Dembele v Souzouroudie Fane, 1 November 1905, Tribunal de Province, Bouguni; Fane v Dembele, 2 November 1905, Tribunal de Cercle, Bouguni. ANM 2 M 110.

21. Rapport sur le fonctionnement de la justice indigène, 1st Quarter 1906, Sikasso, ANM 2 M 93.

22. Rapport sur le fonctionnement de la justice indigène, Bamako, 3rd Quarter 1906, ANM 2 M 54.

23. Rapport sur le fonctionnement des tribunaux indigènes, Gumbu, 4th Quarter 1906, ANM 2 M 65.

24. Rapport sur le fonctionnement des tribunaux, Segu, 1st Quarter 1907, ANM 2 M 92.

25. Rapport sur le fonctionnement de la justice indigène, Mopti, 1st Quarter 1911, ANM 2 M 79.

26. For example, Rapport sur le fonctionnement de la justice indigène, Koutiala, 2nd Quarter 1906, ANM 2 M 75.

27. Janet R. Horne, "In Pursuit of Greater France: Visions of Empire among the Musée Social Reformers, 1894–1931," in *Domesticating the Empire: Race, Gender, and Family Life in French and Dutch Colonialism,* eds. Julia Clancy-Smith and Frances Gouda (Charlottesville: University of Virginia Press, 1998), p. 40.

28. Rapport sur le fonctionnement de la justice indigène, 3rd Quarter 1905, Bougouni, ANM 2 M 59; Rapport sur le fonctionnement de la justice indigène, 4th Quarter 1905, Bougouni, ANM 2 M 59.

29. Rapport sur le fonctionnement des tribunaux indigènes, 3rd Quarter 1906, Bougouni, ANM 2 M 59.

30. Rapport sur le fonctionnement de la justice, 2nd Quarter 1907, Jenne, ANM 2 M 60.

31. Charles Correnson, De l'orientation de la justice et des moeurs chez les populations de la région de Segou, Segu, 5 September 1907, ANM 1 D 55–3.

32. Rapport de M. l'Administrateur de cercle du Bamako sur le fonctionnement des tribunaux indigènes, 1st Quarter 1909, Bamako, ANM 2 M 54.

33. Bernard Cohn, *An Anthropologist among the Historians and Other Essays* (Delhi: Oxford University Press, 1987); Robert Kidder, "Western Law in India: External Law and Local Response," in *Social System and Legal Process,* ed. Harry M. Johnson (San Francisco: Jossey-Bass, 1978), 159–162.

34. Rapport de l'Administrateur sur le fonctionnement des tribunaux indigènes, 4th Quarter 1908, Bamako, ANM 2 M 54.

35. Rapport sur le fonctionnement de la justice, Bouguni, 3rd Quarter 1910, ANM 2 M 59.

36. Rapport sur le fonctionnement des tribunaux indigènes, Bamako, 2nd Quarter 1906, ANM 2 M 54.

37. Rapport sur le fonctionnement des tribunaux indigènes, Gumbu, 4th Quarter 1906, ANM 2 M 65; also Rapport sur le fonctionnement de la justice indigène, Bamako, 2nd Quarter 1906, ANM 2 M 54.

38. Rapport sur le fonctionnement de la justice indigène, Bamako, May 1905, ANM 2 M 54.

39. Rapport sur le fonctionnement des tribunaux indigènes, Gumbu, 4th Quarter 1907, ANM 2 M 65.

40. Rapport sur le fonctionnement de la justice indigène, Koutiala, 2nd Quarter 1909, ANM 2 M 75.

41. Claire Goldberg Moses, *French Feminism in the Nineteenth Century* (Albany: State University of New York Press, 1984), pp. 209–211.

42. Charles Correnson, De l'orientation de la justice et des moeurs chez les populations de la région de Segou, Segu, 5 September 1907, ANM 1 D 55–3.

43. Terence Ranger, "The Invention of Tradition in Africa;" in *The Invention of Tradition,* eds. Eric Hobsbawm and Terence Ranger (Cambridge: Cambridge University Press, 1983); Martin Chanock, *Law, Custom, and Social Order: The Colonial Experience in Malawi and Zambia* (Cambridge: Cambridge University Press, 1985).

44. For the latest discussion on the history of French antislavery policy and its social consequences, see Martin Klein, *Slavery and Colonial Rule in French West Africa* (Cambridge: Cambridge University Press, 1998).

45. Rapport complementaire sur le fonctionnement de la justice indigène, Koutiala, 31 July 1910, ANM 2 M 75.

46. Demba Diara v Dale Tangara, Tribunal de Province, Bamako, 5 February 1907, ANM 2 M 104.

47. Abidou Sidibe v Madine Niamamba, Tribunal de Province, Bamako, 26 July 1907, ANM 2 M 104.

48. See especially Hodgson and McCurdy, *"Wicked" Women.*

49. Sabou Tanaore Lasana Kouma, Tribunal de Province, Segu, 3 August 1905, ANM 2 M 143.

50. Alice Conklin, *Mission to Civilize: The Republican Idea of Empire in France and West Africa, 1895–1930* (Stanford: Stanford University Press, 1997), pp. 109–119; G. Wesley Johnson, "William Ponty and Republican Patenralism in French West Africa (1866–1915)," in *African Proconsuls: European Governors in Africa,* eds. L. H. Gann and Peter Duignan (New York: Free Press, 1978), pp. 141–146.

51. Méniaud also published a two-volume study, *Haut-Sénégal-Niger: géographie économique* (Paris: Larose, 1912); Brevié's project on the Niger military territory was never published.

52. Jean-Louis Triaud, *"Haut-Sénégal-Niger,* un modèle 'positiviste'? De la coutume à l'histoire: Maurice Delafosse et l'invention de l'histoire africaine," in *Maurice Delafosse, entre orientalisme et ethnographie: L'intenéraire d'un africaniste,* eds. Jean-Loup Amselle and Emmanuelle Sibeud (Paris: Maisonneuve and Larose, 1998), p. 212; also Jean-Hervé Jezequel, "Maurice Delafosse et l'émergence d'une littérature africaine à vocation scientifique," in *Maurice Delafosse, entre orientalisme et ethnographie: L'intenéraire d'un africaniste,* eds. Jean-Loup Amselle and Emmanuelle Sibeud (Paris: Maisonneuve, 1998), p. 95.

53. Louise Delafosse, *Maurice Delafosse: un Berichon conquis par l'Afrique* (Paris: Société française d'histoire d'Outre-Mer, 1976), ch. 5, see esp. 271–281; Triaud, *"Haut-Sénégal-Niger,"* 227, fn 7. Delafosse decided to leave behind his long time mistress, Amouï, and his two children he had with her. His eldest daughter was sent to the Catholic sisters' mission school in Dabou.

54. Maurice Delafosse, "Le peuple siéna ou sénoufo," *Revue des études ethnographiques et sociologiques,* vol. 1 and vol. 2.

55. Maurice Delafosse, "Institut ethnographique international de Paris, Actes; Allocution de Maurice Delafosse, président de séance," *Revue d'ethnographie et sociologie* 3 (1912). The journal's name was changed in 1911. For more background, see Emmanuel Sibeud, "Les étapes d'un négrologue" in *Maurice Delafosse, entre orientalisme et ethnographie: L'intenéraire d'un africaniste,* eds. Jean-Loup Amselle and Emmanuelle Sibeud (Paris: Maisonneuve and Larose, 1998), pp. 173–183.

56. William Cohen, *Rulers of Empire: The French Colonial Service in Africa* (Stanford: Hoover Institution Press, 1971); A. Enders, "L'école nationale de la France d'Outre-Mer et la formation des administrateurs coloniaux," *Revue d'histoire moderne et contemporaine* 40 (2) (1993).

57. L. Delafosse, *Delafosse,* 286–291; Triaud, *"Haut-Sénégal-Niger,"* 232, fn. 61.

58. See especially Conklin, *Mission to Civilize,* pp. 109–119; Johnson, "William Ponty and Republican Patenralism," pp. 141–146. For a contemporary discussion of Ponty's administration, see Senator Charles Humbert, "L'Afrique occidentale française sous l'administration de M. W. Ponty," *La Grande revue* 67 (1911): pp. 49–70.

59. Conklin, *Mission to Civilize,* pp. 176–187; also Alice Conklin, " 'On a semé la haine': Maurice Delafosse et la politique du Gouvernement général en AOF, 1915–1936," in *Maurice Delafosse, entre orientalisme et ethnographie: L'intenéraire d'un africaniste,* eds. Jean-Loup Amselle and Emmanuelle Sibeud (Paris: Maisonneuve, 1998), pp. 66–71.

60. Delafosse, *Haut-Sénégal-Niger,* vol. III, p. 2.

61. Delafosse, *Haut-Sénégal-Niger,* vol. III, pp. 127–128.

62. Delafosse, *Haut-Sénégal-Niger,* vol. III, p. 135.

63. Maurice Delafosse, *Les civilisations négro-africaines* (Paris: Stock, 1925), 7; for more detail, see Marc Michel, "Maurice Delafosse et l'invention d'une africanité nègre," in *Maurice Delafosse, entre orientalisme et ethnographie: L'intenéraire d'un africaniste,* eds. Jean-Loup Amselle and Emmanuelle Sibeud (Paris: Maisonneuve, 1998), pp. 84–86. Marie Perinbam applies the same model in her book, *Family Identity and the State in the Bamako Kafu, c.1800–c.1900* (Boulder, CO: Westview Press, 1997).

64. Delafosse, *Haut-Sénégal-Niger,* III, p. 3.

65. Delafosse, *Haut-Sénégal-Niger,* III, p. 21. See Chapter 7 for a fuller discussion of property and property rights within "families."

66. Delafosse, *Haut-Sénégal-Niger,* III, pp. 61–62.

67. Delafosse, *Haut-Sénégal-Niger,* III, pp. 61–62.

68. Charles Monteil, *Les Bambara. du Ségou et du Kaarta: étude historique, ethnographique et littéraire d'une peuplade du Soudan français* (Paris: Maisonneuve, 1924, reprinted Paris: Maisonneuve, 1976).

69. Monteil's relied upon the assistance of two crucial informants, Kare Tammoura and Gran Konate.

70. Prior to his 1924 study of the Bambara, Monteil published a study of Jenne (*Monographie de Djenné* [Tulle: Imprimerie de Jean Mazeyrie, 1903]), a study of songs (*Contes Soudanaises* [Paris: E. Leroux, 1905]), a study on cattle (*L'elevage au Soudan* [Paris: A. Challamel, 1905]), a study on the Peul (*Notice sur l'origine des Peulhs* [n.p., 1911]), and a study of the Khassonkes (*Les Khassonkés. Monographie d'une peuplade du Soudan Français* [Paris: E. Leroux, 1915]).

71. Louise Delafosse, *Maurice Delafosse: un Berichon conquis par l'Afrique* (Paris: Société française d'histoire d'Outre-Mer, 1976), pp. 289–292.

72. Maurice Delafosse, review of *Les Bambara,* originally published in *Afrique française,* March 1924, and reprinted in 1977 edition of *Les Bambara,* xviii.

73. "*Fa* signifies, following the case, seigneur, maitre, patriarche, père . . . It corresponds very well to the family of the status of the high and respectable dignity that Mistral said to his father: mon siegneur père ou le maître." Note in original text.

74. Monteil, *Les Bambara,* pp. 158–159.

75. Monteil, *Les Bambara,* pp. 173–174.

76. Monteil, *Les Bambara,* p. 183.

77. Monteil, *Les Bambara,* p. 185.

78. Rapport complementaire sur le fonctionnement de la justice indigène, Koutiala, 31 July 1910, ANM 2 M 75.

79. Anthony Giddens, *The Construction of Society* (Berkeley: University of California Press, 1984). pp. 9–14.

CHAPTER 6: BRIDEWEALTH AS CONTRACT

1. Quote taken from Richard White, *The Middle Ground: Indians, Empires, and Republics in the Great Lakes Region, 1650–1815* (New York: Cambridge University Press, 1991), p. 102.

2. Camilla Toulmin, *Cattle, Women, and Wells: Managing Household Survival in the Sahel* (Oxford: Clarendon Press, 1992), pp. 4–5, Chapter 13.

3. Coutume Bambara dans le cercle de Gumbu, 1909, ANM 1 D 192.

4. Rapport sur le fonctionnement des tribunaux indigènes, Bandiagara, 4th Quarter 1906, ANM 2 M 56.

5. Coutume Bambara dans le cercle de Gumbu, 1909, ANM 1 D 192. This was clearly Fassanou Dembele's strategy in defense of his failure to reimburse the bridewealth to his daughter's husband after she left him and refused to return. Fassanou Dembele argued in court that because he was not responsible for his daughter's decision to leave her husband, he was not responsible for the repayment of bridewealth. The court obviously found Dembele's defense self-serving in how it narrowed "custom" because it ordered him to reimburse the bridewealth. Bary Soumare v Fassanou Dembele, Tribunal de Province, Bamako, 18 February 1908, ANM 2 M 104.

6. See John Comaroff, ed., *The Meaning of Marriage Payments* (London: Academic Press, 1980); and Jane Collier, *Marriage and Inequality in Classless Societies* (Stanford: Stanford University Press, 1988). See also Veronika Görög-Karady, ed., *Le mariage dans les contes Africaines: Études et anthologie* (Paris: Kathala, 1994).

7. Jean Ortoli, "Coutume Bambara, Cercle de Bamako," in *Coutumiers juridiques de l'Afrique occidentale française* ed. Bernard Maupoil (Paris: Publications du Comité d'études historiques et scientifiques de l'Afrique occidentale française, 1939), vol. II, p. 135. See also René Luneau, *Les chemins de la noce: La femme et le mariage dans la société rurale au Mali* (Lille: Service de reproduction des thèses, Université de Lille, 1975).

8. Such conditions might emerge in famines, epidemics, and other forms of social distress. For more discussion on gender specific spheres of property, see Chapter 7.

9. Cases involving incompletely transferred bridewealth regularly appear in the court records. Marriage disputes are thus simultaneously about marriage and contracts.

10. Toulmin, *Cattle, Women, and Wells,* p. 266.

11. Coutume Bambara dans le cercle de Gumbu, 1909, ANM 1 D 192.

12. Toulmin, *Cattle, Women, and Wells,* pp. 249, 266. Luneux makes the same point, "Mariage coutumier," pp. 151–153. Toulmin's description reflected a normative bias in the nature of her ethnographic data. Real life was certainly different.

13. Ortoli, "Coutume Bambara," pp. 141–142; Alred Aubert, "Coutume Bambara, cercle de Bougouni" in *Coutumiers juridiques,* vol. II, pp. 86–99; Toulmin, *Cattle, Women, and Wells,* p. 299. As I have discussed briefly in Chapter 3, the application of custom in divorce cases in the native courts closely resembled Islamic normative law on divorce. The relationship between changing custom on divorce and Islam needs more attention.

14. Maurice Delafosse, *Haut-Sénégal-Niger* (Paris: originally E. Larose, 1912; reissued Maisonneuve and Larose , 1972), vol. III, p. 41.

15. Coutumes juridiques au Soudan, Cercle de Segu, Segu, 1 April 1897, ANS-AOF 1 G 229. The report emphasized only one aspect of pawning: the transferability of the pawn to a third party. The report elaborated the conditions under which pawns could be transferred. Since pawns were most often girls, the transfer of the pawn resembled the transfer of bridewealth. The transfer of a pawn sometimes constituted part of bridewealth transfers. To compound the situation, the pawn might wind up as a wife of the creditor, further confusing the obligations of debt, credit, and kinship. Exactly these ambiguities emerged on 5 September 1912 when Fadie Coulibaly took Yamadou Kouyate to court in Bamako regarding bridewealth for the marriage of his daughter to Bala Konate. In 1898, Fadie Coulibaly pawned his daughter, Massara Coulibaly, aged seven, to Yamadou Kouyate as guarantee for a loan of Fr 15. Two years later, Yamadou Kouyate married Bala Kouyate's sister. As part of his bridewealth payments, Yamadou Kouyate transferred Massara Coulibaly to Bala Kouyate, thus linking Bala Kouyate to Fadie Coulibaly. In 1903, when Massara Coulibaly was 12, Bala Kouyate took her as his wife with the approval of her father, Fadie Coulibaly, in exchange for Fr 15 the elder Coulibaly owed to Yamadou Kouyate. Bala Kouyate, in his turn, took Yamadou Kouyate to court to recover Fr 15 bridewealth for his sister, who married Yamadou Kouyate. This case captures the complexities of the pawn as security for a debt, which in turn was transformed into marriage for which bridewealth is due. The court ruled that the marriage was valid and ordered each party to pay off their debts to the others. Fodie Coulibaly v Yamadou Kouyate v Bala Kouyate, Tribunal de Province, Bamako, 5 September 1912, ANM 2 M 105. For background on pawning, see Richard Roberts and Martin Klein, "The Resurgence of Pawning in French West Africa during the Depression of the 1930s," *African Economic History* 16 (1987).

16. Gérard Dumestre, *Dictionnaire Bambara-Français* (no publisher, 1981), pp. 527, 1096; Père Charles Bailleul, *Pétit dictionnaire Bambara-Français, Français-Bambara* (Avebury, EN: Avebury Pub., 1981).

17. John Comaroff, "Introduction," in *The Meaning of Marriage Payments,* p. 17–18.

18. M'Pie Diara v Soriba Diara, Tribunal de Province, Bamako, 14 November 1911, ANM 2 M 104.

19. Amadu Kouyate v Ousmane Keita, Tribunal de Province, Bamako, 18 September 1912, ANM 2 M 105.

20. In Kaarta, a griot often played the role of the intermediary. Mid-nineteenth century traveler, Anne Raffenel, wrote, "It is the griot who handles marriage negotiations and who is rewarded when they are successful." Anne Raffenel, *Nouveau Voyage dans le pays des nègres* (Paris: Imprimerie de N. Chaix, 1856), vol. I, p. 164.

21. Fako Dihko v Sienou Koita, Tribunal de Province, Bamako, 3 July 1908, ANM 2 M 104.

22. Kini Coulibaly v Samba Coulibaly, Tribunal de Province, Bamako, 29 August 1908, ANM 2 M 104.

23. Commandant, letter to Lt-gov, Koutiala, 27 June 1911, ANM 2 M 20.

24. Soumoumery Ture v Oualama Kasse, Tribunal de Province, Bamako, 12 May 1908, ANM 2 M 104. I have not examined the records of correctional cases, so I do not know if the court punished individuals for these misdemeanor infractions that plagued the Koutiala district.

25. Nene Tangara v Niani Kone, Tribunal de Province, Segu, 22 February 1911, ANM 2 M 143. While not indicated in the record, the fine was probably levied because the defendant's action was considered a misdemeanor.

26. Demba Ouattara v Mata Sako, Tribunal de Province, Bamako, 3 June 1911, ANM 2 M 104.

27. Makan Kamara v Mama Coulibaly, Tribunal de Province, Segu, 5 February 1909, ANM 2 M 143.

28. Nianguima Sidibe v Alabassane Diara, Tribunal de Province, Segu, 19 March 1908, ANM 2 M 143.

29. Faramata So v Simbo Sangare, Tribunal de Province, Bamako, 4 June 1912, ANM 2 M 105; Mamakan Taraore v Mamdou Kane, Tribunal de Province, Bamako, 23 August 1911, ANM 2 M 104. Qadi courts applied a similar test regarding the health of the husband when considering whether to terminate the marriage contract.

30. For examples from Kenya, see Brett Shadle, "Bridewealth and Female Consent: Marriage Disputes in African Courts, Gusiiland, Kenya," *Journal of African History* 44 (2) (2003).

31. Bala Diallo v Difa Diara, Tribunal de Province, Bamako, 17 July 1905, ANM 2 M 104.

32. Bogori Doumbia v Lamine Soumare, Tribunal de Province, Bamako, 2 September 1911, ANM 2 M 104; Sory Fofana v Dialimoussa Diallo, Tribunal de Province, Bamako, 4 August 1911, ANM 2 M 104.

33. Souley Makasouba v Moussa Diara, Tribunal de Province, Bamako, 4 August 1911, ANM 2 M 104; the same parties appeared again in court for the same dispute three months later. The court probably had ruled for a three months waiting period to see if the fiancé could be located. This is similar to abandonment cases discussed below. Soulay Coulibaly v Moussa Sidibe, Tribunal de Province, Bamako, 11 November 1911, ANM 2 M 104.

34. Sala Doade v Bamba Ballo, Tribunal de Province, Segu, 31 May 1907, ANM 2 M 143.

35. Boa Kamara v Tene Sidibe, Tribunal de Province, Segu, 11 August 1905, ANM 2 M 143.

36. Bandiougou Keita v Fake Soumare, Tribunal de Province, Bamako, 15 November 1907, ANM 2 M 104.

37. Karounga Coulibaly v Fanouma Coulibaly, Tribunal de Province, Bamako, 9 February 1907, ANM 2 M 104.

38. Diara Fofana v Baba Diara, Tribunal de Province, Bamako, 18 May 1911, ANM 2 M 104.

39. Biratigui Keita v Fatoumata Diallo, Tribunal de Province, Bamako, 26 May 1911, ANM 2 M 104.

40. Siradie Doumbia v Togouta Sangare, Tribunal de Province, Bamako, 4 September 1911, ANM 2 M 104.

41. Biratigui Keita v Fatoumata Diallo, Tribunal de Province, Bamako, 26 May 1911, ANM 2 M 104.

42. Aicha Kouyate v Moussa Taraore, Tribunal de Province, Bamako, 25 November 1911, ANM 2 M 104; see also Baba Sidibe v Massa Kone, Tribunal de Province, Bamako, 29 November 1907, ANM 2 M 104, where the judgment orders the plaintiff to complete bridewealth transfers in two installments of Fr 75 every three months.

43. Toulmin, *Cattle, Women, and Wells,* pp. 237–250.

44. Baba of Karo escaped this stigma by adopting a child, see Mary F. Smith, *Baba of Karo: A Woman of the Muslim Hausa* (New Haven: Yale University Press, 1981).

45. On deceased wives, see Barama Diara v N'Pie Sangare and Nieie Sangare, Tribunal de Province, Bouguni, 5 September 1912; on infertile wives, see Dieie Konate v Ouane Konate, Tribunal de Province, Bouguni, 8 February 1912, ANM 2 M 10.

46. Djeli Dembele v Tiemoko Diara, Tribunal de Province, Bamako, 9 April 1907, ANM 2 M 104.

47. Makan Kasse v Ticoura Coulibaly, Tribunal de Province, Bamako, 31 January 1912, ANM 2 M 105.

48. For a general discussion, see Betty Potash, ed., *Widows in African Societies: Choices and Constraints* (Stanford: Stanford University Press, 1986), pp. 9–12.

49. Moro Couolibaly v Masseui Dembele, Tribunal de Province, Bouguni, 17 March 1910, ANM 2 M 110.

50. Zan Doumbia v Fene Kone, Tribunal de Province, Bouguni, 1 April 1910, ANM 2 M 110; Fene Kone v Zan Doumbia, Tribunal de Cercle, Bouguni, 7 May 1910, ANM 2 M 110.

51. Kano Kamite v Nano Cisse and Nale Ba, Tribunal de Province, Segu, 17 November 1910, ANM 2 M 143.

52. Karfa Kone v Meledian Taraore, 11 May 1912, Tribunal de Province, Bamako; Kanda Sidibe v Kemoko Coulibaly, 28 May 1912, Tribunal de Province, Bamako; Initio Ouattara v Manion Diara, Tribunal de Province, Bamako, 30 May 1912, ANM 2 M 105.

53. Dicoumba Keita v Golle Tammoura, Tribunal de Province, Bamako, 9 August 1907; Ma Silla (no defendant identified), Tribunal de Province, Bamako, 10 December 1909, ANM 2 M 104.

54. Kourabe Coulibaly v Fode Sidibe, Tribunal de Province, Bamako, 22 May 1908, ANM 2 M 104.

55. Fatimata Diara v Brahima Fofana, Tribunal de Province, Bamako, 28 July 1908; Sina Sako and Fatimata Sako v Bakary Ba, Tribunal de Province, Bamako, 20 November 1911, ANM 2 M 104.

56. Mama Fane v Oumarou Kamite, Tribunal de Province, Segu, 11 September 1907, ANM 2 M 143.

57. For example, Mamadou Konate v Mamadou Djebril, Tribunal de Province, Segu, 22 January 1909; Tierno Ballo v Demba Oulare, Tribunal de Province, Segu, 7 October 1909, ANM 2 M 143.

58. Digui Diallo v Tene Silla, Tribunal de Province, Bamako 8 October 1907, ANM 2 M 104.

59. Aissate Sy v Amadou Tangare, Tribunal de Province, Bamako, 8 July 1911, ANM 2 M 104.

60. Fako Kouma v Soutoura Diabite, Tribunal de Province, Bamako, 21 December 1910, ANM 2 M 104.

61. Boa Kamara v Tene Sidibe, Tribunal de Province, Segu, 11 August 1905, ANM 2 M 143.

62. Delafosse, *Haut-Sénégal-Niger*, vol. III, p. 62.

63. Rapport sur le fonctionnement des tribunaux indigènes, Bamako, 1st Quarter 1909, ANM 2 M 54.

64. Rapport sur fonctionnement de la justice indigène, Sikasso, 2nd Quarter 1911, ANM 2 M 93.

65. Etat des jugements rendus en matière civile et commerciale par le Tribunal de Province, Bamako, 3rd Quarter 1907, ANM 2 M 104.

66. Delimori Taraore v Lamine Koyate, 2 August 1907. Etat des jugements rendus en matière civile et commerciale par le Tribunal de Province, Bamako, 3rd Quarter 1907, ANM 2 M 104.

67. Rapport sur le fonctionnement de la justice indigène, Sikasso, 4th Quarter 1911, ANM 2 M 93.

68. Emily Burrill explores some of these issues in "Marriage, Divorce, and Child Custody in Bougouni and Sikasso, Haut-Sénégal-Niger, 1905–1912," unpublished paper, Department of History, Stanford University.

69. For example, Rapport sur le fonctionnement des tribunaux indigènes pendant le 2ième trimester 1906, Bamako, ANM 2 M 54. The court records also reveal divorced fathers' strategies to leave children with their mothers until they were ready either to work in the fields or be married off.

70. Rapport sur le fonctionnement de la justice indigène pendant le 4ième trimestre, Koutiala, 1908, ANM 2 M 75.

71. Kelebana Diara v. Kouma Fane, 29 September 1911, Bamako, ANM 2 M 105.

72. Kalfa Toure v. Fatima Fofana, 4 June 1912, Bamako, ANM 2 M 105.

73. Guine Kamite v. Lahi Koita, 14 October 1912, Bamako, ANM 2 M 105.

74. Rapport sur le fonctionnement de la justice indigène, 2nd quarter 1909, Jenne ANM 2 M 60.

75. Rapport sur le fonctionement des tribunaux indigènes, 1st quarter 1908, Gumbu, ANM 2 M 65.

76. Cmdt du Cercle, Rapport complémentaire sur le fonctionnement de la justice indigène, Koutiala, 31 July 1910, ANM 2 M 75.

77. Rapport judiciaire, Sokolo, 2nd Quarter 1911, ANM 2 M 94. The ruling of the tribunal de cercle on the appeal from the tribunal de province was 5 May, only one day after the original court's ruling.

78. Rapport sur la justice indigène, Bamako, 2nd Quarter 1912, ANM 2 M 54.

79. Marlene Dobkin, "Colonialism and the Legal Status of Women in Francophone Africa," *Cahiers d'Études Africaines* 8 (1968): pp. 390–405; and Ghislaine Lydon, "The

Unraveling of a Neglected Source: A Report on Women in Francophone West Africa in the 1930s," *Cahiers d' Études Africaines* 37 (3) (1997): pp. 555–584.

CHAPTER 7: CONFLICTS OVER PROPERTY

1. On the origins of the field of colonial sociology, see especially, Emmanuel Sibeud, *Une science impériale pour l'Afrique: la construction des saviors africanistes en France 1878–1930* (Paris: École des hautes études en sciences socials, 2002), chapters 4–5; see also Emmanuelle Sibeud, " 'Negrophilia', 'Negrology' or 'Africanism'? Colonial Ethnography and Racism in France around 1900," in *Promoting the Colonial Idea: Propaganda and Visions of Empire in France,* eds. Tony Chafer and Amanda Sackur (Houndsmill: Plagrave, 2002), pp. 156–167; David Robinson, "Ethnography and Customary Law in Senegal," *Cahiers d' Études Africaines* 32 (2) (1992): pp. 221–237.

2. Maurice Delafosse, *Haut-Sénégal-Niger* (Paris: originally E. Larose, 1912; reissued Maisonneuve and Larose , 1972), vol. III, p. 1.

3. Mudimbe has analyzed these procedures for what he calls the invention of Africa. V. Y. Mudimbe, *The Invention of Africa* (Bloomington: Indiana University Press, 1988).

4. See Robinson, "Ethnography and Customary Law in Senegal."

5. Louise Delafosse, *Maurice Delafosse,* pp. 77–92; see also Robert Cornevain, "Maurice Delafosse et le *Haut-Sénégal-Niger,*" in Delafosse, *Haut-Sénégal-Niger,* vol. I, pp. vi–x.

6. See Timothy Mitchell, *Colonising Egypt* (Cambridge: Cambridge University Press, 1988); Nicholas Dirks, ed., *Colonialism and Culture* (Ann Arbor: University of Michigan Press, 1992); Paul Rabinow, *French Modern: Norms and Forms of the Social Environment* (Cambridge, MA: Harvard University Press, 1989); Gwendolyn Wright, *The Politics of Design in French Colonial Urbanism* (Chicago: University of Chicago Press, 1991).

7. See Clozel, "Préface de l'Edition de 1912," in Delafosse, *Haut-Sénégal-Niger.* See also Louise Delafosse, *Maurice Delafosse,* p. 292.

8. Delafosse, *Haut-Sénégal-Niger,* III, p. 2.

9. Delafosse, *Haut-Sénégal-Niger,* vol. III, p. 2.

10. Delafosse, *Haut-Sénégal-Niger,* vol. III, p. 3.

11. Delafosse, *Haut-Sénégal-Niger,* vol. III, p. 6.

12. Delafosse, *Haut-Sénégal-Niger,* vol. III, p. 7.

13. From the 1890s through the early decades of the twentieth century, there was a flurry of scholarly research on French rural history and land tenure issues. Delafosse was almost certain to have been familiar with this research, which may account for the "cognitive" filter through which he saw Soudanese civilizations. See Marc Bloch, *French Rural History: An Essay on its Basic Characteristics,* translated by Janet Sondheimer (Berkeley: University of California Press, 1966).

14. Bloch, *French Rural History,* p. 128; Marc Bloch, *La société féodale* (Paris: A Michel, 1968), pp. 169–170, 173–174. For more detail see, Anne-Marie Patault, *Introduction historique au droit des biens* (Paris: Presses Universitaires de France, 1989), pp. 6–9, 18–21, 96–100.

15. Delafosse, *Haut-Sénégal-Niger,* vol. III, p. 15. Delafosse is part of a larger group of pro-peasant colonial officials who sought to prevent colonial economic development in the Soudan along the lines of French Equatorial Africa's concession regime. For more discussion, see Richard Roberts, *Two Worlds of Cotton: Colonialism and the Regional Economy in the French Soudan, 1800–1946* (Stanford: Stanford University Press, 1996), pp. 33–36.

16. Delafosse, *Haut-Sénégal-Niger,* vol. III, p. 7.

17. Delafosse, *Haut-Sénégal-Niger,* vol. III, p. 8.

18. See, for example, Richard Roberts, "Women's Wealth and Women's Property: Maraka Household Textile Industry in the Nineteenth Century," *Comparative Studies in Society and History* 26 (2) (1984).

19. Roberts, "Women's Wealth;" William Allen, *The African Husbandman* (New York: Barnes and Noble, 1965); Claude Meillassoux, "État et condition des esclaves à Goumbou (Mali) au XIXe siècle," in *L'esclavage en Afrique précoloniale,* ed. Claude Meillassoux (Paris: Mapsero), 1975.

20. Martin Chanock, "A Peculiar Sharpness: An Essay on Property in the History of Customary Law in Colonial Africa," *Journal of African History* 32 (1) (1991): p. 87.

21. For a comparative discussion of gender and generational tensions, see Thomas McClendon, *Genders and Generations Apart: Labor Tenants and Customary Law in Segregation-era South Africa, 1920s to 1940s* (Portsmouth, NH: Heinemann, 2002).

22. Jean-Loup Amselle, *Logiques métisses: anthropologie de l'identité en Afrique et ailleurs* (Paris: Payot, 1990), pp. 22–37, 71–88.

23. Roberts, *Two Worlds of Cotton,* pp. 93–96.

24. Félix Dubois, Notre beau Niger, (Paris: Flammarion, 1911), pp. 135–136.

25. Enquête sur les productions animales, 1905, Bamako, ANM 1 Q 257.

26. Interviews with Tijani Sylla, 3 August 1981, Baraweli; Batene Kale, 31 July 1981, Segu.

27. Chanock, "A Peculiar Sharpness;" Claude Meillassoux, *Maidens, Meal and Money: Capitalism and the Domestic Community* (Cambridge: Cambridge University Press, 1981).

28. The term cattle has the same etymological roots as chattel, used to denote property ownership and marketable stores of wealth.

29. The 1906 court registers were sent to Dakar to be examined by the *procureur général.* Only traces of these records can be found in the Senegalese National Archives, ANS-AOF M 121.

30. Brahima Daode v Nana Darako, 14 November 1905, Tribunal de Province, Bamako, ANM 2 M 104.

31. In the period after 1925, when plows became more common, livestock also provided animal traction to increase agricultural productivity. With the use of animal traction, the distinctions and values between breeding stock and work oxen grew. See Camilla Toulmin, *Cattle, Women, and Wells: Managing Household Survival in the Sahel* (Oxford: Clarendon Press, 1992), pp. 159–190.

32. Hinna Camara v Tioubougui Camara, 12 August 1908, Tribunal de Province, Segu. The defendant appealed this ruling, which was heard on 21 and 22 August 1908, Tribunal de Cercle, Segu, ANM 2 M 143.

33. Jacques Méniaud, *Haut-Sénégal-Niger: géographie économique* (Paris: E. Larose, 1912), p. 50.

34. Stock ownership was widely distributed among households in Kala, where Toulmin conducted her research. 55 percent of the households had 10 or fewer cattle. Toulmin also found that size of livestock herds was directly correlated to size of the household and to its overall wealth, *Cattle, Women, and Wells,* chapter 10.

35. Djeneba Togora v Babile Fane, 2 November 1907, Tribunal de Province, Segu, ANM 2 M 143.

36. Baba Kante v Touentou Dembele, 23 January 1908, Tribunal de Province, Segu, ANM 2 M 143.

37. Bakary Kouyate v Souleymane Diabite, 16 September 1912, Tribunal de Province, Bamako, ANM 2 M 105.

38. Yayare Sumare v Bokary So, 20 December 1905, Tribunal de Province, Segu, ANM 2 M 143.

39. Neti Soumare v Soini Kane, 4 October 1911, Tribunal de Province, Bamako, ANM 2 M 104.

40. Neti Soumare v Soini Kane, 14 November 1911, Tribunal de Province, Bamako, ANM 2 M 104.

41. Zele Coulibaly v Djounie Kouma, 23 July 1909; Bani Diara v Moussa Diara, 22 July 1911; Noumouke Doumbia v Buka Keita, 18 September 1911, Tribunal de Province, Bamako, ANM 2 M 104.

42. Samba Barro v Boke Sow, 7 December 1909, Tribunal de Province, Bamako, ANM 2 M 104.

43. Amadou Sako v Sani Ouele, 29 October 1910, Tribunal de Province, Bamako, ANM 2 M 104.

44. Demba Diallo v Isa Ndiaye, 12 July 1910, Tribunal de Province, Bamako, ANM 2 M 104.

45. Naturu v Seribu Gadiagu, 11 October 1911, Tribunal de Province, Bamako, ANM 2 M 104.

46. Moriba Fofana v Naioume Koita, 17 August 1909, Tribunal de Province, Bamako, ANM 2 M 104.

47. See Richard Roberts, "Long Distance Trade and Production: Sinsani in the Nineteenth Century," *JAH* 21 (2) (1980); for the classic social geography of the interior delta, see Jean Gallais, *Le Delta intérieur du Niger, étude de géographie régionale* (Dakar: IFAN, 1967). More recently see, also Mirjam de Bruijn & Han van Dijk, *Arid Ways: Cultural Understandings of Insecurity in Fulbe Society, Central Mali* (Amsterdam: Thela, 1995).

48. Babile Coulibaly v Aliou Diabe, 23 April 1907, Tribunal de Province, Segu, ANM 2 M 143.

49. Kori Keita v Badia Balo, 8 June 1907, Tribunal de Province, Segu, ANM 2 M 143.

50. Koribable Diawara v Mamadou Diko, 7 August 1907 and Boakary Dembele v Lamine Dembele, 3 September 1907, Tribunal de Province, Segu, ANM 2 M 143.

51. Kassa Sangare v Boubou Barro, 20 April 1912, Trbinunal de proinvce, Bamako, AMN 2 M 105.

52. Birama Diara v Mamadi Diabite and Tonemaka Konate, 29 November 1912, Tribunal de Province, Bamako, ANM 2 M 105.

53. Dumbia Kone v Sidi Sow and Baka Barro, 8 January 1912, Tribunal de Province, Bamako, ANM 2 M 105.

54. Diara, Almady Kouyate, Amadou Seck, and Aldiouma Oulare v N'To Dembele, 13 September 1907, Tribunal de Province, Segu, ANM 2 M 143.

55. Gaston Toukoula v Kogue Kasse, 7 February 1908, Tribunal de Province, Bamako, ANM 2 M 104.

56. Koumba Silla v Mamadou Ba, 7 April 1908, Tribunal de Province, Bamako, ANM 2 M 104.

57. Boakary Diawara v Lamine Fane, 3 September 1907, and Bafile Coulibaly v Aliou Sako, 23 April 1907, Tribunal de Province, Segu, ANM 2 M 143.

58. Oumaru Sangare v Bouba Diallo, 1 July 1908, Tribunal de Province, Segu, ANM 2 M 143.

59. Doussa Koro Taraore v Diatouru Samake, 11 January 1911, Tribunal de Province, Bamako, ANM 2 M 104.

60. Moussa Sidibe v Faguinba Koita, 12 November 1912, Tribunal de Province, Bamako, ANM 2 M 105.

61. Notices historiques et géographiques du cercle de Bamako, 1903, ANM 1 D 33, no. 1; Lieutenant Jaime, *De Koulikoro à Tombouctou sur la connonière "le Mage"* (Paris: Les Libraries Associés, 1894), p. 123.

62. See the sections on contacts in Emile Roux, *Manuel a l'usage des administrateurs et du personnel des affaires indigènes de la colonie du Sénégal et des colonies relevant du gouvernement général de l'AOF* (Paris: A Challamel, 1911), pp. 121–22.

63. Satigui Keita v Coumba Keita, 11 June 1911, Tribunal de Province, Bamako, ANM 2 M 104.

64. Babou Demba v Ahmadou So, 1 July 1907, Tribunal de Province, Segu, ANM 2 M 143.

65. Sori Aidara v Gonaufo Keita, 29 January 1912, Tribunal de Province, Bamako; Adama Tangara v Boua Kuma, 20 April 1912, Tribunal de Province, Bamako, ANM 2 M 105.

66. Diogondime Diara v Mory Konate, 5 June 1908, Tribunal de Province, Bamako, ANM 2 M 104.

67. Mahmadou Barro v Bouboukar Tal, 19 April 1907, Tribunal de Province, Segu, ANM 2 M 143.

68. Mody Sangare v Mamadou Kone, 26 May 1908, Tribunal de Province, Bamako, ANM 2 M 104.

69. Koura Seck v Souleyman Diallo, 17 March 1908, Tribunal de Province, Bamako, ANM 2 M 104. The court records indicate that payment was 42 F, but this seems rather high for month service.

70. Kefa Coulibaly v Tiekoura Ouattara, 14 May 1907, Tribunal de Province, Segu, ANM 2 M 143.

71. Diade ould Moctar v Koitee Dembele, 11 December 1908, Tribunal de Province, Segu, ANM 2 M 143.

72. Sidi Balo v Karamoko Koita, 11 June 1908, Tribunal de Province, Segu, ANM 2 M 143.

73. See for example, John Iliffe, *The African Poor: A History* (Cambridge: Cambridge University Press, 1987), chapter 9.

74. Bougani Konate v Brama Konate, 26 June 1908, Tribunal de Province, Bamako, ANM 2 M 104.

75. Willem Bosman, *A New and Accurate Description of the Coast of Guinea, Divided in the Gold, Slave, and Ivory Coasts* (New York: Barnes and Noble, reprinted 1967), p. 202.

76. Roberts, "Women's Wealth and Women's Property."

77. Interview with Sane Tambura, 18 February 1977, Segu.

78. Interview with Cemoko Ture, 5 March 1977, Segu.

79. Jane I. Guyer, "Food, Cocoa, and the Division of Labour by Sex in Two West African Societies," *Comparative Studies in Society and History* 22 (3) (1980); Susan M. Martin, *Palm Oil and Protest: An Economic History of the Ngwa Region, South-eastern Nigeria, 1800–1980* (Cambridge: Cambridge University Press, 1988).

80. John M. Beattie, *Crime and Courts in England, 1660–1800* (Princeton: Princeton University Press, 1986).

81. Aminata Keita v Amady Tamagate, 16 April 1907, Trbunal de Province, Bamako, ANM 2 M 104.

82. Mohamed Diara v Sokono Sissoko, 7 October 1911, Tribunal de Province, Bamako, ANM 2 M 104.

83. Widows might not want to be released from their husbands' households, because such departure would mean leaving children and other corporate ties that they may have developed. See Betty Potash, ed. *Widows in African Societies: Choices and Constraints* (Stanford: Stanford University Press, 1986), pp. 4–10.

84. Kanna Sidibe v Moussa Sidibe, 7 January 1908, Tribunal de Province, Bamako, ANM 2 M 104. We are not told why, but Kanna Sidibe's case was dismissed, probably because she did not have witnesses willing to testify to the loan she claimed to have made to her deceased husband.

85. Aoua Diabite v family of Magate Kone, 11 November 1911, Tribunal de Province, Bamako, ANM 2 M 104. Some of the cases examined in the final section of this chapter deal with the growth of urban rental property in Bamako. With the growth of urban populations, property there was becoming an attractive investment. See Laurent Fouchard, "Propriétaires et commerçants africains à Ouagadougou et à Bobo-Dioulasso (Haute-Volta) fin 19ième siècle-1960," *Journal of African History* 44 (3) (2003).

86. Mariam Cisse v N'Ky Togora, 16 August 1912, Tribunal de Province, Bamako, ANM 2 M 105.

87. Vivian Paques, Les Bambara (Paris: Presses Universitaires de France, 1954), p. 75. This property that brides bring into marriage helps explain some of the confusion in the French archival sources between dowry and bridewealth.

88. Nini Coulibaly v. Ba Ture, 27 March 1907, Tribunal de Province, Segu, ANM 2 M 143. I am not sure how to interpret the appeals, heard on 21 April 1907, in which Ba Ture accused Nini Coulibaly of acquiring her goods by selling his crops. The district administrator overturned the judgment of the provincial court, although the record is not clear how the *tribunal de cercle* ruled.

89. Fatimata Ouele v Mamady Soumare, 28 January 1908, Tribunal de Province, Bamako, ANM 2 M 104.

90. Djeli Kani Diakite v Diani Dembele, 11 December 1908, Tribunal de Province, Bamako, ANM 2 M 104.

91. Nanko Fofana v Mamady Demba, 7 September 1909, Tribunal de Province, Bamako, ANM 2 M 104.

92. Aoua Sako v Diatrou Taraore, 6 May 1911, Tribunal de Province, ANM 2 M 104.

93. Tabara Keita v Dene Balo, 14 June 1907, Tribunal de Province, Segu. The appeal was heard on 17 June at the Tribunal de cercle, ANM 2 M 143.

94. Koko Tamoura v Bala Sidibe, 11 August 1908, Tribunal de Province, Bamako, ANM 2 M 104.

95. Boli Sy v Moussa Dembele, 15 May 1911, Tribunal de Province, Bamako, ANM 2 M 104.

96. Sebe Sankare v Bakary Kouma, 25 January 1911, Tribunal de Province, Bamako, ANM 2 M 104.

97. See Karen Cook, ed., *Trust in Society* (New York: Russell Sage Foundation, 2001).

98. Besides gold and livestock, another store of value for women in particular was amber.

99. Naba Ture v Naibu Ndiaye, 4 November 1907, Tribunal de Province, Segu, ANM 2 M 143.

100. Toyin Falola and Paul Lovejoy, eds., *Pawnship, Slavery and Colonialism in Africa* (Trenton, NJ: African World Press, 2003). See Richard Roberts and Martin Klein, "Resurgence of Pawning in French West Africa during the Depression of the 1930s," in *Pawnship,* eds. Falola and Lovejoy.

101. Oumurou Kamara v Ahmadi Oulare, 5 August 1909, Tribunal de Province, Segu, ANM 2 M 143.

102. Oumarou So v Tenemba Diallo, 12 April 1911, Tribunal de Province, Bamako, ANM 2 M 104. Note that the builder of the canoe sued for payments six months after having delivered the canoe to the owner. For more detail on the commerce in grains and the role of riverine transportation, see Roberts, "Bamako Grain Market"; Richard Roberts, "Fishing for the State: The Political Economy of the Middle Niger Valley," in *Modes of Production in Africa: The Precolonial Era,* eds. Donald Crummey and C. C. Stewart (Beverly Hills: Sage, 1981).

103. Delafosse, *Haut-Sénégal-Niger,* vol. III, p. 97.

104. "Les Bambaras de Segoubougou reclament aux Somonos les lougans . . . " État des jugements rendus en matière civile et commerciale, Month of May 1905, Segu, ANM 2 M 143.

105. Mama Sako of Segoubougou v Sougoba Diara of Segoubougou, 18 May 1905, État des jugements rendus en matière civile et commerciale, Tribunal de Cercle de Segou, 2nd Quarter 1905, Segu, ANM 2 M 143.

106. See Rapport sur le fonctionnement des tribunaux indigènes pendant le deuxième trimestre, 1905, Segu, ANM 2 M 92. If this was, indeed, the case, it would suggest that the early courts could be manipulated instrumentally by the state to reward or punish regardless of the legal issues involved.

107. See interviews with Yusufa Traore, 13 December 1976, Segoubougou; Tene Ture, 1 August 1981, Segoubougou; and Ahmadou Toure, 1 August 1981, Segoubougou.

108. Noumoudion Bale v Dianguiere Yeranangou, 19 November 1909, Tribunal de Province, Segu, ANM 2 M 143.

109. Inchi Konate v Inchi Diallo, 1 June 1908, Tribunal de Province, Segu, ANM 2 M 143.

110. Kori Samake v Ibrahima Diawara, 11 June 1907, Tribunal de Province, Segu, ANM 2 M 143.

111. Bodian Kone v Lamine Fofana, 21 June 1907, Tribunal de Province, Segu, ANM 2 M 143.

112. Mohamed Doade v Boakary Togora, 18 August 1907, Tribunal de Province, Segu, ANM 2 M 143.

113. Amadu Konate v Mahmadouble Konate, 21 June 1907, Tribunal de Province, Segu, ANM 2 M 143.

114. Sibiri Diara v Teneman Sankare, 11 July 1908, Tribunal de Province, Segu, ANM 2 M 143.

115. This section examines urban rental agreements. The records contain some reference also to sharecropping contracts. See, for example, Rapport sur la justice indigène, 4th quarter 1908, Sokolo, ANM 2 M 94.

116. N'Ni Ba v Moussa Ture, 23 June 1908, Tribunal de Province, Bamako, ANM 2 M 104.

117. Issa Silla v Dado Dembele, 2 October 1908, Tribunal de Province, Bamako, ANM 2 M 104

118. Mori Coulibaly v Negueda Coulibaly, 17 August 1909, Tribunal de Province, Bamako, ANM 2 M 104.

119. Mamadou Diko v Mamadou Soumare, 10 May 1910, Tribunal de Province, Bamako, ANM 2 M 104.

120. See Fouchard, "Propriétaires et commerçants africains"; Marie-Louise Villien-Rossi, "Bamako, capitale du Mali," *Bull IFAN, series B* (1966): 249–380.

121. Roberts, "Fishing for the State."

122. Sink Koita and Fa Koita v Konabele Fofana, 14 December 1905, Tribunal de Province, Segu, ANM 2 M 143.

CHAPTER 8: DISPUTING INHERITANCE

1. Charles Monteil, *Les Bambara du Ségou et du Kaarta: étude historique, ethno-graphique et littéraire d'une peuplade du Soudan français* (Paris: Maisonneuve, 1924, reprinted Paris: Maisonneuve, 1976), pp. 129–130.

2. It should not be surprising that Monteil was trained as a lawyer, having received his *licence de droit* in 1906. Emmanuelle Sibeud, *Une science impériale pour l'Afrique: la construction des saviors africanistes en France 1878–1930* (Paris: Ecole des hautes études en sciences sociales, 2002), p. 308.

3. Monteil, *Les Bambara*, p. 183.

4. Rapport sure la justice indigène, Kita, 2nd Quarter 1910 ANM 2 M 73.

5. Sara Berry, *No Condition is Permanent: The Social Dynamics of Agrarian Change in Sub-Saharan Africa* (Madison: University of Wisconsin Press, 1993), p. 29.

6. David William Cohen, "Pim's Doorway," in *Reliving the Past: The Worlds of Social History,* ed. Olivier Zunz (Chapel Hill: University of North Carolina Press, 1985), p. 195.

7. On inheritance and inequality see Josiah Wedgwood, *The Economics of Inheritance* (London: George Routledge, 1929), chapter 3.

8. Boa Kone, Amara Kone of Togo village and Benoko Kone of Togo, all of custom-ary status, 20 October 1905, État de jugements rendus en matière civile et commerciale par le Tribunal de Province de Segou, 4th Quarter 1905, Segu, ANM 2 M 143.

9. Benoko Kone's actions in seeking an appeal to the *tribunal de cercle,* the next high-est court for civil disputes, were highly irregular. Of all the cases brought to the tribunal de province in 1905, only two were appealed. At the *tribunal de cercle,* Benoko reiterated his case, that his two nephews, Boa and Amara Kone, had hidden goods from their father's estate, of which he was the guardian. Benoko again failed to furnish proof of his claim. The court upheld the tribunal de province's judgment against Benoko Kone. It also imposed a fine on him for what it considered a "frivolous" suit.

10. See the classic ethnography by Jack Goody, *Death, Property, and the Ancestors: A Study of Mortuary Customs of the Lodagaa of West Africa* (Stanford: Stanford University Press, 1962), pp. 273–283, 304–327.

11. I have examined Delafosse and his notions of the "double conception of property" more fully in Chapter 7.

12. Maurice Delafosse, *Haut-Sénégal-Niger* (Paris: Larose, 1912; reprinted Paris: Mai-son neuve, 1972), vol. III, p. 26.

13. See especially, Jack Goody, "The Evolution of the Family," in *Household and Fam-ily in Past Time,* ed., Peter Laslett and Richard Wall (Cambridge: Cambridge University, 1972); Jack Goody, *Production and Reproduction: A Comparative Study of the Domestic Domain* (Cambridge: Cambridge University, 1976).

14. Camilla Toulmin, *Cattle, Women, and Wells: Managing Household Survival in the Sahel* (Oxford: Clarendon Press, 1992), pp. 30–31, 264–267. See also John Van Dusen Lewis, "Two Poles of Production in a Malian Peasant Village" (Unpublished Ph.D. disser-

tation, Yale University 1979); John Van Dusen Lewis, "Domestic Labor Intensity and the Incorporation of Malian Peasant Farmers into Localized Descent Groups," *American Ethnologist* 8 (2) (1981): 53–73; and Maria Luise Grosz-Ngate, "Bambara Men and Women and the Reproduction of Social Life in Sana Provice, Mali" (Unpublished Ph.D. dissertation, Michigan State University, 1986).

15. Toulmin, *Cattle, Women, and Wells,* pp. 268–270.

16. For a parallel case, see Babanake Dembele v Meine Dembele, 13 February 1911, Tribunal de Province, Segu, ANM 2 M 143, where one brother sued his uncles on behalf of his other brothers.

17. Eric Pollet and Grace Winter, *La Société Soninke (Dyahunu, Mali)* (Brussels: Editions de l'Institut de sociologie, Universite libre de Bruxelles, 1972), pp. 371, 374.

18. Ba Moa Taraore v Bagoba Taraore, 1 October 1905, Tribunal de province, Segu, ANM 2 M 143.

19. Alfred Aubert, "Coutume Bambara, Cercle de Bougouni," in *Coutumiers juridiques de l'Afrique occidentale française,* ed. Bernard Maupoil (Paris: Publications du Comité d'études historiques et scientifiques de l'Afrique occidentale française, 1939), vol. II, p. 109. Jean Ortoli, "Coutume Bambara, Cercle de Bamako," in *Coutumiers juridiques de l'Afrique occidentale française,* ed. Bernard Maupoil (Paris: Publications du Comité d'études historiques et scientifiques de l'Afrique occidentale française, 1939) in the same volume has little to say about inheritance disputes beyond the enumeration of heirs.

20. Natie Konare v Fadouga Dembele, 15 January 1907, Tribunal de Province, Segu, ANM 2 M 143.

21. Issa Sako v Celouki Sako, 12 August 1908, Tribunal de Province, Segu, ANM 2 M 143.

22. Dienebou Ballo v Hama Kadia Ballo, 18 June 1908, États de jugements, Tribunal de province, Segu, ANM 2 M 143.

23. Baiamory Coulibaly v Alkaro Coulibaly, 5 April 1909, États de jugements, Tribunal de province, Segu, ANM 2 M 143.

24. The debates surrounding Chayanov's theory of the development cycle of domestic groups are voluminous, but the argument about the changes in household size and labor capacity over time remains important. A. V. Chayanov, *The Theory of Peasant Economy,* eds. Daniel Thorner, Basile Kerblay, and R. E. F. Smith (Homeland, IL: R. D. Irwin, 1966); see also Jack Goody's application of Chayanov, *The Developmental Cycle in Domestic Groups* (Cambridge: Cambridge University Press, 1958).

25. Igor Kopytoff and Suzanne Miers, "African 'Slavery' as an Institution of Marginality," in *Slavery in Africa,* ed. Suzanne Miers and Igor Kopytoff (Madison: University of Wisconsin Press, 1977); and Kopytoff, "The Cultural Context of African Abolition," in *The End of Slavery in Africa,* eds. Miers and Roberts, pp. 485–503.

26. Na Koita v Amary Keita, 9 February 1909, États de jugements, Tribunal de province, Segu, ANM 2 M 143.

27. Fatimata Cisse v Zane Kante, 26 December 1907, États de jugements, Tribunal de province, Segu, ANM 2 M 143. Terms such as "domestic" and "servant" were used as proxies for slaves, since the courts did not recognize the legal category of status.

28. Inheritance of Sidiki Sumare, 10 July 1908, Tribunal de province, Segu, ANM 2 M 143.

29. Richard Roberts, "Ideology, Slavery, and Social Formation: The Evolution of Slavery in the Middle Niger Valley," in *The Ideology of Slavery in Africa,* ed. Paul Lovejoy (Beverly Hills: Sage, 1981).

30. Koke Diara v Guimbola Kamite, 4 February 1910, Tribunal de province, Segu, ANM 2 M 143.

31. Inheritance of Birama Konare, 10 July 1908, Tribunal de province, Segu, ANM 2 M 143.

32. Inheritance of Sabou Diallo, 17 November 1905, Tribunal de Province, Segu, ANM 2 M 143.

33. Inheritance of Tene Keita, 10 July 1908, Tribunal de Province, Segu, ANM 2 M 143.

34. Fa Sankare v Ba Kamite, 3 May 1905, Tribunal de Province, Segu, 2nd Quarter 1905, ANM 2 M 143.

35. Ali Taraore v Fatimata Kone, 24 June 1905, Tribunal de Province, Segu, 2nd Quarter 1905, ANM 2 M 143.

36. Ba Diawara v Nia Fane, 27 March 1907, Tribunal de Province, Segu, ANM 2 M 143.

37. Delafosse, *Haut-Sénégal-Niger,* vol. III, pp. 22–23.

38. Emile Leynaud and Youssouf Cisse, *Paysans Malinke du Haut Niger (Tradition et développement rural en Afrique Soudanaise)* (Bamako: Imprimerie Populaire du Mali, 1978), p. 244, also footnote 36. Leynaud and Cisse call this "same sex transmission" of property. See also Vivian Paques, *The Bambara,* translated by Thomas Turner (New Haven: Human Relations Area Files, 1959 [translation of 1954 original]), pp. 96–99. Toulmin, however, notes that in the Kala region, a woman's property devolves to her sons, *Cattle, Women, and Wells,* p. 32.

39. Bafing Kaminke v Ceko Diara, 19 July 1907, Tribunal de Province, Segu, ANM 2 M 143.

40. See Roberts, "Women's Wealth and Women's Property," *Comparative Studies in Society and History* 26 (2) (1984).

41. Modyba Haidara v Aminata Ballo, 20 July 1908, Tribunal de Province, Segu, ANM 2 M 143. A very similar case was Bokary So v Abdoul So, 4 February 1908, Tribunal de Province, Segu, ANM 2 M 143, wherein the wife brought to the household two cows, which had produced a herd of some 30 cattle when the wife died. The case concerns the disputes over who shall inherit the herd.

42. Lewis makes this argument regarding the strategies of accumulation by Muslim Bambara. He also notes that these more nucleated households have distinctive subsistence risks, Lewis, "Two Poles of Production" and "Domestic Labor Intensity."

43. John L. Esposito, *Women in Muslim Family Law* (Syracuse: Syracuse University Press, 1982), pp. 39–44.

44. Inheritance of Dienma Coulibaly, 2 October 1905, États des jugements, Tribunal de province, Segu, ANM 2 M 143.

45. Mohamed Diara and Maire Kouma v Sori Bari, 6 February 1908, États des jugements, Tribunal de province, Segu, ANM 2 M 143. See *Code Musulman, rite Malékite—statut reél, par Khalil ibn Ishak al Jundj,* translated by N. Seignette (Constantine, Impr. L. Arnolet; Alger, Jourdan; Paris, Challamel aîné, 1878).

46. Oumarou Diabite v Ahmadou Barro, 9 May 1908 and Modi Diallo v Sambate Diallo, 19 May 1908, États des jugements, Tribunal de province, Segu, ANM 2 M 143.

47. Rapport sur le fonctionnement des tribunaux indigènes, Segu, 30 April 1905, ANM 2 M 92.

48. Rapport sur le fonctionnement des tribunaux indigènes, Segu, 2nd Quarter 1905, ANM 2 M 92.

49. Petition to the Lt-gov, Kouluba, 12 May 1913, ANM 2 M 236, quoted in Rebecca Shereikis, "From Law to Custom: The Shifting Legal Status of Muslim *Originaires* in Kayes and Medine, 1903–1913," *JAH* 42 (2) (2001): pp. 278–279. See also Rebecca Shereikis, "Customized Courts: French Colonial Legal Institutions in Kayes, French Soudan, ca. 1880–c. 1913" (Ph.D. dissertation, Northwestern University, 2003).

50. Rapport sur le fonctionnement des tribunaux indigènes, Segu, 2nd Quarter 1905, ANM 2 M 92.

51. Fredrik Barth, ed. *Social Groups and Boundaries: The Social Organization of Culture Difference* (Boston: Little Brown and Company, 1969); David C. Conrad and Barbara Frank, eds., *Status and Identity in West Africa: Nyamakalaw of Mande* (Bloomington: Indiana University Press, 1995); Richard Roberts, "The End of Slavery in the French Soudan, 1905–1914" in *The End of Slavery in Africa,* eds. Suzanne Miers and Richard Roberts (Madison: University of Wisconsin Press, 1988).

52. Charles Correnson, De l'organisation de la justice et des moeurs chez les populations de la région de Segu, Segu, 5 September 1907, ANM 1 D 55–3.

53. David Robinson, "Ethnography and Customary Law in Senegal," *Cahiers d'Etudes Africaines* 32 (2) (1992): pp. 234–235. See also N. Seignette, *Code musulmane—statut réel;* para Khalil ibn Ishak al Jundj; tranlated by N. Seignette. Constantine, Impr. Arnolet; Alger, Joundan; Paris, Challamel aîmé, 1878.

54. J.N.D. Anderson, "The Adaptation of Muslim Law in Sub-Saharan Africa," in *African Law: Adaptation and Development,* ed. Hilda Kuper and Leo Kuper (Berkeley: University of California Press, 1965), p. 153.

55. Perignon, "Généralités sur le Haut Sénégal et du Moyen Niger," Segu, 1900, ANS-AOF 1 G 248.

56. Delafosse, *Haut-Sénégal-Niger,* vol. III, pp. 31–32.

57. Between Douba Dialo v Ba Manie Diawara, Tribunal de Province, Segu, 4th Quarter 1905, Segu, ANM 2 M 143.

58. Succession de Sibery Diallo, 10 August 1905, Tribunal de Province, Segu, ANM 2 M 143.

CHAPTER 9: CONCLUSION: THE IMPORTANCE OF "DISPUTES WITHOUT SIGNIFICANCE"

1. For a critique, see Michael Watts, *Silent Violence: Food, Famine, and Peasantry in Northern Nigeria* (Berkeley: The Univeristy of California Press, 1983), pp. 84–89.

2. Being public did not prevent local pressures from being exerted on the court's proceedings. I recently ran across a fascinating 1937 case in which several Africans were accused of seeking to bribe the president of the *tribunal de 1ère degré* of the districts of Baol and Thies to rule in favor of a disputed land claim. Tentative de corruption du Président du Tribunal civil du cercle de Baol à Dourbel, 1937, ANS Affaires contentieux 24. My thanks to Saliou Mbaye for directing me to these newly released sources.

3. I find Jeffrey Herbst's concept of broadcasting power useful in thinking about the spatial dimension of the power of the colonial state. See Jeffrey Herbst, *States and Power in Africa: Comparative Lessons in Authority and Control* (Princeton: Princeton University Press, 2000).

4. Camilla Toulmin, *Cattle, Women, and Wells: Managing Household Survival in the Sahel* (Oxford: Clarendon Press, 1992); Barbara Cooper, *Marriage in Maradi: Gender and*

Culture in a Hausa Society in Niger, 1900–1989 (Portsmouth, NH: Heinemann, 1997); Sean Hawkins, " 'The Woman Question': Marriage and Identity in Colonial Courts of Northern Ghana, 1907–1954," in *Women in African Colonial Histories,* eds. Jean Allman, Susan Geiger, and Nakanyike Musisi (Bloomington, Indiana University Press, 2002), pp. 116–142.

5. Jean Allman and Victoria Tashjian, *"I Will Not Eat Stone": A Women's History of Colonial Asante* (Portsmouth, NH: Heinemann, 2000), pp. xxxvi–xxxvii.

6. Martin Chanock, *The Making of the South African Legal Culture, 1902–1936: Fear, Favour, and Prejudice* (Cambridge: Cambridge University Press, 2001).

7. One of my favorite studies on the unanticipated consequences of social engineering in colonial situations is Gergory Massell, *The Surrogate Proletariat: Moslem Women and Revolutionary Strategies in Soviet Central Asia, 1919–1929* (Princeton: Princeton University Press, 1974).

8. Marlene Dobkin, "Colonialism and the Legal Status of Women in Francophone Africa," *Cahiers d'Etudes Africaines* 8 (1968): 390–405; on Vichy's colonial ideology, see Eric Jennings, *Vichy in the Tropics: Pétain's National Revolution in Madagascar, Guadeloupe, and Indochina, 1940–1944* (Stanford: Stanford University Press, 2002).

9. The most important study of the institutional changes in the native courts is the contemporary report by E. Beurdeley, *La justice indigène en Afrique occidentale française: mission d'études, 1913–1914* (Paris: Publication de comité de l'Afrique Française, 1916). See also Gouvernment general de l'Afrique occidentale française, *Justice indigène: instructions aux administrateurs sur l'application du Décret du 16 Août 1912, portant reorganization de la Justice indigène en Afrique Occidentale Française* (Dakar: Imprimerie Terneux, 1913).

10. William Felstiner, Richard Abel, and Austin Sarat, "The Emergence and Transformation of Disputes: Naming, Blaming, Claiming. . . ." *Law and Society Review* 15 (1980–1981); Susan F. Hirsch, *Pronouncing and Persevering: Gender and Discourses of Disputing in an African Islamic Court* (Chicago: University of Chicago Press, 1998).

BIBLIOGRAPHY

SELECTED READINGS

Abel, Richard. "Introduction." In *The Politics of Informal Justice: Volume 2, Comparative Studies,* ed. Richard Abel. New York: Academic Press, 1982.

———. "Western Courts in Non-Western Settings: Patterns of Court Use in Colonial and Neo-Colonial Africa." In *The Imposition of Law,* ed. Sandra Burman and Barbara E. Harrell-Bond. New York: Academic Press, 1979.

Adewoye, O. *The Judicial System in Southern Nigeria, 1854–1954: Law and Justice in a Dependency.* Atlantic Highlands: Humanities Press, 1977.

Ageron, Charles-Robert. *Modern Algeria: A History from 1830 to the Present,* translated by Michael Brett. Trenton, NJ: Africa World Press, 1991.

Allen, William. *The African Husbandman.* New York: Barnes and Noble, 1965.

Allman, Jean and Victoria Tashjian. *"I Will Not Eat Stone": A Women's History of Colonial Asante.* Portsmouth, NH: Heinemann, 2000.

Amselle, Jean-Loup. *Logiques métisses: anthropologie de l'identité en Afrique et ailleurs.* Paris: Payot, 1990.

———. *Vers une mutliculturalisme française: L'empire de la coutume.* Paris: Aubier, 1996.

Amutabi, Maurice Nyamanga. "Power and Influence of African Court Clerks and Translators in Colonial Kenya: The Case of Khwisero Native (African) Court, 1946–1956." In *Intermediaries, Interpreters, and Clerks: Africans in the Making of Modern Africa,* eds. Benjamin Lawrance, Emily Osborn, and Richard Roberts. Madison: University of Wisconsin Press, forthcoming.

Anderson, J. N. D. "The Adaptation of Muslim Law in Sub-Saharan Africa." In *African Law: Adaptation and Development*, ed. Hilda Kuper and Leo Kuper. Berkeley: University of California Press, 1965.

———. *Islamic Law in the Modern World.* New York: New York University Press, 1959.

Annuaire du gouvernement général de l'Afrique Occidentale françcaise. Paris: Larose, 1904.

Aouli, Smaïl, Randame Redjala, and Philippe Zoummeroff. *Abd el-Kader.* Paris: Fayard, 1994.

Asiwaju, Tony. "Control through Coercion: A Study of the Indigenat Regime in French West African Administration, 1887–1946." *Bull IFAN, Series B* 41 (1) (1979).

Aubert, Alfred. "Coutume Bambara, cercle de Bougouni." In *Coutumiers juridiques de l'Afrique occidentale française,* ed. Bernard Maupoil. Paris: Publications du Comité d'études historiques et scientifiques de l'Afrique occidentale française, 1939.

Bâ, Ahmadou Hampaté. *The Fortunes of Wangrin,* translated by Aina Pavolini Taylor. Bloomington: Indiana University Press, 1999.

Bailleul, Père Charles. *Pétit dictionnaire Bambara-Français, Français-Bambara.* Amersham, England: Avebury Pub., 1981.

Barrows, Leland C. "Louis Léon César Faidherbe (1818–1889)." In *African Proconsuls: European Governors in Africa,* ed. L. H. Gann and Peter Duignan. New York: Free Press, 1978.

Barry, Bouboucar. *Senegambia and the Atlantic Slave Trade.* Cambridge: Cambridge Univeristy Press, 1998.

Barth, Fredrik, ed. *Ethnic Groups and Boundaries: The Social Organization of Culture Difference.* Boston: Little Brown and Company, 1969.

Bazin, Jean. "À Chacun son Bambara." In *Au Coeur de l'ethnie: Ethnies, tribalisme, et état en Afrique,* eds. Jean-Loup Amselle and Elikia M'Bokolo. Paris: Découverte, 1985.

Beattie, John M. *Crime and Courts in England, 1660–1800.* Princeton: Princeton University Press, 1986.

Benda-Beckman, Keebet von. "Forum Shopping and Shopping for Forums: Dispute Settlement in Minangkabau Village in Western Sumatra." *Journal of Legal Pluralism* 19 (1981).

Bender, Thomas, ed. *The Antislavery Debate: Capitalism and Abolitionism as a Problem in Historical Explanation.* Berkeley: University of California Press, 1992.

Benton, Lauren. *Law and Colonial Cultures: Legal Regimes in World History, 1400–1900.* New York: Cambridge University Press, 2002.

Berenson, Edward. *The Trial of Madame Caillaux.* Berkeley: University of California Press, 1992.

Berlin, Ira and Leslie S. Rowland, eds. *Families and Freedom: A Documentary History of African-American Kinship in the Civil War Era.* New York: New Press, 1997.

Berlin, Ira, Marc Favreau, and Steven F. Miller, eds. *Remembering Slavery: African Americans Talk about their Personal Experiences of Slavery and Freedom.* New York: New Press, 1998.

Berry, Sara. *Chiefs Know Their Boundaries: Essays on Property, Power, and the Past in Asante, 1896–1996.* Portsmouth, NH: Heinemann, 2001.

———. *No Condition Is Permanent: The Social Dynamics of Agrarian Change in Sub-Saharan Africa.* Madison: University of Wisconsin Press, 1993.

Beurdeley, E. *La justice indigène en Afrique occidentale française: mission d'études, 1913–1914.* Paris: Publication de la comité de l'Afrique Française, 1916.

Bloch, Marc. *French Rural History: An Essay on its Basic Characteristics,* translated by Janet Sondheimer. Berkeley: University of California Press, 1966.

———. *La société féodale.* Paris: A Michel, 1939.

Bosman, Willem. *A New and Accurate Description of the Coast of Guinea, Divided in the Gold, Slave, and Ivory Coasts.* New York: Barnes and Noble, reprinted 1967.

Bouche, Denise. *Villages de liberté en Afrique noire française, 1887–1910.* The Hague: Mouton, 1968.

Braudel, Fernand. *The Mediterranean and the Mediterranean World in the Age of Philip I,* translated by Sian Reynolds. New York: Harper and Row, 1972.

Brégeon, Jean-Joel. *L'Egypte française au jour le jour, 1798–1801.* Paris: Perrin, 1991.

Bret, Patrice, ed. *L'Expédition d'Egypte: une enterprise des Lumières, 1798–1801.* Paris: Technique & documentation, 1998.

Bruijn, Mirjam de and Han van Dijk. *Arid Ways: Cultural Understandings of Insecurity in Fulbe Society, Central Mali.* Amsterdam: Thela, 1995.

Buell, Raymond. L. *The Native Problem in Africa.* New York: Macmillan, 1928.

Burman, Sandra and Barbara E. Harrell-Bond, eds. *The Imposition of Law.* New York: Academic Press, 1979.

Burrill, Emily. "Marriage, Divorce, and Child Custody in Bougouni and Sikasso, Haut-Sénégal-Niger, 1905–1912." Unpublished paper, Department of History, Stanford University.

Buttinger, Joseph. *Vietnam: A Political History.* New York: Praeger, 1968.

Carlson, Richard A. *Experienced Cognition.* Mahwah, NJ: L. Erlbaum Associates, 1997.

Chafer, Tony and Amanda Sachur, eds. *Promoting the Colonial Idea: Propaganda and Visions of Empire in France.* New York: Palgrave, 2002.

Chanock, Martin. *Law, Custom, and Social Order: The Colonial Experience in Malawi and Zambia.* Cambridge: Cambridge University Press, 1985.

———. *The Making of South African Legal Culture, 1902–1936: Fear, Favour, and Prejudice.* Cambridge: Cambridge University Press, 2001.

———. "A Peculiar Sharpness: An Essay on Property in the History of Customary Law in Colonial Africa." *Journal of African History* 32(1) (1991).

Chayanov, A. V. In *The Theory of Peasant Economy,* eds. Daniel Thorner, Basile Kerblay, and R. E. F. Smith. Homeland, IL: American Economics Association, 1966.

Christelow, Allan. *Muslim Law Courts and the French Colonial State in Algeria.* Princeton: Princeton University Press, 1985.

———. "Theft, Homicide, and Oath." In *Law in Colonial Africa,* eds. Kristin Mann and Richard Roberts. Portsmouth, NH: Heinemann, 1991.

———. *Thus Ruled Emir Abbas: Selected Cases from the Records of the Emir of Kano's Judicial Council.* East Lansing: Michigan State University Press, 1994.

Clifford, James. *The Predicament of Culture: Twentieth Century Ethnography, Literature, and Art.* Cambridge, MA: Harvard University Press, 1988.

Clozel, Marie François Joseph. "Preface." In *Les Attributions judiciaires des administrateurs et chefs de poste en service à la Côte d'Ivoire,* by Roger Villamur. Paris: Libraire de la cour d'appel et de l'ordre des avocats, 1902.

Clozel, Marie François Joseph, Roger Villamur, and Honoré Cartron. *Les coutumes indigènes de la Côte d'Ivoire: Documents publiés avec une introduction et des notes.* Paris: A. Challamel, 1902.

Cohen, Abner. "Cultural Strategies in the Organization of Trading Diaporas." In *The Development of Trade and Markets in West Africa,* ed. Claude Meillassoux. London: Oxford University Press, 1971.

Cohen, David W. " 'A Case for the Basoga': Lloyd Fallers and the Construction of an African Legal System." In *Law and Colonialism in Africa,* eds. Kristin Mann and Richard Roberts. Portsmouth, NH: Heinemann, 1991.

———. "Pim's Doorway." In *Reliving the Past: The Worlds of Social History,* ed. Olivier Zunz. Chapel Hill: University of North Carolina Press, 1985.

Cohen, William B. *Rulers of Empire: The French Colonial Service in Africa.* Stanford: Hoover Institution Press, 1971.

Cohn, Bernard. *An Anthropologist among the Historians and Other Essays.* Delhi: Oxford University Press, 1987.

———. *Colonialism and its Forms of Knowledge: The British in India.* Princeton: Princeton University Press, 1996.

————. "Some Notes on Law and Change in India." *Economic Development and Change* 8 (1) (1959).

Collier, Jane F. *Law and Social Change in Zinacantan.* Stanford: Stanford University Press, 1973.

————. *Marriage and Inequality in Classless Societies.* Stanford: Stanford University Press, 1988.

Colson, Elizabeth. "The Contentiousness of Disputes." In *Understanding Disputes: The Politics of Argument,* ed. Pat Caplan. Providence, RI: Berg, 1995.

————. "Social Control and Vengeance in Plateau Tonga Society." *Africa* 23 (1) (1953).

Comaroff, John, ed. *The Meaning of Marriage Payments.* London: Academic Press, 1980.

Conklin, Alice. *A Mission to Civilize: The Republican Idea of Empire in France and West Africa, 1895–1930.* Stanford: Stanford University Press, 1997.

————. " 'On a semé la haine': Maurice Delafosse et la politique du Gouvernement général en AOF, 1915–1936." In *Maurice Delafosse, entre orientalisme et ethnographie: L'intenéraire d'un africaniste,* eds. Jean-Loup Amselle and Emmanuelle Sibeud. Paris: Maisonneuve, 1998.

Conley, John M. and William M. O'Barr. *Just Words: Law, Language, and Power.* Chicago: University of Chicago Press, 1998.

————. *Rules versus Relationships: The Ethnography of Legal Discourse.* Chicago: University of Chicago Press, 1990.

Conrad, David C. and Barbara Frank, eds. *Status and Identity in West Africa: Nyamakalaw of Mande.* Bloomington: Indiana University Press, 1995.

Cook, Karen, ed. *Trust in Society.* New York: Russell Sage Foundation, 2001.

Cooper, Barbara. *Marriage in Maradi: Gender and Culture in a Hausa Society in Niger, 1900–1989.* Portsmouth, NH: Heinemann, 1997.

Cooper, Frederick. "Islam and Cultural Hegemony: The Ideology of Slaveowners on the East African Coast." In *Ideology of Slavery in Africa,* ed. Paul Lovejoy. Beverly Hills: Sage, 1981.

————. "What Is the Concept of Globalization Good for? An African Historian's Perspective." *African Affairs* 100 (1) (2001).

Cooper, Frederick and Randall Packard, eds. *International Development and the Social Sciences: Essays on the History and Politics of Knowledge.* Berkeley: University of California Press, 1997.

Cornevain, Robert. "Maurice Delafosse et le *Haut-Sénégal-Niger.*" In *Haut-Sénégal-Niger,* ed. Maurice Delafosse. Paris: Maisonneuve, reprinted, 1972.

Curtin, Philip. *Cross-Cultural Trade in World History.* New York: Cambridge University Press, 1984.

Danziger, Raphael. *Abd al-Qadir and the Algerians: Resistance to the French and Internal Consolidation.* New York: Holmes and Meyer, 1977.

Davis, Natalie. *Fiction in the Archives: Pardon Tales and their Tellers in Sixteenth Century France.* Sanford: Stanford University Press, 1987.

Debré, Jean-Louis. *La justice au XIXe siècle: Les magistrats.* Paris: Librarie Académique Perrin, 1981.

Delafosse, Louise. *Maurice Delafosse: un Berichon conquis par l'Afrique.* Paris: Société française d'histoire d'Outre-Mer, 1976.

Delafosse, Maurice. *Haut-Sénégal-Niger.* Paris: originally E. Larose, 1912; reissued Maisonneuve and Larose, 1972.

———. "Institut ethnographique international de Paris, Actes; Allocution de Maurice Delafosse, président de séance." *Revue d'ethnographie et sociologie* 3 (1912).

———. *Les civilisations négro-africaines.* Paris: Stock, 1925.

———. "Le peuple siéna ou sénoufo." *Revue des études ethnographiques et sociologiques,* vol. 1 and vol. 2.

Delavignette, Robert. *Les vrais chefs de l'empire.* Paris: Gaillmard, 1939.

Demogue, R. "La loi française aux colonies." In *Les Colonies françaises,* vol. 1 of *Petite encyclopédie coloniale,* ed. Maxime Petit. Paris: Larouse, 1902.

Despagnet, Frantz. "Les protectorats" in *Les Colonies françaises,* vol. 1 of *Petite encylopédie Coloniale,* ed. Maxine Petit. Paris: Larousse, 1902.

Dewachter, Michel, ed. *L'Egypte Bonaparte et Champollion.* Figeac: Association pour le Bicentenaire Champollion, 1990.

Dike, K. Onwuka. *Trade and Politics in the Niger Delta, 1830–1885: An Introduction to the Economic and Political History of Nigeria.* Oxford: Clarendon Press, 1956.

Dirks, Nicholas. "From Little King to Landlord: Colonial Discourse and Colonial Rule." In *Colonialism and Culture,* ed. Nicolas Dirks. Ann Arbor: University of Michigan Press, 1992.

Dislère, Paul. *Traite de législation coloniale.* Paris: P. Dupont, 1914.

Djata, Sundiata A. *The Bamana Empire by the Niger: Kingdom, Jihad, and Colonization, 1712–1920.* Princeton: M. Weiner, 1996.

Dobkin, Marlene. "Colonialism and the Legal Status of Women in Francophone Africa." *Cahiers d'Études Africaines* 8 (1968).

Dubois, Félix. *Notre beau Niger.* Paris: Flammarion, 1911.

Dumestre, Gérard. *Dictionnaire Bambara-Français.* no publisher, 1981.

Ellis, Stephen. "Writing Histories of Contemporary Africa." *JAH* 43 (1) (2002).

Enders, A. "L'école nationale de la France d'Outre-Mer et la formation des administrateurs coloniaux." *Revue d'histoire moderne et contemporaine* 40 (2) (1993).

Epstein, A. L. "The Case Method in the Field of Law." In *The Craft of Social Anthropology,* ed. A. L. Epstein. London: Tavistock, 1967.

Escott, Paul. *Slavery Remembered: A Record of Twentieth-Century Slave Narratives.* Chapel Hill: University of North Carolina Press, 1979.

Esposito, John L. *Women in Muslim Family Law.* Syracuse: Syracuse University Press, 1982.

Ewick, Patricia and Susan S. Silbey. *The Common Place of Law: Stories from Everyday Life.* Chicago: University of Chicago Press, 1998.

Fage, J. D. *An Introduction to the History of West Africa.* Cambridge: Cambridge University Press, 1955.

Fallers, Lloyd. *Law without Precedent: Legal Ideas in Action in the Courts of Colonial Busoga.* Chicago: University of Chicago Press, 1969.

Falola, Toyin and Paul Lovejoy, eds. *Pawnship, Slavery and Colonialism in Africa.* Trenton, NJ: Africa World Press, 2003.

Felstiner, William, Richard Abel, and Austin Sarat, "The Emergence and Transformation of Disputes: Naming, Blaming, Claiming . . . " *Law and Society Review* 15 (1980–1981).

Foner, Eric. *Nothing But Freedom: Emancipation and Its Legacy.* Baton Rouge: Louisiana State University Press, 1983.

———. *Reconstruction: America's Unfinished Revolution*. New York: Harper and Row, 1988.

Fouchard, Laurent. "Propriétaires et commerçants africains à Ouagadougou et à Bobo-Dioulasso (Haute-Volta) fin 19ième siècle-1960." *Journal of African History* 44 (3) (2003).

François, Georges. *L'Afrique occidentale française*. Paris: E. Larose, 1907.

Frémeaux, Jacques. *Les Bureaux arabes dans l'Algérie de la conqûete*. Paris: Denoël, 1993.

Furet, François. *Revolutionary France, 1770–1880*, translated by Antonia Nevill. London: Blackwell, 1988.

Galanter, Marc. "Justice in Many Rooms: Courts, Private Ordering, and Indigenous Law." *Journal of Legal Pluralism* 19 (1981).

Gallais, Jean. *Le Delta intérieur du Niger, étude de géographie régionale*. Dakar: IFAN, 1967.

Garrigues, Jean. *Le Général Boulanger*. Paris: O. Orban, 1991.

Giddens, Anthony. *The Constitution of Society*. Berkeley: University of California Press, 1984.

Gilbert-Desvillons and Edmond Joucla, *Jurisprudence de la chambre d'homologation: Justice indigène. Jurisprudence de la Chambre d'homologation, publiée sous le patronage de M. William Ponty, gouverneur général*... Gorée: Imprimerie du Gouvernement-général, 1910.

Ginio, Ruth. "Negotiating Legal Authority in French West Africa: The Colonial Administration and African Assessors, 1903–1918." In *Intermediaries, Interpreters, and Clerks: Africans in the Making of Modern Africa*, eds. Benjamin Lawrance, Emily Osborn, and Richard Roberts. Madison: University of Wisconsin Press, forthcoming.

Ginzburg, Carlo. *The Cheese and the Worms: The Cosmos of a Sixteenth Century Miller*, translated by John Tedeschi and Anne Tedeschi. Baltimore: Johns Hopkins University Press, 1980.

Girault, Arthur. *Principes de colonization et de legislation coloniale: deuxième partie: les colonies françaises depuis 1815*, 3 vols., 4th edition. Paris: Sirey, 1921–1923.

———. *Principes de colonization et de legislation coloniale*, 1st edition. Paris: Larousse, 1895.

Glassman, Jonathon. *Feasts and Riot: Revelry, Rebellion, and Popular Consciousness on the Swahili Coast, 1856–1888*. Portsmouth, NH: Heinemann, 1995.

Gluckman, Max. "Introduction." In *The Craft of Social Anthropology*, ed. A. L. Epstein. London: Tavistock, 1967.

———. *The Judicial Process among the Barotse of Northern Rhodesia*. Manchester: Manchester University Press, 1955.

Goody, Jack. *Death, Property, and the Ancestors: A Study of Mortuary Customs of the Lo Dagaa of West Africa*. Stanford: Stanford University Press, 1962.

———. "The Evolution of the Family." In *Household and Family in Past Time*, eds. Peter Laslett and Richard Wall. Cambridge: Cambridge University Press, 1972.

———. *The Logic of Writing and the Organization of Society*. Cambridge: Cambridge University Press, 1986.

———. *The Myth of the Bagre*. Oxford: Clarendon Press, 1972.

———. *Production and Reproduction: A Comparative Study of the Domestic Domain*. Cambridge: Cambridge University Press, 1976.

Görög-Karady, Veronika, ed. *Le mariage dans les contes Africaines: Études et anthologie*. Paris: Karthala, 1994.

Gouvernment-général de l'Afrique occidentale française. *Justice indigène: instructions aux administrateurs sur l'application du Décret du 16 Août 1912, portant reorganization de la Justice indigène en Afrique occidentale française.* Dakar: Imprimermie Ternaux, 1913.

Griffiths, John. "What is Legal Pluralism." *Journal of Legal Pluralism* 24 (1986).

Grosz-Ngate, Maria Luise. "Bambara Men and Women and the Reproduction of Social Life in Sana Provice, Mali." Unpublished Ph.D. dissertation, Michigan State University, 1986.

Guèye, Lamine. *Étapes et perspectives de l'Union française.* Paris: Editions de l'Union Française, 1955.

Guyer, Jane I. "Food, Cocoa, and the Division of Labour by Sex in Two West African Societies." *Comparative Studies in Society and History* 22 (3) (1980).

Guyer, Jane, ed. *Money Matters: Instability, Values, and Social Payments in the Modern History of West African Communities.* Portsmouth, NH: Heinemann, 1995.

Harding, James. *The Astonishing Adventure of General Boulanger.* New York: Scribner, 1971.

Harris, Ruth. *Murders and Madness: Medicine, Law, and Society in the fin de siècle.* Oxford: Clarendon Press, 1989.

Harrison, Christopher. *France and Islam in West Africa, 1860–1960.* Cambridge: Cambridge University Press, 1988.

Hawkins, Sean. " 'The Woman Question': Marriage and Identity in Colonial Courts of Northern Ghana, 1907–1954." In *Women in African Colonial Histories,* eds. Jean Allman, Susan Geiger, and Nakanyike Musisi. Bloomington: Indiana University Press, 2002.

———. *Writing and Colonialism in Northern Ghana: The Encounter between the LoDagaa and "the World on Paper."* Toronto: University of Toronto Press, 2002.

Hay, Margaret Jean and Marcia Wright, eds. *African Women and the Law: Historical Perspectives.* Boston: African Studies Center, 1982.

Herbst, Jeffrey. *States and Power in Africa: Comparative Lessons in Authority and Control.* Princeton: Princeton University Press, 2000.

Hirsch, Susan F. *Pronouncing and Persevering: Gender and Discourses of Disputing in an African Islamic Court.* Chicago: University of Chicago Press, 1998.

Hodgson, Dorothy and Sheryl McCurdy, eds. *"Wicked" Women and the Reconfiguration of Gender in Africa.* Portsmouth, NH: Heinemann, 2002.

Hofmeyr, Isabel. *"We Spend Our Years as a Tale that is Told": Oral Historical Narrative in a South African Chiefdom.* Portsmouth, NH: Heinemann, 1993.

Hogendorn, Jan and Marion Johnson. *The Shell Money of the Slave Trade.* Cambridge: Cambridge University Press, 1986.

Hogendorn, Jan and Paul Lovejoy. *Slow Death to Slavery: The Course of Abolition in Northern Nigeria, 1897–1936.* Cambridge: Cambridge University Press, 1993.

Hooker, M. B. *Legal Pluralism: An Introduction to Colonial and Neo-Colonial Laws.* Oxford: Clarendon, 1975.

Hopkins, A. G. *An Economic History of West Africa.* London: Longman, 1973.

Horne, Janet R. "In Pursuit of Greater France: Visions of Empire among the Musée Social Reformers, 1894–1931." In *Domesticating the Empire: Race, Gender, and Family Life in French and Dutch Colonialism,* eds. Julia Clancy-Smith and Frances Gouda. Charlottesville: University of Virginia Press, 1998.

Hubbell, Andrew. "A View of the Slave Trade from the Margin: Souroudougou in the Late Nineteenth Century Slave Trade of the Niger Bend." *JAH* 42 (1) (2001).

Humbert, Senator Charles. "L'Afrique occidentale française sous l'administration de M. W. Ponty." *La Grande revue* 67 (1911).

Iliffe, John. *The African Poor: A History.* Cambridge: Cambridge University Press, 1987.

Irvine, William D. *The Boulanger Affair Reconsidered: Royalism, Boulangism, and the Origins of the Radical Rights in France.* New York: Oxford University Press, 1989.

Jaime, Lieutenant. *De Koulikoro à Tombouctou sur la connonière "le Mage."* Paris: Les Libraries Associés, 1894.

Jennings, Eric. *Vichy in the Tropics: Pétain's National Revolution in Madagascar, Guadeloupe, and Indochina, 1940–1944.* Stanford: Stanford University Press, 2002.

Jezequel, Jean-Hervé. " 'Collecting Customary Law': Educated Africans, Ethnographic Writings, and Colonial Justice in French West Africa." In *Intermediaries, Interpreters, and Clerks: Africans in the Making of Modern Africa,* eds. Benjamin Lawrance, Emily Osborn, and Richard Roberts. Madison: University of Wisconsin Press, forthcoming.

———. "Maurice Delafosse et l'émergence d'une littérature africaine à vocation scientifique." In *Maurice Delafosse, entre orientalisme et ethnographie: L'inténéraire d'un africaniste,* eds. Jean-Loup Amselle and Emmanuelle Sibeud. Paris: Maisonneuve, 1998.

Jobbé-Duval, M. E. "L'histoire comparée de droit et l'expansion coloniale de la France." *Annales internationales d'Histoire* (1900).

Johnson, G. Wesley. "William Ponty and Republican Paternalism in French West Africa (1866–1915)." In *African Proconsuls: European Governors in Africa,* eds. L. H. Gann and Peter Duignan. New York: Free Press, 1978.

Journal Officiel de l'Afrique Occidentale française. Dakar: Gouvernement général de l'Afrique Occidentale française, 1895–1912.

July, Robert. *An African Voice: The Role of the Humanities in African Independence.* Durham, NC: Duke University Press, 1987.

Kanya-Forstner, A. S. *The Conquest of the Western Sudan: A Study in French Military Imperialism.* Cambridge: Cambridge University Press, 1969.

Kidder, Robert. "Western Law in India: External Law and Local Response." In *Social System and Legal Process,* ed. Harry M. Johnson. San Francisco: Jossey-Bass, 1978.

Klein, Martin. *Islam and Imperialism in Senegal: Sine-Salou, 1847–1914.* Stanford: Stanford University Press, 1968.

———. *Slavery and Colonial Rule in French West Africa.* Cambridge: Cambridge University Press, 1998.

Kopytoff, Igor. "The Cultural Context of African Abolition." In *The End of Slavery in Africa,* eds. Suzanne Miers and Richard Roberts. Madison: University of Wisconsin Press, 1988.

Laissus, Yves. *L'Egypte, une aventure savante, 1798–1801.* Paris: Fayard, 1998.

Lamiral, Dominique. *L'Affrique et le peuple affircain considérés sou tous leurs rapports avec notre commerce et nos colonies.* Paris: Dessenne, 1789.

Law, Robin, ed. *From Slave Trade to 'Legitimate Commerce': The Commercial Transition in Nineteenth-Century West Africa.* Cambridge: Cambridge University Press, 1995.

Lawrance, Benjamin, Emily Osborn, and Richard Roberts, eds. *Intermediaries, Interpreters, and Clerks: Africans in the Making of Modern Africa.* Madison: University of Wisconsin Press, forthcoming.

Léotard, Jacques. "Afrique Occidentale." In *Les colonies françaises au début du XX siècle: Cinq ans de progrès (1900–1905),* eds. Jacques Léotard, R. Teisseire, A. Ramal, and J-B Samat. Marseille: n.p., 1906.

Leynaud, Emile and Youssouf Cisse. *Paysans Malinke du Haut Niger (Tradition et développement rural en Afrique Soudanaise).* Bamako: Imprimerie Populaire du Mali, 1978.

Llewellyn, Karl N. and E. A. Hoebel. *The Cheyenne Way: Conflict and Case Law in Primitive Jurisprudence.* Norman: University of Oklahoma Press, 1941.

Lovejoy, Paul. *Caravans of Kola: The Hausa Kola Trade, 1700–1900.* Zaria, Nigeria: Ahmadou Bello University Press, 1980.

Lowy, Michael J. "A Good Name is Worth More than Money: Strategies of Court Use in Urban Ghana." In *The Disputing Process: Law in Ten Societies,* eds. Laura Nader and Harry F. Todd. New York: Columbia University Press, 1978.

Luneau, René. *Les chemins de la noce: La femme et le mariage dans la société rurale au Mali,* vol. III. Lille: Service de reproduction des thèses, Université de Lille, 1975.

Lydon, Ghislaine. "Thus Ruled the Qadi of Ndar (Senegal): Civil Litigation in a Colonial Muslim Tribunal, 1880s–1920s." Unpublished paper presented at the Muslim Family Law and Colonialism in Africa workshop, Stanford, May 2001.

———. "The Unraveling of a Neglected Source: A Report on Women in Francophone West Africa in the 1930s." *Cahiers d'Études Africaines* 37 (3) (1997): 555–584.

McClendon, Thomas. *Genders and Generations Apart: Labor Tenants and Customary Law in Segregation-era South Africa, 1920s to 1940s.* Portsmouth, NH: Heinemann, 2002.

McDougall, Ann. "Banamba and the Salt Trade of the Western Sudan." In *West African Economic and Social History: Studies in Memory of Marion Johnson,* ed. David Henige. Madison: African Studies Center, 1990.

McWhinney, Edward. "Code Law Systems." In *Encyclopedia of the Social Sciences.* New York: Macmillan, 1968.

Malkki, Liisa. *Purity and Exile: Violence, Memory, and National Cosmology among Hutu Refugees in Tanzania.* Chicago: University of Chicago Press, 1995.

Mamdani, Mahmoud. *Citizen and Subject: Contemporary Africa and the Legacy of Late Colonialism.* Princeton: Princeton University Press, 1996.

Martin, Susan M. *Palm Oil and Protest: An Economic History of the Ngwa Region, Southeastern Nigeria, 1800–1980 .* Cambridge: Cambridge University Press, 1988.

Martin-Fugier, Anne. *La bourgeoise: Femme au temps de Paul Bourget.* Paris: Bernard Grassett, 1983.

Massell, Gergory. *The Surrogate Proletariat: Moslem Women and Revolutionary Strategies in Soviet Central Asia, 1919–1929.* Princeton: Princeton University Press, 1974.

Medick, Hans. *Weben und Überleben in Laichingen 1650–1900: Lokalgeschichte als allgemeine Geschichte.* Göttingen: Vandenhoeck & Ruprecht, 1996.

Meillassoux, Claude. *The Anthropology of Slavery: The Womb of Iron and Gold,* translated by Alide Dasnois. Chicago: University of Chicago Press, 1991.

———. "État et conditions des esclaves à Gumbu (Mali) au XIXe siècle." In *L'esclavage en Afrique précoloniale,* ed. Claude Meillassoux. Paris: Mapsero, 1975.

———. *Maidens, Meal and Money: Capitalism and the Domestic Community.* Cambridge: Cambridge University Press, 1981.

Méniaud, Jacques. *Haut-Sénégal-Niger: géographie économique.* Paris: Larose, 1912.

Merry, Sally Engle. "Anthropology, Law, and Transnational Processes." *Annual Reviews in Anthropology* 21 (1992).

————. "The Articulation of Legal Spheres." In *African Women and the Law: Historical Perspectives,* eds. Margaret Jean Hay and Marcia Wright. Boston: African Studies Center, 1982.

————. *Colonizing Hawaii: The Cultural Power of Law.* Princeton: Princeton University Press, 2000.

————. *Getting Justice and Getting Even: Legal Consciousness among Working-Class Americans.* Chicago: University of Chicago Press, 1990.

————. "Legal Pluralism." *Law and Society Review* 22 (5) (1988).

Merryman, Henry. *The Civil Law Tradition: An Introduction to the Legal Systems of Western Europe and Latin America.* Stanford: Stanford University Press, 1969.

Messick, Brinkley. *The Calligraphic State: Textual Domination and History in a Muslim Society.* Berkeley: University of California Press, 1993.

Meunier, Pierre. *Organisation et fonctionnement de la justice indigène en Afrique occidentale française.* Paris: A. Challamel, 1914.

Meyer, Jean, Jean Tarrade, Annie Rey-Goldzeiguer, and Jacques Thobie, *Histoire de la France coloniale: Des origines à 1914.* Paris: Armand Colin, 1991.

Michel, Marc. "Maurice Delafosse et l'invention d'une africanité nègre." In *Maurice Delafosse, entre orientalisme et ethnographie: L'intenéraire d'un africaniste,* eds. Jean-Loup Amselle and Emmanuelle Sibeud. Paris: Maisonneuve, 1998.

Miers, Suzanne and Richard Roberts, eds. *The End of Slavery in Africa.* Madison: University of Wisconsin Press, 1988.

Mitchell, Timothy. *Colonising Egypt.* Cambridge: Cambridge University Press, 1988.

Monteil, Charles. *Les Bambara du Ségou et du Kaarta: étude historique, ethnographique et littéraire d'une peuplade du Soudan français.* Paris: Maisonneuve, 1924, reprinted Paris: Maisonneuve, 1976.

————. *Contes Soudanaises.* Paris: E. Leroux, 1905.

————. *L'elevage au Soudan.* Paris: A. Challamel, 1905.

————. *Les Khassonkés. Monographie d'une peuplade du Soudan Français.* Paris: E. Leroux, 1915.

————. *Monographie de Djenné.* Tulle: Imprimerie de Jean Mazeyrie, 1903.

————. *Notice sur l'origine des Peulhs.* N.p., 1911.

Moore, Kathleen M. "Legal Studies." In *Encyclopedia of Women and Islamic Cultures: Methodologies, Paradigms and Sources,* ed. Suad Joseph. Leiden: Brill, 2003.

Moore, Sally Falk. "Individual Interests and Organizational Structures: Dispute Settlements as 'Events of Articulation.' " In *Social Anthropology and the Law,* ed. Ian Hamnett. London: Academic Press, 1977.

————. *Social Facts and Fabrications: "Customary" Law on Kilimanjaro, 1880–1980.* New York: Cambridge Univeristy Press, 1986.

Moses, Claire Goldberg. *French Feminism in the Nineteenth Century.* Albany: State University of New York Press, 1984.

Mudimbe, V. Y. *The Invention of Africa.* Bloomington: Indiana University Press, 1988.

Muir, Edward and Guido Ruggiero, eds. *Microhistory and the Lost Peoples of Europe,* translated by Eren Branch. Baltimore: Johns Hopkins University Press, 1991.

Nader, Laura and Harry F. Todd, eds, *The Disputing Process: Law in Ten Societies.* New York: Columbia University Press, 1978.

Nasir, Jamal J. *The Status of Women under Islamic Law and under Modern Islamic Legislation.* London: Graham and Trotman, 1990.

Ndiaye, Seck. "Les tribunaux musulmans du Sénégal de 1857 à 1914." Unpublished mémoire. Dakar: University of Dakar, 1984.

Newbury, C. W. "The Formation of the Government General of French West Africa." *JAH* 1 (1) (1960).

Nord, Philip. *The Republican Moment: Struggles for Democracy in Nineteenth-Century France.* Cambridge, MA: Harvard University Press, 1995.

O'Brien, Donal Cruise. "Towards an 'Islamic Policy' in French West Africa." *JAH* 8 (2) (1967).

Oliver. Roland. *The Missionary Factory in East Africa.* London: Longmans, Green, 1952.

Ong, Walter. *Orality and Literacy: Technologizing of the Word.* London: Metheun, 1982.

Ortoli, Jean. "Coutume Bambara, Cercle de Bamako." In *Coutumiers juridiques de l'Afrique occidentale française,* ed. Bernard Maupoil. Paris: Publications du Comité d'études historiques et scientifiques de l'Afrique occidentale française, 1939.

Osborn, Emily. " 'Circles of Iron': African Colonial Employees and the Interpretation of Colonial Rule in French West Africa." *JAH* 44 (1) (2003).

———. "Power, Authority, and Gender in Kankan-Baté, 1650–1920." Unpublished Ph.D. dissertation, Stanford University, 2000.

Pagden, Anthony. *Lords of All the World: Ideologies of Empire in Spain, Britain, and France, c. 1500–1800.* New Haven, CT: Yale University Press, 1995.

Paques, Vivian. *Les Bambara.* Paris: Presses Universitaires de France, 1954.

Patault, Anne-Marie. *Introduction historique au droit des biens.* Paris: Presses Universitaires de France, 1989.

Perinbam, B. Marie. *Family Identity and the State in the Bamako Kafu, c.1800–c.1900.* Boulder, CO: Westview Press, 1997.

Perron, M. translator. *Précis de jurisprudence musulmane ou principes de législation musulmane civile et religieuse selon le rite malékite.* Paris: Imprimerie Nationale, 1848–1852.

Petit, Emilien. *Droits publics, ou gouvernement des colonies françaises, d'après les loix faites pour des pays.* Paris: Chez Delalain, 1771.

Petit, Maxine, ed. *Petite encylopédie Coloniale.* Paris: Larousse, 1902.

Pluchon, Pierre. *Histoire de la colonisation française: Le premier empire colonial, des origines à la Restauration.* Paris: Fayard, 1991.

Pollet, Eric and Grace Winter. *La Société Soninke (Dyahunu, Mali).* Brussels: Editions de l'Institut de sociologie, Universite libre de Bruxelles, 1972.

Potash, Betty, ed. *Widows in African Societies: Choices and Constraints.* Stanford: Stanford University Press, 1986.

Prochaska, David. *Making Algeria French: Colonialism in Bône, 1870–1920.* Cambridge: Cambridge University Press, 1990.

Quellien, Alain. *La politique musulmane dans l'Afrique occidentale française.* Paris: Emile Larose, 1910.

Rabinow, Paul. *French Modern: Norms and Forms of the Social Environment.* Cambridge, MA: Harvard University Press, 1989.

Raffenel, Anne. *Nouveau Voyage dans le pays des nègres.* Paris: Imprimerie de N. Chaix, 1856.

Ranger, Terence. "The Invention of Tradition in Africa." In *The Invention of Tradition,* eds. Eric Hobsbawm and Terence Ranger. Cambridge: Cambridge University Press, 1983.

Rapport au Président de la République. "Suivi de decret portant réorganisation du service de la justice dans les colonies relevant du gouvernement général de l'Afrique occidentale." *Journal officiel de la République Française,* 24 November 1903.

Renault, François. "L'Abolition de l'esclavage au Sénégal: L'attitude de l'administration, 1848–1905." *Revue française d'histoire d'outre mer* 63 (1971).

Rey-Goldzeiguer, Annie. "La France coloniale de 1830 à 1870." In *Histoire de la France coloniale: Des origines à 1914,* eds. Jean Meyer, Jean Tarrade, Annie Rey-Goldzeiguer and Jacques Thobie. Paris: Armand Colin, 1991.

Roberts, Richard. "The Case of Faama Mademba Sy and the Ambiguities of Legal Jurisdiction in Early Colonial French Soudan." In *Law in Colonial Africa,* eds. Kristin Mann and Richard Roberts. Portsmouth, NH: Heinemann, 1991.

———. "The Emergence of a Grain Market in Bamako, 1883–1908." *Canadian Journal of African Studies* 14 (1) (1980).

———. "The End of Slavery in the French Soudan, 1905–1914." In *The End of Slavery in Africa,* eds. Suzanne Miers and Richard Roberts. Madison: University of Wisconsin Press, 1988.

———. "Fishing for the State: The Political Economy of the Middle Niger Valley." In *Modes of Production in Africa: The Precolonial Era,* eds. Donald Crummey and C. C. Stewart. Beverly Hills: Sage, 1981.

———. "Guinée Cloth: Linked Transformations within France's Empire in the Nineteenth Century." *Cahiers d'Études Africaines* 128 (1992).

———. "Ideology, Slavery, and Social Formation: The Evolution of Slavery in the Middle Niger Valley." In *The Ideology of Slavery in Africa,* ed. Paul Lovejoy. Beverly Hills: Sage, 1981.

———. "Long Distance Trade and Production: Sinsani in the Nineteenth Century." *JAH* 21 (2) (1980).

———. "Text and Testimony in the *Tribunal de Première Instance,* Dakar, during the Early Twentieth Century." *JAH* 31 (3) (1999).

———. *Two Worlds of Cotton: Colonialism and the Regional Economy in the French Soudan, 1800–1946.* Stanford: Stanford University Press, 1996.

———. *Warriors, Slaves, and Merchants: The State and the Economy in the Middle Niger Valley, 1700–1914.* Stanford: Stanford University Press, 1987.

———. "Women, Household Instability, and the End of Slavery in Banamba and Gumbu, French Soudan, 1905–1912." In *Women and Slavery: In Honour of Suzanne Miers,* eds. Gwyn Campbell, Suzanne Miers, and Joseph Miller. London: Frank Cass, forthcoming.

———. "Women's Wealth and Women's Property: Maraka Household Textile Industry in the Nineteenth Century." *Comparative Studies in Society and History* 26 (2) (1984).

Roberts, Richard and Martin Klein. "The Banamba Slave Exodus of 1905 and the End of Slavery in the Western Sudan." *JAH* 21 (3) (1980).

———. "The Resurgence of Pawning in French West Africa during the Depression of the 1930s." *African Economic History* 16 (1987). Reprinted in *Pawnship, Slavery and Colonialism in Africa,* ed. Toyin Falola and Paul Lovejoy. Trenton, NJ: Africa World Press, 2003.

Robinson, David. "Ethnography and Customary Law in Senegal." *Cahiers d'Etudes Africaines* 32 (2) (1992).

———. "French 'Islamic' Policy and Practice in Late Nineteenth Century Senegal." *JAH* 29 (3) (1988).

———. *The Holy War of Umar-Tal: The Western Sudan in the Mid-Nineteenth Century.* Oxford: Clarendon Press, 1985.

————. *Paths to Accommodation: Muslim Societies and French Colonial Authorities in Senegal and Mauritania, 1880–1920.* Athens: Ohio University Press, 2000.

Robinson, David and Jean-Louis Triaud, eds. *Le temps des marabouts: itinéraires et stratégies islamiques en Afrique occidentale française, 1880–1960.* Paris: Karthala, 1998.

Rosen, Lawrence. "Islamic 'Case Law and the Logic of Consequence.'" In *History and Power in the Study of Law: New Directions in Legal Anthropology,* eds. June Starr and Jane Collier. Ithaca: Cornell Univeristy Press, 1989.

Roume, Ernest. *Justice indigène: Instructions au administrateurs sur l'application du Décret de 10 November 1903 portant réorganisation du service de la justice dans les colonies relevant du Gouvernement général de l'AOF.* Gorée: Imprimerie du Gouvernement-général, 1905.

Roux, Emile. *Manuel à l'usage des administrateurs et du personnel des affaires indigènes de la colonie du Sénégal et des colonies relevant du gouvernement général de l'AOF.* Paris: A. Challamel, 1911.

Royer, Jean-Pierre, Renée Martinage, and Pierre Lecocq. *Juges et notables au XIXe siècle.* Paris: Presses Universitaires de France, 1982.

Ruedy, John. *Modern Algeria: The Origins and Development of a Nation.* Bloomington: Indiana University Press, 1992.

Said, Edward. "Orientalism: The Cultural Consequences of the French Preoccupation with Egypt." In *Napoleon in Egypt: Al-Jabarti's Chronicle of the French Occupation, 1798,* translated by Shmuel Moreh and introduced by Robert Tignor. Princeton: M. Weiner, 1993.

Saintoyant, Jules François. *La colonisation française pendant la période Napoléonienne (1799–1815).* Paris: La Renaissance du Livre, 1931.

Salacuse, Jeswald. *An Introduction to Law in French-Speaking Africa.* Charlottesville: Michie, 1969.

Sarr, Dominique. "La Chambre spéciale d'homologation de la Cour d'appel de l'Afrique occidentale Française et les coutumes pénales de 1903–1920." *Annales Africaines* l (1974).

————. "Le chamber spéciale d'homologation de la cour d'appel de l'Afrique occidentale Française et les coutumes pénales de 1903–1920." *Annales Africaines* 1 (1975).

————. "Jurisprudence des tribinaux indigenes du Sénégal: Les causes de rupture du lien matrimonial de 1872 à 1946." *Annales Africaines* 2 (1975).

Schnapper, Bernard. "Les tribunaux musulmans et la politique coloniale au Sénégal (1830–1914)." *Revue historique de droit français et étranger* 39 (1961).

Schneider, William. *An Empire for the Masses: The French Popular Image of Africa, 1870–1900.* Westport, CT: Greenwood Press, 1982.

Scott, James C. *Domination and the Arts of Resistance: Hidden Transcripts.* New Haven: Yale University Press, 1990.

Searing, James. *"God Alone Is King": The Wolof Kingdoms of Kajoor and Bawol, 1859–1914.* Portsmouth, NH: Heinemann, 2002.

Seignette, N. *Code musulmane—statut réel, par Khalil ibn Ishak al Jundj,* translated by N. Seignette. Constantine, Impr. L. Arnolet; Alger, Jourdan; Paris, Challamel aîné, 1878.

Seligman, Edmon. *La justice en France pendant la Revolution (1789–1792).* Paris: Plon-Nourrit, 1901.

Shadle, Brett. "African Court Elders in Nyanza Province, Kenya, c. 1930–1960." In *Intermediaries, Interpreters, and Clerks: Africans in the Making of Modern Africa,* eds. Benjamin Lawrance, Emily Osborn, and Richard Roberts. Madison: University of Wisconsin Press, forthcoming.

Shapiro, Ann-Louise. *Breaking the Codes: Female Criminality in Fin-de-Siècle Paris.* Stanford: Stanford University Press, 1996.

Shepperson, George and Thomas Price. *Independent African: John Chilembwe and the Origins, Setting, and Significance of the Nyasaland Native Rising of 1915.* Edinburgh: Edinburgh University Press, 1958.

Shereikis, Rebecca. "Customized Courts: French Colonial Legal Institutions in Kayes, French Soudan, ca. 1880-c. 1913." Ph.D. dissertation, Northwestern University, 2003.

———. "From Law to Custom: The Shifting Legal Status of Muslim *Originaires* in Kayes and Medine, 1903–1913." *JAH* 42 (2) (2001).

Sibeud, Emmanuelle. *Une science impériale pour l'Afrique: la construction des saviors africanistes en France 1878–1930.* Paris: Ecole des hautes études en sciences sociales, 2002.

———. " 'Negrophilia', 'Negrology' or 'Africanism'? Colonial Ethnography and Racism in France around 1900." In *Promoting the Colonial Idea: Propaganda and Visions of Empire in France,* eds. Tony Chafer and Amanda Sackur. Houndsmill: Palgrave, 2002.

Sierra, Maria Teresa. "Indian Rights and Customary Law in Mexico: A Study of the Nahuas in the Sierra de Puebla." *Law and Society Review* 29 (2) (1995).

Smith, Mary F. *Baba of Karo: A Woman of the Muslim Hausa.* New Haven: Yale University Press, 1981.

Smith, Mary M., Peter E. Morris, Philip Levy, and Andrew W. Ellis. *Cognition in Action.* London: Hillsdale, 1987.

Starr, June. *Dispute and Settlement in Rural Turkey: An Ethnography of Law.* Leiden: Brill, 1978.

Starr, June and Jane F. Collier. "Introduction: Dialogues in Legal Anthropology." In *History and Power in the Study of Law: New Directions in Legal Anthropology,* eds. June Starr and Jane Collier. Ithaca: Cornell Univeristy Press, 1989.

Starr, June and Jane F. Collier. "Historical Studies of Legal Change." *Current Anthropology* 28 (3) (1987).

Szijártó, István. "Four Arguments for Microhistory." *Rethinking History* 6 (2) (2002).

Thiry, Baron Jean. *Bonaparte en Egypte, Décembre 1797–24 Août 1799.* Paris: Berger-Levrault, 1973.

Thobie, Jacques. "La France coloniale de 1870 à 1914." In *Histoire de la France coloniale: des origines à 1914,* eds. Jean Meyer, Jean Tarrade, Annie Rey-Goldzeiguer, and Jacques Thobie. Paris: Armand Colin, 1991.

Toulmin, Camilla. *Cattle, Women, and Wells: Managing Household Survival in the Sahel.* Oxford: Clarendon Press, 1992.

Triaud, Jean-Louis. "*Haut-Sénégal-Niger,* un modèle 'positiviste'? De la coutume à l'histoire: Maurice Delafosse et l'invention de l'histoire africaine." In *Maurice Delafosse, entre orientalisme et ethnographie: L'intenéraire d'un africaniste,* eds. Jean-Loup Amselle and Emmanuelle Sibeud. Paris: Maisonneuve and Larose, 1998.

Tucker, Judith E. *In the House of the Law: Gender and Islamic Law in Ottoman Syria and Palestine.* Berkeley: University of California, 1998.

Van Dusen Lewis, John. "Two Poles of Production in a Malian Peasant Village." Unpublished Ph.D. dissertation, Yale University, 1979.

———. "Domestic Labor Intensity and the Incorporation of Malian Peasant Farmers into Localized Descent Groups." *American Ethnologist* 8 (2) (1981).

Vansina, Jan. *Living with Africa.* Madison: University of Wisconsin Press, 1994.

———. *Oral Tradition: A Study in Historical Methodology,* translated by H. M. Wright. Chicago: Adline, 1965.

———. *Oral Tradition as History.* Madison: University of Wisconsin Press, 1985.

Villamur, Roger. *Les Attributions judiciaires des administrateurs et chefs de poste en service à la Côte d'Ivoire.* Paris: Libraire de la cour d'appel et de l'ordre des avocats, 1902.

Villamur, Roger and Léon Richaud. *Notre colonie de la Côte d'Ivoire.* Paris: A. Challamel, 1903.

Villien-Rossi, Marie-Louise. "Bamako, capitale du Mali." *Bull IFAN, Series B* (1966).

Volney, Constantin-François. *Voyage en Égypte et en Syrie.* Paris: Mouton, 1959.

Ward, Jennifer. "The Bambara-French Relationship, 1880–1915." Unpublished Ph.D. dissertation, UCLA, 1976.

Watts, Michael. *Silent Violence: Food, Famine, and Peasantry in Northern Nigeria.* Berkeley: University of California Press, 1983.

Wedgwood, Josiah. *The Economics of Inheritance.* London: George Routledge, 1929.

White, Luise, Stephen F. Miescher, and David William Cohen, eds. *African Words, African Voices: Critical Practices in Oral History.* Bloomington: Indiana University Press, 2001.

White, Richard. *The Middle Ground: Indians, Empires, and Republics in the Great Lakes Region, 1650–1815.* New York: Cambridge University Press, 1991.

Wiener, Jonathan. *The Social Origins of the New South: Alabama, 1860–1885.* Baton Rouge: Louisiana State University Press, 1978.

Wollschlager, Christian. "Exploring Global Landscapes in Litigation Rates." In *Sociologie des Rechts: Festschrift fur Erhard Blakenburg zum 60. Geburtztag,* eds. Jurgen Brand and Dieter Strempel. Baden-Baden: Nomos, 1998.

Wright, Gwendolyn. *The Politics of Design in French Colonial Urbanism.* Chicago: Chicago University Press, 1991.

Zeldin, Theodore. *France 1848–1945.* Oxford: Clarendon Press, 1973.

ARCHIVES

Archives Nationales, République du Mali. Fonds Anciens. ANM.

ANM B 70. Dèves and Chaumet, letter to Min of Colonies, n.p., n.d., included in a file sent from Min. of Colonies to gov-gen, Paris, 31 January 1900.

ANM B 83. Archinard, letter to Gov. Senegal, 9 January 1890, Kayes.

ANM B 150. Gov. Grodet, letter to Com. Sup., Region Nord-Est (Segu), Kayes, 26 January 1894.

ANM 1 D 15. Archinard, letter no. 149, np, 23 April 1891, cited in Lt. Sargols, Notice sur la justice indigène et la justice musulmane au Soudan, np, March 1896.

ANM 1 D 33, no. 1. Notices historiques et géographiques du cercle de Bamako, 1903.

ANM 1 D 55–3. Charles Correnson, De l'organisation de la justice et des moeurs chez les populations de la région de Segu, Segu, 5 September 1907.

ANM 1 D 192. Coutume Bambara dans le cercle de Gumbu, 1909.

ANM 1 D 206. Rapport sur les coutumes et institutions juridiques, Cercle de Segu, 1909.

ANM 2 D 72. Captain Loyer, commandant of Bamako, letter to commandant supérieur, 5 May 1886, Bamako.

ANM 5 D 44. Archinard, letter to commandant Segu, Kayes, 3 December 1890.

ANM 1 E 19. Rapport du commandant de cercle sur l'affaire de Nyamina, 22 May 1901.

ANM 1 E 19. Rapport politique, Bamako, May 1907.

ANM 1 E 38. Rapport politique, Gumbu, June 1909.

ANM 1 E 38. Thoron de Laur, Rapport sur la tournée de recensement, 5 May 1909, Gumbu.

ANM 1 E 71. Bulletin politique et militaire, Segu, July 1895; various Rapports politiques, Segu, 1897–1903.

ANM 1 E 72. Rapport politique, Segu, October 1906.

ANM 1 E 177. Rapport général sur la politique du cercle pendant l'année 1905, Segu.

ANM 2 M 1. Lt-gov, p.i., letter to gov-gen, Kayes, 5 September 1905. Included in letter was Rapport de l'Administrateur sur le fonctionnement des tribunaux de cercle, Bandiagara, June 1905.

ANM 2 M 2. Ponty, Instructions [regarding 1903 legislation], n.d., n.p., [probably 1904].

ANM 2 M 4. Lt-gov. Colonel de Trentinian, Note circular, Bamako, 3 February 1896.

ANM 2 M 20. Commandant, letter to Lt-gov, Koutiala, 27 June 1911.

ANM 2 M 34. De la Brestesche, letter to lt-gov, Segu, 6 December 1906.

ANM 2 M 40. Gov. Trentinian, circulaire no. 546, Droits des commandants de Région, de cercle et poste en matière de justice, Kayes, 16 December 1896. The same circular appears in file ANM 2 D 155.

ANM 2 M 54. Captain Porion, Étude sur la justice administrative indigène dans le cercle de Bamako, Bamako, 19 July 1894.

ANM 2 M 54. Various Rapport sur le fonctionnement des tribunaux indigènes, Bamako, 1906–1912.

ANM 2 M 56. Rapport sur le fonctionnement des tribunaux indigènes, Bandiagara, 4th Quarter 1906.

ANM 2 M 59. Various Rapports sur le fonctionnement de la justice, Bouguni, 1905–1910.

ANM 2 M 60. Various Rapports sur le fonctionnement de la justice, Jenne, 1906–1909.

ANM 2 M 65. Various Rapports sur le fonctionnement des tribunaux indigènes, Gumbu, 1906–1909.

ANM 2 M 73. Capt. Froment, letter to gov. Soudan, Kita, 20 March 1894.

ANM 2 M 73. Rapport sur la justice indigène, 2nd Quarter 1910, Kita.

ANM 2 M 75. Various Rapports sur le fonctionnement de la justice indigène, Koutiala, 1905–1910.

ANM 2 M 79. Rapport sur le fonctionnement de la justice indigène, Mopti, 1st Quarter 1911.

ANM 2 M 92. Commandant Quiquandon, Rapport sur le fonctionnement de la justice administrative dans le cercle de Segu, Segu, 1 April 1894.

ANM 2 M 92. Various Rapports sur le fonctionnement des tribunaux indigènes, Segu, 1905–1907.

ANM 2 M 93. Various Rapports sur le fonctionnement de la jusitce indigène, Sikasso, 1905–1911.

ANM 2 M 94. Various Rapports sur le fonctionnement de la jusitce indigène, Sokolo, 1908–1911.

ANM 2 M 104. Tribunal de Province, Bamako, 4 April 1905.

ANM 2 M 104. État des jugements rendus en matière civile et commerciale par le Tribunal de Province, Bamako, 3rd Quarter 1907.

ANM 2 M 104/105. Registres des affaires civiles et commerciales, Tribunal de Province, Bamako, 1905–1913.

ANM 2 M 110. Registres des affaires civiles et commerciales, Tribunal de Province, Bouguni, 1905–1912.

ANM 2 M 122. Registres des affaires civiles et commerciales, Tribunal de Province, Gumbu, 1905–1912.

ANM 2 M 143. Registres des affaires civiles et commerciales, Tribunal de Province, Segu, 1905–1912.

ANM 2 M 236. Petition to the Lt-gov, Kouluba, 12 May 1913.

ANM 2 M 459. Minister of Colonies Gaston Doumergue, letter to Gov-gen, Paris, 23 August 1902.

ANM 2 M 459. Ponty, circular to district officers, Kayes, 26 January 1903.

ANM 2 M 459. William Ponty, Délégué permanent du Gouverneur-général, to administrateurs des cercles de la Sénégambie-Niger, Kayes, 5 February 1903.

ANM 2 M 459. Sec-gen Merlin, Instructions aux administrateurs . . . , Gorée, October 1904.

ANM 2 M 459. Lt-gov, circualaire au sujet de la compétence des tribunaux indigènes, to administrators and commandants de cercle de la colonie, Kayes, 2 June 1906.

ANM 2 M 459. Ponty, gov-gen per interim, letter to lt-gov, H-S-N, Instructions et circulaires sur le fonctionnement de la justice, Dakar, 10 October 1907.

ANM 2 M 459. Ponty, serving as interim gov-gen, letter to lt-gov H-S-N, Dakar, 10 October 1907.

ANM 2 M 459. Gov-gen, letter to lt-gov H-S-N, Dakar, 2 May 1910.

ANM 1 Q 257. Enquête sur les productions animales, 1905, Bamako.

ANM 1 R 69. Rapport commercial et agricole, 1st Quarter 1901, Segu.

Archive Nationales, République du Sénégal. Archives de l'Afrique Occidentale Française. ANS-AOF. Archives de la Colonie du Sénégal. ANS.

ANS-AOF 1 D 105. Commandant Superiéur Archinard, Rapport militaire, campagne 1889–1890, nd, np.

ANS-AOF 1 D 137. Archinard, Rapport de campagne, 1892–1893, November 1893, Paris.

ANS-AOF 5 E 1. Procès verbal, Commission permanente du Conseil du Gouvernement, session 6 June 1903, Dakar.

ANS-AOF 1 G 138. Lt-gov. Trentinian, Circulaire to commmandants de cercle, 19 December 1896, Kayes.

ANS-AOF 1 G 229. Coutumes juridiques au Soudan, Cercle de Segu, Segu, 1 April 1897.

ANS-AOF 1 G 229. Étude de Barrat, commis des Affaires indigènes à Nioro, 1897–1900.

ANS-AOF 1 G 248. Perignon, Généralités sur le Haut Sénégal et Moyen Niger, Segu, 1900.

ANS-AOF 2 G 1–14. Rapport politique, Segu, 1901, ANS-AOF 2 G 1–14; Ponty, Rapport politique, H-S-N, February 1901.

ANS-AOF 2 G 3–8/VI. Ponty, Service judiciaire, Justice, Rapport annuel, Haut-Sénégal-Niger, 1903.

ANS-AOF 2 G 4–16. Ponty, Rapport d'ensemble sur la situation générale de la colonie, H-S-N en 1904.

ANS-AOF 2 G 11–9. Lt-gov. Clozel, Rapport politique, Haut-Sénégal-Niger, 1911.

ANS-AOF 2 G 4–16. Ponty, Rapport d'ensemble sur la situation générale de la colonie du Haut-Sénégal-Niger en 1904.

ANS-AOF 4 G 11. Saurin, Rapport concernant la verification du service de M. Faure, administrateur cmdt, le cercle de Sokolo, 20 January 1910.

ANS-AOF 4 G 11. Inspecteur Saurin, rapport concernant la verifcation du service de M. Catalogne, resident à Banamba, 23 February 1910.

ANS-AOF 15 G 58. Ponty, letter to cmdt Bouguni, Kayes, 8 August 1900.

ANS-AOF 15 G 58. Ponty, letter to cmdt Segu, Kayes, 23 April 1900.

ANS-AOF 15 G 58. Ponty, letter to cmdt Nioro, [Kayes], 26 September 1900.

ANS-AOF 15 G 60. Ponty, letter to cmdt Segu, Kayes, 2 May 1901, ANS-AOF 15 G 60; Ponty, letter to cmdt Segu, Kayes, 5 July 1901.

ANS-AOF 15 G 95. Min of Colonies, letter to gov-gen, Paris, 9 November 1898.

ANS-AOF 15 G 172. Palabre, Nyamina, 19 April 1890, signed by Archinard, Mamdou Racine, Mademba, Amadou Kuma, Bonnier, Underberg, and Quinquadon.

ANS-AOF 18 G 2. Commandant Destanve, Projet d'organisation politique, administrative et defensive de l'AOF, n.p., 1898.

ANS-AOF 18 G 2. Trentinian, L'organisation d'un gouverment-général de l'AOF (Soudan, Sénégal, Guinée, Côte d'Ivoire, Dahomey), Paris, 7 October 1899.

ANS-AOF K 19. Brevié, Rapport sur l'esclavage, Bamako, 1904.

ANS-AOF M 79. Gov-Gen Roume to lieut-govs, Dakar, 4 March 1904.

ANS-AOF M 83. Lt-gov Clozel, letter to gov-gen, Bamako, 29 April 1911.

ANS-AOF M 85. Beurdeley, letter to gov-gen, Mission d'études sur le fonctionnement de la justice dans les colonies de l'AOF, 25 June 1914, Dakar.

ANS-AOF M 119–121. Selected 1906 court registers for the tribunaux de province can be found only in Dakar.

ANS-AOF M 122. Procureur-général to gov-gen, 22 December 1908, Dakar.

ANS Affaires contentieux 24. Tentative de corruption du Président du Tribunal civil du cercle de Baol à Dourbel, 1937.

Archives Nationales, République de France. Depot d'Outre-Mer.

ANF-DOM AOF I-1. Ministre des Colonies, confidential instructions to Gov-gen Chaudié, Paris, 11 October 1895.

ANF-DOM AOF I-4. Gov-gen Chaudié, letter to Min of Colonies, St Louis, 6 December 1897.

ANF-DOM AOF I-6. Minister of Colonies, letter to gov-gen, Paris, 3 October 1899.

ANF-DOM AOF I-8. Instructions données par telegramme du 5 May 1900 en vue de la revision de sentences prononcés par vois d'action disciplinaire contre des indigènes dans l'ancienne colonie du Soudan Français, Principaux actes du Ministre des Colonies, Paris, January 1901.

ANF-DOM AOF I-8. Gov-gen, Rapport sur la situation politique de l'AOF, St Louis, 11 July 1901.

ANF-DOM AOF VII-2. Ministre des Colonies, Rapport au Président de la République française, Paris, 16 June 1895.

ANF-DOM AOF VII-2. Exposé sommaire de la reglementation concernant l'organisation administrative de l'Indo-Chine française, nd, np.

ANF-DOM AOF VII-2. Min. of Colonies, Projet de decret, Institue un conseil supérieur du gouvernment-général de l'AOF, Paris, 12 September 1895.

ANF-DOM AOF VII-4. Le Directeur des affaires d'Afrique, Note pour le Ministre, Paris, n.d. [1899].

ANF-DOM AOF VII-4. Gov-gen Chaudié, Rapport à M. le Ministre des colonies sur les modifications politiques et administratives à introduire dans l'organisation du Soudan, Paris, 26 September 1899.

ANF-DOM AOF VIII-1. Liontel, letter to Minister of Colonies, Porto-Novo, 15 January 1901.

ANF-DOM AOF VIII-1. Gov Liotard, letter to Minister of Colonies, Porto-Novo, 18 January 1901.

ANF-DOM AOF VIII-1. Liontel, President du conseil d'appel, chargé de mission, letter to Minister of Colonies, Grand Bassam, 31 January 1901.

ANF-DOM Sénégal et Dependences IV-95. Archinard, telegram to Gov Senegal, Bamako, 12 April 1890.

ANF-DOM Soudan I 1 a. Archinard, letter to under secretary of state for colonies, 9 January 1891, Nioro.

ANF-DOM Soudan I-4. Sous sec d'état des colonies, Instructions à M. le Colonel Archinard, Commandant sup du Soudan, Paris, 12 September 1892.

ANF-DOM Soudan III-3. Lt. Voulet, letter to capt., resident of Bandiagara, Tagarou, 24 February 1896.

ANF-DOM Soudan VIII-2. Le Chef du cabinet, Ministre des Colonies, Note pour le 1ère Direction, 1ère Bureau, Application dan les territoires de l'ancien Soudan du decret du 30 September 1887, Fonctionnement de la justice indigène, Paris, n.d. [but mid-late April 1900].

ANF-DOM Soudan VIII-2. Chaudié, telegram to Ponty, Saint Louis, 20 February 1900; Ponty, telegram [to gov-gen], Kayes, 22 February 1900, regarding the clemency of Médoune Gueye.

ANF-DOM Soudan VIII-2. Chaudié, letter, St. Louis, 19 March 1900.

ANF-DOM Soudan VIII-2. Chaudié, letter to govs of Guinée Française, Côte d'Ivoire, and Dahomey, St Louis, 19 March 1900.

ANF-DOM Soudan VIII-2. Gov.-gen. Chaudié, letter to Minister of Colonies with copies to 1ère Direction, 1ère Bureau, and Sec-gen 3ème Bureau, St. Louis, 21 March 1900.

ANF-DOM Soudan VIII-2. Chaudié, letter to Minister of Colonies, St Louis, 21 March 1900.

ANF-DOM Soudan VIII-2. Etat nominatif de individus condamnés à la prison, various dates.

ANF-SOM AP 1645/3. Procès verbal, Commission permanente du Conseil du Gouvernement, session 18 May 1903 and 20 May 1903.

ORAL INTERVIEWS

Baye, Fofana. 20 July 1981, Banamba.

Diakite, Idrissa. Hamdullaye, 21 December 1996, Bamako.

Kale, Batene. 31 July 1981, Segu.

Kone, Sidi Yahaya. 1 February 1977, Sinsani.

Kulibali, Santa. 21 March 1977, Sinsani.

Kuma, Binke Baba. 21 March 1976, Sinsani.

Simpara, Mustafa, Baasi Simpara, Bafu Simpara, Danguien Simpara, Fasumara Simpara, Baramu Simpara, Sadybu Simpara, Mayhamy Simpara, Moktar Simpara, and Sory Konate, 18 July 1981, Banamba.

Sukule, Binke. 21 March 1977, Sinani.

Sylla, Tijani. 3 August 1981, Baraweli.

Tambura, Sane. 18 February 1977, Segu.

Toure, Ahmadou. 1 August 1981, Segoubougou.

Traore, Yusufa. 13 December 1976, Segoubougou.

Ture, Cemoko. 5 March 1977, Segu.

Ture, Tene. 1 August 1981, Segoubougou.

INDEX

About the Author

RICHARD ROBERTS is Professor of African History and Director of the Center for African Studies at Stanford University. He has published widely on the social and economic history of French West Africa and has edited two volumes that have appeared in the Social History of Africa series (*Law and Colonialism in Africa*, coedited with Kristin Mann, and *Cotton, Colonialism, and Social History of Sub-Saharan Africa*, coedited with Allen Issacman).